Beyond
Postcolonial
Theory

ALSO BY E. SAN JUAN, JR.

From Exile to Diaspora

The Philippine Temptation

Hegemony and Strategies of Transgression

Allegories of Resistance

Racial Formations / Critical Transformations

From the Masses, to the Masses

Reading the West / Writing the East

History and Form

Mediations: From a Filipino Perspective

Writing and National Liberation

Beyond Postcolonial Theory

E. San Juan, Jr.

St. Martin's Press
New York

ISBN 0-312-17426-8

Library of Congress Cataloging-in-Publication Data

San Juan, E. (Epifanio), 1938-
   Beyond postcolonial theory / E. San Juan, Jr.
     p. cm.
   Includes bibliographical references and index.
   ISBN 0-312-17426-8
   1. Developing countries. I. Title.
  D883.S16 1998
  909'.09724—dc21   97-19890
                                                            CIP

Design by Acme Art, Inc.
First edition: January, 1998
10 9 8 7 6 5 4 3 2 1

To all political prisoners in the world, north and south

No uprising fails. Each one is a step in the right direction.
—Salud Algabre,
leader of the Sakdal rebellion
in the Philippines, 1935

The tradition of the oppressed teaches us that the "state of emergency" in which we live is not the exception but the rule. We must attain to a conception of history that is in keeping with this insight. Then we shall clearly realize that it is our task to bring about a real state of emergency.
—Walter Benjamin,
"Theses on the Philosophy of History" (1940)

Resolution in hardship, perseverance to the end. [O]nly those who have aims and ambitions for the benefit not of the individual, but of humankind as a whole, can persevere to the end.

—Ding Ling,
"Thoughts on March 8"

To the socialist, no nation is free whose national existence is based upon the enslavement of another people, for to him colonial peoples, too, are human beings, and, as such, parts of the national state. International socialism recognizes the right of free independent nations, with equal rights. But socialism alone can create such nations, can bring self-determination of their peoples. This slogan of socialism is like all its others, not an apology for existing conditions, but a guidepost, a spur for the revolutionary, regenerative, active policy of the proletariat. So long as capitalist states exist, i.e., so long as imperialistic world policies determine and regulate the inner and the outer life of a nation, there can be no "national self-determination" either in war or in peace.
—Rosa Luxemburg,
The Crisis in German Social Democracy (1916)

Contents

Acknowledgments ix

Introduction. 1

1. Interrogations and Interventions:
     Who Speaks for Whom? 21

2. Postcolonial Theory versus the Revolutionary Process
     in the Philippines. 53

3. "Unspeakable" Subalterns: Lessons from Gramsci,
     El Saadawi, Freire, Silko. 83

4. The Multicultural Imaginary: Problematizing Identity
     and the Ideology of Racism .113

5. Revisiting an "Internal Colony": U.S. Asian
     Cultural Formations and the Metamorphosis
     of Ethnic Discourse 155

6. Globalization, Dialogic Nation, Diaspora 195

7. Beyond Postcolonial Theory:
     The Mass Line in C. L. R. James's Works 227

8. Imagining the End of Empire:
     Emergencies and Breakthroughs. 251

Notes. 275

Bibliography. 286

Index 315

ACKNOWLEDGMENTS

It has been over two decades since I edited one of the first collections of Georg Lukác's writings in English translation (published in 1973 in New York City); despite the vicissitudes of the struggle during the Cold War era, the ideals of the great revolutionary thinker still exercise a catalyzing influence on the minds of my generation, including myself. One of these ideals is condensed in fact in the third part of Marx's "Theses on Feuerbach": "The coincidence of the changing of circumstances and of human activity can be conceived and rationally understood only as revolutionizing practice." Whether conceived as radicalizing "theoretical practice" or united-front/coalition work, most of these essays were first tried out as lectures, "interventions" if you like, or remarks on various occasions and then, with the benefit of the antagonisms and challenges from those arenas of contestation, rethought and revised in a new format. No doubt many of the themes and arguments found here continue the projects begun in my earlier works, among them *Racial Formations/ Critical Transformations, Hegemony and Strategies of Transgression,* and *The Philippine Temptation.*

Most of those occasions took place in the Philippines, particularly at the Ateneo de Manila University in Quezon City and at various campuses of the University of the Philippines (in Metro Manila, Iloilo City, Miag-ao, and Baguio City), and also at the International Academy of Management and Economics (IAME) in Makati City, Philippines. I want to thank in particular Professors Soledad Reyes and Lulu Torres of Ateneo de Manila University, Dr. Elmer Ordoñez of the University of the Philippines, Professor Tomas Talledo (UP Visayas), Professors Roland Simbulan and Ed Villegas (UP Manila), and President Emmanuel T. Santos of the IAME for their hospitality and encouragement in inviting me to lecture at the aforementioned institutions.

Here I also want to acknowledge the comradeship of Dr. Giovanna Covi and Mark Beitel of the Universita degli studi di Trento, Italy, for giving me the opportunity to share my ideas with the members of the English Seminar in Trento during May 1995. Thanks also to Professor Donald Pease who instigated the composition of parts of "The Multicultural Imaginary" for his NEH Seminar at Dartmouth College. The second chapter as well as many parts of this book owe their origin from the talk I gave to Professor Arif Dirlik's Asian/Pacific Workshop at Duke University. I thank my colleagues who have given support throughout the years of the Cold War, among them: Alan Wald (University of Michigan), Arif Dirlik (Duke University), James Bennett (University of Arkansas), Robert Dombroski (CUNY Graduate Center), Bruce Franklin (Rutgers University), Sam Noumoff (McGill University, Canada), Neil Larsen (Northeastern University), Evelyn Hu-Dehart (University of Colorado), W. F. Haug (Free University, Berlin), Paul Buhle (New York University), Donald Wesling (University of California, San Diego), Manning Marable (Columbia University), Roger Bresnahan (Michigan State University), Nancy and Norman Chance (University of Connecticut), Jim Zwick (Syracuse University), and especially Dean Karen Gould of Old Dominion University. Professor Michael Martin, chair of the Department of Ethnic Studies, Bowling Green State University, has also been supportive. Last but not least, Delia Aguilar (Bowling Green State University), Eric San Juan (University of Chicago), and Karin Aguilar-San Juan (Brown University) have given me ideas, advice, and inspiration in all my work, for which I am eternally grateful. All errors and oversights are of course my responsibility.

I would like to thank the staff of the Scholarly and Reference Division of St. Martin's Press, in particular Maura E. Burnett, for their help in the editing, production, and promotion of this book.

Some of the chapters in this work appeared in earlier versions in the following journals and series to whose editors and publishers I owe profound gratitude: *The Journal of Commonwealth Literature, Weg und Ziel, AsianWeek, Left Curve, Ariel, Working Papers in Asian/Pacific Studies* (Duke University), *Diliman Review, Philippine Resource Center Monitor,* and *Das Argument.*

Introduction

Consonant with the globalization of capital, the rise of a new discipline and scholarly industry called "postcolonial" discourse affords us the occasion for addressing issues central to the field of cultural studies and the human sciences in general.[1] Postcolonial theory's claim to institutional authority deserves careful scrutiny for the questions about knowledge, power, and value it rehearses. Of pivotal importance are the question of identity and the multiple logics of inter alia difference, individuality, temporality, and singularity articulated with it; the question of agency and history that Arif Dirlik, in his insightful opus *The Postcolonial Aura* (1997), has thoroughly explored; and the question of reason, value, and structural transformation in history, both subsumed and sanitized in the current talk on "ethics," the "body," and "desire." Changes in the power alignment of nation-states with the end of the Cold War, the elevation of "terrorism" and human rights as international concerns overshadowing communist totalitarianism, ethnonationalist conflict, labor migration, and the traffic in women (to mention only the most topical) have all registered their varying pressures on the curriculum and research agenda in the humanities and social sciences. While neoconservatism remains the hegemonic ideology, cracks are beginning to appear in the walls of the fortress. On the horizon's edge, the winds of change are rising. Just as the civil rights and national-liberation struggles in the sixties reconfigured the canon and the priorities of traditional disciplines, the antiracist revolts in the eighties and nineties together with continuing militancy in the ecological, peace, and women's movements continue to shape the vocabulary and parameter of the debates now designated as the "culture wars."[2]

With the dissolution of an alternative to predatory capitalism in the form of state/bureaucratic "socialism" in the Soviet Union and its satellites, there is an assumption that the planet has now suddenly become empty, free, and open to improvisations of all sorts. Ecological, feminist, and anti-nuclear movements may have been co-opted if not pacified temporarily by beggar-thy-neighbor individualism, religious or New Age fundamentalisms, and assorted reactionary trends. Progressive and emancipatory projects are on hold. In this interregnum, a notion of "transculturology" has even appeared that makes the future an enigmatic, fluid, and slippery border on which transmigrants are domiciled. Temporality becomes equivalent to a realm of vague possibilities, "locomotion without goal," according to the Situationist International, parallel to development without progress, growth without improvement. There are also ambiguous "Third Spaces" that Homi Bhabha and others have conjured from a Disneyland of industrial waste and ecological disasters, amorphous and hybrid forms that seem to play on polyphonic chords of differences and thrive on them.

Before starting our journey, we are advised to invent new relational logics, new concepts of communal border-crossing and transnational habitats, inaugurated and sustained in multiplicity. Proscriptions, however, have not disappeared. We are not allowed to generalize, much less "totalize" (sheer abomination for cyborg denizens of postmodernism). Appeals to Enlightenment metanarratives of progress and liberation are not tolerated in this realm of deconstructive "free play." It is curious that amid this exhortation to reject essentialism so as to undermine the discourses of power and its displacements onto other hierarchies and asymmetries, we never encounter any specific scenario of injustice, domination, or actual resistance from which we may gather intimations of the passage through the postcolonial ordeal (this comment also applies to the deployment of the rubric "diasporic" and "subaltern" as opposites of Eurocentric; see Stratton and Ang 1996). Between the "thick description" of a Salman Rushdie inscribed in a beleaguered position in the United Kingdom and the diagnosis of such a predicament by the postcolonial critics in the poverty-stricken South, we are left with speculations about the pleasures of random identifications and syncretic, ad hoc fetishisms of all sorts. Indeterminacy seems to abide forever. Postcoloniality is, for some, whatever you want to make of it that will allow individual compromises and opportunisms to flourish.

Postcolonial theory is, to my mind, more than a cultural or literary phenomenon limited to those who have undergone the colonial experience. That experience, a relation of conqueror and conquered, is in fact universal. European colonialism, which ushered the division of the world into the core industrialized powers and the peripheral underdeveloped societies, has distinguished the history of humankind from the Renaissance up to the present. The advent of imperialism (in Lenin's reckoning) in the late nineteenth century, however, also marks the beginning of its demise. Our stage of late capitalism or postmodernity is pervaded with spectacular crises and catastrophes: world wars and revolutions, including counterrevolution (the degeneration of the socialist projects in the Soviet Union and China, among others). Like postmodernism, postcoloniality—for some the condition of the "comprador intelligentsia" from the South (Appiah 1992)—marks an epochal shift of sensibility, a mutation in the expectant "structure of feeling" (to borrow Raymond Williams's oxymoron), among the intelligentsia of the former colonized world that reflects these vast changes, in particular the failure of national liberation struggles to achieve a complete radical break with the past of shame and invisibility, a past that was, to adapt Hobbes's terms, "nasty and brutish" but not short.

Before remarking on this epistemic shift, I want to situate postcolonialism within the framework of the structural crisis of international capitalism outlined by Ernest Mandel. This crisis is characterized by the "overaccumulation of capital and a crisis of overproduction of commodities, triggered by a decline of the average rate of profit" (1995: 438). To increase the average rate of profit, more precisely the average rate of surplus value (the rate of exploitation of wage labor), the capitalist rulers and their administrators seek to introduce technological innovations—computerization, for example—and a rearrangement of the social conditions of accumulation into a "dual society" to undermine the collective solidarity of the working class mainly composed of "Third World" wage earners (Figueroa 1997; see Chapter 6 for my discussion of Overseas Contract Workers), youth, the unemployed, ethnic minorities, immigrants, women, and so on. While a historical stalemate between capitalists and working class has existed in the "postindustrial" societies since the end of World War II, the crisis in the South has worsened with the perpetuation of unemployment and underemployment as a consequence of uneven, unsynchronized underdevelopment. United Nations reports indicate that about one billion people in the postcolonies live below the poverty line; 16 million children die every year from hunger and curable diseases—the quantity equals the combined total number of victims of World War II, Auschwitz, Hiroshima, and the Bengal famine. Mandel calls our attention to the destructive effects of imperialist barbarism on the environment and world health situation, including the "third worldization" of the bureaucratized postcapitalist countries.

Evidence of this repercussion is found in our backyard, the downtown redevelopment of Los Angeles, a city already acknowledged as the true capital of the postcolonial "Third World." It epitomizes the uneven quality of globalization. Contrary to Fredric Jameson's thesis that postmodernism as a cultural dominant of late capitalism saturates the urban architecture and landscape of the city, Michael Davis (1985) points out that the Warholesque transformation of buildings like John Portman's Bonaventure Hotel is determined by two coordinates: the emergence of new international rentier circuits in the present crisis phase of capitalism, and the new class polarization leading to the abandonment of the ideal of urban reform. Segregation worsens; conflicts across class, race, nationality multiply: the 1992 Los Angeles urban rebellion is one portentous sign of things to come.

The future is here with us, incarnate in the contemporary. What has swept rapidly through the synapses of the most powerful transnational conglomerates is something that I think, for all their incommensurable disparities, postmodernist/postcolonial artists and critics are trying to make intelligible. But their attempts are vitiated by an egregious flaw that inheres in their inability and/or refusal to grasp the fact of determinate social changes occurring not just at the margins but right at the heart of the circumnavigating behemoth:

> This transformation of a decayed precinct of downtown LA into a major financial and corporate-control node of the Pacific Rim economy (battening also on Southern California's runaway real-estate inflation and its booming defence industries) has gone hand-in-hand with a precipitous deterioration of the general urban infrastructure and a new-wave immigration that has brought an estimated one million undocumented Asians, Mexicans and Central Americans into the Inner City. The capitalism of postmodernism, far from eliminating the last enclaves of precapitalist production as Jameson suggests, has brazenly recalled the most primitive forms of urban exploitation. (M. Davis 1985: 110)

In addition, Davis notes the presence of at least one hundred thousand superexploited garment workers of various nationalities, including children, within a few miles' radius of the postmodern hotels. This restructuring of capitalist relations of production and productive process betokens not a new stage but rather "a return to a sort of primitive accumulation," with absolute surplus value being produced through the superexploitation of a multiethnic urban proletariat (the mechanics of racism underpinning this transition is discussed in Chapter 4). The Latino artist Coco Fusco (whose 1992 performance of *Two Undiscovered Amerindians Visit* revealed atavisms in the present) labels this conjuncture "late feudalism" (1995: 24). Such a return to "primitive accumulation" finds its intelligibility in the narrative erased from postcolonial memory.

One axiomatic proposition of materialist historiography orients this collection of essays: capitalism as a world system has developed unevenly, with the operations of the "free market" being determined by the unplanned but (after analysis) "lawful" tendencies of the accumulation of surplus value. With the rise of merchant capitalism, diverse modes of production with varying temporalities and "superstructural" effects have since then reconfigured the planet (Jalee 1977; Nabudere 1977; Brewer 1980; Wallerstein 1983). In a new cartography, we find metropolitan centers subordinating peripheral territories and peoples. Colonialism and, later, finance-capitalism (imperialism) compressed time and space, sharply juxtaposing variegated cultures linked to discrepant economies and polities, with the colonizing center dictating the measure of modernity. After World War II, the accelerated migration of former colonial subjects into the metropoles together with the refinement of technologies of communication and transportation heightened the spectacle of heterogeneous languages and practices coexisting with the homogenizing scenarios of everyday life both at center and margin (Featherstone 1990). I consider postcolonialism as the cultural logic of this mixture and multilayering of forms taken as the ethos of late modernity, a logic distanced from its grounding in the unsynchronized interaction between the civilizations of the colonial powers and of the colonized subalterns.

The controversy about postcoloniality's genealogy stems from a denial of historical causation by way of reifying unevenness itself. Although inseparable from the postalization of modernism in such trends as "poststructuralism" and the more inclusive term "postmodernism" (and variants like "postcommunism," "postrevolutionary," and so on), postcoloniality dates back to the emergence of immigrant and refugee intellectuals from the Empire's hinterlands in Western institutions of higher learning. The debate may have begun with Aijaz Ahmad's interrogation of a certain romantic idealization of the "Third World" by Western intellectuals. In his provocative manifesto *In Theory* (1992), Ahmad expressed objections to Jameson's concept of a "national allegory" that distinguishes the physiognomy of writing in social formations crisscrossed by revolutionary movements of decolonization in contrast to writing spoiled by the reification and atomization prevalent in "First

World" nations. Such allegories, whether or not they extend transcendent meaning or purpose to metropolitan intellectuals, do not represent (Ahmad insists) the variety of cultural practices in the "Third World." Ahmad also posed questions about Edward Said's *Orientalism,* in particular Said's expurgation of Marxism from postcolonial critique and his implicit compromise with bourgeois ideology in general.

In a recent essay, Ahmad (1995a) moved on to interrogate the "politics of literary postcoloniality" as exemplified by Gayatri Spivak and Homi Bhabha, two cult figures of postcoloniality (no conspiracy is implied here by dint of spatial contiguity or guilt by association). What Ahmad bewails is the postcolonial denial of history, specifically the histories of peoples with their distinctive trajectories of survival and achievement. More reprehensible is the complicity of such an eclectic, sometimes dilettantish, approach with the rule of instrumentalizing capital: "Within this context, speaking with virtually mindless pleasure of transnational cultural hybridity, and of politics of contingency, amounts, in effect, to endorsing the cultural claims of transnational capital itself. . . . It is not at all clear how the celebration of a postcolonial, transnational, electronically produced cultural hybridity is to be squared with this systematic decay of countries and continents, and with decreasing chances for substantial proportions of the global population to obtain conditions of bare survival, let alone electronic literacy and gadgetry" (1995a: 12-13). Together with a species of indiscriminate relativism that Ahmad labels "cultural differentialism," in which the insider's version is presumed authentic and immune to falsification by any objective criterion, postcolonial politics is revealed as complicit with late capitalism's drive to maintain its ruthless hegemony over the world's multitudes, chiefly working people of color (Ahmad 1995b).

Postcolonial doctrine assigns ontological priority to the phenomenon of cultural difference between colonized and colonizer. The articulation of such difference in "in-between" spaces produces hybridization of identities: "It is in the emergence of the interstices—the overlap and displacement of domains of difference—that the intersubjective and collective experiences of nationness, community interest, or cultural value are negotiated" (Bhabha 1994b: 1-2). Since capital ethnicizes peoples to promote labor segmentation, hybridity and other differential phenomena result (Wallerstein 1991). But for Bhabha, ambivalence arises from the poststructuralist "*différance* of writing" that informs any cultural performance, not from encystment and historical social catalepsy (Memmi 1965). Such performances are found in certain privileged positionalities and experiences: "the history of postcolonial migration, the narratives of cultural and political diaspora, the major social displacements of peasants and aboriginal communities, the poetics of exile, the grim prose of political and economic refugees" (Bhabha 1994b: 5). Callinicos calls Bhabha's approach "an idealist reduction of the social to the semiotic" (1995: 111; see also the wide-ranging essay by Parry 1994). Indeterminacy, interruption of the signifying chain, aporia, infinite displacements, translations, and negotiations characterize postcolonial literary theory and practice. Aside from the ambiguity of historical references in postcolonial discourse, Neil Larsen points out that the postcolonial hypnosis by the mysteries of discourse prohibits the postcolonial evangelist to pose "the awkward question of the nation and nationalism as the historical product (neither origin nor telos) of capitalism," thus allowing no alternative "between classical historicist ideology of nationalism and the anti-historicist discovery of the nation as the 'liminality of cultural modernity' " (1995b: 15). In the discursive realm of floating signifiers and exorbitant metaphors, the objective asymmetry of power and resources between hegemonic blocs and subaltern groups (racialized minorities in the metropoles and in the "third world"), as well as the attendant consequences, disappears.

Of primary importance in this debate on the politics of difference and identity is the salient question of agency, the intentionality of transformative practice, enunciated in concrete historical conjunctures. This crucial aspect (explored in Chapters 1, 3 and 5) has been elided by orthodox postcoloniality. Its claim to be more radical than neo-Nietzschean anarchism (Foucault, Lyotard, Deleuze) is problematic, especially for people of color seeking to affirm their communal identities and autochtonous traditions. Its reduction of political economy, of the facts of exploitation across the categories of race, gender, and class, to the status of discourse and intertextuality has canceled the possibility of the intervention of social subjects and collectivities in the shaping of their lives. A transcendental politics of difference is substituted for critique of hegemony and its material practices of social reproduction and of assigning value.

In their notes to *The Post-Colonial Studies Reader*, Bill Ashcroft, Gareth Griffiths and Helen Tiffin claim that postcolonial theory disavows the postmodern project of deconstructing Eurocentric master-narratives involving concepts of progress, essentialist subjectivity, teleology, and so on. Rather they uphold the aim of dismantling the Center/Margin binarism of imperial discourse, thus generating the political agency of postcolonials. Such agency, however, is not really theorized as an immanent historical process but merely as verbal dexterity and ludic rhetorical games. What strikes me as fatal is the repudiation of foundations and objective validity that undermines any move to produce new forms of creative power and resistance against globalized inequalities and oppressions. Hybridity, heterogeneous and discrepant lifestyles, local knowledges, cyborgs, borderland scripts—such slogans tend to obfuscate the power of the transnational ideology and practice of consumerism and its dehumanizing effects. Postcolonial discourse generated in "First World" academies turns out to be one more product of flexible, post-Fordist capitalism, not its antithesis.

Postcolonial ventriloquism has even ventured to deprive subalterns of speech (see Chapter 3) even though in some cases the choice of not-speaking can be deemed a proactive mode of subversion. Speaking positions are, after all, also axes of struggle; language is multiaccentual precisely because the speaker's silence is constituted by voices coming from within and without, from all directions. This resonance configures the vectors of emergencies, interventions, and breakthroughs of those hitherto repressed and excluded. This can be vividly illustrated in the countrapuntal montage of voices/images in Tomas Alea's unforgettable film *Memories of Underdevelopment;* examine the ending of the film when, at the height of the missile crisis, the petit-bourgeois intellectual Sergio's confession of futility ("The island is a trap. . . . It's a very expensive dignity") is juxtaposed with Fidel Castro's cry of defiance: "We know what we are doing and we know how to defend our integrity and we know how to defend our sovereignty" (1990: 95). To label this moment "hybrid" pastiche would be to miss the point entirely, appropriating its potency and defusing it as one more fungible consumer item. We have residual, emergent, and dominant currents all converging in the protean arenas of struggle. Nor can the energies of subalterns be completely deflected, neutralized, or exhausted by the sublimations of hedonistic consumption and spectacles of commodified pleasures. Power is always situational, not dispersed in abstract space (contrast Smith and Katz [1993] with Soja and Hooper [1993]). Moreover, social analysis is fundamentally spatiotemporal and historical (Rosaldo 1994). In short, crisis is where we work, suffer, meditate, rejoice, and fashion our destinies. This provides access not only to dangers and solipsistic dead ends but also to opportunities for rupture and liberation.

The ironies of postcolonial theory become more flagrant when contraposed to the resistance of colonized subalterns themselves (which

I address in the first three chapters, with particular focus on C. L. R. James in Chapter 7). Clearly the postcolonial fixation on the manifestations of "unevenness" has undergone fetishization, divorced from its concrete social determinations. What postcolonial theory seeks to carry out in the name of individualist resistance is the valorization of reified immediacies—the symptomatic effects of colonization in various forms of "orientalisms" and strategies of adaptations and cooptations—unconnected with the institutions and instrumentalities that subtend them. Viewed from the perspective of late-capitalist political economy, the figures of difference, fragmentation, liminality, and diaspora that Lawrence Grossberg (1996) considers the principles of identity for postmodern cultural studies (of which postcolonialism is a subspecies) are modes of regulating the social relations of production, in particular the division of global social labor and its reproduction. But postcolonial critics not only remove them from their circumstantial ground, from their situational contexts; they also treat them as autonomous phenomena separate from the structures of cultural production and political legitimation in late modern societies. In Henri Lefebvre's formulation, "Each of these 'moments' of the real [i.e., hybridity, fragmentation, etc.], once isolated and hypostatized, becomes the negator of the other moments and then the negator of itself. Limited and transposed into a form, the content becomes oppressive and destructive of its own reality" (1968: 167).

Postcolonialism is then culpable for what it claims to repudiate: mystification and moralism. What postcolonialism ultimately tries to do is to reify certain transitory practices, styles, modalities of thought and expression that arise as attempts to resolve specific historical contradictions in the ongoing crisis of moribund transnational capitalism. Cultural difference is the single ambivalent result of colonialism that can be articulated in plural ways. Unevenness is no longer an abstract categorizing term but an empirical one-sided description that affords the subaltern's newly discovered agency some space for the display of libertarian disingenuousness. What Georg Lukács (1971) calls "ethical utopianism," the lapse into subjectivism, afflicts postcolonial theory because it denies the internally complex determinants that are its condition of possibility. This mediation of the hybrid, interstitial, and borderline experience with the overdetermined totality of the social formation is rejected as "essentialism" or "totalization."

Postcolonial theory, in brief, can be read as metaphysical idealism masking its counterrevolutionary telos by denying its own worldly interests and genealogy. It occludes its own historical determinacy by deploying psychoanalytical and linguistic conceptual frameworks that take market/exchange relations for granted. It takes as given the ideological assumptions of utilitarian individualism as normative and natural. Despite claims to entertaining visions of community by denouncing power and commercialism, postcolonial theory advances reactionary goals by ultraleft, opportunist adventurism. Its partisanship for the "disjunctive borderline temporalities" of minority and marginalized cultures is itself an intermediary link to the totality's project of extending the instrumental freedom of the gendered, stratified subject to its erstwhile "subjects" (preponderantly people of color), this time under the aegis of a more tolerant procedural pluralism that recognizes "the outside of the inside," the part in the whole, *e pluribus unum*. In effect, the totality of the marketplace is thereby reaffirmed while giving the impression that everyone is now included in the decision-making process. Lacking the dialectical mediation of the part to the whole that historical materialism considers imperative for theorizing the possibilities of change and the sublation of historically specific contradictions, postcolonial orthodoxy dissolves mediations and generates exactly the predicament that it claims to prevent: the antinomy of transcendentalizing idealism and mechanical determinism.

In the post–Cold War environment in which history (ideology having self-destructed in the fifties) is supposed to meet its apocalypse, the postcolonial mode seems to flourish as a peculiar excrescence of the geopolitical climate in the metropolis. Amid mindless uniformity and standardized taste, the liberal consensus needs the illusion of competition and the compensatory relief of variety. If work is alienating, the imagination can be programmed to yield instant gratifications. The signature brands of hybridity, indeterminacy, and multiplicity find warrant in the universalization of what Leslie Sklair calls the "culture-ideology of consumerism": "The transnational corporations strive to control global capital and material resources, the transnational capitalist classes strive to control global power, and the transnational agents and institutions of the culture-ideology of consumerism strive to control the realm of ideas" (1991: 82). It is within this milieu of bureaucratic accumulation via the Society of Consumption and massification that postcolonial discursive practice (including neoconservative apologetics which I examine in Chapter 6) can be judiciously appraised.

In this context, postcoloniality can be interpreted as a refurbishing of the liberal individualist ethos geared to the "free play" of the market.

It is articulated with archaic tributary impulses revitalized and displaced into commodity-fetishism and other hallucinatory sublimations. This ludic exchange is, however, unequal since the relations between rich and poor classes, between dependent periphery and "advanced" industrial nation-states, whatever the rhetoric of mutual advantage, are ruled by chicanery and diplomatic machinations, by covert and open violence. Much of the celebration of postcolonial versatility and freedom is, on closer analysis, an integral part of what James Petras (1993) calls "cultural imperialism" or the "Americanization of Third World cultures," the universalization of anomie and bureaucratic subordination of the masses. The exiled Kenyan novelist Ngugi Wa Thiong'o asserts with moral conviction that "Western cultural dominance has been underwritten by post-colonial political practices" purveyed in the mass media (1993: 90).

We cannot therefore understand postcolonial pseudoresistance apart from its metropolitan context. Recent U.S. interventions into Central America, the Middle East, Africa, Bosnia, and other flashpoints of the hinterland (Mexico and Zaire are next in line) confirm the ascendancy of the Hobbesian principle (the *Realpolitik* of free trade) in international affairs. The exercise of foreign policy, as many studies have demonstrated, depends on the pacification of citizens through a variety of regulatory and disciplinary mechanisms (G. William Domhoff 1969; Gilbert and Joris 1981; Parenti 1995). Such trends as multiculturalism, globalization, the decline of the nation-state, diasporic communities (treated in Chapters 4, 5, and 6), and the return of the rhetoric/lexicon of civil society need to be reinscribed in the vicissitudes of the "culture wars."

Mediated through racial/ethnic and class antagonisms, the sharpening of class and racial conflicts in the United States today has revived a hegemonic project of reconstituting a pluralist multiracial nation that recuperates traditional ideas of individualism and "American exceptionalism." National identity, however, has always been the political and ideological effect of a managed consensus based on material inequality and hierarchical stratification. A common identity or public culture is rendered untenable by the logic of capital in reproducing class and other sectoral divisions marked by cultural differences. Faced by economic crisis, demographic changes, and the counterhegemonic resistance of people of color, U.S. capitalism refunctions racism through the ideology of differential culturalism—making "militant particularisms" somehow suspect—centered on ethnicity, immigration (the code word here is "undocumented aliens"), and "humanitarian"-motivated interventions around the world.

Cultural pluralism via what I call the "multicultural Imaginary" (Chapter 4) may be regarded as the principal ideological strategy of the ruling bourgeoisie in the post–Cold War era. The legitimation crisis broached in the sixties is now neutralized by the culturalization of old forms of racist practices articulated with new flexible, disaggregated class-formation processes (as those mentioned by Davis; see Appelbaum 1996). Contradictions arise, however, whenever nation-states and corporations try to reduce the practicosensory realm, the body, and socialized spatial practices to reified marketable space (Lefebvre 1991). Interposing here the debate on canon revision, we move into the terrain of the politics of Sameness versus the politics of identity, the recognition of difference: Menchu and Silko versus the Great Books, Afrocentrism versus Eurocentrism, and so on.

Uneveness here reasserts itself in textual heterogeneities and discrepant narrative models and representations. If we re-situate the question of ethics in this terrain of "the battle of the books" (books, it is understood, are figures for assemblages and collectivities competing for allegedly scarce resources [Bourdieu 1993]), the bottom-line philosophical question may be better ascertained. It involves understanding both the failures of deconstructive essentialism that has underwritten postmodernist identity politics, and the reformist program exemplified in many textbooks on how to translate cultural diversity into syllabi and workplace guidelines. Nancy Fraser contends that both traditionalists and multiculturalists "fail to connect a cultural politics of identity and difference to a social politics of justice and equality. Neither appreciates the crux of the connection: cultural differences can only be freely elaborated and democratically mediated on the basis of social equality" (1996: 207). It is, I submit, a formidable challenge. Just consider the following queries: how can we mediate the cultural differences between Menchu's account and the canonical texts of Plato, Shakespeare, T. S. Eliot, and others? How can we so easily shift from the paradigm/ worldview of the Quiche people that refuses to recognize the separation of humans from nature, of individual from the community, to the central premises of a liberal polity centered on possessive, exclusivist, racializing individualism?

We need to discriminate as a prior issue the singularity of an antipostcolonial text, one that questions, among others, the innocence of the Judaeo-Christian tradition. Notwithstanding the recent Christian theology of liberation utilized by Menchu, this tradition has legitimized the conquest of the continent and the genocide of its aboriginal peoples,

and today sanctions their continued repression by an oligarchic government armed and supported by various United States administrations. In
such confrontations, the usual asymmetry of civilization (the West) and
barbarism (the Rest) is scrambled, reversed, or discombobulated. In this
new field of counterhegemonic projects, the terms of market liberalism
(whether *laissez faire* or post-Fordist) no longer apply.

Urgent life-or-death questions are ignored by postcolonial theory
outside of the multiculturalism debate. Questions of inequality of power
and control over resources are elided (Epstein 1996). It might be an ad
hominem tactic to ask: Where were the postcolonial gurus during the
Gulf War? What is their stand on political prisoners like Mumia Abu
Jamal, Elizam Escobar, Leonard Peltier, and many others languishing in
U.S. jails? Lacking any alternative vision or self-reflexive critique of the
status quo, postcolonial proselytizers valorize their own dilemma as
paradigmatic—a symptom of amnesia, malaise of *ressentiment,* and self-
serving willfulness in late imperial culture (Sprinker 1995). How does
postcolonial theory, for example, explain the plight of millions of
"overseas contract workers"—women domestics, "hospitality girls," and
mail-order brides comprise this large, horizontally mobile cohort—all
over the world? Postcolonial theory does not understand the interpellation of bodies by the "law of value" in the international stratification of
labor. This is not to obscure or marginalize the narratives of other
populations that are being subjected to unconscionable treatment such
as systematic brutalization and genocide: for example, the aboriginal
communities of the Americas, the Maoris in New Zealand, and so on.
Menchu's explosive account of her ordeal and that of the indigenous
collectivities in Central America is testimony that escapes the deracinated
sensibility of the postcolonial intellect (see Chapter 1). Witness also the
horrendous plight of child prostitutes in India, Thailand, and other
impoverished countries; the suffering of refugees in strife-torn countries
in Africa, in Chechnya, in the former Yugoslavia, and elsewhere—these
do not register in the postcolonial sensorium. Likewise, the struggles of
colonized peoples in East Timor (Chomsky 1978-92), Puerto Rico
(Fernandez 1994), Northern Ireland, Hawaii (Blaisdell 1994), and
elsewhere elude representation in the postal conversation.

Let me interpolate here one scandalous incident virtually ignored by
everyone: On 10 May 1993, a fire gutted a factory outside Bangkok,
Thailand, which manufactured stuffed toys and other playthings for
children for American corporations (Toys R Us, Fisher Price, Hasbro,
J.C. Penney, among others); of 3,000 workers, 188 died and 469 were

injured (Greider 1997). But none of this aroused outrage from the world public, much less the U.S. citizenry. To be sure, the damage exceeded the burning of the Triangle Shirtwaist Company in 1911; the death of 146 young immigrant women electrified the country then and ushered in laws to guarantee safety at work. What happened in Thailand is replicated a thousand times in the plight of the Mexican *maquiladoras,* Filipina domestics in the Middle East, and the exploitation of child labor around the world. In textualizing or aestheticizing such realities, postcolonial theory has virtually "postalized" and consigned them to a transcendental and reified locus beyond rescue, a domain that the distinguished Brazilian educator Paolo Freire (1985) once called "the culture of silence" (see Chapter 3).

Whatever one's persuasion or creed, it cannot be denied that geopolitical faultlines have shifted of late. But we have not arrived yet at the end of either history or ideology, contrary to the propaganda and publicity stunts of the hegemonic power bloc. Arif Dirlik (1994a) has accurately characterized the North/South division after the collapse of the Soviet Union as that between the first world of transnational capital and a third world of underdevelopment, with the second world subsumed into the latter within the configuration of a globalized capitalist economy. Of course, there are still "internal colonies" within the advanced industrial countries, not only American Indian reservations but the "inner cities" inhabited by what has been called "the truly disadvantaged," the now proverbial lumpen "underclass." However novel and unparalleled the ongoing reconfiguration of transnational production systems, it is still the law of uneven and combined development that effectively shapes the context for the cultural production, circulation, and consumption of neoliberal ideas and practices (Amin 1994; Mandel 1995). Despite the drastic time-space compression of the last thirty years and the profound impact of electronic multimedia communication on everyday life (Harvey 1989), we still have to grapple with the concept of uneven geographical development for the reason that it "captures (a) the palimpsest of historically sedimented socio-ecological relations in place, (b) the multilayered and hierarchically ordered mosaic of socio-ecological configurations, and aspirations that order space, and (c) the often chaotic motion of socio-ecological (particularly under contemporary conditions capital and migratory) flows that produce, sustain, and dissolve geographical differences in the landscape over time" (Harvey 1996: 429-30). And I think this complex of overlapping determinants also sets the stage for the performance and evaluation of postcolonial theorizing.

Globalization as "historic change without history" (Wood 1995) inaugurated by microchip technology seems to frame all assessment of modernity for the mainstream public. In *Cultural Imperialism* (1991), John Tomlinson argues at the end that it is the "cultural experience of globalisation" that we need to deconstruct. This vacuous "social imaginary" (Cornelius Castoriadis's term) of late capitalist modernity has replaced earlier notions of colonial subordination, with the autonomized global institutions having displaced the "national community of fate" that energized cultural will. There is certainly a large truth to this. But, as Ellen Meiksins Wood and others contend, the nation-state has not vanished precisely because it functions as "the main conduit through which national (or indeed multinational) capital is inserted into the global market" (1997: 28). In Chapter 6, I present a Bakhtinian approach to the multiaccented decolonizing nation, a chronotope and speech-genre that transcodes the Other into the semantics of popular sovereignty, equality, and justice. The nation becomes equivalent to a "third" participant, the insurgent people/nation, which I locate as a utopian "utterance-becoming-apostrophe" in the texts of Filipino nationalism during the Filipino-American War of 1899-1902.

In articulating both the performative and constantive dimensions of the "Third World" nation, I hope to disclose also the political economy of subject-ification. The archaeology of self-identity can be traced in the uneven social formation of colonized polities, as illustrated by the Philippines, the only direct Asian colony of the United States from 1898 to 1946 and a neocolony thereafter (see Chapter 2). Disclosure of spatiotemporal contexts on which meaning and value hinge can show how postcolonial liminality is itself a delayed symptom of the "primal scene" of collective violation. The United States imperial state and its ideological apparatuses, in particular the scholarly legitimization of the West's "civilizing mission," have inflicted incalculable damage on most Filipinos to the point at which it is not possible at all to call Filipino society "postcolonial." Even "neocolonial" seems an understated and trivializing epithet to measure the pain and transmogrifications wrought by decades of subservience. This much can be affirmed despite all manner of evasion, self-rationalizations, and delusion. My caveats will perhaps recall Chinua Achebe's (1988; see Amuta 1996) cautionary reminders to Western scholars to proceed slowly before making any final judgment on the natives.

Postcoloniality is therefore a moment in this worldwide crisis of late imperial culture. Cultural practice registers this historical moment as difference, hybridity, fragmentation—the illusory and often deceptive manifestations of a process of large-scale changes. Current events confirm that the ultimate untenability of the established global order inheres in the built-in antagonisms not only between the bourgeoisie of the "postindustrial" capitalist states but between these states and what has been called the "ethnic pandemonium" of the South (Meszaros 1995: 155-56). Between the uneven and fractured surface, we discern "the old mole" working through. Only a historical materialist mode of synthesizing these changes, to my mind, can grasp their substance and comprehend the power of human agents in guiding their direction. Like neoliberal pragmatists, postcolonial critics dismiss historical materialist analysis as obsolete or useless, or "circumscribed."[3] Yet this analysis is the only one that is truly radical in the sense of being able to probe and grasp the roots of the crisis. As Raymond Williams reminds us in his partisan assessment *The Year 2000* (1983a), the North-South polarity is still based on the capitalist "international division of labor" and the foundational inequality of market exchange. At the very least, the postcolonial critic shares the master's peremptory stance of determining the terms of equivalence for any exchange of ideas according to prior Establishment canons. But mastery is not just a matter of discourse or linguistic intertextuality. The postcolonial critic labors under the burden of limitations shared by the white bourgeois feminist who, in Maivan Lam's words, has yet to come to terms "with her given status as heir of an imperial-colonial order" that has subjugated people of color. What she needs is to "hear, rather than talk, the lives of these [subjugated] women, in the fullness of their complexities—lives that these women may hope to modify, even radically, but not jettison" (1994: 871).

Recognition of material power differences, then, is the prime desideratum of solidarity and practicable alliance (on its relevance to anthropology, see Fabian 1990). In the space of contingent and aleatory happenings to which the subaltern has been consigned by postcolonialism, protracted and durable histories of resistance persist (Harlow 1987). It is no longer called Vietnam, Palestine, Chile, Nicaragua, El Salvador, Grenada, Panama, or Iraq. It is definitely no longer South Africa and its postapartheid order. It is, for sophisticated commentators of the cultural scene, "an uninhabitable, an impossible place" (Robbins 1993: 127). But against the grain of "received" wisdom, I want to postulate a "Third World" domain of subjects-in-process that is not so much geographical as political and social. This is a theme elaborated further in my concluding chapter (see also San Juan 1994b). I have in mind a community of persons who inquires into the way things are, how they have been, and how they can be and should be. Conflated with a naive view of the interdependence of nations, the "Third World" mystique can and has been used to hide class conflict. Paul Gilroy (1993) advises us to guard against absolutizing the "unstable, profane categories" of race and ethnicity as an escape from the fixed insider-outsider duality. In the same vein Roberto Schwarz's reminder may also be prophylactic: "In aesthetics as in politics, the Third World is an organic part of the contemporary scene" (1992: 174). This stance of globalizing would be perfectly in keeping with Marx's own prescient observations about the agrarian unrest in China in 1850 when he commented on its possible consequences: "When our European reactionaries, on their next flight through Asia, will have finally reached the Chinese Wall, the gates that lead to the seat of primeval reaction and conservatism—who knows, perhaps they will read the following inscription on the Wall: *Republique Chinoise—Liberté, Egalité, Fraternité!*" (1968: 23).

Lest I be accused of homogenizing a diverse ensemble of peoples and collectivities, I want to assert here that I am referring to all places in which an actual movement of resistance or opposition to imperial domination exists (for the Asia-Pacific region, see Wilson and Dirlik 1995). "Third World" then becomes more a trope as well as a site of dissent and insurgency, less a fixed physical setting, that anticipates change and renewal. And lest I be charged with indulging in a nostalgic celebration of national liberation movements of yore, of clientelist "postcolonial" regimes that have rivaled the Western colonizers in all kinds of crimes against their peoples (circumstances described by such novelists as Ngugi Wa Thiong'o, Gabriel Garcia Marquez, Pramoedya Ananta Toer, Naguib Mahfouz, and others), I can only cite my own historical critique of the "postcolonial" Marcos dictatorship in a nominally independent country, *Crisis in the Philippines* (1986; see also San Juan 1990, 1994a). Despite the tragedies and predicaments of excolonized societies, I still uphold the principle of self-determination (as Lenin expounded it in rebutting Rosa Luxemburg's class reductionism [Dunayevskaya 1981]) for all communities and peoples tyrannized by capital and other irrational forces.

The recognition and appreciation of the complexities of "Others" mark the space of absence, of erasure, in postcolonial orthodoxy. What is needed is, I think, a recovery of that historical materialist sensibility embodied in the works of C. L. R. James, a vision and praxis of transformation I call "the mass line" (Chapters 1 and 7). Of course, Lu Hsun, Fanon, Kim Il Sung, Mariategui, Hikmet, Rodney, and countless others already alluded to in this book have articulated eloquently the empowering virtue of the national-popular, the inexhaustible creative resources of the people in taking control over their lives. In Chapters 5, 6, and 8, I survey diverse modes of cultural production articulating a popular anticolonialism premised on historical memory and symbols of belonging and solidarity. Rejecting postcolonial antifoundationalism, the thesis of situated cultures in process of emergence—cultures that in their concrete dynamics of engagement with global capitalism express militant resistance to commodification—also calls attention to the invention of native traditions that defy postmodernist relativism and offer resources of hope absent from Enlightenment thought and its mirror-image, postcolonial nominalism. The wars of national liberation in our century have dramatized the mobilization of these resources and their regenerative, inspiriting vitality.

Twentieth-century history is indeed, to echo a platitude, the chronicle of the struggles for freedom by people of color. Despite the setbacks and retreats of the three decades since the end of the Vietnam War, current developments attest to the emancipatory potential of emergencies erupting in the most unlikely places and the dreams of multitudes breaking through. The prototypical diasporic artist Wilson Harris sums up the scene quite poignantly: "Wherever one looks, whether in the West or in the societies of the Third World, it would seem that moral being cannot be divorced from a deepened cycle of creativity through which we may visualize a breakthrough from absolute violence. Such a breakthrough requires us to accept the adversarial contexts in which cultures wrestle with each other but to descend as well into camouflages and masks as flexible frames within the mystery of genuine change" (1985: 128; other exemplary witnesses are Retamar [1989] and Turki [1978]). Reality, to be sure, exceeds all hypothetical speculations, schematic blueprints, and futuristic extrapolations. As witness to that maxim, I invoke here the testimonies of two other figures to convey the spirit of solidarity presiding over these essays and endowing them with an ethicopolitical if not organic consistency: first, Salud Algabre, one of the leaders of the 1935 Sakdalista uprising against U.S. imperialism and the neocolonial government of the Philippines. Interviewed in the sixties about the failure of the peasant revolt, Algabre enunciated the vernacular faith in historical becoming—the permanent cultural revolution of the New anchored in the principle of Hope that Ernst Bloch (1970) so eloquently theorized—that continues to speak truth to power and the triumphalism of her conquerors: "No uprising fails. Each one is a step in the right direction" (Sturtevant 1976: 296). Second, I excerpt from an impassioned and astute statement of Subcomandante Marcos, head of the Zapatista rebellion in Chiapas, Mexico, who responded to rumors that he was a homosexual:

Marcos is gay in San Francisco, Black in South Africa, an Asian in Europe, a Chicano in San Ysidro, an anarchist in Spain, a Palestinian in Israel, a Mayan Indian in the streets of San Cristobal, a gang member in Neza, a rocker in the National University, a Jew in Germany, an ombudsman in the Defense Ministry, a communist in the post–Cold War era, an artist without gallery or portfolio, a pacifist in Bosnia, a housewife alone on Saturday night in any neighborhood in any city. . . . So Marcos is a human being, any human being, in this world. Marcos is all the exploited, marginalized and oppressed minorities, resisting and saying "Enough!" (quoted in Parenti 1995: 209-10)

CHAPTER ONE

Interrogations and Interventions: Who Speaks for Whom?

That which is most yielding overcomes what is most resistant. That which is not becomes that which is.
—Tao Te Ching

. . . Only with a burning patience can we conquer the splendid City which will give light, justice, and dignity to all mankind. In this way the song will not have been sung in vain.
—Pablo Neruda, *Toward the Splendid City*

In her introduction to a recent *PMLA* (Publications of the Modern Language Association of America) issue devoted to "Colonialism and the Postcolonial Condition," Linda Hutcheon placed her imprimatur on the institutionalization of postcolonial theory and discourse, ascribing to it the "complexities" that scholars privilege as the mark of legitimacy. "Heterogeneity" is the salient code word that characterizes this "broad anti-imperialist emancipatory project," a "counter-discourse" of dissensus that is also "performative, provisional, and situated" (1995: 12). Indeed, the term "post," for Hutcheon and like-minded colleagues, becomes emblematic of "the dynamics of cultural resistance and retention" (1995: 10): "post" implies not only "after" but also "inclusive," even more explicitly anticolonial in its task of valorizing the "multiplication of identities." Next to the *PMLA*'s official blessing, the entry on "Postcolonial Cultural Studies" in *The Johns Hopkins Guide to Literary Theory and Criticism* surveys the variety of this genre from a historical perspective. Postcolonial cultural studies (PCS), according to Georg

Gugelberger, "is the study of the totality of 'texts' (in the largest sense of 'text') that participate in hegemonizing other cultures and the study of texts that write back to correct or undo Western hegemony" (1994: 582); but he also observes that the term "postcolonial" has a "jargonizing quality and lacks precision" (583). While asserting that PCS inadequately problematizes Western hegemonic discourse paradigms, Gugelberger claims that it is "essentially radical in the sense of demanding change" (584). Change from what to what? one may ask.[1]

Despite its prima facie radicalism, I contend that in general post-colonial discourse mystifies the political/ideological effects of Western postmodernist hegemony and prevents change. It does so by espousing a metaphysics of textualism, as in Gayatri Spivak's (1985) fetishism of "the archives of imperialist governance," or in Bhabha's (1990) analogous cult of linguistic/psychological ambivalence. Such idealist frameworks of cognition void the history of people's resistance to imperialism, liquidate popular memory, and renounce responsibility for any ethical consequence of thought. Decentering a unitary discourse of Enlightenment modernity or, conversely, repudiating Eurocentric models to advance a unique postcolonial mode of decolonization (for example, Katrak 1989), does not liberate oppressed people of color such as the Guatemalan Indians, nor overturn in any way the World Bank/International Monetary Fund conditionalities imposed on super-exploited nations like the Philippines, Jamaica, Tanzania, and others. I endorse Kumkum Sangari's timely intervention here: "To believe that a critique of the centered subject and of representation is equal to a critique of colonialism and its accoutrements is in fact to disregard the different historical formation of subjects and ways of seeing that have actually obtained from colonization" (1995: 146; see also Callinicos 1989; Appiah 1995).

Postcolonial theory entrenched in the Establishment institutions of the West denounces historical specificity and with it projects of national-popular liberation and socialist transformation. By ignoring or discounting the actual efforts of "Third World" communities to survive the havoc of global imperialism, postcolonial critics and their subtle stratagems only serve the interests of the global status quo, in particular the asymmetry between North and South (Magdoff 1992). One suspects complicity with transnational and "transculturological" interests. If the postcolonial desire is "the desire of decolonized communities for an identity" (During 1987), this desire is negotiated neither through the imagination enabled by print capitalism nor an uncontaminated indigenous language equivalent to a precolonial culture. It is negotiated through diverse counterhegemonic struggles (both in wars of position and of maneuver, to use Gramsci's terms [1971]) that dismantle the intricate play of sameness and difference in the constitution of Otherness in material practices and institutions. Such struggles (three examples of which I allude to below) are historically specific, with their own infinitely variegated strands of residual, dominant, and emergent formations that need to be inventoried and configured within the world-system of "actually existing" global capitalism. To label these struggles "totalizing" and "totalitarian" only confirms the presence of the enemy's not-so-invisible hand.

SCENARIOS OF THE "POSTCOLONIAL" STIGMATA

One site for this struggle may be instanced in the semantic historicity of the term "postcolonial" and its politically determinate inflections. In terms of the genealogy of sedimentations, I would like first to record the semantic shift of the term "postcolonial" by registering its initial usage within the seventies debate on the "postcolonial state." Hamza Alavi, among others, argued then for the relatively autonomous nature of the postcolonial state: "The role of the bureaucratic-military oligarchy is relatively autonomous because, once the controlling hand of the metropolitan bourgeoisie is lifted at the moment of independence, no single class has exclusive control over it" (1973: 147). The petite bourgeoisie in newly independent countries is credited with playing a progressive role in such institutions as the civil service bureaucracy and the military; hence the Arusha Declaration in Tanzania is interpreted as an initial victory for the progressive wing of the petite bourgeoisie. Following the failures of the radical experiments of Nkrumah in Ghana, Lumumba in the Congo, and Sukarno in Indonesia, the idea that the postcolonial state is independent of foreign interests (the former colonizer, among others) and can be harnessed for nationalist goals has been definitively refuted. From a historical-materialist perspective, the postcolonial state can only reproduce the general conditions needed to perpetuate the unequal property/power relations and their effects. In most of the "Third World," the weakness of the capitalist fraction of the native elite forces it to depend on the military or on a despot to administer the state apparatus; hence a ruling junta or Bonapartism as the form of the state in underdeveloped capitalist formations. The structural legacy of colonialism thus includes the postcolonial state, a mechanism to replace direct by indirect ideological/economic domination.

After the demise of the classic imperial system in 1945, the United States as the successor to the debilitated European states opted for a strategy of neocolonialism (Woddis 1972) or neoimperialism (Parenti 1995). In this framework, the postcolonial state may appear independent or sovereign, but in reality its economic and political policies are dictated by the former colonizer and other foreign interests through the indigenous elite, the civil service, and the military with its network of ties with Western governments during the Cold War and after. Aside from economic control, the ideological/cultural stranglehold of the West reduces political independence to mere formality: "Through its control of the institutions of education, the media and communication systems, the West is in a position to subvert whole spheres of Third World social life" (Hadjor 1993: 216). Neocolonialism designates then the persistence of economic ascendancy and cultural hegemony underneath the mask of political independence, demarcating the real democratic right of the people to exercise self-determination (which is effectively undermined by built-in mechanisms) from the formal or nominally procedural right.

But instead of the rubric "neocolonial" to describe the discrepancy between, and paradoxical imbrication of, formal independence and real subservience, the specter of the "postcolonial state" now revives to fabricate the illusion that we have gone beyond the neocolonial stage. In fact, some argue that we have entered the postimperialist era, one in which transnational corporations are integrating national economies into one supranational world market. Dependency theory in the 1960s failed to account for the growth of the power of the transnational corporations. Today, world-systems theory (Wallerstein 1983; Amin 1994) seeks to comprehend the new globalizing trend of capital by a systemic cosmological trope of center and periphery. Consequently, "postcolonial(ism)" is offered, according to Vijay Mishra and Bob Hodge, because "it foregrounds a politics of opposition and struggle, and problematizes the key relationship between centre and periphery" (276). They qualify this, however, by postulating a complicit postcolonialism underpinning *The Empire Writes Back (EWB)*, one that confuses self-misrecognizing mastery of difference with empowerment of citizens. Because postcolonial critics are heavily invested in the complicitous critique offered by postmodernism via irony, allegory, and self-reflexive tropes of doubleness, they reduce everything to metanarratives of contingency and indeterminacy. By reifying terms like "nation," "people," and so on, they commit the same fallacies they ascribe to everyone else except their disciples. In defense, the Australian authors of *EWB* argue that their position cannot be conflated with a postmodernist consensus. Disavowing the link between the deconstruction of Eurocentric master-narratives (concepts of progress, logocentric subjectivity, essentialism, teleology) and the project of "dismantling the Center/Margin binarism of imperial discourse," they assert that postcolonial critics confirm the "political agency of the colonized subject." Such agency, however, is posited but not really theorized or concretized as an immanent historical process that subverts worldwide commodification.

FUNDAMENTALIST DISSEMINATIONS

Postcolonial theory acquires its most doctrinaire instigator in Homi Bhabha. For Bhabha, the poststructuralist paradigm of linguistic or textual difference legitimizes a new master-narrative of indeterminism and contingency. The triumphalist note in the celebrations of the "coming of age" of postcolonial theory (exemplified by Hutcheon and Gugelberger) is epitomized by Bhabha's chapter on "Postcolonial Criticism" in an Establishment guidebook, *Redrawing the Boundaries: The Transformation of English and American Literary Studies*. We find here a distillation of Bhabha's axioms concerning cultural translation, deferred or postponed meanings, and the "incommensurability of cultural values and priorities that the postcolonial critic represents" (1992: 439). The fundamental premise is that the colonial experience of marginality and displacement can be figured as analogous to the arbitrary position of the signifier in a system of differences; following Lacan, the signifier is constantly suspended in a chain that never connects with the signified, forever caught in perpetual slippage, because of differential temporalities and spaces that resist comprehensive, systematic explanations. The postcolonial discourse of cultural difference is essentially ambivalent, liminal, hybrid, disjunctive, chockful of ironies and aporias; unpresentable by definition, it refuses the logic of representation and all principles of intelligibility (Bhabha 1990).

It is somewhat of a surprise, indeed, that Bhabha or I can speak of postcolonial themes and rhetoric in this manner. But let us proceed anyway in a hypothetical mode, since plenitude of meaning or communicative "good faith" is unwarranted here.

Because of the experience of oppression, diaspora, migration, exile, and so on, the postcolonial subject—the most controversial prototype is Salman Rushdie—occupies the locus of enunciation (contradistinguished from the enunciated) and inhabits it indefinitely. For Bhabha,

postcolonial culture as enunciation or enunciative practice is an uninterrupted process of performance, never achieving the closure of *enoncé* or
the sentence. Because it refuses to be bound to fixed referents or
significations, postcolonial discourse undermines the logic of representation that accompanies "consensual and collusive" liberal society, the
"holistic and organic notions of cultural value" (1992: 441). Postcolonial
culture/identity privileges "the enunciatory present as a liberatory discursive strategy. . . . The contingent and the liminal become the times
and the spaces for the historical representation of the subjects of cultural
difference in a postcolonial criticism where the dialectic of culture and
identification is neither binary nor sublatory" (1992: 444-45). With
structuralism and dialectics refused, Bhabha elevates the "language"
metaphor to transcendental aprioristic status. In this context, Barthes'
playful and agonistic semiotics is invoked as a model. Its performative
textuality, the libertinism of the signifier, the "hybrid moment outside
the sentence" finally leads to Derrida, whose example "opens up
disjunctive, incommensurable relations of spacing and temporality
within the sign," ushering us into a borderland filled with time-lags,
alterity, mimicry, and sly civility. Authorities proliferate. Bhabha invokes
Guha, then Bakhtin and Arendt (revised accordingly to fit Bhabha's
purpose), then Rorty and Foucault, and stops in an anticlimactic orgy
of archival legerdemain.

What is symptomatic in this version of postcolonial ratiocination (if
it can be called that) is its claim to plausibility. Except for the allusions to
Guha and Fanon, none of the authorities mentioned really belongs to any
conceivable geopolitical milieu—unless the imperial metropoles already
are included in the slippage of the signifier "postcolonial." What is more
a telltale index of this exercise in eclectic citatology and paraphrase is the
way Bakhtin's idea of dialogism is appropriated in complete opposition
to Bakhtin's politico-ethical commitment (see Bakhtin 1981). Bhabha,
for instance, attempts to impute a deconstructive motive to Bakhtin:
"Bakhtin's use of the metaphor of the chain of communication picks up
the sense of contingency as contiguity, while the question of the 'link'
immediately raises the issue of contingency as the indeterminate" (1992:
454). On the contrary, Bakhtin precisely rejects the contingency of parole
or utterance because the speech-act is triangulated by the constitutive roles
of speaker/theme/addressee. In other words, utterance addressed to a
specific listener in a specific situation is concretely determinate, not
contingent; moreover, utterance considered as "a link in the chain of
communication" (quoted by Bhabha himself) is rooted in an intersubjec-

tive, hierarchical totality of social assemblages locked in ideological-political antagonisms, hence the "multiaccentuality of the sign" (Voloshinov/Bakhtin 1986: 23). Utterance or acts of communication are thus a crucial arena of class warfare. Whereas Bhabha repudiates the categories of history and class subjects, Bakhtin situates language and speakers in an "uninterrupted process of historical becoming" (271) where official and oppositional discourses fight for supremacy.

IMMOBILIZING FANON

While Bhabha's fallacies and inadequacies have been examined already by Parry (1994), Callinicos (1995), and others, I would like to show how Bhabha's subordination of everything to the language metaphor and its exorbitant implications compels him to distort and thus render inutile the praxis-oriented voice of Frantz Fanon.

One example of Bhabha's relentless insistence on the grammatological syndrome can be demonstrated by analyzing his essay "Remembering Fanon: Self, Psyche and the Colonial Condition." In a typical move, Bhabha situates Fanon in the topos of ambivalence, in the "uncertain interstices of historical change." Challenging Enlightenment historicism (Hegel, Marx) and the "representative structure of a General Will," Fanon's *Black Skin/White Masks* (according to Bhabha) "rarely historicizes the colonial experience. There is no master narrative or realist perspective that provides a background of social and historical facts against which emerge the problem of the individual or collective psyche" (1994a: 115). This incredible claim that the primordial question Fanon asks, "What does the black man want?" is posed in a vacuum—in spite of the numerous references to "colonial racism" in Africa, Algeria, the United States, and elsewhere—blunts the political edge of the text and mystifies Fanon's argument. It also undercuts Bhabha's thesis that "The emergence of the human subject as socially and psychically authenticated depends upon the negation of an originary narrative of fulfillment or an imaginary coincidence between individual interest or instinct and the General Will" (1994: 118). Lacking that "originary narrative," any negation seems pointless. Bhabha insists that the answer to Fanon's question is the psychoanalytic, more precisely Lacanian, doctrine of "the splitting moment of desire" that defines the Other. The black man wants "the objectifying confrontation with otherness." Bhabha posits this injunction: the "Other must be seen as the necessary negation of a primordial identity—cultural or psychic—that introduces the system of differentiation which enables the 'cultural' to be signified as a linguistic, symbolic, historical reality" (1994: 119). In plain language, the psyche can be understood as a sociohistorical construction inserted into a web of cultural artifices and artificial boundaries.[2] From this semiotic anatomy of Fanon's desire, Bhabha makes Fanon reject the Hegelian "dream for a human reality in itself-for itself" for a nondialectical Manicheanism. Bhabha thus reifies the colonial Manichean world that Fanon poignantly delineated in *The Wretched of the Earth* for the sake of freezing Fanon in that twilight zone of difference, the in-between of displacement, dispossession, and dislocation that Bhabha hypostatizes as the ineluctable essence of postcoloniality. Reductive closure of Fanon is complete.

This hermeneutic sabotage would not be a serious matter if we were to take Bhabha's version of Fanon as one possible reading or interpretation, albeit a highly fanciful one. To claim that this version captures the substantive, integral, and most subversive quality of Fanon's thought is, however, to expose the pathos if not reactionary function of postcolonial theorizing. Fanon analyzed the case of a real patient, relied on empirical research, and interrogated the conclusions of O. Mannoni and Jean-Paul Sartre. His observations of everyday life and the general conditions of blacks in Africa, the Caribbean, the United States, and Europe led him to an existentialist affirmation of creative freedom enabled by a Hegelian problematic that, according to Bhabha, Fanon abandons. In the concluding chapter of *Black Skin/White Masks,* Fanon writes:

> [The] former slave wants to make himself recognized. At the foundation of Hegelian dialectic there is an absolute reciprocity which must be emphasized. . . .
>
> The only means of breaking this vicious circle [of colonial, racist domination] that throws me back on myself is to restore to the other, through mediation and recognition, his human reality, which is different from natural reality. The other has to perform the same operation. "Action from one side only would be useful because what is to happen can only be brought about by means of both . . . "; "they recognize themselves as mutually recognizing each other." (1967: 217; the quotes are from Hegel's *The Phenomenology of Mind*)

Because he distrusted Western philosophy as complicit with the ruses of racism, Fanon relied on his own experiences and his diagnosis of others to liberate blacks from the "epidermalization" of the inferiority complex produced by historical structures and economic circumstances. His book ends with a humanistic shibboleth reminiscent of Rousseau, Voltaire, and the philosophes anathema to postcolonial bricolage: "I am my own foundations. . . . It is through the effort to recapture the self and to scrutinize the self, it is through the lasting tension of their freedom that men will be able to create the ideal conditions of existence for a human world" (1967: 231). His ultimate "prayer" already signals a departure from the positions enunciated in the book: "O my body, make of me always a man who questions!" Three years after, Fanon criticized his formulaic psychoanalysis of racism thus: "Here we have proof that questions of race are but a superstructure, a mantle, an obscure ideological emanation concealing an economic reality" (Zahar 1974: 34). But even then, as he immersed himself in the unequivocal exigencies of anticolonial revolution, Fanon never succumbed to a purely dualistic or Manichean metaphysics nor did he accept a formalist valorization of anarchistic decentering and dispersal.[3] Like Rigoberta Menchu, C. L. R. James, and Maria Lorena Barros, my other exemplars here, Fanon sought solidarity with Europe's "Others" and communicated this desire to all who shared his anti-imperialist principles and their potential for generating communities of activists. Feeling responsible to the mass of "Calibans" constructed by the West's "civilizing" hubris, he decided to serve the cause of the victims and their project of collective transformation.

The victims in fact multiply at the hands of postcolonialists. The premium assigned to hybridity, pastiche, parodic performance, and so on, as constitutive of the postcolonial *Weltanschauung* is rendered suspect when we encounter the dissidence of aboriginal peoples. Diana Brydon argues that the claim to authenticity of Canada's native peoples "condemns them to a continued marginality and an eventual death" (1995: 141). In order to transcend the impasse of liberal pluralism manifest in the postmodernist cult of difference, to move beyond "myths of cultural purity or authenticity" that isolate natives from "contemporary life and full citizenhood," Brydon urges a strategy of "contamination" that will not homogenize or coopt. She envisions a "new globalism that is neither the old universalism nor the Disney simulacrum" in a postcolonial recuperation of deconstructive energies (1995: 141). As a "white Inuit," this white middle-class intellectual intends to bring "differences together into creative contact" (136). From these notions of the "multiple, shifting, and often self-contradictory identity" of the postcolonial subject, can we properly appreciate the political sagacity embedded in North American Native vernacular speech—say, those by Pauline Johnson (Tekahionwake) or by Alootook Ipellie (Caws and Prendergast 1994: 2517-19, 2704-07)?

The claim of postcolonial theory (as exemplified by assorted Australian, Indian, and Canadian ventriloquists of "speechless" subalterns) to be more radical than avant-garde modernism is problematic especially for people of color seeking to affirm their autochtonous traditions of resistance. What is at stake is their survival, their authentic and incommensurable dignities. Also cast in the wager is their counterhegemonic projects to recover/reaffirm the integrity of their cultures often anchored to the land/habitat, to events of dwelling and communion with their environment. What we have discerned so far is that a transcendental politics of aporia and equivocation is substituted for a critique of hegemonic authority. The ironic or minimal self of the theorist intervenes to mediate between Western epistemes and the self-empowering expression of multitudes, thus recuperating in "bad faith" the fraud of representation originally denounced.

Critics ranging from Arif Dirlik (1994b) and Aijaz Ahmad (1995a) to indigenous partisans in the frontline have contended that the postcolonial repudiation of "foundations" undermines any move to generate new forms of resistance against globalized capitalism and its centrifugal hierarchies (Magdoff). Hybrid contrivances, discrepant local epistemes, cyborgs, border crossings, creole or *metissage* texts—such performative slogans tend to obfuscate the realities of what Leslie Sklair (1991) calls the transnational ideology of capitalist consumerism. Postcolonial theory generated in "First World" academies turns out to be one product of flexible, post-Fordist capitalism, not its antithesis. I suggest a dialectical counterpoint to this orthodoxy (satirized by Jacoby) in the practices of Guatemalan activist Rigoberta Menchu and of the socialist revolutionary thinker C. L. R. James from Trinidad. In contrast to the postcolonial posture of recalcitrance, I offer the lifework of a guerilla combatant of the New People's Army in the Philippines, Maria Lorena Barros, whose martyrdom speaks more eloquently about the human condition under imperialism than any hyperreal, labyrinthine discourse from the metropole. These are three possible embodiments of the Fanonian figure who questions; their identities cannot be "postalized" or romanticized because their illocutionary force rests in the border between trauma and utopia.

IN QUEST OF THE SPEAKING SUBJECT

Not too long ago, Jean Baudrillard, a formidable sage of postmodernism, shocked the public by claiming that the 1992 Gulf War did not really take place. In a world governed by the principle of reversibility, where the code that enables reproduction generates the hyperreal and abolishes the difference between the real and the imaginary so that "everything becomes undecidable," we begin to doubt that ordinary words mean anything, including what I am saying here. We are said to live in a world of simulation, feigned images, and simulacra where everything (nature, culture) becomes interchangeable, where there is neither true nor false, beautiful nor ugly, useful nor useless—such binary opposites either collapse or implode. Who can tell what is real from what is fake? Naivete or faith seems to be the desideratum, as Dostoevsky's Grand Inquisitor once counseled the perplexed, in confronting such enigmas and mysteries.

Before we can face the postmodernist Grand Inquisitor, we need to establish the basis for dialogue. What is the background to our text, *Me Llamo Rigoberta Menchu Y Asi Me Nacio La Conciencia* (1983)? Obviously, given its condition of production—the encounter in Paris between a Venezuelan anthropologist and an activist Indian—Menchu's text needs to be distinguished from the Western genre of autobiography, interview, or even the innovative ethnographic discourse. Suffice it to mention a few facts to establish the parameters of exchange.

By the time Menchu's book came out, a conservative estimate is that at least 100,000 indigenous peoples (Guatemala is the only North America country with a predominantly Indian population) have been killed by the U.S.-supported government; at least 40,000 have disappeared, 450 villages destroyed, and 250,000 people turned into refugees because of "antiguerilla" campaigns against the native population together with labor, human rights, and church activists (Brecher 1993). This "Mayan holocaust, . . . a wave of violence unparalleled in this hemisphere in modern times," can also be summed up this way: "Out of a total population of fewer than nine million people living in a territory the size of Tennessee, one million Guatemalans endured internal displacement and another 100,000 fled the country" (Hawkins 51). In *Open Veins of Latin America* (1973), Eduardo Galeano recounts the orgy of violence from 1954 to 1967, a carnage unprecedented in the history of the American hemisphere.

The roots of this horrendous situation can be traced to the colonial underdevelopment of the country as a "banana republic" in which 98 percent of the land is owned by fewer than 150 people (counting each foreign corporation as a person). U.S. foreign investments dominate the country (the United Fruit Company was once the biggest landowner). When Guatemalans elected a democratic government headed by Jacobo Arbenz (1952-54), Arbenz began to institute a mild land reform program. This triggered a 1952 CIA report that "Communist influence . . . based on militant advocacy of social reforms and nationalistic policies" was dominant, leading to "the persecution of foreign economic interests, especially the United Fruit Company" (Chomsky 1992: 47-48). President Eisenhower sanctioned the CIA's destruction of his regime. The president of the United Fruit Company then happened to be Allen Dulles, CIA director; and Walter Bedell Smith, who directed the CIA before Dulles, became president of the United Fruit Company after Arbenz was overthrown. Included in the directorship of the Company were Henry Cabot Lodge, U.S. Ambassador to the United Nations, and John Cabot, Assistant Secretary of State for Inter-American Affairs; U.S. Secretary of State John Foster Dulles was legal adviser to the Company (Greene 1970).

After the military coup, the Kennedy and Johnson administrations gave massive aid to the Guatemalan military that quickly transformed it into the "killing fields" of the last four decades. Carter's "human rights" administration did not change anything. It was in the period of Reagan's support of Rios Montt in the early 1980s that the genocidal slaughter of tens of thousands of Indians occurred, decimating entire regions. Julio Godoy, a Guatemalan journalist, returned from Europe in 1989 and contrasted the situation there with that in Central America. He found the East Europeans luckier because while the Moscow-imposed government in Prague would degrade and humiliate reformers, the Washington-made government in Guatemala would kill them. It still does, in a virtual genocide that has taken more than 150,000 victims [in what Amnesty International calls] "a government program of political murder. . . . One is tempted to believe that some people in the White House worship Aztec gods—with the offering of Central American blood. (Chomsky 1992: 50)

To appreciate the substantive context of Menchu's book, we need to frame it within the present social conditions: Today, 2 percent of the population still owns 67 percent of the land. One third of those in the countryside (mainly Mayan Indians who constitute 60 percent of the population) live on plots "the size of a grave" (Hawkins 50). Six million don't have health care; illiteracy stands at 75 percent. Thousands of homeless children living in the streets are brutalized by the police; a series of authoritarian dictatorships "use security forces as instruments of intimidation and terror," with over a hundred thousand political murders since the CIA-backed coup in 1954 (Demko 1992). According to a 1990 UNICEF report, 87 percent of the people live below the poverty line while 14 percent (*ladinos,* or mixed blood, and people of European descent) exploit the cheap labor of workers in coffee, bananas, and other export crops.

Such tabulation of facts has no meaning unless it is contextualized in the history of unequal international exchange. Before there can be a real social basis of equality as prerequisite for multicultural dialogue, I think we need to understand the complex links and interdependencies between what used to be called "center" and "periphery," between the dominant hegemonic military-economic powers and nation states and the subaltern societies, in the world-system. Clearly the basis for egalitarian communicative exchange is lacking. This perhaps explains why most critics experience difficulty in locating Menchu's authority as narrator/representer. Ma. Josefina Saldaña Portillo astutely locates Menchu's articulation of revolutionary transformation in an ambiguous borderland or shifting locus that escapes our theoretical categories. Portillo writes: "In her self-representation, Menchu strategically vacillates between the position of autonomous liberal subject and the Other of Western discourse to critique modernization from a gendered, classed, and ethnic position; and to critique teleologies of consciousness put forth by her male counterparts and predicated on the 'transcendence' of her present subject position" (109-110). While Menchu's authorial "I" preserves a precarious distance from the tactical "We" who claim to represent others, this interlocutor at least belies the old Guatemalan attitude of self-defense expressed by Luis Cardoza y Aragon: "We do not go out of ourselves and, if we do, it is not to start a dialogue but to explode over our own monologue" (Franco 1967, 232). Menchu initiates a conversation, staging contradictions and differences, utilizing the versatile modality of this genre as the chief agent of revolutionary articulation.

MENCHU: SPEAK TRUTH TO POWER

In 1992, Rigoberta Menchu, a Quiche Indian from Guatemala, was given the Nobel Peace Prize for her work "for social justice and ethno-cultural reconciliation based on respect for the rights of indigenous peoples" (*New York Times* 17 October 1992). We read in the same news report that Menchu's parents and brother were killed by government troops in the

1980s, part of the more than 50,000 poor, rural Indians and 120,000 Guatemalans slain during the three decades of insurrections. Could these figures be interpreted as mere signs in a self-contained logic of difference? If the sign value of the Nobel Peace Prize depends on a code instead of context of reference, then it self-destructs. Baudrillard proposes that in order to resist the closed system of the hyperreal and obfuscating media hype, we need "seduction" and "fatal strategies"—that is, ecstasy, risk, and vertigo—before the object that seduces and to which we need to submit (for a sample of reader's vertigo, see Sommer 1993).

How is it then possible to submit to Menchu's *testimonio* and not risk the stigma of being duped by a presumed reality out there? Since the genre of *testimonio* mediates the documentary sociohistorical context and authorial ego, reference and intentionality (Tatum 1992), does Menchu's intertextual performance, her "speaking truth to power," overcome the disingenousness of postmodernist aesthetics?

One can say that Menchu's *testimonio* evokes a reality-effect homologous to what she experienced. Whether the actual events occurred or not, what is certain is that the transcription of acts of barbarism tests the limits of ordinary language and the genre of classical expressive realism. Let us take one episode for verification. In Chapter 24, Menchu recounts the torture and death of her sixteen-year old brother who was burned alive in front of members of her family and the whole community. She recalls thus:

> So they inflicted those dreadful tortures on him. Day and night they subjected him to terrible, terrible pain. They tied him up, they tied his testicles, my brother's sexual organs, they tied them behind with string and forced him to run. Well, he couldn't stand that, my little brother, he couldn't bear that awful pain and he cried out, he asked for mercy. And they left him in a well, I don't know what it's called, a hole with water and a bit of mud in it, they left him naked there all night. There were a lot of corpses there in the hole with him and he couldn't stand the smell of all those corpses. There were other people there who'd been tortured. He recognized several catechists there who'd been kidnapped from other villages and were suffering as badly as he was. My brother was tortured for more than sixteen days. They cut off his fingernails, they cut off his fingers, they cut off his skin, they burned parts of his skin. Many of the wounds, the first ones, swelled and were infected. He stayed alive. They shaved his head, left just the skin, and also they cut off the fleshy part of his face. My brother suffered tortures on every part of his body, but they took care not to damage the arteries or veins so that he would survive the tortures and

not die. They gave him food so that he'd hold out and not die from his wounds. There were twenty men with him who had been tortured or were still undergoing torture. There was also a woman. They had raped her and then tortured her. (174)

The narrative elaborates the outrage for another six or seven pages until we witness all the bodies of the suspected guerillas doused with petrol and set afire. Pathos is foiled by raw spectacles too horrible to contemplate.

The next chapter offers no catharsis or relief. It describes the death of Rigoberta's father along with comrades who occupied the Spanish Embassy in Guatemala. Her father died when the Embassy building burned down after intense government assault. Menchu recounts several versions of what happened, whether the peasants were armed or burned themselves or were killed by bombs thrown by the police. She pursues a scientific approach, using the evidence that her father's body showed five bullet holes in the head and one in the heart, "and he was very stiff" (186). What actually transpired can be reconstructed on the basis of the bodies that "were stiff, rigid, and all twisted."

As though plotting a climactic trajectory, Menchu's narrative leads to what one might call the return of truth-claims in a time when the real has supposedly evaporated into a pastiche of kaleidoscopic images. The next chapter details the kidnapping and death of her mother, indubitably a much more horrendous scene of mutilation and rape than the previous one, until her body is eaten by animals. "We were relieved to know my mother wasn't suffering any longer . . . " (200). We later discover that these confessions are not meant simply to sensationalize the subject or scandalize the readers. Its logic is soon revealed as part of an ethnographic craft. Bracketed by chapters that describe in prodigious detail the customs and traditional folkways of the Quiche Indians, these three episodes provide the explanation why at the end Menchu decides to offer her life to the cause of defending and saving the cultural integrity and dignity of her people: "The world I live in is so evil, so bloodthirsty, that it can take my life away from one moment to the next. So the only road open to me is our struggle, the just war. . . . I am convinced that the people, the masses, are the only ones capable of transforming society. . . . My commitment to our struggle knows no boundaries nor limits" (246-47). Even as she goes into exile to arouse international solidarity for her people's struggle, Menchu affirms something that escapes or defies textualization: "I've traveled to many places where I've had the opportunity to talk about my people. . . . Nevertheless, I'm still keeping my Indian identity a secret. I'm still keeping secret what I think no-one should know" (247). Something is left over, an excess, after so much disclosure.

Counterpointing the postcolonial devaluation of the Cartesian unitary subject, Menchu's narrative may be interpreted as an act of reconstitution of a destroyed community. Like dream-work, it proceeds by means of displacement and condensation. It strives for a synthesis of the fragmented lives and the disintegrated families of the Guatemalan Indians, the Quiche people, as well as the *ladinos* and other indigenous groups. Menchu asserts that her story is not just a private or purely personal confession; it speaks for "all poor Guatemalans" exploited and manipulated by the local elite and their foreign patrons. Pursuing this avowal of intent, John Beverley considers Menchu's testimonio an example of "an emergent popular-democratic culture" transcending bourgeois humanism, the Eurocentric decorum of "proper" style, and all existing ideological apparatuses of alienation and domination. Menchu's narrative may be said to approximate a plot of education, the personal/collective learning of the operations of a brutal racist system based on combined tributary-capitalist property relations (for U.S. intervention in Guatemala, see Greene 1970; Chomsky 1992; Hawkins 1994). It is also a reciprocal interrogation of the self and others, of accounting for one's responsibility to beleaguered communities traversed by one's labor and suffering.

For Menchu, the impulse to communicate is integral to the liberatory and nurturing *conatus* of her life. Her speech-act is also a "form of survival" (Rice-Sayre 52) and a cognitive mastery of necessity as knowledge of determinations. From Chapters 1 to 15 of her *testimonio,* we are given an ethnographic account of the life cycle of the Quiche Indians, their traditional beliefs and rituals, as experienced by a young woman whose maturation coincides with our exposure to the degradation suffered by the Indians.[4] This montage of scenes, conveyed in the style of expressive realism, culminates in the torture and burning of her brother in Chapter 24, followed by the killing of her father in a revolutionary engagement and then by the torture and murder of her mother. Despite the decimation of her family followed by her exile, Menchu is reunited with her sister; her "family" becomes all the *compañeros* in the Peasant Unity Committee (rubric abbreviated as CUC) and the Quiche people. She reaffirms her commitment:

> My life does not belong to me. I've decided to offer it to a cause. . . . The
> world I live in is so evil, so bloodthirsty, that it can take my life away from

one movement to the next. So the only road open to me is our struggle, the just war . . . [W]e can build the people's church . . . a real change inside people. I chose this as my contribution to the people's war. I am convinced that the people, the masses, are the only ones capable of transforming society.

That is my cause . . . it wasn't born out of something good, it was born out of wretchedness and bitterness. It has been radicalized by the poverty in which my people live. It has been radicalized by the malnutrition which I, as an Indian, have seen and experienced. And by the exploitation and discrimination which I've felt in the flesh. And by the oppression which prevents us performing our ceremonies, and shows no respect for our way of life, the way we are. (246-47)

Menchu is then both a singular person and an allegorical figure. Her testimony is less an autobiography in the conventional sense than a history of lived experience, a cosmography of the indigenous peoples of Central America and by extension of the Fourth World. One cannot deny a unifying telos immanent in the unfolding of Menchu's lived experiences. The autobiographical redaction unites in a precarious but heuristic tension the political and scientific concerns of both the anthropologist Elizabeth Burgos-Debray and the protagonist Menchu. Ethnography mutates into a unique practice of dissent combining both alternative and oppositional stances (Sommer 1993; Portillo 1995).

In her study of this anticanonical genre, Barbara Harlow underscores the dynamics of resistance in the narrative blending of "the social transformation of traditional family structure into a political organization and the personal transformation of the daughter into a political organizer" (1987: 191). While Menchu, the signified subject-position, may be conceived as an effect interpellated by a rhetoric of exposure and indictment, such a discourse is itself inscribed in the overdetermined specificity of the Guatemalan sociopolitical formation judged in the context of geopolitical Cold War conflicts of the 1960s and 1970s: U.S. support for the Guatemalan military in order to contain the threat of the Nicaraguan Sandinistas, the Cuban revolution, and so on. Formulated another way, one can characterize Menchu's discourse as both referential and self-reflexive: it speaks truth to power. Its illocutionary force lies in its truth-effect, its programmatic resonance, more exactly, in the provocation of agencies or instrumentalities committed to destroying the system of injustice in Guatemala and the entire hemisphere.

Contamination by a received agenda of popular-democratic socialism as well as a Latin American theology of liberation may be apprehended in the "silences" of the narrative. But this does not result in an infinitely polysemous and finally unintelligible, playful text. Quite the contrary. Menchu's project is in diametrical opposition to the postcolonial one of undecidable mixture: an integration of the personal and the communal, the forging of a new universality (to use a term C. L. R. James frequently deploys) that will connect the Quiche people with all humans fighting for equality, justice, and respect for each people's integrity and right to self-determination. This quest for a radical universality is sustained by an impulse to preserve something unique, something distinctive, whose substance can be only precariously named by the term "ethnic"—the aboriginal signature—that resists codification, hermeneutic gloss, cooptative translation. Menchu's act of witnessing is rooted in the call for solidarity sanctioned by the community's distinctive, inviolate ethos:

> Therefore, my commitment to our struggle knows no boundaries or limits. This is why I've traveled to many places where I've had the opportunity to talk about my people. . . . Nevertheless, I'm still keeping my Indian identity a secret. I'm still keeping secret what I think no one should know. Not even anthropologists or intellectuals, no matter how many books they have, can find out all our secrets. (247)

Menchu's "secrets"—not just her Indian *nom de guerre*—will continue to resist the appropriation/abrogation strategy of postcolonial theory as long as imperialism and the client "postcolonial" state seek to destroy the habitat and spiritual ecology of the Indian peoples in Guatemala (Beverley and Zimmerman 1990). As the *testimonios* of the silenced multiply, I am confident that this genre is bound to neutralize any postcolonial ludic machinery geared to destabilizing representation and obstructing communication.[5]

In a formalist perspective, Linda Hutcheon has suggested that postmodernist representation bears an ambivalent politics: while it denaturalizes "realism's transparency and modernism's reflexive response," it retains "(in its typically complicitously critical way) the historically attested power of both" (1989: 34). Realism's assumption of a logic of the social can coexist with parody and irony. While postmodernism nourishes incredulity toward metanarratives of progress and freedom, it recognizes the legitimacy of local narratives or language games (in Wittgenstein's sense). Menchu is self-critical—but the self here acquires individuality only in historical situation or habitat of revolutionary performance.

One can say then that Menchu, against the grain of documentary mimicry, anticipates the postmodern decentering of the subject, the bifurcation of the enunciator (the speaking voice) and enunciation (the grammatical subject, or subject of the predicate). In withholding her "Indian name," Menchu approximates Lyotard's notion of *differend*—the silencing of a player in a language game. While others may demand that for the existence of the Nazi gas chambers to be confirmed, a victim as witness needs to appear before the court—as some postmodernists claim, "only a dead person can testify"—Menchu appears here as the sign of an injustice that defies expression in cognitive or commonsensical fashion. But can we really accept the argument that she, or her utterance (taking this word in the dialogistic sense conceived by Bakhtin), is the subject of a *differend* and thus marks either a silence or impossibility of presenting/representing injustice? Lyotard's thesis follows Kant in that no universal can refer to a real object; an ethical universal can only be theorized in the mode of the sublime, something unrepresentable or exceeds all means of representation. In short, there is no existing genre of discourse that can capture the *differend,* or the ontological primacy of the Other in the realm of pure heterogeneous space. Given that, we avoid the totalitarian delirium of metanarratives—progress, equality, justice—as well as the performativity of technological and instrumental rationality.

C. L. R. JAMES: DETERRITORIALIZING INDIVIDUALISM

Let us examine another transcription of *la vida real.* In *The Empire Writes Back,* Bill Ashcroft, Gareth Griffiths, and Helen Tiffin uphold the Caribbean as "the crucible of the most extensive and challenging postcolonial literary theory" on account of the works of Edward Braithwaite, Wilson Harris, and others. But what I find revealing is that there is not a single mention in their book of C. L. R. James, the great West Indian Marxist innovator (more on James in Chapter 7). Throughout his entire oeuvre spanning the interwar years and the Cold War, from *The Black Jacobins* to *Mariners, Renegades, and Castaways* to *American Civilization* and *Beyond a Boundary,* James exemplified the dialectical incorporation of Western thought and art in a peculiar "Third World" sensibility that is neither hybrid, syncretic, nor pastiche but singular in its commitment to the popular overthrow of the imperial world system. James's thesis of a "permanent revolution" in the domain of cultural practice may be illustrated by his insightful commentaries on popular culture (cinema, detective novels) and especially by his chronicle of cricket as performed in the colony, *Beyond a Boundary.*

James's text is less an autobiography than a discourse on the Caribbeanization of British/European culture. On the surface, it may be read as an endeavor to syncopate the chronological sequence of his life with his exploration of the aesthetic pleasure and ethical value of cricket in the national life of Trinidad and the West Indies. James serves both as witness and experiencer of contradictory forces, the lines of power/difference generated in a typical colonial milieu. Cricket happens to be the terrain of hegemonic compromise in which the natives are given access to an imported "form of life." James's interest centers on the pedagogical and symbolic function of cricket. While cricket is appraised as an educational and moral force in shaping Anglophone West Indian identity and social mores, it also serves as "a privileged site for the playing out and imaginary resolution of social antagonisms" (Lazarus 1992: 78). In other words, cricket functions as an ideological apparatus that can interpellate subjects as colonized natives or independent agents. In chapter 16, James conceives of cricket as an art form that resembles classic Greek drama, "so organized that at all times it is compelled to reproduce the central action," in which the characters are engaged in a conflict that is both personal and representative of social groups. James expounds on the allegorical character of the players and movements of the game, especially the "significant form" of stylized bodily motion:

> This fundamental relation of the One and the Many, Individual and Social, Individual and Universal, leader and followers, representative and ranks, the part and the whole, is structurally imposed on the players of cricket. . . . Thus the game is founded upon a dramatic, a human, relation which is universally recognized as the most objectively pervasive and psychologically stimulating in life and therefore in that artificial representation of it which is drama.
>
> [Hence] the greatness of the great batsman is not so much in his own skill as that he sets in motion all the immense possibilities that are contained in the game as structurally organized. (1983: 197, 198)

But aside from this aesthetic "heightening of vitality," James focused on the game's political resonance by analogy with Greek drama and the Olympic games, both of which are associated with the birth of democracy and individualism. The striving for a "more complete human existence" (1983: 211) is not expressed just by individual players but by the mass audience that, for James, participated in the rendering of its socially "significant form."

Beyond a Boundary is James's genealogy of his intellectual and ethical formation. It is a memoir of how questions of race, class, and nationality (no matter how elided or peripheral) could not be repressed from the texture of everyday life in the colony. Loyalty, restraint, moral discipline, a critical attitude, adherence to a code of conduct or a structure of feeling—these are what for James constitute the positive legacy of colonial sports. His life history coincides with the political struggle to define the emergence of West Indian integrity and initiative within this imperial scaffolding in a way that transforms this material, together with the indigenous elements, into something new and original, not a mimicry or counterfeit image. Although James acknowledges his debt to colonial schooling, to British literature (from Bunyan to Thackeray and Arnold), in the end he affirms his rootedness in place: "We are of the West Indies West Indian" (255). The "Puritan sense of discipline" he discerns in his own extended family is not something foreign but already indigenized, not a mimicry of Western "Othering" but a creative response to imposed circumstances.

In the public arena, James always acknowledged himself as a product of European learning. In the lecture "Discovering Literature in Trinidad: The 1930s," James located himself in a world-system and took his bearings from this extraterritorial vantage-point: "We live in one world, and we have to find out what is taking place in the world. And I, a man of the Caribbean, have found that it is in the study of Western literature, Western philosophy and Western history that I have found out the things I have found out, even about the underveloped countries" (238). If he was a "hybrid" from a postcolonial optic, he can also claim to have made himself an "original" in his own terms.

Following the Marxian vision that capitalism begets its own gravediggers, James suggested that artists like Wilson Harris, St. John Perse, and Aimé Césaire, and others who broke away from the Eurocentric tradition, disavowed the premises but operated within the same parameters. It is an instance not of syncretic adaptation but of dialectical sublation, a simultaneous canceling and preserving of selected cultural materials. The process, however, occurs within the new horizon of an emancipatory agenda. The center/periphery dualistic paradigm is thereby problematized. If English literature is largely a creation of "foreigners" like Conrad, Henry James, Ezra Pound, T. S. Eliot and an assemblage of Irish writers from Shaw to Yeats, Joyce and O'Casey, then James contends that the Caribbean artist can also participate in modifying or de-Westernizing "civilization" as both insider and outsider: "And it is when you are outside, but can take part as a member, that you see differently from the ways they see, and you are able to write independently" (1980b: 244). From this standpoint that problematizes outside/inside boundaries, we can appreciate by way of a symptomatic reading James's idea of British colonialism in the West Indies as a mode of begetting its "gravediggers." His association with the celebrated cricket player Learie Constantine witnessed the manner of its begetting via James's pioneering advocacy for West Indian self-government. We should qualify this, however, by interpolating here the subsequent catalyzing role of the militant socialist tradition: it was the influence of Marxism, particularly American Trotskyism, radical French historiography, Herman Melville's fiction, and United States popular culture filtered through the mass media, that all together served as midwife to the antiimperialist rebirth of cricket as an allegory of the West Indian quest for national recognition/self-determination. In this framework, the process of mediation/transition becomes thematized. The Jamesian text becomes the site for calculating the precise determinants of native agency, what postcolonial critics would call the self-referential "happening" of translation and intractable displacement.

The profoundly instructive value of James's trajectory—from historian of the Haitian slave revolt as part of the European bourgeois revolution to the cultural activist of *American Civilization* and *Beyond a Boundary*—cannot be captured by the postcolonial epistemology of hybridity and ambivalence. Nor can it account for the difference between influence and reception. Within the framework of permanent world revolution challenging state capitalism in the East and West, James discovers new life in the "weak links" of the system. This is shown by his wide-ranging inventory of struggles foregrounded in "From Toussaint L'Ouverture to Fidel Castro," "The People of the Gold Coast," and "The Revolutionary Answer to the Negro Problem in the USA" (James 1992). More than thirty years after his departure from Trinidad, he discovers the moment of autonomy, his Caribbean voice/persona, in the search for the universality first claimed by the European Enlightenment but already forfeited by Cold War capitalism in a stage of protracted crisis. There is a lesson for postcolonials in recalling that James was languishing as a prisoner in an Ellis Island facility when he completed his magisterial cultural study, *Mariners, Renegades and Castaways.*

BARROS: HOPE AND THE WILL FOR TRANSFORMATION

In an insightful critique of postcolonial dogma, Aijaz Ahmad argues that within the orbit of transmigrant, multinational capitalism and its consumerist ethos the nation-state remains as an effective horizon of politics. Popular-democratic struggle for national liberation, not identity politics based on ethnic particularisms, is a legitimate and historically timely response to the structural offensive of transnational corporations and their instrumentalities (such as the World Bank/International Monetary Fund): "It is in this framework that the nation-state remains, globally, the horizon for any form of politics that adopts the life-processes of the working classes as its point of departure, and which seeks to address the issue of the exploitation of poorer women, the destruction of the natural environment by national as well as transnational capitals, or the rightward drift of ideological superstructures, all of which are deeply connected with labour regimes, gender-related legislations and ideologies, and investment and extraction plans guaranteed by the nation-state" (1995a: 12-13). It is in this context that I call attention to the cultural politics of the National Democratic Front in the Philippines (which includes the partisans of the New People's Army [NPA] led by the Communist Party of the Philippines) spearheading the struggle against the neocolonial U.S.-supported regimes from the time of the Marcos dictatorship (1972-86) to Corazon Aquino (1986-92) and the present Ramos administration.

Anticolonial insurrections against centuries of Spanish tyranny in the Philippines climaxed in the 1896 revolution, but complete and genuine independence was aborted with the intervention of the United States military forces. The Filipino-American War (1899-1902) marked the beginning of U. S. political, ideological, and economic domination over the Filipino people. This conquest was punctuated by numerous peasant revolts for half a century, culminating in the Huk uprising of 1949-51 at the height of the Cold War. Amid world-epochal upheavals, notably the Cultural Revolution in China, popular uprisings in Africa and Latin America, and the protest against intensified U.S. aggression in Indo-China, the founding of the NPA in 1969 initiated a new epoch of popular-democratic resistance throughout the archipelago.

The vicissitudes of the armed struggle against the postcolonial state (the Philippines was granted formal independence by the United States in 1946) can be emblematized by the life of Maria Lorena Barros, founder of the pioneering women's organization, Makibaka (*Malayang Kilusan ng Bagong Kababaihan,* or Movement of New Nationalist Women). This appraisal is not intended to romanticize a single individual, but to deploy a life history as a condensation of the rich, durable tradition of women's resistance to colonialism and patriarchy beginning with figures like Gabriela Silang, Teresa Magbanua, and Melchora Aquino to twentieth-century heroines like Salud Algabre, Consolacion Chiva, Liza Balando, and many others now enshrined in the pantheon of Filipina feminism.

Born on 18 March 1948, Barros matured during the 1968 student rebellions and mass demonstrations against the Marcos government's complicity in the Vietnam War. Deeply influenced by her mother's views about social injustice and inequality, Barros graduated in 1970 with a degree in anthropology from the University of the Philippines where she taught for some time. She led in organizing Makibaka with a program of action linking women's emancipation from male domination with class exploitation and national oppression. On the "woman question," her stance was profoundly oppositional: "In our system of values, a woman who uses her brains is regarded as an anomaly. The women in our society are encouraged to be passive creatures good only for bearing and rearing children" (San Juan 1986: 156). In this she concurs with the finding of the 1980 Permanent People's Tribunal that Filipina women suffer "double oppression and exploitation" by the dominant classes and by "male authority" *(Komite ng Sambayanang Pilipino* 1981).

Given the uneven, tortuous development of the Filipino struggle for genuine independence amid persistent U.S. domination of civil society and state, the issue of gender equality and the potential of women as an autonomous force for radical transformation remain contentious for all sides (Aguilar 1988). But it is difficult even during Barros's lifetime to ignore the specificity of women's oppression that defies the peremptory foreclosure of postcolonial eclecticism and ambivalence.

I review the most relevant background facts here (Evasco et al 1990; Eviota 1992). Composing more than one-half of the population, the majority of Filipino women live in the countryside, performing two thirds of the work but receiving only one tenth of the usual income of peasants and rural workers. In the urban regions, women are subjected to substandard wages, limited benefits, sexual abuse, and degrading substandard conditions. In the seventies, the unemployment rate for women was

75 percent compared to 10 percent for men. Sexist segregation of the labor force confined women to traditional female jobs with lower wages, longer hours, and accelerated pace: domestic servants, nursing, sales, clerical work, rank-and-file workers. Prostitution was the source of livelihood for over 300,000 women in the cities, with at least 60,000 (many of them teenagers) earning subsistence wages around the U.S. military bases. With martial law under the Marcos dictatorship, the lives of women considerably worsened, driving many of them to engage in the "hospitality" trade, their bodies converted into exchangeable commodities or fetishized as "mail order brides" or "warm body export." That was the sociopolitical context of Barros's decision to join the national-democratic struggle against U.S. neocolonialism and its client regime.

In line with Barros's agenda of transgressing patriarchal and neocolonial borders, Makibaka urged women's total participation in politics. It targeted traditional sexist practices that quarantined women in the domestic sphere of civil society. It sought to unleash "the vigor, intelligence and creativity of Filipino women," to mobilize them (particularly students in the Catholic colleges) in programs combatting sexual discrimination and exploitation. After studying the roots of women's oppression in the history of the Filipino family, Barros observed that "You have to convince them [women in the middle stratum of society] that there really is exploitation in the Philippines. . . . The principal problem is our culture, a culture that subordinates women to men. Makibaka aims to project this problem in the context of the national democratic struggle. Its purpose is to present more dramatically the need for emancipation and involvement" (Davis 1989: 139).

After experiments in consciousness-raising (influenced by Paulo Freire's conscientization pedagogy) of petit-bourgeois women, Makibaka decided to widen its range of action by trying to organize peasant women in the rural villages as well as women in the factories. Barros realized that the right to abortion was not a priority for peasant women in the countryside where the basic needs for food, clothing, and medicine (including reproductive health care) were urgent concerns. The major demands of tenant farmers and workers concerned land reform, elimination of usury, reduction of land rent, and improvement of the quality of life in general. Various chapters of Makibaka were established throughout the islands: workers' bureau for peasants and urban poor, the Mother's Corps for housewives who were more pressured by the rising prices of basic staples, high tuition fees, and so on. Barros set up nursery classes for preschool children in cooperation with her mother's co-activists. In the course of her work, Barros discovered how the majority of women workers were not aware of their individual human rights, accepting subhuman working conditions. In actualizing participatory democracy, Barros was forced to go underground when the writ of habeas corpus was suspended in August 1971; the government had already announced a reward of 500 pesos for her capture.

At this juncture, I want to interject some background information for those not familiar with political events in the Philippines in the last three decades. Since the re-establishment of the Communist Party of the Philippines in 1968, tremendous efforts have been made to involve women in both the legal and the clandestine sectors of the national-democratic struggle (Chapman 1987). Of immense significance is the direct participation of women in guerilla actions, with the formation of a Red Detachment of Women in the New People's Army, part of the coalition called the National Democratic Front. Women partisans of the NPA have distinguished themselves in ambushes, raids, organizing work, and so on, on all fronts. They have assisted in consolidating the liberated base areas and supervising the creation of Barrio Revolutionary Committees, the chief administrative body for initiating revolutionary land reform, building up the people's army, and strengthening the united front of all progressive forces (see the interview with Makibaka by Prairie Fire Organizing Committee 1989; Justiniani 1987; Aguilar 1993). The opportunities of reclaiming territory (physical and spiritual) from patriarchal capitalist control had considerably expanded by the time Barros fled the city in 1971 for the battlefield in the northern province of Isabela.

After Marcos imposed martial law in 1972, Barros married a fellow activist and subsequently gave birth to her first child in a private clinic in Manila. But she had to return to the hills, leaving her son in the care of relatives. In October 1973, four months pregnant, Barros was arrested while engaged in organizing the rural masses; she was supposedly armed with a .32 caliber gun and bound for Sorsogon City, Sorsogon province, several hundred miles south of Manila, in order to establish a revolutionary base. She was first detained at Camp Vicente Lim for interrogation. She refused to cooperate and so was placed in *bartolina* (isolation), where she remained for several months. When she was allowed to mix with other prisoners, Barros began to organize them and counter the demoralization they suffered, prompting the military to transfer her to the seclusion of the Ipil Rehabilitation Center in Fort Bonifacio, on the outskirts of Manila.

In January 1974, Barros was interviewed by a correspondent of the *Manchester Guardian*. She had refused to disclose the whereabouts of other guerilla partisans in exchange for milder prison treatment. She recalled the attempt of a mercenary government officer:

> He told me, "You'll be inside for thirty years and then you'll be an old woman and you won't be able to get married." I was shocked that he thought that such a threat would frighten me. I told him, all right, I said, "I've been married once already, and that was enough to last until I die." (San Juan 1986: 159)

As noted earlier, she was married to an NPA combatant who was killed five months after in an encounter with government troops. In her work as organizer of village committees of peasants, Barros immersed herself in the lives of over 75 percent of Filipinos who live in the impoverished countryside. In the rigor of integrating with the people, she grasped what Raymond Williams (1977) calls the peculiar "structure of feeling" immanent in communities desiring and wanting revolutionary change. She found that "the people in the villages wanted to know all about communism. We tell them that under communism there will be no landlords, that the land will really be theirs and their families'; we teach them the problem of bringing about communism in a feudal society like the Philippines; that the first stage of the struggle would be to industrialize the Philippines, but that this cannot be done as long as we are a semi-colony of U.S. imperialism" (San Juan 1986: 159).

Barros's artistic sensibility envisioned breaks, transitions, rituals of passage. It was during her confinement in July 1974 that she wrote about her distress, her grief at being separated from her loved ones, which she compares to "a tear shed for a leaf, / pain unassuaged / by the promise of a new bud / at the tip." She invokes the "rich soil of people's war" that will fructify and sustain the cycle of natural life. In another poem entitled "Sampaguita" (written a year earlier), she engages in "cross-addressing," emphasizing commonalities instead of singularities, and inscribing directions on what would otherwise be a site of undecidability or postcolonial ambiguity:

> This morning Little Comrade
> gave me a flower's bud.
> I look at it now
> remembering you, Felix,

dear friend and comrade
and all the brave sons and daughters
of our suffering land
whose death
makes our blades sharper
gives our bullets
surer aim. . . .

How like this pure white bud
are our martyrs
fiercely fragrant with love
for our country and people!
With what radiance they should still have unfolded!
But sadness should not be
their monument.
Whipped and lashed desperately
by bomb-raised storms,
has not our Asian land
continued to bloom?
Look how bravely our ranks
bloom into each gap.
With the same intense purity and fragrance
we are learning to overcome.

Partisans of the New People's Army in the Philippines, one of the
organizations participating in the united front of progressive forces called
the National Democratic Front, Phillippines.

In another poem, Barros shifts to a relaxed mood reminiscent of the "exteriorism" of the Nicaraguan poet Ernesto Cardenal and the Cuban writer Roberto Fernandez Retamar. She abandons the sentimental exuberance of images derived from organic nature and recounts her talk with an old man who spoke "of patience, / in his voice a whole season / of cool, summed-up sorrows." The dialogic evocation of differences engenders the occasion for learning the wages of responsibility: "Comrade, dear friend, / teach me how not to flinch" through adversities. In such verses, the architectonic of exchange mediates both realism and utopian longing. I call this genre of interlocution "emergency writing" after Walter Benjamin's reminder that for the oppressed the state of emergency is not the exception but the rule (San Juan 1995a: 103).[6]

Barros's writings are dispersed in many underground publications and private archives, still uncollected. We can infer that because of their insistence on recovering agency and rational critique, on transcending multiplicity and striving for wholeness via solidarity and cooperation with others, her art goes against the grain of orthodox postcolonial theory. It is an art of decision and risk-taking, an imagination sworn to determining accountability and articulating responsibility for what is going on in her part of the world. On the whole, Barros's militant melancholy foresees personal defeat but inscribes this in the public sphere created by the struggle, in the immortal life of the community of workers and peasants.

On 1 November 1974, Barros and four companions escaped with the help of other political prisoners who distracted the guards. She rejoined the NPA and became the leader of a squad operating in the Bicol provinces. Even while engaged in military operations, Barros reserved time to listen to people's problems, especially women combatants. Surrounded by literally endangered lives, Barros had to sacrifice the luxury of claiming an oxymoronic, shifting, and plural identity expressed in tropes of positional/border identities. In such situations of unmitigated and unrelenting emergency, the strategy of self-positioning requires drawing up priorities during the interval of defense and attack, a nuanced maneuver that affords a sense of wholeness from which one is enabled to defamiliarize the status quo:

> Considering the quality of the young people today, the country has a good future. . . . The interests of the ruling class and of the exploited masses are diametrically opposed; the former will never allow the latter to wrest power without a struggle. . . . The revolution is inevitable, it is dictated by

necessity. The Philippines might become another Vietnam. If we don't endure and do something about it now, the succeeding generations will suffer even more. . . . If an armed conflict does arise, we will fight alongside the men. We should take up arms, if necessary. We are working for a better society for men and women alike, so why should the men always bear the brunt of the struggle? (San Juan 1986: 156)

Such retrieval and inventory of trends in the geopolitical terrain may serve as Barros's autograph in unifying the particular and the universal. In the early morning of 24 March 1976, in the town of Mauban, Quezon Province, Barros was killed in an encounter with ruthless government troops. She was twenty-eight years old. Her mother commented on her daughter's funeral: "Whenever there is a struggle there is a sacrifice, and death is a common occurrence" (Davis 1989: 142).

Postcolonial indeterminacy breaks down here in the site of the destroyed female body. Refusing the strangeness of the Other, of death as ultimate sovereign boundary, Barros's mother and all her comrades sought to read the young woman's life as performance of a feminist identity beyond the category of "national allegory" (Jameson 1986). From the perspective of the embattled subalterns, Barros's life may be construed as a project (in the Sartrean sense) of achieving subjecthood and enfranchisement beyond Bhabha's "interstices" or "Third Space," beyond Rushdie's "imaginary homelands." Among engaged feminists in the Philippines today, Barros functions as a model of a learning process, a resource for discovering the nexus between personal experience and history. She serves as a legible sign, an intelligible configuration, of life's value as deeply imbricated in communal desires, concerns, aspirations. I might add here that for thousands of underground revolutionaries in the Philippines, the homeland is not imagined nor fantasized but actually lived, suffered, endured; their collective experiences signify the questioning body that Fanon celebrated as an icon of permanent resistance (San Juan 1994a).

SIGNS OF INDIFFERENCE

Whether those of the Quiche Indians, Filipina women, or Caribbean intellectuals, the practices of national-popular struggle (in Gramsci's sense) are richer than any categorical description. Nonetheless we might venture some theoretical reflections on the inadequacy of orthodox postcolonialism. My three examples of alternative anti-postal practice in the domain of expression are all attempts to counter the universal deracination, loss of foundations, and totalized marginality posited by postcolonial theory. They are concerned with initiatives, discovering roots and sources, laying the groundwork for partisanship that would bind "we" and "they," "you" and "I"—all shifters that acquire determinate concreteness in actual projects. Alterity is inscribed in a situation of permanent emergency—Menchu's beleaguered people, James's diasporic quest, Barros's theme of metamorphosis—that temporalizes space. Time becomes fundamental for emergence of the new, the *Novus*.

In this alternative cultural milieu, we become enmeshed in a web of significance constituted by a literature of reconnaissance and transition—all three activists perform inventories of their lives in the act of surpassing the past, of valorizing the transitional moments of decision and existential becoming. So instead of the in-between, we have transition and the interregnum as privileged sites of self-recognition via the community; instead of ambivalence, we have resolve, commitment, determination to face specific problems and crisis. Instead of the local, we have a striving for coalitions and counterhegemonic blocs to prefigure a universal public space. Instead of the syncretic and hybrid, we have creative demarcations and the crafting of the architectonic of the new, the emergent, the *Novus*. Instead of the polyvocal, we have the beginning of articulation from the silenced grassroots, the loci of invention and resourceful innovation. Here the trope of difference is displaced by the trope of possibilities, the binary impasse of reified hegemonic culture deconstructed by the imagination of materialist critique and extrapolation. Utterance is neither private nor solipsistic but an utterance of the mass line, not heteroglossic but triangulated; not contingent but charted by cognitive mapping and provisional orientations.

What is at stake in this counterpointing of standpoints is the future—justice for the oppressed, equality for the deprived, liberation for all. Out of necessities and limited possibilities, oppressed people of color endeavor to shape a future freed from the nightmare of colonial history. Such endeavors are central, not marginal, to any attempt to renew humane learning everywhere. What Edward Said (1994) calls "the centrality of imperial culture" insinuates itself into the postcolonial claim to speak for all "the Rest," thus negating its self-proclaimed commitment to difference and radical alterity.

As though repudiating the ventriloquism of postcolonial experts, James and Menchu in their disparate ways provide a strategy of popular anticolonialism premised on historical retrospection and narratives of "belonging" and solidarity (Eagleton 1990). In Barros's laconic verses, we also encounter a synthesis of the personal and the collective in the process of trying to dismantle neocolonial repression and its floating signifiers of "free enterprise," "individual freedom," and mass consumerism (Featherstone 1991). After this complex encounter with the unequal division of intellectual labor, we return to history, the repressed corpus, via popular memory (in Menchu's *testimonio*), by tracing the variable genealogy of cricket (in James's memoir), and by documentary witnessing (in our appraisal of Barros's trajectory as feminist underground combatant). All three reject the academic historicist renunciation of conflicts and apotheosis of museumized fragments. They welcome "thick description" of events, of accountabilities—the conflicted texture of experience of change, discontinuity, transmutations, breakthroughs. What happened? Who is responsible? After all, we are complicit in the fate of humanity anywhere on this planet.

All three figures I have surveyed here represent modalities of cultural production different from the mainly British Commonwealth "subaltern" archetype that today dominates postcolonial doctrine. Overall, I opt for replacing "postcolonial" foundationalism with a hypothesis of situated "national-popular" cultures that in their concrete dynamics of engagement with global capitalism in specific sites express the varied forms of responses by people of color (aborigines, women, peasants and workers, ethnic communities, dissident petite bourgeoisie) to commodification. (One example that quickly comes to mind is the work of Basil Davidson on African history [1982]). Such responses also illustrate their modes of inventing autochtonous traditions that defy postmodernist skepticism or irony and offer materials for articulating hopes and dreams not found in the classic European Enlightenment and its mirror-opposite, postcolonial relativism and pragmatic nominalism.

CHAPTER TWO

Postcolonial Theory versus the Revolutionary Process in the Philippines

A life not consecrated to a great ideal is a useless one. . . .
There are no tyrants where there are no slaves.
— Jose Rizal

I repeat, on my word of honor, that the so-called anarchists, Nihilists, or, as they say nowadays, Bolsheviks, are the true saviours and disinterested defenders of justice and universal brotherhood. When the prejudices of these days of moribund imperialism have disappeared, they will rightfully occupy our altars.
— Isabelo De Los Reyes

Our people's war is part and supportive of the worldwide struggle against imperialism and reaction being waged by the proletariat and people, national liberation movements, revolutionary parties and progressive states. Our struggle contributes to their victories, just as these help advance our revolutionary movement. The Philippine revolutionary forces can best contribute to the cause of national liberation, democracy, socialism, and peace by winning our own revolutionary struggle.
— National Democratic Front, Philippines

THE POSTCOLONIAL MYSTIFICATION

In the wake of the post–Cold War triumphalism of the neoliberal West wracked by recession and the terror of "ethnic cleansing," it seems that a new ideology of recuperating "Manifest Destiny" and "The White Man's Burden" has captured the attention of former subjects of U.S. tutelage: postcolonial theory. Whose "civilizing mission" is at stake this time? This belated notion of defamiliarizing reality and reaffirming Western hegemony has invaded the Philippines under the aegis of postmodernist cultural studies and its subdepartment, postcolonial studies and its local inflections. Globalizing entails localizing (Friedman 1990). What is the effect of this incursion?

For intellectuals in the periphery of late capitalism who function as "transmission belts" of ideas from Europe and North America, this mimicry of "posting" reality has produced negative repercussions. For one, it has resulted in aggravating further the alienation of the petit bourgeois intellectual in a compradorized uneven milieu (Dirlik 1994a). Such "First World" theorizing can be used to detach those with subaltern roots from their initial sympathy with the ideals of national liberation, popular democracy, and anti-imperialist "people's war." Rejecting the Enlightenment narrative of the conquest of people's freedom from predatory capital, the eclectic stance of diasporic academics (many from the Commonwealth territories) has mainly served to refurbish a bankrupt program of a paternalistic but ultimately racializing utilitarianism. Whose lives are at stake in the postcolonial refusal of socialist revolution? After the Hobbesian *diktat* of Marcos and the pseudo-Nietzschean carnival of the "People Power" converts, can "low intensity warfare" (Klare and Kornbluh 1988) be far behind?

Perhaps I am overestimating the impact of postmodernist thinking in a terrain (such as Filipino society in general) customarily inhospitable to the imperatives of radical critique. But among our migrant compatriots disillusioned with "national democracy" (see, for example, Hidalgo and Legasto 1993) as well as Filipinos in "First World" professional niches and NGOs (Non-Governmental Organizations) vulnerable to the seduction of "Theory," disorientation prevails.

We can rehearse here the platitudes of fundamentalist postcolonialism. Since the classic colonial predicament has allegedly dissolved or at least entered a phase of obsolescence, we are urged to mimic the West in the paradigm shift of rejecting the totalizing and essentializing universals of "national liberation," equality, social justice—in short, of humanity's progress in controlling the forces of Necessity. Instead we have to catch up and somehow log on to the televised new gadgets and gimmicks in the global marketplace. We are urged to shop in the cosmopolitan bazaar of ludic pluralism and negotiate our syncretic identities in the emporium of *différance*. Meanwhile, despite claims to the contrary, has there been a let-up in transnational corporate profitmaking? Or in the "warm body export" (Anderson 1993), the perennial exodus of Overseas Contract Workers to the Middle East? With the opening of the erstwhile Soviet empire to business, has the draconian logic of capital accumulation not become the present and probable future of humankind? Faced with the unconscionably dehumanizing poverty, brutalization of women and children, severe exploitation of peasants and workers, and state violence afflicting 70 million Filipinos, can we really accept that things have changed for the better? Or have they only suffered a surface mutation and assumed new disguises?

In the post–Cold War era that opened with the war on Iraq (an episode in the ongoing crusade against Iran, Libya, North Korea, Cuba, and other "unruly" states), the Enlightenment vision of an evolving planetary culture epitomized by Goethe's notion of *Weltliteratur* has allegedly evaporated. It has given way to a melange of ethnic particularisms amalgamated with relics of Eurocentric universalisms all expediently labeled "postcolonial" literature (Bhabha 1992). At the same time, clichés about "globalism," world citizenship, and the supposedly benign dispensation of transnational business abound today amid reports of vicious ethnonationalist strife and racially motivated violence everywhere (Hall 1992a). With the celebration of newly discovered, residual, or hitherto muted differences, the last judgment of the "hyperreal" has reputedly arrived. Regardless of one's opinion on these disparate phenomena, I think there can be no worthwhile exchange on culture and art today without acknowledging the existence of the capitalist world system as its condition of possibility, its enabling complex of presuppositions and theorems (Wallerstein 1983; Harvey 1989; Sklair 1991). In other words, one cannot theorize on the vicissitudes of the "culture wars" in the United States (or in Europe) without being implicated in their geopolitical resonance, in that paradoxically normalized excess called the "Third World" that threatens market stability but makes cultural sublimations ("Western democracy" signifying "free" elections, "free" speech, etc., is still referenced as a norm to be emulated) possible. Postcoloniality, in other words, can be considered one flagrant symptom of the persistence of inequality and injustice everywhere in the world.

The fashionable transculturalizing trend called "postcolonial criticism" is well exemplified by *The Empire Writes Back* (Aschroft et al. 1989). Writing from the Australian end of the former British empire, the authors of this now scriptural text consider the United States as the first postcolonial society to fashion a "national" literature ("national" is never defined in the book). This is an astonishing claim from the viewpoint of Puerto Ricans, Cubans, Hawaiians, Native Americans, and other victims of Anglo-Saxon/European settlement in the post-Columbian Americas. Not only is it "first" in this, but these experts also believe the United States can be "the model for all later post-colonial writing." Such an exorbitant proposition is either a joke in bad taste or a disingenuous trope to outrage "politically correct" fellow travelers (McClintock 1994). Can the United States ever be postcolonial by any stretch of the imagination? Can we seriously view the Puritan settlement of New England as a precursor of the Mau Mau uprising in Kenya or of Ho Chi Minh's peasant guerillas? Ashcroft and his colleagues have formulated a hypothesis that functions like a mirror-image of the U.S. discourse of pacification—from the "Trail of Tears" and the Mexican-American War to the invasion of Grenada, Panama, and so on. We are reminded of the old rhetoric of the "civilizing mission" that was used to legitimate the violent subjugation of Filipinos— "thirty thousand [American soldiers] killed a million [Filipinos]," to use Mark Twain's (1992) expression. On certain appropriate occasions, the victims of "postcolonial" writers like Emerson and Faulkner may still commemorate the ideals of Locke, Adam Smith, and the Enlightenment philosophes; but to celebrate Euro-American culture as a paragon for the Third World simply exceeds the limits of liberal open-mindedness and even utilitarian prudence.

The genealogy of this style of postcolonial speculation betrays symptoms worth diagnosing. Prejudiced against foundational scripts by indigenous "minorities" and aborigines (such as Leslie Marmon Silko or Toni Morrison), the postcolonial critic—one can cite any number of them, from Bhabha (1990) and Spivak (1991) to Trinh Minh-ha (1989) and other Commonwealth intellectuals—usually begins with the critique of Western logocentrism or identitarian metaphysics, at once a self-undermining teleological move. Unless she wants to sanction the permanence of Eurocentrism, she must prefigure in the same move of inversion and distanciation her autonomous trajectory. She thus needs to expose and repudiate the constitutive effects of the intellectual division of labor in the world system that she has just erased from her account (Parry 1987; Ahmad 1992)). In this catachrestic performance, the "post" in "postcolonial," which replicates First World conservatism, is thus sublated to a stance of displacement begging recognition not from the masses in Africa, Asia, or Latin America but from their tutors, Western master-theoreticians of the "sublime." The postcolonial sage then turns out to be the new comprador of post-Fordist, "disorganized" accumulation. Postcoloniality is thus one of those language games of positionalities whose rules global capitalism has devised and deployed in order to refurbish its worn-out ideological apparatus for subjugating people of color and service its new flexible production scheme (Callinicos 1989; Chomsky 1989). I agree with Arif Dirlik (1994b, 1997) in his view that postcolonial theorizing is the name of a symptom produced by poststructuralist theories (Derrida, Lacan, Foucault) when regurgitated and worked over by intellectuals from the former colonies disclaiming *inter alia* totality, foundations, telos, or the idea of any intelligible, comprehensive historical process. However, I believe that postcoloniality (like the Indian subcontinent) has no ideal-typical essence, as its practitioners claim; consequently, this anatomy I delineate becomes a shadowy persona in the larger allegory of the crisis of Western imperial domination grasped as a symptom of the internal contradictions and intensifying crisis of late capitalism (Bush, Johnston, and Coates 1987; Turner 1994).

While there is no doubt that imperialism (as once defined by Lenin [1939]) has altered in the wake of corporate globalization, the collapse of Soviet "communism," and the rise of new social movements (ecological, feminist, indigenous, etc.) not anticipated by revolutionaries of the last century, the most powerful analytic framework for understanding social processes and for creating feasible agencies of change remains, to my mind, the Marxist perspective and its rich, complex tradition. Mark Solomon reiterates Marx's principles concerning "the root contradiction within capitalism between developing productive forces (machines and workers) and constraining production relations (social production, private appropriation) as well as his insight into the nature of exploitation/surplus value (appropriated in the form of profits derived from commodity exchange) leading to crises of overproduction, the emergence of . . . revolutionary consciousness and ultimately revolution itself" (1994, 28). Such principles have been deepened and refined by Western Marxism (Lukács, Gramsci, Althusser) and by "Third World" revolutionaries like Mao, C. L. R. James, Che Guevara, Cabral, and others.

In the world-system of historical capitalism, the relations between peoples and nation-states have been characterized by inequalities at all levels. Contradictions between oppressor and oppressed overdetermine cultural/ideological, political, and economic exchanges. What needs more conscientious application is the axiom of "uneven and combined development" (Mandel 1979) that should orient all knowledge of metropolis-periphery transactions so as to avoid a one-sided fetishism of cultural trends. By applying materialist dialectics, we can also avoid the narrow focus on either market exchange or its obverse, local power relations. If one rejects (as postcolonialists would) this metanarrative of "uneven development," then how is comparatist study feasible? If the serial instances of the local become incommensurable and we are prohibited from distinguishing one from the other, forbidden to grasp determinate qualities and discriminate among particulars in the field of antagonisms and antinomy-laden processes, how can we make judgments about the direction of historical change? How is the production of knowledge even possible?

Complex historical reality always defies "postcolonial" wish-fulfillments. For example, within the global context of nation-states, one finds a pattern of hierarchical ranking that openly discriminates among the various national and regional literatures. Born from the violence of colonial occupation, Filipino writing in English, for example, has never been recognized by U.S. arbiters of high culture upholding canonical standards of taste. Texts by major writers like Jose Garcia Villa or Nick Joaquin have never been admitted into the mainstream anthologies of U.S. literature (San Juan 1984, 1991, 1992a). The anomalous, marginal if not completely invisible status of Filipino writing in English in U.S. literary annals explodes the myth of cultural pluralism and questions the claim of transhistorical universality attached to neoliberal "free market" icons. "Difference" in the asymmetrical marketplace after all is what constitutes the dominant mode of U.S. self-identification, a disciplinary mode of agency-formation whose reifying power seems infinite until it encounters the refusal of the outcast, the pariah, the "lazy native," the "terrorist," and communist—enemies of the "American Way of Life" (Vidal 1986-92).

Recent events in the Philippines—the withdrawal of U.S. military bases, a minor renaissance of vernacular writing and performance art, the unprecedented migration of Filipino workers to the Middle East and around the world (over 6 million and still accelerating), the regrouping of nationalist forces leading to the revival of peace talks between the government and the National Democratic Front begun during the Aquino interregnum, and so on—have problematized the status and future of English as a literary language in the Philippines. This crisis is irreversible.[1] If we deploy a historical contextualization of the field of writing practices, one will see that English is only one "language game" or one choice in the means of indigenous cultural production amid a space where electronic visual communication (television and cinema) predominates. In fact, Filipino English can be construed as one kind of vernacular or sectoral idiom with a limited audience within a decolonizing but not yet postimperial milieu (San Juan 1994a).

To democratize the U.S. liberal marketplace as the first stage in reordering priorities, we need to problematize the received consensus of U.S. cultural history. At the same time we need to appraise and critique the position of reactionary nativism and the chauvinism of the "international style" purveyed by the parasitic comprador elite. After surveying the texts of U.S. critics judging Filipino cultural practices, I would like to propose for further inquiry the thesis that Filipino writers (excluded from the horizon of Commonwealth postcolonial scholarship) can offer a challenge to U.S. academic hubris predicated on the inferiorization of the cultures of "Others" for its own self-validation (Kaplan and Pease 1993). As part of the excluded "Others," Filipino writers implicitly problematize the possibility, in late capitalism, of composing a U.S. "national" literary history in a space constituted by multiple nationalities and racialized diasporic communities—all internal colonies of a still hegemonic nation-state. In the context of world literature written in English, one can ask: Can there be a reciprocal and mutually creative dialogue between the resistant, emergent Filipino imagination and the "power/knowledge" constellation of the dominant U.S. polity? Is it possible to expect a rupture of the status quo by the "postcolonial" hybrid nomad and its ludic virtuosity?

A review of how the reality of U.S. colonial domination and its peculiar mode of exercising hegemony in the Philippines have been "produced" and circulated by liberal discourse with "postcolonial" pretensions may be instructive here.

THE PRODUCTION OF "CIVILIZING" DISCOURSE

For the first time since the outbreak of the Spanish-American War in 1898 and the fall of Bataan and Corregidor to the Japanese invaders in 1942, the Philippines dominated the world's attention for a few days in February 1986: an urban mass insurrection of over a million people overthrew the long-entrenched Marcos dictatorship without too much bloodshed, in the face of tanks and soldiers armed to the teeth (Davis

1989). Scenes of this uprising were televised throughout the world, images exuding an aura of the miraculous. Distanced from the original context, those images and representations that mediated this singular event became an inspiration to the popular rebellions that soon exploded around the world, particularly in Eastern Europe, China, Pakistan, Haiti, and other national-security states of the "free world."

Less publicized is one epochal achievement of the nationalist resurgence that began with the "First Quarter Storm" in 1970 and persists up to this day: in 1992, the U.S. government finally yielded to Filipino resolve and abandoned its two huge military installations (Clark Air Field and Subic Naval Base), symbols of colonial suzerainty for over half a century. Despite some attenuation, the Philippines today has the only viable communist-led guerilla insurgency in all of Asia and perhaps in the whole world.

But like most "Third World" societies plagued by vestiges of the past (three hundred years of Spanish rule and conquest by the United States in 1898 up to the present), the Philippines today suffers from neocolonial bondage. Although nominally independent, its economy is controlled by the draconian "conditionalities" of the IMF-World Bank, its politics by semi-feudal warlords, bureaucrats, and military officials beholden to Washington, its culture by U.S. mass media—in general, by Western information/knowledge-production monopoly (also known as the culture/consciousness industry) (Richardson 1989; Constantino 1975, 1978). Although direct colonial rule was finally terminated in 1946, the cultural and political hegemony of the United States persists to this day. When the Reagan administration intervened in 1986 to shore up the ruins of empire by rescuing its client despot from the wrath of Filipinos in revolt and install a new set of overseers (namely Corazon Aquino and her successor, General Fidel Ramos, former "impresario" of Marcos's martial law), it was less nostalgia than a tactical defensive retreat (Sison 1986). Desperate maneuvers to salvage the military bases confirmed a long-range strategy of retrenchment (Schirmer 1995). There was definitely no retreat in the realm of politics, ideology, and culture, given the claim of academic pundits (for example, Buss 1987) that such intervention demonstrated the U.S. goodwill to preserve its investment in its long-revered "showcase of democracy" in Asia after its debacle in Vietnam.

Whatever the status of the U.S. civic memory, the day will soon be here when the public will celebrate the centennial anniversary of Admiral George Dewey's defeat of the Spanish armada in Manila Bay on 1 May 1898. Perhaps the commemoration will not be accompanied by the usual jingoistic fanfare of yore though no doubt hoary veterans will rehearse the familiar nostalgia for the days of Empire. We are after all inhabiting today a "New World Order" characterized by U.S. triumphalist incursions in the Middle East and its post–Cold War saber-rattling toward Iran, Libya, Cuba, and socialist Korea (Bennis and Moushabeck 1993).

Contrary to the claim that the first U.S.-Philippines contact began when Filipino recruits jumped off the Spanish galleons in the seventeenth century and settled near what is now New Orleans, Louisiana, I would contend that the inaugural scene points to the intrusion of Dewey into Manila Bay in 1898. That was immediately followed by the Filipino-American War (1899-1902), which suppressed the revolutionary forces of the first Philippine Republic—when "thirty thousand [Americans] killed a million [Filipinos]." And this domination continues today in covert, mediated or sublimated forms—proof that what Mark Twain called the Philippine "temptation" (McWilliams 1973, xxii) persists amid profound mutations in the world system of transnational capital. But for the moment I want to cite here Twain's comment on the U.S. adventure which (in Carey McWilliams' s [1964] view) prompted the government to "guide the natives in ways of our own choosing," especially when the "lesser breeds" or "little brown brothers occupied a potentially rich land" (548). The ironic resonance of this self-proclaimed "civilizing mission" is registered in Twain's distinctive idiom:

> We have pacified some thousands of the islanders and buried them; destroyed their fields, burned their villages, and turned their widows and orphans out-of-doors; furnished heartbreak by exile to some dozens of disagreeable patriots; subjugated the remaining ten millions by Benevolent Assimilation, which is the pious new name of the musket; we have acquired property in the three hundred concubines and other slaves of our business partner, the Sultan of Sulu, and hoisted our protecting flag over that swag. And so, by these Providences of God—and the phrase is the government's, not mine—we are a World Power. (quoted in Zinn 1992, 20)

In his nuanced satire, Twain marveled at the report that thirty thousand American soldiers killed a million Filipinos: "Thirty thousand killed a million. It seems a pity that the historian let that get out; it is really a most embarrassing circumstance" (62). In February 1899, the month in which the Filipino-American War began and the U.S. Senate ratified the treaty formalizing the annexation of Spain's former colonies, Rudyard Kipling's poem, "The White Man's Burden," appeared. In it the poet echoed U.S. Senator Albert Beveridge's claim of "the mission of our race, trustee under God, of the civilization of the world" (1987, 23; see also Parenti 1989).

This inaugural event in the chronicle of U.S. territorial expansionism is not without precedent, a fact thoroughly documented and argued by Gareth Stedman Jones (1970), William Appleman Williams (1962), and others. From the Monroe Doctrine to the Tonkin Gulf resolution, a narrative of intervention gives intelligibility to U.S. foreign policy. In his perspicacious commentary on the U.S. war machine, *Star Wars* (1986), H. Bruce Franklin remarks: "The warfare waged against the Cuban and Philippine nationalists, for whose ostensible benefit we had defeated Spain, was an export of the genocidal campaigns against the 'savages' and 'redskins' who had inhabited North America" (92). In a penetrating essay, "Cuba, the Philippines, and Manifest Destiny," the political analyst Richard Hofstadter (1967) delineated the configuration of "psychic crisis" that mixed several elements: the chauvinist self-aggrandizement of the 1890s, the imperialist ethos of duty and populist self-assertion, the disappearance of the frontier, and the bureaucratization of business amid cyclical economic depression. Reappraising the origins of the United States as a modern world power, the influential historian Gabriel Kolko returns us to Twain's insight with perspicuous force:

> Violence in America antedated industrialism and urban life, and it was initially a product of an expansive rural-commercial economy that in the context of vast distance and a hastily improvised and often changing social structure saw barbarism, violence, and their toleration ritualized into a way of life. Slavery consisted of institutionalized inhumanity and an attack on the very fiber of the black's personal identity and integrity. . . . Against the Indians, who owned and occupied much coveted land, wholesale slaughter was widely sanctioned as a virtue. That terribly bloody, sordid history, involving countless tens of thousands of lives that neither victims nor executioners can ever enumerate, made violence endemic to the process of continental expansion. Violence reached a crescendo against the Indian after the Civil War and found a yet bloodier manifestation during the protracted conquest of the Philippines from 1898 until well into the next decade, when anywhere from 200,000 to 600,000 Filipinos were killed in an orgy of racist slaughter that evoked much congratulation and approval from the eminent journals and men of the era who were also much concerned about progress and stability at home. From their inception, the great acts of violence and attempted genocide America launched against

outsiders seemed socially tolerated, even celebrated. Long before Vietnam, that perverse acceptance of horror helped make possible the dominating experiences of our own epoch. (1976, 286-87)

This critical framework, an intellectual stance enabled not by Foucault and Nietzsche but by the now much maligned "national liberation" struggles of "Third World" peoples, has been expunged from approved textbooks and from civic memory. But despite the neoconservative atmosphere and endemic amnesia, it is now being slowly grasped and applied in the canon-revising program of progressive scholars throughout the country.[2] Admittedly, this orientation is still marginal and even taboo when it comes to understanding the complicated cultural-ideological relations between the United States and the Philippines. This field is, to be sure, muddled and constrained by substantial and long-standing military, political, and financial interests easily confirmed by the latest negotiations over the Philippine debt to the World Bank/International Monetary Fund and other transnational investors (Catholic Institute 1989; Canlas et al 1988; Putzel 1992; Boyce 1993).

The major obstacle to any scientific and judicious exploration of U.S. imperialist hegemony in the Philippines inheres in the controlling paradigm of philosophical idealism that has founded academic disciplines and legitimized their regimes of truth. I suggest that this paradigm hinges on a positivistic, evolutionary theory of culture—traditional patterns of conduct, norms, beliefs, attitudes, together with their corresponding practices of symbolic translation and signification—as the explanatory key to the subaltern condition of the Filipino. That constellation of action, meaning, and *habitus* also explains the production/reproduction of dependency relations (already criticized by Virgilio Enriquez and others; see Pe-pua 1989). Reduced to a few pivotal notions like *hiya,* "mutual loyalties," internal debt (*utang na loob*), and so on, culture with its symbolic economy is divorced from its circumstantial anchorage and becomes a generalizing formula used to unravel affairs of extreme "thickness" and complexity (for a sophisticated elaboration of the formula, see Kerkvliet and Mojares 1991). The functionalism of deploying the patron-client dyad is not of course totally without value in shedding light on specific empirical phenomena. Further refinements have been introduced by Benedict Kerkvliet (1990) in theorizing the everyday small-scale politics of resistance in a Philippine village. But the effects of neocolonial exploitation, racism, and gender oppression are absent or concealed. Lacking the historical world-system dynamics involving the "asymmetrical relations" (to use social science jargon) between exploitative occupier and subjugated people, devoid of any sensorium for registering the unequal power relations between contending subjects who necessarily impinge on each other's physiognomies, what we have in such accounts is nothing but a banal exercise in apologetics.

From a more theoretical vantage point, Stanley Karnow's *In Our Image* (1989) may be taken as emblematic of a classic problem in defining the Self via representing the Other from the Self's interested optic (San Juan 1992a). In this framework, the Filipino becomes both an empirical referent and a construct of cross-hatched narratives. Of half a dozen texts that have invented and disseminated the received "truths" about the Philippines and Filipinos, texts central to the constitution of the discipline called "Philippine Studies," one may cite three that are acknowledged to be influential in crafting state policies and fabricating mass consensus: W. Cameron Forbes, *The Philippine Islands* (1924); Joseph Hayden, *The Philippines: A Study in National Development* (1942); and George Taylor, *The Philippines and the United States: Problems of Partnership* (1964), generally construed as the Cold War primer for Filipinologists of that period. Together with other institutional practices, these commissioned texts constructed the object of knowledge and exercised mastery over it. They were in turn authorized by a whole panoply of regulations (economic, political, cultural), at once hortatory and conciliating, governing the relations between the United States as a colonizing sovereignty and the subjugated inhabitants of the territory labeled "the Philippine islands." Now the theme of "imperial collaboration" between the Filipino elite and the U.S. colonial administration has been a recurrent leitmotif in the canonical archive of U.S. diplomacy since Forbes's two-volume inventory of U.S. accomplishment in the Philippines. Hayden focused on its resonance in the Commonwealth period (1935-40) while Taylor examined its fit with Cold War geopolitics. Notwithstanding their authors' claims to objectivity, these texts have now been compromised by the reality of massive social injustice, unmitigated poverty of millions, rampant atrocities by the military, exploitation of women and children, and widespread violation of human rights by business and government (De la Torre 1986; San Juan 1986; De Dios et al 1988). Aspects of this reality have been exposed by concerned Filipinos (see, for example, Hernando Abaya's [1984] exposé of the shady deals of General Douglas MacArthur and Paul

McNutt in his autobiography)—proof that subalterns can speak and represent themselves.

In retrospect, this legitimation crisis of imperial power frames all discourse on U.S.-Philippines relations. Conceived as one ideological discourse mobilized for the post-Marcos era of mending "fences" and "bridges," Karnow's journalistic chronicle is symptomatic not only of the U.S. Establishment's need to redefine periodically its global mission in the context of international rivalries, especially in the light of its economic decline, but also of the urge to rewrite the past—precisely to represent many "other" wills and events purged from the official records—in order to define the "American Self" anew.[3] Since the dogma of white supremacy is deeply embedded in all Western discourse (Fanon 1963; Cesaire 1972; Retamar 1989; Williams 1995), this act of U.S. self-definition operates within that episteme and seeks mainly to recover lost ground. Friend (1989), for instance, shifts the blame to the "Hispanic tradition" for all the social ills afflicting the Philippines. Karnow's discourse can be perceived as the latest in a long series of recuperative strategies to represent the Filipino people as a reflection of Anglo-American "manifest destiny" in its various mutations, particularly urgent at this conjuncture when U.S. ascendancy has eroded and is being challenged or threatened by other states (Davis 1987; Callari et al 1995).

Karnow's book should be appraised within this specific conjuncture. His tendentious summary of over eighty years of strenuous American archival labor to understand the dynamics of U.S. involvement in the Philippines has yielded only what the aforementioned classics of "Philippine Studies" have repeatedly posited: the effort to Americanize the Filipinos partly succeeded in terms of introducing the forms of institutions like electoral democracy, mass public education, civil service system, and so forth; but it completely failed in altering traditional "Filipino" values, in particular those sanctioning the patron-client tributary relationship and its effects.[4] In short, the Philippines continued to be represented by imperial discursive practice (U.S. State Department reports, U.S. official pronouncements and their academic counterparts) as a realm of irrational passion, chaos, internal disorder, corruption, and inefficiency to which only the "disciplinary technology" of counterinsurgency (if the surveillance of legal apparatuses for securing consent fails) can be the appropriate remedy (Doty 1996). Lacking agency, the "uncivilized" Filipinos from the gaze of U.S. administrators cannot enjoy full, positive sovereignty.

What happened then to this much-touted U.S. experiment in colonial entrepreneurship that claimed to produce the miraculous "showcase of U.S. democracy" in Asia after World War II? Why did it fail?

In 1947, the great Marxist philosopher Karl Korsch turned his attention to the new form of imperialist control being set up in the Philippines based on puppets, Quislings, and variegated collaborators, with the concession of political independence being used to increase economic and social dependence (Taruc 1953). In general, Korsch observed that Western colonization violently disrupted "all the traditional living habits in the indigenous community," but the rise of neocolonialism after World War II has resurrected the nineteenth-century slogan of tutelage for benighted natives. Korsch warns us about U.S. stratagems in this regard:

> It would be false, however, to expect that the old fine-sounding justifications of Western colonial policies would perish with the historical preconditions on which they are based. It is in the nature of an ideology to gain severity as it loses practical validity. And thus it is by no means paradoxical that the most obstinate support for the theory of evolution and education by capitalist colonization is found today in the public opinion of the one country [United States] which cannot even furnish a real basis in experience for the theory in its history. (1990, 42)

Aside from repudiating the spurious rationale of "tutelage," Korsch points to the degeneration of ideology (white supremacy, civilized capitalism) into fascist barbarism when it "loses practical validity." CIA and U.S. counterinsurgency measures diluted with Agency for International Development (U.S. AID), Peace Corps, and assorted NGOs confirm the veracity of this insight from the Magsaysay administration to those of Marcos, Aquino, and Ramos (Catholic Institute 1992; BAYAN International 1994).

From the beginning, the entire disciplinary apparatus of U.S. academic scholarship has been organized to provide an explanation for such eventuality. Challenged by mounting popular resistance from the late sixties on, the rationale for U.S. support of the Marcos dictatorship—from Nixon to Ford, Carter, Reagan, and Bush—for almost three decades has drawn its logic and rhetoric from the scholarship of American historians, political scientists, sociologists, and functionaries in various disciplines. Complicit with state policies since the advent of Empire, their intellectual authority in the field of actual implementation remains to be scrutinized and evaluated.

Logos yields to the exigencies of praxis, transcendence to historical contingency. Given the renewed threat of Filipino nationalism to expunge once and for all the myth of U.S.-Philippines "special relations," the compulsive desideratum of contemporary U.S. discourse on the Philippines (as demonstrated by the works of David Steinberg [1982], Theodore Friend [1986], and particularly Peter Stanley [1974]) is to re-conceptualize the fact of U.S. domination as a transaction of equal partnership between Filipinos and Americans. It is essentially an interpretive strategy to revise the canonical, orthodox narrative of imperial success. This project of revaluation—what I would call a post-hoc-ergo construal to underscore its retrograde instrumentalism—would center on a refurbishing of the patron-client paradigm; the notion of reciprocal obligations entailed by it would arguably serve as the theoretical framework within which one can then exorcise the burden of U.S. responsibility for what happened in the Philippines from 1898 to 1946 by shifting the cause of the failure of American tutelage to the putative shrewdness of Filipinos in "manipulating" their masters.[5]

We tried to do our best, but . . . This is the basic thesis of Peter Stanley's *A Nation in the Making: The Philippines and the United States, 1899-1921* (1974), an updated sequel to the family of metanarratives cited earlier. It is an argument replicated by Karnow and other commentaries before and after the February 1986 insurrection. A dialectical twist of historical sensibility seems to have occurred. The sharp contrast between these reconstructive texts and previous works critical of U.S. imperialism—to cite only the most accessible, James Blount's *The American Occupation of the Philippines* (1912), Leon Wolff's *Little Brown Brother* (1961), Benedict J. Kerkvliet, *The Huk Rebellion* (1977), and Stuart Creighton Miller's *"Benevolent Assimilation": The American Conquest of the Philippines 1899-1903* (1982)—may be read as symptomatic of a cleavage in the hegemonic consensus, perhaps a change in tactics attuned to the reactionary climate of opinion now ascendant since the mid-seventies. It can also be conceived as a defensive mechanism set into play to counter a resurgent anti-U.S. imperialism around the world in the wake of the Vietnam defeat and the exfoliating revolutionary ruptures in Central America, South Africa, the Middle East, and elsewhere (Amin 1994).

This mutation needs to be clarified because of its impact on contemporary cultural politics and the function of intellectuals in both metropolis and periphery. In reviewing a volume edited by Peter Stanley entitled *Reappraising an Empire, New Perspectives on Philippine-American History* (1984), Robert B. Stauffer (1987) acutely points to the dogmatic ideological framework of the new apologetics mentioned earlier. The revisionary thrust of scholars employing the paradigm of patron-client linkage instead of a concept like dependency or even (in pedantic terminology) "asymmetrical relation" within the capitalist world-system is meant to recast the exploitative relationship of dependency into a reciprocal one where responsibility is equalized if not dispersed. By downplaying any serious U.S. influence on Philippine social structures and inflating the ingenious duplicity of the colonized, Stauffer contends, Stanley and his colleagues make "empire" into a romantic ideology. Since a seemingly immutable patron-client pattern of relationship determined political life during U.S. ascendancy, Filipino nationalism is relegated to the "manipulative underside of the collaborative empire," a phrase that euphemistically reformulates McKinley's "benevolent assimilation proc-lamation" of 21 December 1898, the foundation of U.S. rule over the island colony. Stauffer's reservation is amplified by Peter Tarr (1989) in another context. Tarr attributes the fallacy of the new apologetics to the "Immaculate Conception" view of American imperial policy as a glorious and selfless "civilizing mission," this last phrase evoking the period of a socioeconomic transition from European mercantilism to a new inter-national division of labor subtending capital's strategy of "counterrevo-lution," to use Arno Mayer's (1971) terminology. In retrospect, one can describe this "civilizing mission" as the ideological impetus behind the march of Anglo-Saxon progress over the conquered territories and subjugated bodies of African slaves, American Indians, Mexicans, Chi-nese workers, and so on, from the erection of the pilgrim settlements to the closing of the western frontier at the end of the nineteenth century.[6]

FORGING MODALITIES OF RESISTANCE

In a provocative essay on United States interventions in the "Third World," Eqbal Ahmad underscores the tradition of bargaining, co-optation, or management in U.S. political culture for those located within the boundary of the liberal marketplace. For those defined outside this boundary (American Indians, blacks, etc.), violence and extermina-tion are the chosen modes of maintaining the consensus. Within this authoritarian superstructure exists "a well-defined but extremely permis-sive infrastructure." Displaced onto a global arena, the practice of technocratic-managerial discourse (as exemplified in the texts cited earlier) underwrites the way American experts on the Philippines have sought to reconcile the everyday violence suffered by impoverished peasants and workers with the accumulation strategy of transnational business. Stauffer has already described the reality of democracy in the Philippines as "that form of intra-elite competition for office via elections during the colonial era, and under conditions where elected officials were given a great deal of symbolic public space but were denied real power which remained firmly anchored in U.S. hands" (1990, 36).

Revisionist historians have suggested that the predicament of the "institutional invisibility" of Philippine Studies is a result of the absence of any serious discussion of imperial American "exceptionalism" in the academy. Everyone knows that American scholars of Philippine affairs occupy a marginal or subordinate slot as a function of the low geopolitical status of the Philippines in the U.S. global profit-making horizon, a status fixed earlier by the successful hegemonic scheme of "Filipinization" (Paredes 1988). This astute cooptative scheme implemented by William Howard Taft, first civil governor of the colony, may indeed be taken as the originary inspiration for the current vogue of holding the victims responsible for their plight (the most recent example is Glenn Anthony May's [1996] debunking of the Filipino "mythmakers" responsible for the cult of the Filipino revolutionary hero Andres Bonifacio).

However, I do not think that this minor status of American Filipinologists involves simply the question of representation whether political, semiotic, or ethnographic. I believe that the structural cause has something to do with this persistent failure to critique the process of U.S. hegemonic rule in the Philippines celebrated by Karnow, Eggan (1991), and others, due to the nature of their training and the apologetic mission of the discipline. This is compounded with the usual compensatory reward in the metropolitan expert gaining mastery over "others" that is so integral a part of Western racist culture (as David Goldberg [1994] has so persuasively demonstrated). This then, I submit, is the hard lesson that the Philippine "temptation"—the "civilizing" ethos assuming new disguise at every stage of uneven development—must reinculcate for every generation: oppositions and contradictions cannot be converted into a series of differences for the sake of celebrating a neoliberal pluralism without sacrificing the ultimate goal of justice, participatory democracy, and self-determination of peoples. An aesthetics of "postcolonial" difference is a poor substitute for a politics of thoroughgoing popular-democratic transformation. What makes a real difference is the moment of recognition by the millions of the powerless and disenfranchised that the world can be changed if they can organize and act in order to change iniquitous property/power relations radically. When performed by the masses, cultural criticism within the tradition of Fanon, C. L. R. James, Lu Hsun, Ngugi, Retamar, and others becomes a handmaiden to this process of seizing the initiative and demanding full recognition.

A more pressing if vexed issue needs to be addressed at this point. Is the Filipino intellectual's position one of hybridity, "part of the colonized by ancestry while aligning with the colonizer by franchise," and therefore complicitous? Is the Filipino from this angle simultaneously part of the problem and part of the solution?[7] This hypothetical positionality is tied to the larger problematic of utilitarian pluralism. It is entailed by the logic of pragmatic individualism whereby a stratified and hierarchically ordered polity is legitimized whenever the terms *freedom* and *democracy* are brandished. "Hybridity" is a term that one can choose or reject. But the central issue is: what is the actual alignment of power relations and political forces in which we find ourselves imbricated? This is a key question that remains bracketed and "unspoken" in and by postcolonial theory.

Given the predominance of elite careerism and other varieties of petit-bourgeois opportunism among postcolonials, I am afraid the inventory of ourselves that Antonio Gramsci (1957) once prescribed as a preliminary heuristic imperative might take some time to accomplish. Meanwhile, a few modest proposals in this context may not be supererogatory. What I think is salutary is the attitude of being conscious and critical of one's framework as a point of departure, predisposed to analyzing events in terms of their multiple determinants and extrapolating the internal relations that comprise their differentiated and overdetermined unity. I would urge here a critical orientation geared to historicizing and cognitively demarcating the limits of theory (vis-à-vis social practices and forms of life) and assigning responsibility. In this way, the praxis of producing knowledge—one inevitably asks for what purpose? and for whom?—recognizes its multiple determinants, its condition of possibility, in the terrain of popular struggles across class, gender, "race," nationality, and so forth. Thus we come to understand the process whereby the knower becomes an integral part of the known; the educator is educated, to rehearse the old adage, when reading/writing ceases to be an end in itself and coincides with the act of transforming and transvaluing the world.

The acquisition of such a critical sensibility, transgressive and radically utopian at the same time, is an arduous task for the excolonized sensibility. Paulo Freire (1972) once taught us the elementary lesson of decolonization via "conscientization." Fanon (1967) outlined the vicissitudes of this Manichean ordeal in the native psyche in his essay, "On National Culture," a trial of cunning, resourcefulness, and endurance. What any subject of colonial bondage faces in this attempt to liberate his psyche from the temptations of servility has been intimated by the great Caribbean revolutionary thinker C. L. R. James when he discerned how the colonial myth of white/Western supremacy, now become an organic part of the colonized thought process, is so difficult to disgorge: "It is not that the myth is not challenged. It is, but almost always on premises that it has itself created, premises that (as with all myths) rest on very deep foundations within the society that has created them" (1993b, 109). Demystification of idols and their dethronement then becomes the first order of the day.

Historical experience teaches us that some idols may last as long as imperial capitalism survives its periodic and ineluctable crisis. In the spectrum of reactions to the ravages of white supremacy, the most common (in the Philippines) seems to be the nativist glorification of traditional pieties, feudal customs, and tributary rituals, often labelled by well-intentioned educators as "Filipino values." These values are then privileged to be what distinguishes the warm organic community of the pristine countryside as the authentic homeland counterposed to the alienating, diabolic, and strife-torn postindustrial cities. This type of "nationalism" is understandable but scarcely defensible. Of late that essentialism has given way to the cult of the hybrid and heterogeneous, the indeterminate and fragmented—in short, the decentered subject (for recent examples, see Campomanes 1995; Rafael 1995). In this disaggregated context, should we Filipinos then make a virtue of the neocolonial predicament, celebrating our syncretic identities as our avant-garde sublime? Disavowing the perils of essentialism and the proverbial "grand narratives," we sometimes succumb to the sirens of totalizing anomie in our endeavor to affirm our dignity, our autochtonous tradition, our right to self-determination. There is something intriguing in the characteristic gesture of "postcolonized" intellectuals embracing their schizoid fate as a virtue or at least a springboard for future amphibious quests. On the other hand, the transnational corporate system proves clever enough to utilize this posture of sophistication to promote touristic ventures and their profitable manipulation of spectacles.[8]

Symptomatic of over four hundred years of oppression and resistance, this valorization of the fissured and sedimented identity of the "Filipino"—of any survivor of imperial tutelage, for that matter—may be read as the trademark of intellectuals uprooted from the popular-democratic struggles of the working masses whose aspiration for freedom and dignity demand the prior satisfaction of basic needs as a fundamental human right. In the era of flexible capitalism, we Filipinos as participants in a process of nationalitarian reconstruction seem to be still on the threshold of modernity. We are still inventing allegories of the birth of *Pilipinas,* a process of collective imagining and praxis, a project begun at the time when a local tribal chief killed Magellan (shortly after his "discovery" of the islands in 1521) but later on aborted by Admiral Dewey's incursion into Manila Bay.

A crisis of the logic of representationalism—the mode of representing "others" criticized by Edward Said (1978) as "Orientalism," also known in the lexicon as *mission civilizatrice*—has furnished the pretext for prematurely drawing up a "postal" balance sheet. But I submit that we have not yet reached the final reckoning. Witness the anticolonial struggles in Puerto Rico, East Timor, Hawaii, Kurdistan; in states ruled by the comprador bourgeoisie, as well as the resistance of subjugated indigenous or aboriginal peoples in all continents. Amid the turbulence of global realignment, Haiti, the country of "marvellous realism" (Alexis 1995), is still struggling to escape the stranglehold of U.S. neocolonial intervention under the guise of democratic reform and humanitarian assistance. Not yet postcolonial, we, "hewers of wood and drawers of water," still languish in the hinterlands of the Empire's outposts, which overlook armadas of nuclear gunboats.

What seems imperative now is to insist on a more dialectical comprehension of the global process that subsumes both the United States and the Philippines in the text of a world-system crisscrossed by antinomies, schisms, contradictions, and so on. Cultural representations are always being constructed and deconstructed along race, class, gender, and ethnic lines relative to the multifarious struggles going on, a situation that seems to defy the codes and assumptions of the traditional disciplines. To heed Freire's advice, it is necessary not only to demystify neocolonial myths but also to expose the insidious working of the entire commodity system that we have inherited and continue to inhabit often without our knowing it. Such a system includes the whole network of mass media production and distribution of signs and spectacles. Central to this is the tourist/entertainment circuit of exchange, the fabrication of tokens and images repackaging the Philippines for quotidian mass consumption. Voyeurism substitutes for actual financial investments and complements the export-oriented economy of the "free trade zones." While one travel writer bewailed the price the Philippines paid for its "mutual intoxication with the West" (thus lacking the magic of Thailand or Indonesia because it is Asia sanitized) (*The Guardian,* 20 September 1982), another hymned the country as "a paradise waiting for those [Western businessmen] who wish to avoid citiscape and . . . sit amidst Mother Nature's ethereal beauty" (*The Daily Yomiuri,* 20 September 1989).

Commodification reaches its apogee in a cinematic media event of some consequence. In the last days of the Marcos dictatorship, the Philippine countryside was suddenly transformed into a stage prop for Francis Ford Coppola's $35 million extravaganza, *Apocalypse Now* (ostensibly based on Joseph Conrad's novella, *Heart of Darkness*), which reprised the Vietnam War as both spectacle and therapy, utopian dream and technological nightmare.

One might suspect at the outset that reality succumbed to seductive "simulation" and hyperreal pastiche in this film—but only on the surface. Shot in Baler, Quezon province, Philippines, Coppola's block-buster production featured a cast of hundreds of Vietnamese "boat people," Filipino extras, and specimens of the immortal "water buffalo" (carabao) that colonial governor Taft once honored with his buttocks. Initially hyped as an attack on U.S. aggression in Vietnam, the film actually collaborated with imperial policy in endorsing the Pentagon's version of the "foreign invasion" of South Vietnam. It also aided the U.S.-backed Marcos dictatorship in fighting the New People's Army combatants led by Marxist-Leninist cadres. Beyond that, Coppola's "conspicuous consumption" poisoned the local environment with prostitution, racist discriminatory treatment of Vietnamese and Filipino participants, and other con games that usually gravitate around Hollywood big-time spending (Sussman 1992). In retrospect, Conrad's vision of the "heart of darkness" seems to have materialized again in those islands subjected since Magellan's fateful intrusion in 1521 to the violence and fantasies of Western travelers, missionaries, and hustlers who have produced the stereotyped knowledge and doxa of the "Philippines" and "Filipinos" for everyone's profit except for the Filipinos themselves.

This caesura of commodification and reification punctuates the vicissitudes of U.S.-Philippines relations in a way that allows us to appreciate, next to specimens of the "ugly American," Fredric Jameson's exhaustive reading of Kidlat Tahimik's *The Perfumed Nightmare* (1992). Composed in the midst of Marcos's dictatorship, Tahimik's film adopts Aesopian language and seriocomic techniques in satirizing the "colonial mentality" and foregrounding the historical linkages between the Philippine authoritarian regime and U.S. imperial dominance. The American Marxist critic Jameson, however, is fascinated with the film's aesthetics of revolt sublimated in the formal qualities of a unique innovation of the *naif* film genre, an experiment that opens up, for "First World" activists," a pretext for the "constant re-functioning (Brecht's *Unfunktioneirung)* of the new into the old, and the old into the new." Kidlat's jeepnies, Jameson informs us, "mark the place of a properly Third-World way with production which is neither the ceaseless destruction and replacement of new and larger industrial units (together with their waste by-products and their garbage), nor a doomed and nostalgic retrenchment in traditional agriculture, but a kind of Brechtian delight with the bad new things that anybody can hammer together for their pleasure and utility if they have a mind to" (1992, 211). And Filipino cultural activists "have a mind" to salvage (a term refunctioned during the martial-law era to signify political assassination) from the wreckage of U.S. superpower hubris the invaluable lesson that "weak links" exist in the heterogenized and dereified postindustrial metropolis. We do not have to eschew the political for the economic, or the economic for the social—all three levels of the historical-materialist hermeneutic crystallized in specific crisis points are addressed here as well as in the projects of seasoned national-democratic forces in Philippine cities and countryside.

In the global process of commodification, the gurus of postcoloniality have contributed their share of promoting fetish worship. I do not know whether to laugh or be outraged when Jean Baudrillard, in his notorious essay "The Precession of Simulacra" (1984), uses a group of aboriginal Filipinos known as "Tasaday" (which the Marcos dictatorship fabricated for its commercial and publicity needs) for his virtuoso ruminations. When the Marcos government for a time supposedly returned the Tasadays to "their primitive state," this withdrawal (according to Baudrillard) afforded ethnology "a simulated sacrifice of its object in order to save its reality principle." The French shaman performs his own magical number here in updating the myth of the "noble savage": "The Indian thereby driven back into the ghetto, into the glass coffin of virgin forest, becomes the simulation model for all conceivable Indians before ethnology. . . . Thus ethnology, now freed from its object, will no longer be circumscribed as an objective science but is applied to all living things and becomes invisible, like an omnipresent fourth dimension, that of the simulacrum. We are all Tasaday" (1984, 257-58). A trope indeed to end all rhetoric, all discourse dealing with truth, reality, life-and-death issues.

What escapes this postmodern thinker but not the victims of his tropology is the quite ordinary staple of quotidian politics: publicity utilized for speculation and profit making. We are confronted by the hoax perpetrated by the Marcos regime, by elite bureaucrats and the military (not by ethnologists), who stand to gain by driving the Manobos (members of whom were forced to pose as a Stone Age tribe) from their mineral-rich homeland. This fabrication was then processed into a commodity-form by the National Geographic Society and other Western media apparatuses, reinforced by a gallery of spectators including Gina Lollabrigida, relatives of General Francisco Franco invited by Elizalde and Imelda Marcos, and other celebrities to which Baudrillard ascribes a tremendous *mana*-power of transforming all reality into simulation. But this item is not a simulation: one of those who testified in an international conference in 1986 to expose this hoax, Elizir Bon, was killed in September 1987 by paramilitary agents near the Marcos-declared Tasaday reservation (Berreman 1990) while the rest of the "Tasaday" have been silenced by a machinery of terror that Baudrillard would rather ignore.

The duplicities of neocolonial life thus interrogate the ethics of postmodern theory and expose the inconsistencies of postcolonial aesthetics. In complicity with Western rationality, Baudrillard punishes the "Indians" (the Manobos are indiscriminately dissolved into this erroneous generic classification) by depriving them of their history, their embeddedness in a specific sociocultural setting—in short, their integrity as humans. This is the textualizing revenge of imperial power on the world that dare claim precedence over it.

How can one recognize the Other as more than a distorted projection of all the negativity and lack in one's Self? Is this case of unconscionable fraud entangled in the wake of dead bodies reducible to a disposable pastiche of information, simulacra, and language games, to the *jouissance* of hyperreal bricolage? What is really at stake here?

IMAGINING ALTERNATIVES: WHO LIVES DANGEROUSLY?

Crossing boundaries wedding fear and hope, we return to native ground: free-fire zones, quarantined quarters, long contested terrain where the conflict stages the *agon* of hearts besieged and minds beleaguered, the homeland as permanent battleground.

The legacy of the past centuries of colonialism—three hundred years under Spain, almost a century under the United States (compounded by the traumatic Japanese Occupation of World War II)—has proved devastating, exorbitant, even incommensurable. Next to the Filipino-American War, this competes for the title of the Filipino postcolonial sublime. Our witnesses among the living and the dead (who never heard Nietzsche's cry to "live dangerously") to this truism are legion.

Statistics can only give an abstract index of what Filipinos have inherited from the past whose effects profoundly mark their present lives. Of about 70 million Filipinos today, 72 percent are impoverished; mostly peasants and workers, they are scattered throughout seven thousand islands once endowed with abundant natural resources but that are now almost one unrelieved ecological disaster. In 1950 the country had 52 million hectares of tropical forest; now only a million hectares remain (*Christian Science Monitor,* 8 May 1992). In the primate city of Manila, 38 percent live below the poverty line; 40 percent inhabit sub-standard squatter settlements. Almost 40 percent of the entire work force are unemployed or underemployed. Despite the temporary recovery due to OCW (Overseas Contract Workers) remittances, the Philippines has one of the lowest per capita income and one of the lowest wage rates in the world (Tujan 1996). Filipinos are the second most malnourished people in the whole world despite the country being a top producer and exporter of food, minerals, and labor power, one of the most vital resources for transnational capital: about 6 million Filipino OCWs fulfill the needs of the world for cheap semiskilled, nonunionized labor with destructive implications for the health of women, families, and entire communities (Pineda-Ofreneo and Ofreneo 1995). With a per capita income of $2,3000 (gross domestic product), the Philippines is easily ranked the poorest in the region. Given the rising unemployment, inflation and high prices for basic foods, lack of capital goods industries, corruption in government, and an onerous foreign debt, the immediate prospect for amelioration of the lot of the majority (despite the current frenzy of privatization and deregulation) is practically nil.

The major source of political and economic inequality in Filipino society, all recent studies concur (Putzel 1992), is the control of land and other resources by an oligarchic minority—former President Aquino's family counts among the most wealthy—who also manipulate the bureaucracy, the legislature, courts, and the military in order to preserve their power and privileges. State power in a disarticulated formation like the Philippines encroaches deep into the trenches and ramparts of civil society; consequently, the sphere of private life and ego-centered interests cannot be considered an inviolable refuge of peace and liberty. It is primarily owing to U.S. support of this parasitic and moribund elite since the turn of the century that 54 million Filipinos, according to human rights lawyer Romeo Capulong (1986), "will never forget that it was U.S.

tanks, guns, bullets, bombs, planes and even chemicals that the Philippine military used to kill them." Hundreds of political prisoners, according to Amnesty International (1992) reports, still languish in jails where they are now classified as common criminals. U.S. "low intensity" warfare (initiated by the Reagan administration and fostered by its successors) proceeds without much impediment (Bello 1987). Senator Wigberto Tanada warned us recently: "Despite the demise of the Cold War, ship visits by nuclear-armed U.S. naval vessels continue to make port calls in the Philippines. A pre-positioning agreement between the Clinton and Ramos governments is quietly being negotiated to pave the way for continued U.S. military access to Philippine territory, despite the clear-cut prohibition against this kind of deployment of foreign forces by the Philippine Constitution" (5).

We can now comprehend how the much ballyhooed "Philippines 2000" promoted by President Ramos as a scheme to convert the Philippines into a newly industrialized country (NIC), underwritten by the IMF/World Bank and transnational corporations, is bound to worsen the plight of ordinary working people and deepen the stagnation all around (BAYAN International 1995; for an eulogistic report, see Luce [1996]). No transitory reform from above, in my opinion, can alter deeply entrenched property relations or effect a redistribution of wealth and power without sustained and voluntary mass actions. Only the perseverance and sacrifices of the national-democratic forces across the spectrum (including the Moro, Lumads, and Igorots with their long record of anticolonial intransigence [Rodil 1993; Scott 1993]), in wars of position and of maneuver—the most durable has been the National Democratic Front and its guerilla army, the New People's Army (San Juan 1986; Chapman 1987)—gives hope to the masses of a possible change for the better in their situation, an improvement of their everyday lives, a vindication of their exuberant spirit, a renewal of their integrity and dignity. Despite the government's claim that the insurgent forces had declined from its peak strength of twenty-five thousand armed combatants in the mid-1980s to about eight thousand, the reality disavows the illusion of stability: the material conditions fueling oppression and exploitation remain and, as noted earlier, have even worsened. Meanwhile the old "mole" keeps burrowing, crafting new weapons, drawing up an inventory, planning for the next offensive. There seems to be no alternative but refusal and insurgency, always bearing in mind too that (as De la Torre [1986] puts it) "politics is a choice among realities, among possibilities"—a condition of indeterminacy evolving into the ruptural unity of tensions and polarizations, a convergence of forces that constitutes the innovative and redemptive power of popular-democratic interventions.

The culture of the Filipino resistance possesses a long memory, drawing sustenance from four centuries of anti-imperialist rebellion against Spain, the United States, and Japan. We can go back to Father Jose Burgos and the 1872 martyrs of nascent Filipino nationalism, to Jose Rizal and the *propagandistas,* to Apolinario Mabini's audacity epitomized by his declaration: "I hope the Americans will understand that the present state of culture of the Filipino people shall not put up with subjugation by force as a permanent condition. The Filipinos may be vanquished now and again, but as long as they are denied every kind of right, there will not be lasting peace" (1974, 231). Salud Algabre, woman leader of the 1935 Sakdal uprising, attests to this insurrectionary legacy: "We did what we ourselves [peasant masses] had decided upon— as free people, and power resides in the people. What we did was our heritage . . . We decided to rebel, to rise up and strike down the sources of power. I said 'We are Sakdals! We want immediate, complete, and absolute independence.' No uprising fails. Each one is a step in the right direction" (Sturtevant 1976). These voices articulate what Otto Bauer (1970) once called "the community of fate" that defines a people affirming the right of self-determination, of national autonomy.[9] They all refute the "postcolonial" argument that subaltern actors/protagonists cannot speak because they are paralyzed by an insurmountable psychic crisis, or else are hostage to a past of betrayals, "false consciousness," and forfeited opportunities. A "negation of negations" is in order here.

The restoration of neocolonial democracy in 1986 ushered a new stage for the revival of neocolonial apparatuses of domination to which I have alluded earlier, agencies of hegemonic rule designed to protract the nation's subservience to transnational corporations and the IMF/World Bank (Diokno 1987). The comprador-oligarchic elite retains the same qualities discerned by Pedro Abad Santos during the thirties: "It is timid because it is aware of its weakness. It is ignorant, for even its intellectual leaders lack understanding of advanced political and economic thought" (Allen 1993). Western bourgeois values persist in saturating the media, fueling consumerism, and the individualist lifestyle glamorized by U.S. music, films, and advertisements in the mass media. Patriarchal and authoritarian habits pervade the organs of the state and the institutions of civil society. Commodification is the modernizing engine running over all. While the censorship of films like Lino Brocka's *Orapronobis* can be

considered a symptom of the shriveled "democratic space" for oppositional practices (as the confiscation by the military of Behn Cervantes's
film *Sakada* in the seventies signaled the enlarged role of underground
cultural activity), the cultivation of anticommunist religious fundamen-
talism that flourished for a while with the Aquino-sponsored "vigilante"
groups has been displaced with other forms of "low intensity" warfare
against liberationist impulses. Splittist and divisive tendencies in the
progressive organizations are being fomented by the counterinsurgency
apparatuses of the government. Unwarranted arrests of activists, militari-
zation of villages and towns, and extrajudicial summary execution of
suspected subversives are continuing. Political prisoners are multiplying,
with the courts functioning as instruments of the military. Schools and
the mass media continue to shape cultural policy geared toward supplying
cheap labor for the global market, particularly for despotic Middle Eastern
sheikdoms as well as for the domestic needs of Singapore, Taiwan, Hong
Kong, and the sex-entertainment industries of Japan (Medel-Anonuevo
1990; Center for Women's Resources 1996).

Meanwhile, resistance smolders on, flaring up at times. The popular-
democratic forces ranging from sectoral groups of peasants, workers,
women, ethnic communities, youth, teachers, religious assemblages, and
other dissident formations are inventing new initiatives to fill the vacuum
created by the dissolution of the Cory mystique and the exposed
bankruptcy of any successor regime. Oligarchic comprador rule, though
obsolescent, still prevails owing to the force of inertia and the divisions
among the oppressed—proof that we live between a past in its death
throes and a future still struggling to be born. The exhausted logic of
cynical compromise formerly indulged in by *trapos* (traditional politicians) is now being artificially revived by its sponsors from Japan, Hong
Kong, and assorted surrogates of the United States. Aquino's and
Ramos's victims point the way to future emancipatory projects far
beyond the ironic recuperation of "people power" for profit and class-
conflicted peace, far beyond any mock-utopian promise of the elite's
"Philippines 2000."

We have thus reached a turning point in our itinerary of collective
self-discovery, a goal anathema to postcolonial anti-essentialism. Everyone in the progressive ranks soon realized that Aquino and her cohort
stood not for real change but only for the restoration of the status quo,
this time much worse than Marcos's "constitutional authoritarianism"
because of its reformist facade and parliamentary chicanery. Systematic
violation of human rights and impoverishment of the majority of

Filipinos worsened in the years of the Aquino presidency, without a single military officer being punished for human rights violations. With the failure of the Aquino regime in consolidating an elite conservative order, the movement for participatory democratic transformation has to renew its project of shaping a national-popular agenda of land reform, gender equality, autonomy for indigenous peoples, vindication of the victims of military-landlord abuses, and a sweeping redistribution of wealth. Whatever strategy is pursued to achieve such long-range goals— all means are necessary provided the masses after sufficient deliberation support them, it is necessary to bear in mind that the plotting of mass mobilization is itself overdetermined by the changed landscape of post– Cold War global alignments.[10]

In this framework, it appears certain that the fate of U.S. cultural hegemony as well as U.S. business, cultural, and political interests will soon be decided by the unfolding of manifold contradictions, primarily by the action of Filipino workers and peasants and middle strata, in the first decades of the twenty-first century. Meanwhile, democratic socialist thinking inspired by "Western Marxisms" is being "supplemented," enriched, and historicized by in-depth studies of indigenous social movements and local resistances involving feminists, ecologists, cultural activists from all walks of life, and other partisans of grass-roots initiatives. The "postcolonial" alternative is arguably one possible route (Said 1994), not the best to my judgment, in arriving at the correct bearing—correct, that is, in that it catalyzes and enriches popular-democratic initiatives and agendas. After all the detours and zigzags, the task of the cultural opposition (literary critics included) and organic intellectuals of the people remains clear: to participate with the masses in the discovery and charting of the Filipino road to national liberation and democratic socialist reconstruction in the next millenium.

The Philippines, a country undergoing profound social and political transformations, exemplifies a "Third World" society in which the major contradictions of our time—forces embodying the categories of class, ethnicity, gender, nationality, religion, sexuality, and so on—converge into a fissured and disjunctive textual panorama open for interpretation, critique, and ecumenical exchanges. My contribution to these exchanges is a modest one, that of endeavoring to survey the domain of signifying practices via a radical critique of United States–Philippines literary contacts, transactions, displacements. At the same time it strives to express a Third World perspective on the impact of Eurocentric power (specifically the United States) on a hitherto unexplored multicultural tradition of protest and resistance. It seeks to elucidate the ruses and resonance of hegemonic ideology, its encounter with oppositional discourses and cultural practices, foregrounding in the process the creative and critical power of those victimized by capital accumulation and its reifying racist-patriarchal technologies. What this counterhegemonic narrative of mine hopes to valorize is the emancipatory project of Filipino artists incarnating a popular-democratic vision and praxis of national liberation attuned to the multilayered struggles of other oppressed, subjugated, and exploited peoples wherever they are found.

With the Philippines as a figure for the revolutionary impulse everywhere, one can now conceive of the cultural production of two thirds of the planet's inhabitants—people of color in Africa, Asia, and Latin America, as well as the "internal colonies" in the developed industrialized societies—as indivisible from their struggle for self-determination, justice, equality, and the affirmation of dignity. Those heterogeneous projects of resistance and revolt, inscribed in poems, stories, *testimonios,* and other performances of those formerly silenced and made invisible, are what ultimately reproduce the "Third World" as a permanent political-cultural agency of global transformation. As I have said with reference to texts like Philip Vera Cruz's autobiography (San Juan 1995a), these performances can be used to fashion emancipatory agencies equipped with "a memory of the future," a recollection of hopes and dreams from which a life-enchancing future is extrapolated. They can restore to primacy the value-creating practice of associative labor, the power of the multitude (first theorized by Baruch Spinoza and elaborated by Marx, Lenin, and Third World revolutionaries), including the network of productive cooperation that generates society and mediates the state. They can help recover the rights of racialized collectivities (especially in the United States and Europe) that are marginalized or excluded by the bourgeois system of contracts, laws privileging private property and the machinery of commodification so as to renew the revolutionary practice of the masses—the autonomy, productivity, and the constitutive drive (*conatus*) of people of color. This axiom bears reiteration even when it has become dangerously commonplace, as circumstances warrant: wherever there is imperial domination in any form or disguise in our "postcolonial" transculturalized planet, there will always be a "Third World" protagonist fighting for national-popular liberation, whether in Haiti, Somalia, East Timor, Brazil, Hawaii, Palestine, the Philippines, or (to use an old but still militant metaphor) in the "belly of the beast" itself.

CHAPTER THREE

"Unspeakable" Subalterns: Lessons from Gramsci, El Saadawi, Freire, Silko

From Pennsylvania's Death Row in Pennsylvania, USA, this is Mumia Abu Jamal.
—Mumia Abu Jamal

The key issue is to regain our sovereignty.
—Leonard Peltier

I asked myself how could I effectively offer the reader a vivid description of prison so that he or she can understand the conditions under which I live and create my work.
—Elizam Escobar

Giambattista Vico, the eighteenth-century philosopher of culture and history, once said that humans can know only what they have made or enacted. This is possible because humans express an almost unlimited sequence of desires and needs through language; *homo faber* becomes the subject as *homo loquens,* who at the same time begets the Other—what one is not or does not have. From this standpoint, the Other (object, world) defines the self/subject by negation, the ultimate signifier of everything that the "I" is not. In Western phallogocentric discourse, the Other is often acknowledged as the woman, people of color, whatever is deemed monstrous and enigmatic: all are excluded from humanity (to which, it goes without saying, the definer belongs) by being so categorized. The Other is outside or marginal to the regnant system of beliefs, an amorphous and deviant figure against the background of conventional standards. Stereotypes and "Orientalisms" with panoptical reach normalize a gallery of others who remain fixed, passive, recalcitrant, irrational, depraved, and so on. But, to reverse Simone de Beauvoir's proposition (1952), is the category of the Other an *a priori* given as primordial as consciousness itself? And does speech distinguish its life-world?

In Jacques Lacan's psychoanalysis, the Other is the site in which the subject finds confirmation; the Other's response of recognition establishes the location of the "I." Echoing Hegel, Lacan states that the discourse of the Other is ascribed to the unconscious "in order to indicate the beyond in which the recognition of desire is bound up with the desire for recognition. . . . This other is the Other that even my lie invokes as a guarantor of the truth in which it subsists" (1977: 172). In a symptomatic reading, we grasp the Other as "the locus from which the question of [the subject's] existence may be presented" (1977: 194). Inscribed in a determinate historical setting, this Other is not neutral nor pure formality, since its embodiment in language implicates it with the patrocentric class ideology of the dominant culture (Wilden 1972). Acquisition of language by the child, in Lacan's epistemology, leads to its separation from the undifferentiated world of objects and precipitates the discovery that desired objects are not gone *(fort)* but have only gone somewhere else *(da)*—as per Freud's commentary on the *fort/da* game in *Beyond the Pleasure Principle*—and can return, with the child's anxiety henceforth assuaged by the discovery of difference in time and space. Parasitic on the Other and so constituted by the aleatory play of language and its chain of shifting signifiers, the subject on this poststructuralist reckoning possesses no self-contained integrity or permanent coherence—except in illusion, fantasy, and other pathological excess.

In contrast to this currently fashionable notion of the subject as unfixed by the other, Mikhail Bakhtin contends that others are needed precisely to substantiate and complete ourselves. To see the "I" as an other is required for dialogue to occur. Exotopy signifies the writer's attempt to break her empathy or identification with her characters and so posit their alterity, the condition of possibility for dialogue and reciprocal exchange; in short, without self-estrangement, there is no self-knowledge. From this angle, the negativity of the other becomes positive and enabling: marginalized others (like women, peasants, colonized subalterns) can thus comprehend the dominant and determining structures of their lives more accurately and fully than those who occupy the center and the commanding heights of society.

There is a sense in which Bakhtin's idea of exotopy anticipates and interrogates Jacques Derrida's notion of supplementarity. All forms of representation and interpretation require more than what is represented or interpreted; they necessarily presuppose a supplementary element that exists in the margins or borders of the thing and that is summoned to complete it. Derrida argues that writing becomes dangerous "from the moment that representation there claims to be presence and the sign of the thing itself" since "in the very functioning of the signs . . . the substitute makes one forget the vicariousness of its own function and makes itself pass for the plenitude of a speech whose deficiency and infirmity it nevertheless only supplements. . . . The sign is always the supplement of the thing itself" (1976: 144-45). Within this deconstructive analytic, Lacan's "Other" may be conceived as supplementary and speechless, given the contingency that the listener at the other end of the communication line may refuse to listen or be deaf, dead, or missing.

Not so long ago, a proponent of Derridean grammatology startled a few academic circles with the proposition that the "subaltern" cannot speak or represent herself; she must be spoken for and represented (Spivak 1988). In a later interview, Spivak clarifies her view: "[E]ven when one uttered, one was constructed by a certain kind of psychobiography that neutralizes one's utterance. . . . So, 'the subaltern cannot speak,' means that even when the subaltern makes an effort to the death to speak, she is not able to be heard, and speaking and hearing complete the speech act" (1996: 291-92).

Etymologically, the "subaltern" soldier is subordinate to the captain in the military hierarchy; hence subalterns refer to non-elite or subordinated social groups. However, from the perspective of the Indian Subaltern Studies group, the term "subaltern" has been redefined to encompass all subordinated populations oppressed by colonial/postcolonial regimes in various ways (economic, racial, sexist) to which the "supplement" of resistance acts as a contrapuntal chord: the category then refers to "the demographic difference between the total Indian population and all those whom we have described as the 'elite'" (Spivak 1996: 203). The agency of change in decolonizing formations is sought in the insurgent subaltern (1987: 197-221) conceived as the product of "a network of differential, potentially conflicting strands." The practitioners of "Subaltern Studies" seek to deconstruct those colonial narratives that determine the subjectivity of subalterns by positing a sphere of resistance original to those subjugated and enslaved. Their search for a "subaltern consciousness" exhibits a "strategic use of positivist essentialism" complicit with subaltern insurgency. Summarizing Ranajit Guhas's study of peasant resistance in India, Partha Chatterjee (1993) isolates the fundamental social character that underlies peasant insurgency: the notion of community. With the paradigmatic form of peasant subalternity ascertained, Chatterjee then argues that peasant consciousness is capable of a "vast range of transformations" that defy "objectivizing." In this writerly context, "community" becomes an ideal type that escapes "universal categories" because of its complexity and variability, thus dissolving subaltern otherness and its paradoxes into the abyss of its infinite empirical manifestations.

In contrast to the "Subaltern Studies" line of investigation, the historical materialist approach to domination employs a relational "cognitive mapping" (Jameson 1988) of situations with historically determinate properties. It stresses the movement of political antagonisms arising from the dynamics of specific social formations in which divergent modes of production (residual, dominant, emerging) coalesce or collide. Ignoring such concrete specificities, Spivak distorts Gramsci by imputing to the text of "The Southern Question" "an allegory of reading taken from or prefiguring an international division of labor" (Spivak 1988: 283) antecedent to the situation of subalterns. For Gramsci, however, the critical task is unequivocal: he is endeavoring to theorize the problem of transition in Italy from one mode of production and social formation to another, making the national question prior to the international question of geopolitics. Revolution, Gramsci's topic, is surely concerned with more than a grammatology of supplementary otherness and difference.

GROUNDING DISCOURSE IN HISTORY

What follows is an extended detour through Gramsci's texts on the question of the subaltern, historically the peasantry in Italy, as a way of recuperating the voices of those rendered mute by the terrorism of "undecidable" magisterial texts. "Peasantry" here can be taken as a synecdochic figure for the predicament of all victims of imperialist oppression in the North and South.

Since 1930, Gramsci has composed a series of notes with the heading "History of the Subaltern Classes." Notebook Q25 (written in 1934), for instance, carries the general title: "On the margins of history: history of the subaltern social groups" (1985: 294). Subaltern classes have no history of their own in the sense that the official historical documents do not notice them, or else submerge them in the master-narrative of the conquerors. From Gramsci's point of view, the "subaltern" cannot be conceived apart from the totality of social relations at any given historical conjuncture. In contrast to conventional usage, the "subaltern" is not so much an empirical fact as a theoretical element in understanding order and change in society.

Given the consensus that Gramsci's claim to distinction as a Marxist thinker lies in problematizing the process of hegemony, the controversy over subaltern representation cannot be resolved without engaging in the analysis of hegemony itself. I construe "hegemony" here in the sense not just of political leadership of an alliance of classes but also moral and intellectual leadership of a historical bloc of forces engendered in the process of revolutionary transformation. A subaltern group, for Gramsci, is one "deprived of historical initiative, in continuous but disorganic expansion, unable to go beyond a certain qualitative level, which still remains below the level of the possession of the State and of the real exercise of hegemony over the whole of society" (1971: 395-96; see also Sassoon 1980). In this sense, "subaltern" becomes a moment in the strategy of a fundamental class striving for hegemony (consent armored with force) by establishing the "integral state" via a political party as leader of a historic bloc striving to universalize an expansive, self-reflexive, critical world view.

As everyone knows, Gramsci was the first Italian Marxist to foreground and grapple seriously with the "Southern question" as "the central problem of Italian national life." And he is perhaps, after Lenin, the first to theorize the *problematique* of what Mao later called the "new democratic" or "national democratic revolution" in the "Third World" based on a worker-peasant united front: "The problem of the Italian revolution is therefore the problem of the unity of the workers and peasants" (quoted in Pozzolini 1970: 100).

In the course of archival investigation, I have found two articles by Gramsci before the founding of the Communist Party of Italy in 1921 whose insights into the historical configuration of forces surrounding the peasantry enable him to define the subaltern physiognomy. In the *Avanti!* (6 June 1918) article, Gramsci examines the historical evidence of the peasantry's resistance to the emergent institutions of the French bourgeois state during the French revolution. Extolling the mass of peasants as "the reservoir of all of society's wealth and energies," Gramsci inquires into the level of its political culture: "To what extent do they succeed in reaching the abstraction necessary for 'comprehending' the collectivity, for 'sensing' the 'others,' for solidarity with others, and for breaking out of the closed circle of egotism?" (1975: 77). By "egotism," Gramsci means corporatism based on "the principle of private property." He speculates to what extent the agricultural proletariat can exercise solidarity with the urban proletariat in a collectivist experiment for the socialist reconstruction of society. Peasants distrust and hate collective organizations so long as they do not feel the state as their "economy," a state based not on blood relation but on a concept of law and on obedience to it sanctioned by inner conviction and a historicist consciousness. Peasants regard landed property as equivalent to the family and ownership as a religious bond. Peasants conform to a concept of honor— "the recognition of a social capacity"—in submitting to military service under despotic rule; it is not solidarity with the state but self-love. When the landowners begin to identify with the state, the peasants react and begin to free themselves of "their habitual idolatry of central authority" and become antagonistic to it.

For Gramsci, the subalternity of the peasant springs from the survival of "the institutions and mental habits of feudalism" based on tribute and privilege, which preserve castes; hence peasants lack the mentality to understand the "needs of the collectivity" and their corresponding duty. What the peasantry has not acquired yet is the "historicist mentality" possessed by the industrialist who knows that property is a "historical category which remains only as long as the conditions which support it remain" (1975: 78). In sum, the peasant lacks a knowledge of the institutions of the modern state, the citizen's habit of solidarity, "an integral sense of the economic solidarity of classes," a lack caused by "his absence from public life" and the notion that political force is ultimately what prevails in society.

Gramsci applies his notion of subalternity as corporatism and ahistoricism in the anatomy of peasant psychology in the *L'Ordine Nuovo* (2 August 1919) article. Here it is not the French revolution but World War I that frames his materialist diagnosis of the divide between city and countryside, proletariat and peasantry. First, Gramsci observes that in backward countries like Italy, Spain, and Russia, the modern liberal State has not penetrated the masses deeply enough so that economic and political institutions, instead of being perceived as "natural, perpetual, irreducible categories," are considered "historical categories" (1977a: 83). Because the State has juridically perpetuated the feudal "investitures and privileges" of the big landowners, the peasantry subsists in virtual serfdom, erupting in violent revolts but unable to be an effective historical force:

> [The peasant] is incapable of seeing himself as a member of a collectivity (the nation for the landholders, the class for the proletarians), nor can he wage a systematic and permanent campaign designed to alter the economic and political relations of society. . . .
>
> Under such conditions, the psychology of the peasants was inscrutable: their feelings remained occult, entangled and confused in a system of defense against exploitation that was merely individualist, devoid of logical continuity, inspired largely by guile and feigned servility. Class struggle was confused with brigandage . . . it was a form of elementary terrorism, without long-term or effective consequences. Objectively, therefore, the peasant's psychology was restricted to a tiny number of elemental feelings dependent upon the social conditions created by the democratic-parliamentary State. The peasant was left completely at the mercy of the landowners and their hangers-on. . . . The peasant has always lived outside the rule of law—he has never had a juridical personality, nor a moral individuality. He lives on as an anarchic element, an independent atom in a chaotic tumult, constrained only by his fear of the police and the devil. He had no understanding of organization, of the State, of discipline. Though patient and tenacious in his individual efforts to wrest a lean harvest from nature and capable of making unheard of sacrifices in his family life, he was impatient and savagely violent in class struggle, incapable of setting himself a general goal for action and pursuing it with perseverance and systematic struggle. (1977a: 84)

The war, the material conditions of exploitation and concentrated interaction, radically transformed peasant psychology. It gave the peasant soldiers a historical mentality and sense of solidarity, the lack of which condemned them to subalternity:

> Selfish, individual instincts were blunted; a common, united spirit was fashioned; feelings were universalized; the habit of social discipline was formed. The peasants came to see the State in all its complex grandeur, its measureless power, its intricate construction. They came to see the world no longer as something infinitely vast like the universe and as circumscribed and small as the village bell-tower, but as a concrete reality consisting of States and peoples, social strengths and weaknesses, armies and machines, wealth and poverty. Links of solidarity were forged which

would have taken decades of historical experience and intermittent struggles to form. Within four years, in the mud and blood of the trenches, a spiritual world emerged that was avid to form itself into permanent and dynamic social structures and institutions. (1977a: 84-85)

Gramsci then points out how in Russia the councils of delegates harnessed that sense of solidarity and historicity to develop "a consciousness of the unity of the working class." In Italy, the class unification of workers and peasants will be achieved through "the practice of the socialist State and will be based on the new psychology created by communal life in the trenches." Gramsci then envisions these trenches to be re-created in "communist labour units" that would begin to set up centralized industrial farming led by a socialist State. His later theory of social/historic bloc derives from a firm belief in the imperative of a worker-peasant coalition founded in turn on a thoroughgoing cultural revolution, one that acknowledges "the necessities" and ideological horizon of the peasantry's life:

> Factory workers and poor peasants are the two driving forces of the proletarian revolution. For them, especially, communism is a vital necessity: its advent signifies life and liberty, while the continued existence of private property signifies the imminent danger of being crushed, of losing everything, including life itself. . . . They represent the backbone of the revolution, the iron battalions of the advancing proletarian army. . . . For them, communism represents civilization: it stands for the system of historical conditions in which they will acquire a personality, a dignity, a culture, and through which they will become a spirit creating progress and beauty. (1977a: 86)

In sum, Gramsci sees the peasantry as an irrepressible revolutionary force whose "diffuse mentality" needs a structure. For him, the communist revolution "is essentially a problem of organization and discipline"; therefore, for the spiritual gains acquired during the war not to be wasted, every individual needs to be involved in "organs of a new collective life," for only "in the functioning and practice of these, the advances can be consolidated, the experiences developed, and linked and directed consciously towards the accomplishment of a concrete historical goal." Again, Gramsci stresses that the transcendence of subalternity requires organization and education: "Organized in this way, the peasants will become an element of order and progress; left to themselves, incapable as they are of waging any systematic and disciplined action, they will become a disordered rabble, a tumultuous horde driven to the cruellest barbarities" (1977a: 86-87). Subalternity is thus a condition of disintegration, heteronomy, subjection to contingency and brute matter.

In his 1926 essay "Some Aspects of the Southern Question," Gramsci pursues the theme of class alliance and proletarian leadership in organizing and education. He clarifies the Turin communist group's argument for stressing the "political alliance between the Northern workers and the Southern peasants to oust the bourgeoisie from State power" (1995: 17). Proletarian hegemony depends principally on winning the "consensus of the large peasant masses," and that can only be secured, Gramsci points out, if the Italian proletariat incorporates the class demands they represent in its revolutionary program of transition. In other words, it is necessary for the proletariat to change its ideologically limited and distorted understanding of the peasantry.

Of prior importance is the purging of "every residue of corporatism, every syndicalist prejudice or incrustation," prejudices and egoism, if they want to "lead the peasants and intellectuals. . . . If this is not achieved, the proletariat does not become the leading class" and the majority of the population under bourgeoise leadership will enable the State to crush the socialist advance" (1995, 28). Even here, Gramsci already deploys the notion of class alliance and "political class blocs" skillfully exercised by the "politics of bourgeois democracy" to frame the anatomy of subalternity. Gramsci inscribes his findings within the historicopolitical trajectory of the South:

> The South can be defined as a great social disintegration. The peasants, who make up the largest part of the population, have no cohesion among themselves. . . . Southern society is a large agrarian bloc made up of three social strata: the large peasant mass, amorphous and disintegrated; the intellectuals of the petty and medium rural bourgeoisie; and the large landowners and the great intellectuals. Southern peasants are in perpetual ferment, but as a mass they are unable to give a centralized expression to their aspirations and needs. The middle strata of intellectuals receives the impulses for its political and ideological activity from the peasant base. In the last stage of analysis, the large landlords in the political field and the great intellectuals in the ideological field centralize and dominate the whole complex of manifestations. Naturally, it is in the ideological field that centralization is verified with major efficiency and precision. (1995: 38)

After several paragraphs analyzing the character of the Southern intellectuals (including the clergy), their class background and nuances of disposition, Gramsci proceeds:

> The Southern peasant is bound to the large landowners through the mediation of the intellectual. The peasant movements, insofar as they do not take even formally, the form of autonomous and independent mass organizations . . . always end up by finding their place among the ordinary articulations of the State apparatus. . . . [T]he Southern peasant is bound to the large landowners through the mediation of the intellectual. . . . It creates a monstrous agrarian bloc which functions wholly as intermediary and overseer for Northern capitalism and the large banks. . . .
>
> The alliance between the proletariat and the peasant masses requires this formation [of an intellectual mass oriented toward the revolutionary proletariat]. It is required that much more by the alliance between the proletariat and the peasant masses of the South. The proletariat will destroy the Southern agrarian bloc insofar as it succeeds, through its Party, in organizing increasingly significant masses of poor peasants into autonomous and independent formations. (1995: 38, 40, 47)

The subalternity of the peasant masses then consists in their disintegration as a collectivity and their dependency on intellectuals who are agents for large landowners and the bourgeoisie. The production of the subaltern position is thus performed in the ideological sphere, mainly characterized by the absence of any counterhegemonic force against the bourgeoisie or its preemption by the traditional intellectuals. In his remarks on the state and civil society, Gramsci distinguishes what is "subversive" or negative in the subaltern populace: "Not only does the people have no precise consciousness of its own historical identity, it is not even conscious of the historical identity or the exact limits of its adversary. The lower classes, historically on the defensive, can only achieve self-awareness via a series of negations, via their consciousness of the identity and class limits of their enemy; but it is precisely this process which has not yet come to the surface, at least not nationally" (1971: 273).

In his "Notes on Italian History" in *Prison Notebooks,* Gramsci outlines the failure of the Risorgimento in shaping a Jacobinist agenda to resolve the contradiction between the city and countryside. The tradition of the Action Party harks back to the example of the medieval communes in which the city functions "as a directive element . . . which deepens the internal conflicts of the countryside and uses them as a politico-military instrument to strike down feudalism" (1971, 64). Gramsci asks: "Why did the Action Party [of Mazzini and Garibaldi] not pose the agrarian question globally?" The answer: because they thought like the Moderates who considered as "national" the aristocracy and the landowners, not the millions of peasants (1971, 101). In short, the radical wing of the Risorgimento was not able to forge a national-popular will that would liberate the peasantry from both the property owners and the influence of clerical reaction and impelling them toward a more democratic and egalitarian path.[1]

Before Gramsci was imprisoned, he discussed again in February 1926 the agrarian question within the framework of his unique analysis of the relations of forces. This time he broke down the peasant masses into culturally specific groupings: the Slav peasants engaged in the national question, the "non-confessional" peasants of Piedmont led by the Peasant Party; then the peasants in central and northern Italy organized by the Church apparatus; and those in southern Italy and the islands who, after the agricultural and industrial proletariat of northern Italy, comprise "the most revolutionary social element." Gramsci elucidates the nature of subalternity in historically specific terms:

> What is the material and political basis for this function of the peasant masses in the South? The relations which link Italian capitalism and the southern peasants do not consist solely in the normal historical relations between city and countryside, as they were created by the development of capitalism in all countries in the world. In the context of this national society, these relations are aggravated and radicalized by the fact that, economically and politically, the whole zone of the South and the islands functions as an immense countryside in relation to Northern Italy, which functions as an immense city. This situation leads to the formation and development in southern Italy of specific aspects of a national question, even though in the immediate these do not assume an explicit form of such a question as a whole, but only that of an extremely powerful struggle of a regionalistic kind, and of deep currents in favor of decentralization and local autonomy.
>
> What makes the situation of the southern peasants a specific one is the fact that, unlike the three groupings described previously, they do not—taken as a whole—have any autonomous organizational experience. They are incorporated within the traditional structures of bourgeois society, so that the landowners, an integral part of the agrarian/capitalist

bloc, control the peasant masses and direct them in accordance with their own aims. . . .

The only possible organizer of the mass of peasants in the South is the industrial worker, represented by our party. But for this work of organization to be possible and effective, it is necessary for our party to draw close to the southern peasant: for it to destroy in the industrial worker the prejudice instilled by bourgeois propaganda, that the South is a ball and chain which hinders the greatest developments of the national economy; and for it to destroy in the southern peasant the yet more dangerous prejudice, whereby he sees in the North of Italy a single bloc of class enemies. (1977b: 396-97)[2]

In sum, the lack of autonomous organizational experience has perpetuated plebeian servility to the rural bourgeoisie. Without an educational/propaganda attempt to win them over, the fascist petite bourgeoisie will utilize the region as "the marshalling-ground of counter-revolution." Hence Gramsci condemns ultraleft corporatism that simply relies on the automatic development of objective conditions instead of political training and mobilization by the party of the working class to fight for revolutionary goals.

CLASS "SUICIDE"

Intellectuals of the embattled classes at certain conjunctures become key players in the scenarios of representing others. In describing the historical "formation of intellectuals," Gramsci stressed the role of organic intellectuals as the agents for endowing a group with the "homogeneity and an awareness of its own function not only in the economic but also in the social and political fields" (1971: 5). But intellectuals (priests, lawyers, and others with organizational skills) who originate from the peasantry cease to be organically linked to the peasantry by virtue of the feudal or semifeudal configuration of forces in Italy, particularly the hegemonic apparatus of the Church and its cosmopolitan universalism. Gramsci states that "the mass of the peasantry, although it performs an essential function in the world of production, does not elaborate its own 'organic' intellectuals, although it is from the peasantry that other social groups draw many of their intellectuals and a high proportion of traditional intellectuals are of peasant origin" (1971: 6). Given its place in the uneven development of Italian capitalism, the peasantry cannot supersede its subalternity because it cannot become really independent and dominant unless it constructs a new type of State and with it a new intellectual and moral order. The peasantry then is not a fundamental social group because its position in the historical relation of forces signifies a level (the "primitive philosophy of common sense") of development that has already been transcended by the critical philosophy of the proletariat—that is, by Marxism as the unity of theory and practice that articulates a "coherent and unitary conception of the world," "actually coherent and systematic consciousness, precise and decided will" (1957: 67, 69).

To recapitulate, Gramsci holds that subalternity is a condition marked by the absence of a will or project on the part of a social group to achieve an integral, organic, critical self-consciousness. This project is of course part of the Enlightenment master-narrative of the conquest of freedom by recognizing necessity. What Gramsci says of individuals in the 1916 article "Socialism and Culture" can be applied to whole groups: "To know oneself means to be oneself, to be master of oneself, to distinguish oneself, to free oneself from a state of chaos, to exist as an element of order—but of one's own order and one's own discipline in striving for an ideal. And we cannot be successful in this unless we also know others, their history, the successive efforts they have made to be what they are, to create the civilization they have created and which we seek to replace with our own" (1977a: 13). Further, Gramsci believes that the critique of capitalist civilization has generated the goal-directed consciousness of the proletariat, "not simply a spontaneous and natural-istic evolution" that "can judge facts and events other than in themselves or for themselves but also in so far as they tend to drive history forward or backward." Such a culture, mediated through the philosopher-politician and the party as the "collective intellectual," changes thought into life, into the theorized praxis of the masses. It would serve as the basis for a socialist expansive hegemony where active consensus of the masses results from the integration of their interests in a genuine national-popular program of revolutionary transformation.

Of crucial significance, then, is the interlocutory and interpellating function of intellectuals for the peasantry, especially the rural type of intellectuals linked to the small-town petite bourgeoisie "not as yet elaborated and set in motion by the capitalist system" in the context of Italian history. While Gramsci compares the urban intellectuals operat-ing in industry to "subaltern officers in the army," he describes the rural intellectual as a "social model" for the peasants, a means of interfacing with the gentry (the landowning class), even though that attitude is a mixture of respect, envy, and resentful anger. Gramsci emphasizes the extreme dependence of the peasantry on this sector: "One can understand nothing of the collective life of the peasantry and of the germs and ferments of development which exist within it, if one does not take into consideration and examine concretely and in depth this effective subordination to the intellectuals. Every organic development of the peasant masses, up to a certain point, is linked to and depends on movements among the intellectuals" (1971: 14-15).

The concept of "subaltern class" thus assumes a different valence when Gramsci theorizes it as a product of ideological interpellation by intellectuals. Subalternity is produced by an ideological practice of subordination through apparatuses of displacement and absorption. In antithesis, the task of the revolutionary class that has moved beyond corporatism (sectarian *oeuvrierisme* or *operaismo*) is to establish a firm, conscious alliance with the peasantry and mobilize this solidarity to destroy the ground for subalternity. Gramsci reflects on the link between "class struggle" and "peasant war" in two articles in *L'Ordine Nuovo* in December 1919, citing the example of the Russian revolution: "[In the council or soviet], class struggle and peasant war fused their destinies inseparably. . . . Factory control and land seizure must be seen as a single problem. North and South must work together, and together lay the preparations for the nation's transformation into a productive community" (1977a: 141). As John Cammett (1967) observes, the directors of the PSI (Italian Socialist Party) failed to promote a strategy of peasant-worker alliance, the key to building hegemony, such as the one envisioned in Gramsci's analysis in an article of January 1920:

> The Northern bourgeoisie has subjugated the South of Italy and the Islands, and reduced them to exploitable colonies; by emancipating itself from capitalist slavery, the Northern proletariat will emancipate the Southern peasant masses enslaved to the banks and the parasitic industry of the North. The economic and political regeneration of the peasants should not be sought in a division of uncultivated or poorly cultivated lands, but in the solidarity of the industrial proletariat. This in turn needs the solidarity of the peasantry and has an "interest" in ensuring that capitalism is not re-born economically from landed property; that southern Italy and the Islands do not become a military base for capitalist counter-revolution. . . . By smashing the factory autocracy, by smashing the oppressive apparatus of the capitalist State and by setting up a workers' State that will subject the capitalists to the law of useful labor, the workers

will smash all the chains that bind the peasant to his poverty and desperation. By setting up a workers' dictatorship and taking over the industries and banks, the proletariat will swing the enormous weight of the State bureaucracy behind the peasants in their struggle against the landowners, against the elements and against poverty. (1977a: 148-149)

What Gramsci is targeting here is the need to launch a campaign of revolutionary education among the broad masses with the aim of winning a majority to support a communist program upholding the thesis that the problems of both industrial and agricultural economy can be "resolved only outside Parliament, against Parliament, by the workers' State." Opposed to transformism and the bourgeoisie's "passive revolution" (see Buci-Glucksmann 1979), this combined pedagogical, agitational, and propaganda effort strives to give the masses a "theoretical consciousness of creating historical and institutional values and being a founder of States. The union of 'spontaneity' and 'conscious leadership,' or 'discipline,' is the real political action of subaltern classes, since it is mass politics and not simply an adventure of groups who address themselves to the mass" (Cammett 1967: 199). The agrarian or peasant question, then, and the corollary theme of subaltern classes devoid of their own history, cannot be fully grasped outside of the social totality and the relations of forces in a given historical conjuncture. The subaltern subject is a product of bourgeois ideological practice that occludes the constitutive nature of "complex social relations" in articulating identity and also the fact of human practical agency in historical becoming.

In surveying Gramsci's ideas on folklore, Alberto Maria Cirese (1982) identifies "subaltern" as those classes "lacking in or deprived of historical force," subaltern being associated with epithets such as simple, unorganic, fragmentary, passive, derivative. The opposite term is "hegemonic," which connotes the qualities of being organic, unitary, original, active. The condition of subalternity can be surpassed through the mediation of the organic intellectual and the communist political party that can effect "the decisive passage from the structure to the sphere of the complex superstructures" so as to realize not only "a unison of economic and political aims, but also intellectual and moral unity, posing all the questions around which the struggle rages not on a corporate but on a 'universal' plane, and thus creating the hegemony of a fundamental social group over a series of subordinate groups" (Gramsci 1971: 181-82).

One other way of defining the subaltern condition is to consider it as a terminal point before the beginning of self-awareness, before the critical elaboration of the inventory of infinite "traces" deposited by the historical process. It is thus the moment before what Gramsci calls "catharsis," the passage from the purely economic (the egoisms of civil society) to the ethicopolitical level, the translation of structure into the superstructure. This dialectic is, for Gramsci, the starting point for the philosophy of praxis, for Marxism: "the passage from 'objective to subjective' and from 'necessity to freedom.' Structure ceases to be an external force which crushes man, assimilates him to itself and makes him passive; and is transformed into a means of freedom, an instrument to create a new ethico-political form and a source of new initiatives" (1971, 367). This narrative of causality introduces the condition of possibility for writing the history of the subaltern peoples without claiming to deprive them of voice, or presuming their lack of speech or agency for creative transformation.

Can we make an extrapolation from Gramsci's historically determinate use of "subaltern" to redeploy it in illuminating our contemporary situation? That is, can the *problematique* of subaltern/hegemonic shed light on the relation between the industrialized countries of the North and the underdeveloped countries of the South, as Immanuel Wallerstein, Samir Amin, and others have explored this phenomenon of uneven and unequal development? Can we describe what used to be called the "Third World," now renamed the "global South," as subaltern? Only, I think, in a provisional sense. If "subaltern" signifies lack of historical initiative, disintegration, and dependency of recent independent nation-states, yes. In retrospect, the underdeveloped ex-colonies could not for various reasons sustain the revolutionary impulse of the fifties and sixties that challenged Western oppression and exploitation. By the eighties, these "postcolonial" formations had no choice but to accept the pernicious structural adjustments of the IMF–World Bank, with their economies buried in debt, their citizens impoverished and repressed, and their cultural/political institutions manipulated by Western governments in obedience to transnational corporate mandates.

Only with the rise of the now defunct Non-Aligned Movement— from the Bandung Conference of 1955 to its demise in the Jakarta Summit of 1992—were the "subaltern" nation-states able to generate unprecedented initiatives in distancing themselves from the Western and Soviet blocs, "insisting on an independent ideological judgment, i.e., socialism with varying democratic structures" (Maksoud 1993: 32). Intimations of hegemonic power surfaced in the Non-Aligned Movement's influence in the United Nations in the sixties, particularly through the Group of 77. Internal dissension (such as that between India and China) thereafter weakened the role of the Movement as "organic intellectual" of the South; the Jakarta Summit reconfigured the North-South paradigm with the aim of thwarting the hegemonic propensities within the new "unipolar system" of global capitalism led by the United States, Japan, and the European Community. It is during the Earth Summit of June 1992 in Brazil that the "subaltern" voices seemed to have re-emerged and displayed a new vitality for oppositional initiatives and historical self-awareness as many of these subordinated societies rallied around common economic, environmental, developmental and social concerns. The South's identity, despite their differences, crystallizes in their sharing the common traits of poverty, weak and defenseless economies, and powerlessness vis-à-vis the prosperous North (Maksoud 1993).

One can discern in current manifestos by intellectuals from the South the rhythm of a quest for solidarity, a directive will to "project the South as a collective grouping on the global scene," subsuming the Non-Aligned Movement within it and superseding any corporatist introspection as it prepares to engage in a principled contestation with the affluent North. In this sense, the global South as "subaltern" begins to be visible as soon as it endeavors to be hegemonic—that is, to pose a series of historical problems in a way that can only be resolved in the reorganizing of power relations among nation-states in the global arena, a new alignment that dialectically supersedes the old iniquitous system and its permanent crisis. From this perspective, perhaps, the working-class parties of the North—following Gramsci's strategy—would find unity with the "subaltern" masses of the south, mainly people of color, in a united-front resistance to the force of global capitalism. Only then will Marx's call for an otherwise utopian dream, the not-yet posited by *The Communist Manifesto*—"Workers of the World, Unite!"—be finally realized.

VARIETIES OF SUBALTERN RESISTANCE

The law of contradiction pervades the geotopical cartography of subaltern plight. Marx certainly distanced himself from what he called the "idiocy" of village life perhaps to the same extent that in reverse Mao approached it when the 1927 insurrection of the Chinese proletariat in Shanghai, Canton, and other cities was defeated. With Chiapas, Mexico, as the latest incarnation of peasant intransigence, city and countryside need to be remapped as dialectical twin in the tortuous, uneven narrative of the division of social labor within the metamorphosis of the capitalist

mode of production. Framed within the noncapitalist mode of production, however, the peasantry has defied any simple diagrammatic evaluation in terms of its retrograde or liberatory potential. One may cite here
the case of the Russian Narodniks and populists who considered the
peasantry part of a distinct mode of petty commodity production
without any exploitation, discordant to capitalism and invested with
utopian possibilities. Contemporary scholars investigating the peasant's
subsistence ethic, while acknowledging the reality of its exploitation as
determined by rent for landlords and taxes for the government, tend to
glamorize peasant culture as "an alternative moral universe in embryo—
a dissident subculture, an existentially truthful and just one, which helps
unite its members as a human community and as a community of values"
(Scott 1976: 240).

The peasantry, however, cannot be so easily hypostatized as a
monolithic and self-sufficient collectivity. From Marx's *The Class Struggles in France* and *The Eighteenth Brumaire of Louis Bonaparte* to the
analysis of class differentiation and mobilization of the peasantry in
varying social formations by Lenin, Gramsci, Mao, Fanon, Cabral, and
others, the consensus is that the subaltern plight of the peasantry cannot
be appreciated by itself detached from the level and intensity of the class
struggles of specific societies. The detailed inquiries of Eric Wolf (1966,
1971), Hamza Alavi (1965), and Theodor Shanin (1971) all direct our
attention to the protean and multifaceted nature of peasant life-forms,
with its discursive regularities inflected by economic determinants and
altered by political circumstances.

In the present crisis of transnationalizing capitalism, institutions like
the World Bank and various United Nations agencies seek to define
peasant subalternity within familiar schemes like "integrated rural
development" and civil-society "rural reconstruction movement." Latin
American populism in the past has succumbed to such illusions of local
empowerment and amelioration (Vilas 1992-93). So far it has not
discouraged new experiments at self-representation and self-activity.
Arturo Escobar (1995) has sharply criticized the "panoptic gaze" and
normative scopic regime imposed on farmers, women, workers, and
indigenous groups by multilateral institutions tied to corporate business,
all intended to maximize the extraction of surplus labor and exchange
value. What is significant in terms of speaking subalterns is the politics
of cultural affirmation contrived by peasants in the Peruvian Andes, a
mode of emancipatory representation centered not on profit but on
caring for the household economy (natural resources, mores, people) and

habitats. A pan-Andean "heterogeneous re-ethnicization" as a strategy of decolonization can be illustrated by the counterdiscourse and hermeneutics of the PRATEC (Proyecto Andino de Tecnologias Campesinas):

> The prescription of norms for "proper" cultivation is alien to Andean agriculture. Practices and events are never repeated out of a preestablished scheme; on the contrary, knowledge is continually recreated as part of a commitment to strengthening and enriching reality, not to transforming it. Language is alive, its meaning always dictated by the context; language is never permanent or stable. Conversation implies the reenactment of events talked about; words refer to what has been lived rather than to far-off happenings. (Escobar 1995: 169)

If the indigenous Other—in this case, the Andean community—can speak in its vernacular idiom of ceaseless recontextualization and reinvention, does this fact overcome the social, political, and economic grids and cultural codes that police language?

The issue of subaltern speech as an artificial construction precipitates the urgent dilemma of whether we can truly speak for others. If the hegemonic censor always screens thought and culture overdetermines speech, can we even claim to represent ourselves justly and with adequate fidelity? If these others (usually the alien, foreigner, pariah) cannot speak for themselves, dare we speak for them? Linda Alcoff (1991-92) argues that speaking for others is always "a desire for mastery," resulting in "erasure [of others] and a reinscription of sexual, national, and other kinds of hierarchies," though such suspect motives and subterfuges do not suffice to repudiate her claim of representing others as a whole. Edward Said's *Orientalism* is a sustained demonstration of Europe's project of mastering its colonial subjects via an array of insidious discursive practices (for the Western objectification of China, see Longxi 1988). The nature of the dilemma has been succinctly formulated by R. S. Khare: "Given the unavoidability of some form of cultural hegemony and power discourse when representing the Other, the practical question now is whether such a power and privilege can be consciously rendered genuinely reciprocal (and put to good use), rather than be totally eliminated" (1992: 5).

Take the exemplary case of the Egyptian writer and physician, Nawal El Saadawi, a militant feminist with outspoken views on women's sexuality and the practice of clitoridectomy. In her *Memoirs of a Female Physician,* she explores the maturation of an Egyptian

woman in a milieu of repressive surveillance, delineating her protagonist's psychological tensions when she challenges the authorities of her
parents and the fiats of her society. At the end of this phase of her
growth, the narrator confesses:

> I finished my secondary studies and I was first in my class. . . . Then I sat
> thinking: What course do I follow?
>   What course can I follow since I hate my femininity, detest my
> nature, and disown my body?!
>   None but denial . . . challenge . . . resistance!
>   I will deny my femininity . . . I will challenge my nature . . . I will
> resist all the desires of my body. (1994: 1689)

The persona of course cannot be discredited for insincerity; the require-
ment of verisimilitude and the didactic/polemical tone explain her
impassioned response to the constrictive space granted to women in that
milieu. But is the psyche the womb of truth? Reflecting on her sojourn
in the United Kingdom in the mid-eighties, El Saadawi writes: "What
really matters is the economics and the policies of the system under which
women live. What matters is the interests of the class or classes which
hold sway over the system. What matters is the political awareness of
women, the strength of their organizations and their ability to fight"
(1985: 267). Postcolonial reification of antinomies is challenged by El
Saadawi in this forthright, uncompromising stance.

The problem of representing others is more intractable in the case
of the narrative point of view of El Saadawi's novel *Woman at Point Zero*.
The narrator functions here as vehicle or transmitter of the life story of
Firdaus, a woman prisoner condemned for killing an abusive pimp and
scheduled for execution at the end of the novel. Can we trust her speaking
for the Other? According to the publisher, the novel is based on the
author's experience as a psychiatrist at the infamous Qanatir Women's
Prison (El Saadawi herself was incarcerated in this prison in 1981 by the
Sadat regime), where she came across a woman in solitary confinement
awaiting her execution; her conversation with the writer furnished the
material for the quasi-fictional biography of a prostitute. After Firdaus
is taken to be hanged, the narrator concludes:

> I saw her walk out with them. I never saw her again. But her voice
> continued to echo in my ears, vibrating in my head, in the cell, in the

prison, in the streets, in the whole world, shaking everything, spreading fear wherever it went, the fear of the truth which kills the power of truth, as savage, and as simple, and as awesome as death, yet as simple and as gentle as the child that has not yet learnt to lie.

And because the world was full of lies, she had to pay the price. (1975: 105-06)

Who can say that she, the "unspeakable" subaltern, has not spoken as honestly and fully as circumstances warrant? Here, in the Egypt of 1978, which banned the book and thus released it to the world, subaltern speech is validated by an exchange of seemingly incommensurable experiences, one life for another: the truth of the utterance is confirmed by death, just as for Walter Benjamin the authority of narrative ultimately resides in the lethal silence that surrounds it.

Like her protagonist, Nawal El Saadawi herself suffered: she was dismissed from her position in the Ministry of Health and penalized interminably. As a feminist activist, she has exposed the multiple faces of Arab patriarchy and the sexual exploitation of Arab women in books like *Woman and Sex, Man and Sex, The Female Is the Origin,* and *The Hidden Face of Eve.* Because of her anti-imperialist politics and her opposition to the Camp David agreements, she was imprisoned; later, the feminist group she founded that opposed the Gulf War, the Arab Women's Solidarity Association, was banned by the Mubarak government. Speech must be denied to women fighting for equal rights, for recognition as humans, not sex objects or slaves. Is the predicament of subaltern speech then somehow mortgaged to a "culture of silence" (Fanon) that, as in Gillo Pontecorvo's 1966 film *The Battle of Algiers,* can only be disrupted by explosions of dynamite killing hundreds of civilians all deemed accomplices and accessories?

Sovereignty is indeed inalienable, Rousseau insisted, and one's testimony cannot be duplicated. If so, then delegated representation— or even variants like symbolic, microcosmic, and elective (Birch 1971)— is always counterfeit and fraudulent. Better mute or speechless than be misrepresented or misspoken. In the work of the Brazilian educator Paulo Freire and in the novel *Almanac of the Dead* by Leslie Marmon Silko, we find alternative proposals in which agency is reconstructed and speech regained, in trajectories of activism and imagination that span both sides of the American hemispheres and penetrate up to the continental heartlands of Europe, Asia, and Africa.

DIALECTICS OF TEACHING/LEARNING

In the culture of speechlessness or illiteracy that one encounters in most "Third World" societies, the most urgent task is what Paulo Freire called "conscientization" and education reinvented as "the practice of freedom." When Freire began the National Literacy Program in northeastern Brazil in the sixties, the country was experiencing a transitional crisis in which the fatalistic and passive population was beginning to awaken to possibilities of change. Freire's project of trying to actualize the semantics of "liberty," "democracy," and "participation" was crushed by the military coup of April 1964, which led to his imprisonment and subsequent exile.

We encounter the leading principles of Freire's philosophy of education condensed in the proposition that the adult literacy process is cultural action for freedom, a praxis that produces knowing subjects equipped with a critical awareness "both of the socio-cultural reality which shapes their lives and their capacity to transform that reality" (1970: 27). This denotes Freire's seminal method of conscientization, a rigorous critical reading of commonsense experience. According to his most eloquent North American exponent Peter McLaren, Freire's pedagogy "reflects Gramsci's notion that the structural intentionality of human beings needs to be critically interrogated through a form of conscientization, or *conscientizacao*" (1997: 52).

What Freire accomplished in the pre-coup period, however, is significant to our inquiry of how subalternity can be transcended. The answer is "critical education" oriented toward the practice of social and political responsibility, a practice that requires movement from a naive (submission to forces not understood and interrogated) to a "critical consciousness." Critique implies historical awareness of the structures that determine action and speech, a cognitive mapping of one's place in the sociohistorical trajectory of changes occurring every day. This takes place in "circles of culture" where peasants and workers gather after the day's work and, with the help of an "animator" or moderator, learn key words commonly used in their life. Ferreted from the "thematic universe" of the social group of illiterates, these generative words translated into visual images not only facilitate the learning of the language but also catalyze the mode of critical reflection on the concrete situation of their lives. Words from their lived situation or lifeworld serve as themes for reflection, dialogue, and investigation. Freire recounts one event of decodification of lived experience from the theoretic context of learning:

The word struggle, for instance, aroused lively discussions among various groups at different *asentamientos* [individual settlements for the former tenants of large estates, the latifundium]. Peasants talked about what acquiring a deeper knowledge meant for them, specifically, the struggle to obtain the right to the land. In these discussions they related a little of their history not found in conventional textbooks. To dramatize these facts not only stimulates peasants' self-expression but also develops their political consciousness. (1985: 26)

In "Peasants and their Reading Texts," Freire underscored the utility of generative words elicited from the codification of reality because the mystifying legitimacy of the dominant society is then decodified. In the process, "peasants analyze their reality and in their discourse they express levels of seeing themselves relative to an objective situation. They reveal the ideological conditioning to which they were subjected in the 'culture of silence' and in the latifundium system" (1985: 24). This literacy method induces the extrojection of the slave mentality that the oppressors have introjected into the subaltern's personality. A critical recodification of terms/meanings geared toward action involves a problematizing of the natural, cultural, and social reality of peasants and workers, a stance opposed to technocratic problem-solving formulas derived from the banking technique of education.

Adult literacy presupposes the dialectical interaction between human sensuous practice and objective reality in which language functions as the prime mediation. Literacy as the learning of a linguistic code and conscientization as a collective decoding of the experienced reality constitute the dynamics of Freire's critical pedagogy. When the everyday experience of peasants and workers becomes the content or raw material of the learning process, education is no longer a banking mechanism in which stockpiled information is deposited into the mouth of inert consumers, the students. The relationship between teacher and learner is no longer unilateral, authoritarian, or hierarchical; dialogue among participants structures the acquisition of language and the comprehension of reality. This does not, however, imply that social reality by itself can psychologically motivate its transformation.

After three decades of fieldwork and self-reflection, Freire engaged in self-criticism by pointing out that there are two moments—the knowledge of reality and its transformation—that need to be dialectically syncopated. Understanding reality does not translate or coincide immediately with its transformation. Due to a belief in the reformist possibilities of Brazil in the sixties, Freire somehow neglected the gap between awareness and action, specifically the lack of political organization and perspective on the part of workers and peasants. In 1972-73, Freire warned against the psychologistic and idealistic connotations that may be ascribed by reactionary interpreters to his method:

> There can be no conscientization (which necessarily transcends a simple process of awareness) separated from radical and transforming action on social reality. . . . We certainly do not see it as a magical solution, miraculous, and capable in itself of humanizing all people while leaving in place a world which blocks their existence as human beings. Humanization, permanent liberation, is not accomplished with consciousness. It is found in history where human beings have the task of creating and transforming without interruption . . . By reducing such expressions as "humanism" and "humanization" to abstract categories, the modern churches empty them of any real meaning. Such phrases become mere slogans whose only contribution is to serve the reactionary forces. In truth, there is no liberation without a revolutionary transformation of class society, for in class society all humanization is impossible. Liberation becomes concrete only when society is changed, not when its structures are simply modernized. (IDAC 1974: 24, 27)

In *Pedagogy of the Oppressed* (1970), Freire formulated his trenchant criticism of the traditional banking education that induced in subalterns feelings of inferiority, powerlessness, and isolation, opposing to it a political/agitational pedagogy—a mode of unmasking the sources of oppression, inequality, and injustice. Conscientization requires the unity of reflection and action, inciting the learning of democracy through collective participation. After the Brazilian experience, Freire reaffirmed his conviction that pedagogy can become revolutionary only if its goal is the conscious and creative reflection/action of the oppressed masses themselves to attain their own liberation. Education as the vigilant practice of liberty needs to evolve into a permanent cultural revolution embracing the whole society.

In 1986, writing to North American teachers from Sao Paolo where he was former Secretary of Education, Freire reiterated the essentially political function of the teacher's vocation (for which she should assume full responsibility), a practice of knowing and reknowing that fashions creative and critical learners/subjects: "Reading and writing words encompasses the reading of the world, that is, the critical understanding of politics in the world" (1987: 212-13). When Freire's group, the Institute of Cultural Action based in Geneva, Switzerland, visited Guinea-Bissau in 1975, they learned that campaigns for literacy fail if they are not related to "production, the community's taking charge of basic services, and to political mobilization" (1976). Pedagogy or education is an integral element in the larger project of political liberation engaged in by whole communities locked in struggle with exploitative power.

Freire is definitely not a postcolonial guru of schizoid selves or avatar of postmodernist indeterminacy and aporia. He has always emphasized the historical determinations of the subaltern's passage from an intransitive to a naive transitive consciousness on the way to full conscientization. The pivotal mediation between one stage to another is praxis, "the authentic union of action and reflection" (1970: 48).[3] In his insightful *Letters to Cristina,* Freire reiterates his privileging of the reading of the world as a totalizing integration of multiple objects and events in social existence. This dialectical epistemology synthesizes object and subject, means (technique) and ends (value): "In the education and training of a plumber, I cannot separate, except for didactic purposes, the technical knowledge one needs to be a part of the polis, the political knowledge that raises issues of power and clarifies the contradictory relationships among social classes in the city" (1996: 115). Ethics, pedagogy, and politics are joined in the practice of socially accountable freedom. In this Freire echoes Gramsci's elevation of human work as the fundamental educational principle that can equip every citizen with the skills of governing: "The discovery that the relations between the social and natural orders are mediated by work, by man's theoretical and practical activity, creates the first elements of an intuition of the world free from all magic and superstition. It provides a basis for the subsequent development of an historical, dialectical conception of the world, which understands movement and change, which appreciates the sum of effort and sacrifice which the present has cost the past and which the future is costing the present, and which conceives the contemporary world as a synthesis of the past, of all past generations, which projects itself into the future" (1978: 52). Instead of exacerbating the fragmented, schizophrenic and boundaryless condition of subalterns, in particular those occupying the borderlands of the capitalist metropolis and the "postcolonial" hinterlands, Freire employs a radical critique of the ideological mechanisms (schooling being one of the most crucial) that program the hybrid, exotic "Others" into repetition or silence. In this enterprise, he charts the limits of the possible on the faultlines of what is practical, committed to destroying a Euro-American hegemony "forged in the crucible of patriarchy and white supremacy" (McLaren 1997).

ON NATIVE GROUND

Let us turn now to Leslie Marmon Silko's testimony vis-à-vis the postcolonial problematic of otherness and servitude. Can we claim that "unspeakable" subalterns, unaware of Freire or Gramsci, have now learned by themselves how to speak? Faced with Lyotard's theory of the incommensurability of phrase regimes and the agonistics of representation, they might be persuaded again to retreat to silence. What about the "terrorism" exerted by those theoreticians of European high culture often quoted by Bhabha and Spivak (Foucault, Derrida) who condemn the error of essentialism manifest in, for example, the American Indians' claim to their aboriginal land, the foundational principle of their fight for survival and self-determination?

This quasi-essentialist world outlook and strategy lies at the heart of Silko's magnificent novel *The Almanac of the Dead*. Essentially, the novel explores the idea of how the interpretation or deciphering of texts can transform the world and liberate Native Americans whose rich manifold resistance symbolizes those involving all oppressed people of color around the world. The interweaving of diverse struggles universalizes the life process of indigenes associated with the care and redemption of the earth, transfiguring it into a paradigm of global emancipation. If there is any contemporary discourse of the oppressed that aims to unify the fragmented and specific knowledges of subjugated individuals and groups, and in the process also seeks to project a vision of the common good, this text is its eloquent embodiment. For in Silko's text, the subject and its agencies, already proclaimed dead or erased or decentered by ludic nihilism, are resurrected. The subalterns perform with polyphonic if sometimes dissonant voices and registers. Against the master discourse of the Panopticon and the omnipresent regularities of bureaucratic/administrative power, Silko dramatizes the crisscrossing lines of power—political, economic, military, ideological—that traverse the conflicted terrains of the United States, Latin America, and the geopolitical South in general.

This is not the occasion to elaborate on Silko's conception of the "Other" as an epiphany of natives sacrificed to the material progress of capital. Her rich and subtle texts, for example, *Ceremony* and stories like "Yellow Woman" (see San Juan 1995c), demonstrate the inexhaustible power of subaltern speech to abrogate and appropriate the enemy's designs. Suffice it for me to call attention to the section in the novel in which the political education of Angelita, also called La Escapia, is summarized (309-17). We have here a kind of "negation of the negation," a sublation of subaltern fatality by allegory and exemplum. It also marks the overturning of Eurocentric hubris. This is where all postmodernist doctrines (the decentered subject, hybridity, border-crossing) are subverted and refused, staging the moment in which the metanarrative of Marx/Marxism becomes organic and germinal to the making of American Indian histories and traditions:

> Later when enemies in the villages, people related to her by clan or marriage, accused La Escapia of being a "communist," she let them have it. Didn't they know where Karl Marx got his notions of egalitarian communism? "From here," La Escapia had said, "Marx stole his ideas from us, the Native Americans. . . ."
>
> For hundreds of years white men had been telling the people of the Americas to forget the past; but now the white man Marx came along and he was telling people to remember. The old-time people had believed the same thing: they must reckon with the past because within it lay seeds of the present and future. They must reckon with the past because within it lay this present moment and also the future moment . . .
>
> The stories of the people or their "history" had always been sacred, the source of their entire existence. If the people had not retold the stories, or if the stories had somehow been lost, then the people were lost; the ancestor's spirits were summoned by the stories. This man Marx had understood that the stories or "histories" are sacred; that within "history" reside relentless forces, powerful spirits, vengeful, relentlessly seeking justice.
>
> No matter what you or anyone else did, Marx said, history would catch up with you; it was inevitable, it was relentless. The turning, the changing, were inevitable.
>
> The old people had stories that said much the same, that it was only a matter of time and things European would gradually fade from the American continents. History would catch up with the white man whether the Indians did anything or not. History was the sacred text. The most complete history was the most powerful force. (1991: 310-11, 315-16)

Interspersed with the episodes dealing with Bartolomeo, La Escapia, and El Feo is the fantastic and grotesque story of Menardo and the "bulletproof vest," emblematic of the technological superiority of Europe and all colonizers. Together these two thematic strands tie in with the mother's quest for the lost son and the recovery/deciphering of history indexed here by the Almanac. The serialized episodes corresponding to the stories of the major protagonists—Seese, Lecha, and Sterling; Max and Leah; Menardo and Alegria; La Escapia, El Feo, and Bartolomeo; Clinton, and so on—syncopate the themes of power, sexuality, and knowledge within the framework of the American Indian struggle for land, for freedom and dignity, indivisible from a humane environment. Silko's attempt to incorporate the truth of "uneven and combined development," with its multisided contradictions of race, gender, sexuality, nationality, and locality, goes beyond the Foucaultian project of genealogy. While Silko does intervene to reappraise the past in the light of present commitments and concerns, her prophetic motive harbors within it a universal emancipatory purpose that is anathema to neoliberal hedonism.

Silko's staging of a speech festival in Part Six provides the occasion for superimposing on the novelistic heteroglossia a vision of an impending apocalypse. At the International Holistic Healers Convention, Wilson Weasel Tail delivers the agenda of the "green vengeance" and announces the advance of the spirit army of all the oppressed from the South (with the help of the Africans and Caribbeans). Analogies link ramifying subplots. At the same time, Clinton, organizer of the army of the homeless, commemorates the history of rebellions of black slaves (742-46) while Angelita La Escapia envisages all hell breaking loose and the best yet to come: "Now it was up to the poorest tribal people and survivors of European genocide to show the remaining humans how all could share and live together on earth, ravished as she was" (749). She muses that Europeans have not understood "that the earth was mother to all beings, and they had not understood anything about the spirit beings. But at least Engels and Marx had understood the earth belongs to no one. No human, individuals or corporations, no cartel of nations, could 'own' the earth; it was the earth who possessed the humans and it was the earth who disposed of them" (749).

In a shrewd transvaluation of Eurocentrism, the novel naturalizes Marxism and converts the Western socialist tradition into an offshoot of indigenous history-making. This surpasses the postcolonial formula of differing/defering, abrogation/appropriation premised on syncretic layering, in-between hybridity, and mechanical juxtaposition of consumer items, to overcome subalternity. Silko's method is rooted in the indigenous peoples' resistance to the system of profit-making and commodification. In a 1977 interview, she relates how she combined storytelling and community, in particular Laguna as locale for her mixed ancestry, to serve as the matrix of her art (1980: 18-19). In *Almanac*, those two terms are conflated to become the avenging spirit of the "earth mother" counterpointed by the history of rebellions against private property by all victims of exploitation.

While Silko conceives history as both genealogical and prophetic, *Almanac* reaffirms the historical materialist commitment to hopes and possibilities of change. She does not endorse Foucault's "technology of the body" and his account of the regularity of discursive practices imposing their logic and strategy on humans. Power, for Silko, is still embodied in certain institutions (ideological state apparatuses like schools, media, churches) constructed by humans and alterable by their united wills. In a recent essay published in *Hungry Mind Review*, Silko presents an anti-Foucaultian view that the power of a racist system is visibly incarnated in the Border Patrol that terrorizes the Southwest. It is the antithesis to the hallucinations of the hyperreal and the instability of *différance*. I would like to conclude by quoting Silko's unashamedly totalizing perspective that links the Guatemala of Rigoberta Menchu, Mexico, and the United States in a revealing constellation of relations and figures that rescue the Others (like the political prisoners quoted in the epigraphs to this chapter) from the dragnet of the masters of Alterity. Underlying it is a metanarrative of world revolution articulated by subalterns:

> The Border Patrol exercises a power that no highway patrol or country sheriff possesses: the Border Patrol can detain anyone they wish for no reason at all. . . .
>
> But I feel anger too, a deep, abiding anger at the U.S. government, and I know that I am not alone in my hatred of these racist immigration policies, which are broadcast every day, teaching racism, demonizing all people of color, labeling indigenous people from Mexico as "aliens"— creatures not quite human.
>
> The so-called "civil wars" in El Salvador and Guatemala are actually wars against the indigenous tribal people conducted by the white and mestizo ruling classes. These are genocidal wars conducted to secure Indian land once and for all. The Mexican government is buying Black Hawk helicopters in preparation for the eradication of the Zapatistas after the August elections. (1994: 20, 59)

Eluding the border patrols of the "postcolonial" United States, we journey from the domain of peasants and exploited women to the realm of the multicultural Imaginary and the subterranean regions of "internal colony" and civil society before we reach at last the threshold of the globalized arena of nations and diasporic communities—emergencies, interventions, and breakthroughs converging at the apocalypse of Empire.

CHAPTER FOUR

The Multicultural Imaginary: Problematizing Identity and the Ideology of Racism

Spending a week in mid-February 1995 in the space once called "El Pueblo de Los Angeles," the archetypal postmodern city—megalopolis of the "New World Order" of transnational, globalized capitalism—can be disorienting (despite its "orientalisms"), dislocating (because of uneven, contradictory loci of appearances), and revealing for reasons that can only be apprehended by analyzing surfaces and conceptualizing totalities. On 18 February, while touring the old Spanish settlement just a few blocks from the Bonaventure Hotel—Jameson's example of postmodern, decentered hyperspace—I was swept into a rousing march and rally of a few hundred people against Proposition 187. Proposition 187 aims to deny education, health, and social services to illegal immigrants by requiring service providers to identify all persons suspected of being in illegal immigrant status.

Last November, Proposition 187 won 20 percent of the 35 percent of the California electorate who turned out to vote. Roughly 60 percent white voters joined 45 percent African Americans, 25 percent Latinos, and a good number of Asian Americans to target the civil and human rights of California's large, diverse, and fragmented immigrant communities as scapegoats for the state's economic decline and the deteriorating standard of living. What is at issue ultimately is the failure of the "liberal democratic" free-enterprise system to deliver, this failure being indexed by the erosion of economic well-being, opportunity for advancement, social stability, and personal safety for people of all nationalities and the middle class generally. It is the profound crisis of market-centered liberal society, of multinational corporations and globalized capital, that we are witnessing in events in California. The Los Angeles-based Labor/Community Strategy Center has outlined the horrendous consequences entailed by the implementation of Proposition 187 in the following observations.

Extending a worldwide racist and xenophobic phenomenon following the collapse of the "Evil Empire," Proposition 187 will focus on Latin American and Asian immigrants (not just "illegals" or "undocumented workers") as the major cause of social breakdowns. Racism motivates this political movement since it is mainly Latinos and Asians, not the "illegal" Canadian, German, and Scandinavian immigrants jostling with the Orange County crowd, who are targeted for selective enforcement. In the process, the law will create a growing police state institutionalizing an army of informers: social workers, doctors, nurses, and teachers will be enlisted as immigration officers patrolling the "borders" of public schools and hospitals, throwing school children out into the streets, investigating parents, and obstructing people needing medical care. Meanwhile, sharp divisions will plague these communities as native-born Latinos and Asians as well as recently "legalized" immigrants will want to distance themselves from the new immigrants, now associated with derogatory stereotypes inducing self-hatred, shame, and distrust in all people of color. This divide-and-conquer rule has already materialized in the vote. Finally, Proposition 187, asserts the Strategy Center, "is a calculated campaign by the two-party political Right to enlist the middle-class and low-income communities in a campaign to scapegoat ABBB—'Anybody But Big Business'" (1994: 3). In the history of California and of the United States as a whole, as every student knows, anti-immigrant and racist movements erupt during periods of economic recession and depression "to deflect anger away from the recurring crises of the social system and to serve as springboards for the political careers of right-wing politicians—both Republicans and Democrats" (1994: 4). One can cite here in particular the wave of anti-Chinese riots in the 1870s that led to the Chinese Exclusion Act of 1882, the first state legislation stigmatizing a specific racialized group (thought threatening and inassimilable) for prohibition from entering the national territory (Daniels and Kitano 1970).

The history of U.S. immigration laws may help frame the NEH-sponsored "National Conversation on American Pluralism and Identity" within the limits of a clearly marked "racial pattern" that deconstructs the ideal of "an America of shared values and commitments" amid cultural differences. In the Naturalization Law of 1790, Congress legislated that only free "white" immigrants are eligible for naturalized citizenship. This law prevailed for 162 years until cancelled by the McCarran-Walter Act of 1952. The need for manpower in the early years of independence explains the absence of any federal law regulating immigration until the late nineteenth century. Not only the Chinese and Japanese but also immigrants from southern and eastern Europe, according to the Dillingham Report of 1910, were considered racially inferior and incapable of becoming "Americanized." This prompted the enactment of the 1917 Immigrant Act, the first in a series of severely restrictive statutes that introduced literacy tests, ranked eligible immigrants (no limits on the western hemisphere), and drew up the Asiatic "barred zone" (India, Indo-China, and other countries); the quota system based on national origin followed, privileging northern Europe. This quota system, reinforced by the McCarran-Walter Act of 1952 curbing entry of black immigrants from the West Indies, was abolished in the 1965 Hart-Celler Act; while the preferential treatment for European countries was curtailed in 1976, priority was given to western immigrants with training, skills, or family ties—a class discrimination system (Cashmore 1984: 143).

The most recent immigration reforms of 1986 and 1990 reveal the salience of economic imperatives underlying foreign policy and humanitarian considerations. Tracing the vicissitudes of Mexican migrant labor from the bracero program to the case of undocumented aliens (comprised mainly of between 1 and 8 million Mexicans, with half a million deportations occurring every year), the mainstream historian David Reimers underscores the persistence of the economic factor and the power of the corporate business lobbies (1992: 207-52, 261). The general impact of these reforms was to revitalize the myth of laissez-faire individualism, immigrant success, and self-reliance that is integral to the constitution of an American ethnic identity. The astute analyst Colin Greer observes how the national culture centered on public ethnicity validates a politics of inclusion as well as exclusion and thus of permanent inequality and injustice:

> The broadening of national image via ethnic characterization of the populace coincided with the relocation of economic and industrial tension in the political arena, a thrust which meant a shift away from the explicit class focus of the Depression years to an increasingly origins-based focus which identified individuals in groups, regardless of class—thereby attaching them to achievement in society. . . . Key in this framework is the continuing stream of immigration which has remained a basic ingredient

in society. It is at once an aspect of active ethnic self-definition and a focus of the struggle between capital and labor in the context of which ethnic ideology derives. Ethnicity, then, can be seen as a central characteristic of American identity which is most clearly observed in relationship with, not by any means simply as a successor to, immigration. (1984: 128, 131)

Given the logic of capital's dependence on mobilizing social labor in buying labor power in the market and imposing its dictates on the state apparatus, the movement of bodies historically started with the "internal" flow of the displaced peasantry into the industrializing centers. The second flow involved about 50 million Europeans leaving permanently between 1800 and 1914 during the period of the growth of industrial capitalism and the commercialization of agriculture. The United States received about 32 million immigrants between 1820 and 1915, an influx that sustained the country's industrialization. A third wave witnessed contract workers of diverse origins heading for the mines and plantations of the tropics (including the Chinese, Japanese, and Filipinos who headed for Hawaii and the West Coast). The anthropologist Eric Wolf stresses the distinctive characteristics of the third wave:

> The trajectories of the "people without history" on the various continents of the globe dovetail and converge within the larger matrix created by European expansion and the capitalist mode of production. . . . The migrant's position is determined not so much by the migrant or his culture as by the structure of the situation in which he finds himself. Under the capitalist mode of production, this structure is created by the relation of capital to labor in its particular spatial and temporal operation, that is, the structure of the labor market. People may move for religious, political, ecological, or other reasons; but the migrations of the nineteenth and twentieth centuries were largely labor migrations, movements of the bearers of labor power. (1982: 355, 362)

The historian Gabriel Kolko has also pointed out that "the internationalization of the Western world's labor supply after 1800 is perhaps the most ignored phenomenon . . . but this escape valve for the human consequences of economic crisis in one state by relying on the growth of others is among the central events of modern history" (1963: 84). Through the geographical mobility of capital and labor, the spatial integration of world capitalism proceeded apace through recurrent crises, interrupted for a time by the Bolshevik and Third World revolutions, until the contradictory dynamics of capital accumulation at this turn of the century acquires its new transnational, postmodern configuration.

In the mainstream scholarship on immigration, however, the crucial linkage between immigration flow and the labor requirements of an industrial crisis-ridden society has been obscured by the orthodox theory of push/pull factors first enunciated by British geographer Edward Ravenstein in 1889 and updated by U.S. demographer Everett S. Lee in 1966 (Bouvier and Gardner 1986: 5-6). It has also hedged in acknowledging the validity of Robert Miles's claim that "The intervention of the state has become central to the articulation of migration and capital accumulation" (1986: 50). The empiricist and managerial ideology of this dominant approach, which occludes the imperatives of accumulation on a world scale, may be gleaned in the Final Report of the 86th American Assembly on "Threatened Peoples, Threatened Borders: World Migration and U.S. Policy."

In this summary, we find the Establishment consensus on international migration expressed in a tabulation of three equally important contexts that define the migration problematic (1994: 4-5):

> . . . the *domestic setting* matters: unemployment, or the fear of unemployment; disappointed expectations about standards of living; claims for public expenditure; race and ethnicity issues; changing cultural values.
>
> The *international setting* matters: instabilities following the end of the cold war; forced migration and "ethnic cleansing"; flagrant violations of human rights; the reappearance of genocide; rapidly growing populations and deteriorating environments; increasing economic differentials and stagnating economies; and new visibility for these via global communication channels.
>
> The *characteristics of the migration* itself matter: migration flows seen as large, rapid, and uncontrolled; heavy concentrations of migrant groups in particular regions, cities, or neighborhoods; anxieties about rapid ethnic and racial change in regions of settlement; views about whether migrants are integrating; concerns over illegal entry or residence; and whether migrants are identified with violence, crime, terrorism, or drugs, or seen as hardworking contributors to society.

What is clearly erased in this tabulation of multiple causal settings is not only the centrality of the labor market, but the global dynamics of industry deregulation, the shifting of the accumulation crisis to the middle and working classes, and above all the undermining of the sovereignty of Third World economies and people of color—from Mexico to El Salvador, Haiti, Vietnam, Cambodia, to Iraq. An expert on this global phenomenon, Saskia Sassen asserts that "the central role played by the United States in the emergence of the global economy over the past 30 years lies at the core of why people migrate here in increasing numbers" (Strategy Center 1994: 16). U.S. political-military interventions and support of Third World dictatorships have not only generated immigrants, but also displaced persons and refugees by the thousands, not to speak of unwanted orphans or children of American servicemen left as victims of war.

ANATOMY OF RACISM

It might be useful at this juncture to inquire into the ideology of contemporary racism, its complex articulation with the dynamics of market society and the constitution of subjects or agencies, before moving into the controversy over multiculturalism and its implications for people of color in the diaspora and other "postcolonial" niches in global capitalism. How is the multicultural imaginary enabled by commodity-fetishism as its chief condition of possibility? How are we implicated in the myth and mystification of pluralism?

After the Rodney King trial and the subsequent "people's festival" otherwise known as the Los Angeles city riots, public commentary on the outburst of racism and racially motivated violence in the United States focused on the interethnic rivalries, especially between Koreans and African Americans, that complicate the traditional black-white dichotomy on which the social order has for a long time been grounded. Ironically this led Richard Rodriguez (1994) to celebrate the city's accession to a "redeeming maturity" when the inhabitants of this multicultural capital, a paradoxical city founded on separateness, division, and fragmentation, the postmodern metropolis par excellence, now realizes that each person is related to everyone else. In other words, violence and expenditure (sacrifices yielding no surplus value in this instance) conduce to a discovery of social bonds and community, that longed-for national "common culture" (often equated with the hegemonic consensus) that seems to be the politically correct ideal for parties on the right or left who bewail competitive consumerism, individualist anarchy, revolt against hierarchy, antagonisms of class, race, gender, and ethnicity—in short, all the ills of late capitalism.

In the past, racial and ethnic conflicts like King's beating and trial have been invariably construed by radical thought as manifestations of class conflict. Race is the mask of class, in the ultimate analysis. The sophisticated doyen of cultural studies Stuart Hall, though acknowledging that race as a sociohistorical category possesses a distinctive and "relatively autonomous effectivity," nonetheless asserts that race is "the modality in which class is 'lived,' the medium through which class relations are experienced, the form in which it is appropriated and 'fought through'" (1980: 341). So it seems we are back to what some call a totalizing or essentializing approach.

Meanwhile, the poststructuralist revolution has produced not only the "structuralist Marxism" of Althusser but also the power/knowledge deconstruction of Foucault. The most influential application of the Foucauldian analytic on race/ethnic relations are Michael Omi and Howard Winant's *Racial Formation in the United States* (1986) and recently David Theo Goldberg's *Racist Culture* (1993). I have benefited greatly from Omi and Winant's study in writing my book, *Racial Formations/Critical Transformations* (1992), though I register some disagreements in its dismissal of contrastive paradigms. Goldberg's substantial achievement claims to offer "an anti-essentialist and non-reductionist account of racialized discourse and racist expression." Indeed, Goldberg judges as reductive and invalid the anthropologist-historian Eric Wolf's explanation of slavery as a matter of exploiting the coerced labor of whole populations and expropriating the surplus value they produce. Goldberg argues that "racial definition and discourse . . . have from their outset followed an independent set of logics related to and intersecting with economic, political, legal, and cultural considerations, to be sure, but with assumptions, concerns, projects, and goals that can properly be identified as their own" (1993: 27). In pursuit of a semiotics of racialized discourse, Goldberg has emulated Foucault in formulating its preconceptual elements such as classification, order, value, and hierarchy; differentiation and identity, discrimination and identification; exclusion, domination, subjection, and subjugation; as well as entitlement and restriction. Classification is what principally enables racial differentiation while other factors are historically articulated with it to authorize various forms of racial exclusions. Epistemes or regimes of rationality account for the construction of the social subject. While the Law of Authority defines individual subjectivity by social discourse, Goldberg holds that subjects in modern society are defined in general by the discourses of difference and otherness:

> It is thus in the constitution of alterity itself that the hold of racialized discourse and racist exclusions over subject formation and expression is rendered possible. For it is in the very making of otherness by discursive technologies that the modernized modes of racial distinction and distancing can be invested in and through the bodies of social subjects and, accordingly, that this investment can be extended into the body politic. Racisms become normalized through modernity's discursive technologies of subject formation; they acquire their 'naturalism' in the creation of modern moral selves and social subjects. (1993: 60)

Despite his oft-repeated reminder that sociodiscursive praxis needs to be historically contextualized, Goldberg's privileging of epistemes and concepts that hypostatize the exchange of utterance or speech-genres and behavior within a capitalist, market-centered political economy incurs his reproach of essentialism and reductionism. While Goldberg's strategy of drawing up a pragmatic antiracist practice is certainly commendable, the refusal to examine racist discourse and action as indissociable from, and virtually integral to, the dynamics of historically specific capitalist social relations somewhat vitiates Goldberg's research program. The same comment applies to the exorbitation of racial politics in Omi and Winant's perspective.

Not being an economistic Marxist, Marx was also sensitive to questions of identity—the need of individuals to affirm and satisfy the need for self-identification immanent in social labor, the need to identify with collectivities (nation, religious community, etc.). But Marxism, according to the philosopher G. A. Cohen, cannot agree to making racial exploitation on a par with economic exploitation: "It is false that 'closure on racial grounds plays a directly equivalent role to closure on the basis of property.' Unlike racism, property is not, in the first instance, a means of protecting privilege. It is privilege" (1989: 158).

Before we confront the "racial" or "racialized" subject, it might be instructive to deal first with how individuals become subjectified, that is, constructed as social agents in a historical formation. The most influential recent theory of the constitution of the subject in the Western Marxist tradition is Louis Althusser's (1971), a controversial but heuristic one. In trying to answer the key question for the revolutionary project of transforming the labor-capital asymmetry—How is the reproduction of the relations of production secured?—Althusser devised what has been judged a functionalist scheme: they are secured by the Repressive State Apparatuses (coercive institutions of army, police, etc.), "the shield" behind the more crucial Ideological State Apparatuses (ISA; for example, education, religion, family, politics, trade union, communications, culture) comprised of institutions, rituals, and practices that sustain the ideological hegemony of a historic bloc of classes indispensable to the reproduction of relations of exploitation. In the precapitalist period, the dominant apparatus was the Church; in capitalism, it is the educational ideological apparatus, although a "specific familial ideological configuration" subtends the whole capitalist formation.

Althusser then defines ideology as "a representation of the imaginary relationship of individuals to their real conditions of existence." This mode of representation cannot be separated from an institutional apparatus and its material rituals or practices; and this apparatus "hails or interpellates concrete individuals as concrete subjects, by the functioning of the category of the subject" (162). Now Althusser engages in some rather cumbersome prestidigitation when he uses the example of the policeman hailing or interpellating the ordinary pedestrian—white avatar of Rodney King!—and then concludes that "individuals are always-already subjects" who, ignorant of how they have thus been subjectified, accept their role within the system of production relations. His chief model of interpellation concerns the function of "Christian Religious Ideology" from which the political scientist Paul Hirst draws the judgment that Althusser confuses the subject with the "unitary identity of the individual," whereas the individual should be conceived as "the support of a decentered complex of practices and statuses which have distinct conditions of existence" (quoted in Rossi-Landi 1990; see also Hirst 1979). Moreover, Hirst contends that the notion of representation presupposes an empirical construal of the subject-object structure of knowledge, whereby the represented object becomes the measure of subjective representation. Other critics argue that Althusser's concept of the subject is deterministic and so rules out the autonomous agency of individuals who may refuse domination and thus subvert the imperatives of reproduction.

Upholding the key notion of overdetermination, the economists Stephen Resnick and Richard Wolff explain Althusser's theory of the process of subjectivation as a thought-concrete overdetermined by and participating in the overdetermination of the social totality (concrete-real)—hence not empirical but dialectical. Given the mutual effectivities and interplay of concrete-real and thought-concretes, Althusser provides us "a class knowledge of social being in which each human subject occupied specific class and nonclass positions . . . constituted by all the processes of the social totality" (Resnick and Wolff 1987: 98). So human subjects are overdetermined in their location in the fundamental (production and appropriation of surplus labor) or subsumed (distribution of already appropriated surplus) class processes involved in effecting quantitative and/or qualitative changes in those class processes; they are sites of multiple social processes informed by complex contradictions that develop unevenly and where humans are active insofar as "they are held within" these mutually constitutive social and natural processes that comprise aspects of the social totality (1987: 64). Both empiricism and rationalism that yield essentialist and humanist assumptions are rejected.

Let me return to Althusser's formulation of ideology and its import. Ideology is a system of representations (images, myths, ideas, etc.), possessing its own logic and rigor, exercising a historical influence/function within a given society. "Representation" here refers to how human express "the way they live the relation between them and their real conditions of existence," an imaginary relation "that expresses a will (conservative, conformist, reformist, or revolutionary), a hope or a nostalgia, rather than describing a reality" (1969: 233-34). Ideology expresses "the (overdetermined) unity of the real relation and the imaginary relations" between humans and their real conditions of existence. Contrary to allegations, Althusser stressed that given the mutual overdetermination of the real and the imaginary, the action of ideology is "never purely instrumental"; rather, it is constitutive. He gives the example of how the bourgeoisie as ruling class "lives in the ideology of freedom the relation between it and its conditions of existence: that is, its real relation (the law of a liberal capitalist economy) but invested in an imaginary relation (all men are free, including the free laborers)" (234). The categories of law in capitalism—Subject, Object, Freedom, Will, Property, Representation, Person, Thing, etc.—define the subject as one with "the general capacity" of mastery and of being acquisitive, one subject to the law and held responsible (Coward and Ellis 1977: 76; Derrida 1991).

To elucidate the mode of interpellation as the constitution of subjects, Rastko Mocnik (1993) construes it as comprised of two interdependent mechanisms: subjectivation proper, a stereotypical and purely formal symbolic function; and identification, an imaginary relation in which ideological conflict (class struggle) occurs. Mocnik posits the construction of the subject as an articulation of "social demand" (the relation of subjects with one another) and individual desire: "The individual act of identification with the social instance of the subject supposed to believe . . . makes the individual accede to the social dimension of ideological beliefs . . . and assume them for her/his own account. But the act of identification is impossible if, within the socially 'pre-existent' belief-background, it cannot find support for the individual's idiosyncratic 'wishful fantasies." In other words, ideology can only constitute subjects if and when the socially oriented and conscious demand for sense or intelligibility (the normal course of everyday life) can be translated into the individual's unconscious and specific desire/fantasy (a string of signifiers capable of various interpretations), a translation that triggers identification with the hailing Subject (ISAs), what is other than individual consciousness. Behind this fantasy is the "hiatus of the class struggle" which makes the social structure untotalizable. Mocnik's conceptualization of ideology is far more nuanced than this summary suggests, but it raises a number of questions that are also evoked with respect to Lacan's positing of the Imaginary and the Symbolic registers. This Lacanian interpretation of Althusser no doubt shifts the inquiry into power relations of groups to a psychoanalytic construal of individual cases, opening the way to a substitution of cultural categories for structural ones.

In any case, let us pursue this trail further. The fantasy that connects the identification process and the subjectivation mechanism may be defined as the locus of stereotypes, among them racist ones, connecting the facade of coherence and intelligibility (the effect of ideological discourse) with the social exterior. Just to give a brief example. In Studs Terkel's *Race* (1992), we meet C. P. Ellis, former Exalted Cyclops of the Durham, North Carolina, chapter of the Ku Klux Klan, whose childhood years of working-class poverty and suffering are summed up by his statement: "I worked my butt off and never seemed to break even. They say to abide by the law, do right and live for the Lord, and everything'll work out. It just kept getting worse and worse." Subjectivation is effected here by the legitimizing discourse of religion and official bureaucratic norms, but the fantasy level is missing. This will soon be supplied by the initiation into the Klan, mediated by his love for his father. The narrative becomes scenic and allegorical, conflating past and present voices:

> I began to say there's somethin' wrong with this country. I really began to
> get bitter. I tried to find somebody. I began to blame it on black people.

I had to hate somebody. Hatin' America is hard to do because you can't see it to hate it. You gotta have somethin' to look at to hate. [Laughs.] The natural person for me to hate would be black people, because my father before me was a member of the Klan. As far as he was concerned, it was the savior of the white people. So I began to admire the Klan.

The first night I went with the fellas, they knocked on the door and gave the signal. They sent some robed Klansmen to talk to me and give me some instructions. I was led into a large meeting room and this was the time of my life! It was thrilling. Here's a guy who's worked hard all his life and struggled all his life to be something, and here's the moment to be something. I will never forget it. Four robed Klansmen led me into the hall. The lights were dim and all you could see was an illuminated cross. I knelt before the cross. I had to make certain vows and promises. We promised to uphold the purity of the white race, fight communism, and protect white womanhood.

After I had taken my oath, there was loud applause goin' through the buildin', musta been at least four hundred people. It was a thrilling moment for C. P. Ellis. . . .

I can understand why people join extreme right-wing or left-wing groups. They're in the same boat I was in. Shut out. Deep down inside, we want to be part of this great society. Nobody listens, so we join these groups. (272-73)

Obviously here, the constitution of the subject occurs in the intersection of the Imaginary and the Symbolic registers (to use Lacan's terms)—that is, the class (working class) position of Ellis is subsumed in the Imaginary interpellation of his identity as Klansman in which race, politics, and sexual position are cast in binary, paranoid terms. The syncopation of social demand and individual desire, however, as his testimony demonstrates, leads later to a rejection of Klan ideology and adoption of a Christian liberal position filled with *ressentiment:* "I think Christ was a god in the flesh. He cares about individuals. . . . I think if He came back today, he'd be extremely disappointed" (280).

While it is plausible that interpellation—the constitution of subjectivity—will not work unless the "secondary elaboration" of the "preconstructed" (the "always-already" there of ideological formation) by fantasy takes place, the Lacanian ahistorical approach is vulnerable to the charges brought by Deleuze and Guattari (in *AntiOedipus*) and others. The encyclopedic social critic Anthony Wilden sees in Lacan's theory the operation of bourgeois political economy and its legitimization of oppression across class, race, and gender lines: "The trap opened up for the subject in the Lacanian theory is precisely that of the institutionalized LEGALISM of the Judaeo-Christian culture itself. . . . The rationalistic and legalistic categories of reification which underlie the theory thus remain a simple representation of the doublebind of the theological discourse itself [that is, the Father says to the son: 'You must (but you may not) be I, who am what I am.'] This is the inevitable result of defining all dialogue in the terms of language alone, rather than also in terms of the LABOR of relation" (1972: 472-73). Based on the misrecognition of the ego in the mirror-stage, Lacan's conception of ideology functions in a way analogous to the circularity and speculary transparence of the definitions in Flaubert's *Dictionnaire des idées reçues* (circa 1880) ascribed to his fictive characters Bouvard and Pecuchet. Here are sample entries from Flaubert's unfinished satire:

NEGROES. Express surprise that their saliva is white and that they can speak French.

NEGRESSES. Hotter than white women. (See BLONDES and BRU-NETTES.)

BLONDES. Hotter than brunettes. (See BRUNETTES.)

BRUNETTES. Hotter than blondes. (See BLONDES.) (1954: 18-19, 61)

So much for speculary misrecognitions!

Althusser, as many commentators have pointed out, mistook the Lacanian ego formed via the misrecognition of the mirror-stage as the subject of ideology, whereas the Lacanian Subject is an unstable effect of the Unconscious transpiring between the Imaginary and the Symbolic Registers (Eagleton 1991). Subjectivity, in other words, is what may be apprehended in the gap between the I of enunciation/the speaking subject and the I of the grammatical subject.

Now, what I think redeems the core of Althusser's theory of ideology, despite its avowed "theoreticism" and untenable opposition between ideology and science, is the fact that its theory of overdetermination and critique of essentialism (in its empiricist and humanist versions) hinge on the grasp of fetishism as "the necessary mode of existence of social relations" (Callinicos 1976: 105). From this perspective, racism as an ideological practice or process in late capitalism can be fully understood as an integral component of the dynamics of commodity fetishism. As Robert Miles (1989) has pointed out, racism is "a representational form which, by designating discrete human collectivities, necessarily functions as an ideology of inclusion and exclusion"; it operates dialectically when, in the process of racialization (defining group boundaries and allocation of persons accordingly), the negative representation of Others reflect/refract the positive characteristics of Self. Such boundaries and representations deploy qualities supposedly inherent (biological) or permanent (cultural; transcendental) in order to construct and legitimize social contradictions and problems so as to manipulate them to promote one collectivity's advantage. As a naturalizing of what is artificial or invented, racism analogically replicates the general problematic of commodity fetishism.

We now confront this enigmatic "stuff" called the "commodity." The commodity represents not only the elementary form of wealth in bourgeois society but also the result and precondition of the whole system. A commodity manifests two powers or aspects: it satisfies human needs (use value) and it can exercise the power of exchangeability (value). Use value—the concrete heterogeneous qualities that are virtually incommensurable and make commodities qualitatively different—functions as the material basis for the commodity's exchange value. Commodities exchange with each other on the basis of definite quantitative proportions. Commodities can be compared because the quanta of abstract human labor objectified in them can be measured. Abstract labor, the source of value in general, comes from reducing all concrete labor into the amount of socially necessary labor time needed for its production. Exchange value appears when commodities interact in exchange, presupposing the emergence of one particular commodity that can function as the general equivalent of all other commodities, namely, money. In the realm of classic liberal thought, the general equivalent for money is "human nature," defined according to variable and specific sociohistorical coordinates. Within this schema of equivalence, "use value is turned into the form of appearance of its opposite, of value" while concrete labor is turned into "the form of appearance of its opposite, abstract human labor" and private labor into "the form of its opposite, into labor immediately social in form" (Marx 1975: 175).

Exchange value mediated through money transforms the social relationship between individuals who produce commodities into a relationship between things (the products of labor). This "relationship hidden under a reified veil" demonstrates the fetish character of commodities, a mystified relation; the mystery of the commodity form, Marx writes in *Capital* (Chapter 1, section 4), "consists in the fact that in it the social character of men's labor appears to them as an objective characteristic, a social natural quality of the labor product itself . . . The commodity form, and the value relation between the products of labor which stamps them as commodities, have absolutely no connexion with their physical properties and with the material relations arising therefrom. It is simply a definite social relation between men that assumes in their eyes, the fantastic form of a relation between things." The products of humans then acquire a life of their own, independent but related to other products and to humans—products as fetishes in the usage of nineteenth-century anthropology.

In the third volume of *Capital* (Chapter 48), Marx describes how the economic trinity of capital interest, ground rent, and labor wage exemplifies the "complete mystification of the capitalist mode of production, the reification *[Verdinglichung]* of social relations and immediate coalescence of the material production relations with their historical and social determination. It is an enchanted, perverted, topsy-turvy world, in which Monsieur le Capital and Madame la Terre do their ghostwalking as social characters and at the same time directly as things." Reification prevails when the social relationship between individuals is defined in terms of the ratio (abstract labor quantified and translated into money) at which their products exchange with each other. Such a relationship is not false but rather misleading since it conceals actual relationships: "To them their own social action takes the form of the action of things, which rule the producers instead of being ruled by them."

In the chapter on "Reification and the Consciousness of the Proletariat" in *History and Class Consciousness,* Georg Lukács analyzes the objective and subjective dimensions of commodity fetishism, the "phantom objectivity" of the marketplace extending itself to the estrangement of human activity, its reduction to object status determined by natural laws (1971: 86-87). While capitalism unfolded the "socialization of society" as the groundwork for the birth of a new social individual, it also reduced humans to atomized fragments, abstracted into commodities (commodified labor power), devoid of any connection to any social whole or totality. Following Lukács, the social critic Joseph Gabel analyzed the schizophrenic structure of racist ideology, focusing on social

Darwinism as the rationale for the racist subsumption of the social into the organic world.

But Marx located the matrix of reification not in psychology but in the historical contingency of a society based on commodity exchange. In his essay, "On the Jewish Question," Marx perceived the index of reification in the split between the monadic egos of civil society and the abstract ensemble of citizens in the state, the division between social power and political power (Meszaros 1970; Arthur 1986). Marx anticipated the idea of commodity fetishism when he discerned in bourgeois society the conflict between individual sensuous existence and species-existence (sensuous practice; individuality as the totality of social relations). He elucidated how juridical, political freedom in capitalism is premised on a double abstraction:

> Political emancipation is the reduction of man on the one hand to the member of civil society, the egoistic, independent individual, and on the other to the citizen, the moral person.
>
> Only when real, individual man resumes the abstract citizen into himself and as an individual man has become a species-being in his empirical life, his individual work and his individual relationships, only when man has recognized and organized his forces propres [own forces] as social forces so that social force is no longer separated from him in the form of political force, only then will human emancipation be completed. (1975a: 234)

In sum, then, commodity production in capitalism determines the contour and substance of everyday practice: the simultaneous personification of things and the reification of its producers. Humans become subordinate to circumstances that are the result of their own activities, to powers that appear independent and transcendental although they incarnate or express human labor. The genealogy of the usage of the term "race," according to cultural critic Raymond Williams, illustrates how the methodology of biological classification (instanced in the physical anthropology of Blumenbach, 1787) acquires a life of its own when articulated by Gobineau (in *Essai sur l'inégalité des races humaines,* 1853-55) and by the proponents of eugenics: "Physical, cultural and socio-economic differences are taken up, projected and generalized, and so confused that different kinds of variation are made to stand for or imply each other" (Williams 1983: 250). But are we simply faced here by a philological problem as Williams suggests? Various authors, from Albert

Memmi to Anthony Giddens, have defined racism as having to do with the false attribution of inherited characteristics of personality or behavior to individuals on the basis of physical markers, and using this to judge inferiority or superiority. Note that racism is a property of dominance relations between groups (Van Dijk 1993) and cannot be reduced to psychological processes involving individuals and the knowledge-claims of biological and other physical sciences. In contemporary racism, cultural difference (ethnicism) serves as the most efficacious modality of racializing interpellation.

In order to illustrate in a more timely way this commodity-fetishism syndrome—the objective form of appearance of human relations (including its complex cultural network or "superstructure")—and how value (quantitatively measurable in the market) becomes ascribed to an attribute or notion called "race," allow me to use a photograph from the 11 May 1992 issue of *Newsweek* with the caption "This is not America."

Applying the decoding method of Roland Barthes, David Palumbo-Liu (in the Winter 1994 issue of *Public Culture*) demonstrates how this photographic distancing and sublimation of the traumatic Los Angeles riot projects the crisis of the political economy onto the geopolitical theater of black/Asian (Korean) antagonism. It elides the key agent behind this spectacle (the corporate elite) who stands apart as spectator, shifting "the trauma of racial violence onto Asian America" even while "the decontextualized voice of Malcolm X meets the voice of the Korean American ventriloquized through the Asian body in the photograph" (1994: 379). Palumbo-Liu concludes that the programmatic effect of this representation, the "structures of feeling" and silences it deploys, obscures "the political, economic, and ideological apparatuses that set the stage for the Los Angeles uprising of the spring of 1992" (380). Of course his deconstruction of the text-image by contextualizing it seeks to expose the workings of those apparatuses, their mechanisms of interpellation, that generate the racial subjects of blacks and Korean Americans.

Such a reading is demystifying, in the manner of Barthes, undoing the myth created by text/image by showing the mutual distortions of meaning and form. But the photograph as myth is "neither a lie nor a confession; it is an inflexion" in which history is transformed into nature, a semiological into a factual system. But this is precisely also the way in which the wage form functions, inflecting the social into the natural, an acknowledgment but also disavowal of reality. In the Freudian paradigm proper, the fetish is actually a metonymic displacement: the fixation on an object that was once strongly desired [the mother's penis] is transferred to a "reverence for a woman's foot or shoe" (Freud 1989: 461). The fetish here is a substitute that simultaneously affirms castration (what is absent) and disavows it. What the fetishism of this image acknowledges is the right of individuals to protect property; Malcolm X's gesture and words are thereby distorted by a paradigmatic substitution of the Asian figure's stance. At the same time it disavows the origin of the right in the schism between civil society and state—of which the Korean merchant's predicament is a symptom. The caption "This is not America" performs a disavowal of wanton violence, at the same time affirming the sacred right of property. While it may be granted that whites are invisible, the firetrucks representing a faceless state agency, with Asian America standing in for white supremacist ideology, I think the whole staging or composition of this photograph conveys the pathos of petit-bourgeois individualism, which has become somehow anachronistic in urban mass society but which still functions in a limited way as key icon/motif of liberal "free enterprise" ideology.

We have noted earlier that only in capitalism, in a generalized production and exchange of commodities, is labor expressed and measured as an objective property of products regulated by an impersonal market. Labor and its use value in production, a historically specific social process, becomes "naturalized" in its products. In the alienated world we live in, humans are guardians, proprietors, or owners of commodities or property. Radical economists Amariglio and Callari argue that for "the exchange of unequal actual labor times to be also an exchange of equivalents" in a capitalist social formation, "it is necessary for the agents of exchange to have the attributes of economic rationality, economic and political equality, and private proprietorship," attributes necessary to conduct exchange, the site in which the symbolic order of society is partially constituted and learned (1983: 28-30). Agency or subjectivity is thus an effect of a discursive practice linked to an ideological formation that ensures class division based on commodity exchange—the chief commodity being labor power—and guarantees the conditions of exploitation and its social/ideological reproduction.

Here, in our newspaper photograph, the Korean American individual displaying a semiautomatic handgun in this now familiar setting of urban riots (in which blacks are perceived by the mass media as lawless bands of looters, arsonists, etc.) becomes the bearer of a whole social process involving merchant middlemen in the ghetto and also the product of racial interpellation. Just as in market exchange, commodity A becomes the form of existence, or material embodiment, of the abstract value (value form) of commodity B, the physical body of commodity A serving as a mirror for the value of commodity B, so this Korean becomes—in the circulation of bodies with socially defined racial markers—the syntagmatic or metonymic embodiment of the abstract value of individual freedom (to buy, sell, etc.), and also a metaphor (like Malcolm X) for group self-assertion.

The fetishism of the text/image makes the racial distinctions natural/ legitimate even while converting the Korean to represent the dominant society which, though visually absent, is nevertheless present in the content and structure of the enunciation. The image/text interpellates readers and viewers as individuals who, concurring with the caption "This is not America," also disagree with the idea of individual revenge and call for Law and Order in order for "business as usual" to proceed.

On the other hand, one can argue that readers are sutured here into the signification process in a contradictory mode that reproduces the hierarchy of classes and races across the uneven and combined development of the urban social formation. While the background conveys water from the firetrucks putting out the fire, the male with a gun becomes a signifier for a narrative thread: the hunt/search for the culprit or criminal who caused the damage to property. The street crossing positions the subject (the armed Korean male) in a way that hides the labor of construction behind this image and also exposes its spurious transparency: what is this Asian with a gun doing in the streets of America? The will expressed in this fantasy is that of the fetishist who recognizes the absence of freedom in the market/business society (the real relations) but also disavows it (the imaginary sphere of lived experience) in responding to a tacit hailing voice: "Now that your business is wrecked, what do you do?" In unraveling the contradictory impulses locked in the hypostatized image, we are able to grasp the nature of racism as a mode of social semiotic production inscribed in the terrain of political-cultural struggle.

U.S. racial politics today is no longer chiefly mediated by biological and naturalistic ascriptions of value, but rather by symbolic cultural interpellations (the psychoanalyst Joel Kovel [1984] calls it "metaracism") pivoting around the affirmation of "a common culture," around the question of "What is America? What is an American?" The legitimacy of a Eurocentric pluralist society is in crisis. The discursive practice of racism in the media, for example, cannot be understood apart from this ideological formation or reference-system in crisis that underlies its claim to rationality. In this new ideology of culturalism lies the fetish-character of the photograph in question.

In our example, following Michel Pecheux's extension of Althusser's insights, the discursive formation underlying the photograph, the system of linguistic rules and relations that determine what can be said meaningfully, pertains to the framing of an individual in a dramatic moment that connotes anxiety, determination, forcefulness, in a scene that makes the caption either one attributable to the figure framed or a comment on the whole situation. Journalistic style and decorum, as well as the rhetoric of photographs in mass media, all form part of the discursive formation. This formation is situated within an interdiscourse, a structured totality of various discursive formations, that is inscribed within a complex of ideological formations—in particular, the jurisprudence of individual rights (right of ownership, self-defense, etc.), its grammar and lexicon. It is this ideological formation, whose function in generating the image-text is "forgotten" by the reader or viewer, that needs to be recalled by the analyst. This is part of the reification process: by repressing or occluding the process whereby a discursive sequence linked to its ideological context is produced, the photograph creates the illusion that the subject precedes discourse and lies at the origin of meaning. Whereas it is the subject that is "always already produced" by that which is "preconstructed" (the forgotten sociohistorical determinants of Los Angeles' political economy, Korean immigration and global politics of the Pacific Rim, deindustrialization and its impact on African Americans, demographics of the Latino community, and so on) in the sequence. Pecheux explains the constitution of the subject by its identification with the discursive formation and its domination by the ideology underwriting it:

> . . . the functioning of Ideology in general as interpellation of individuals into subjects (and specifically into the subjects of their discourse) is realized through the complex of ideological formations (and specifically through the interdiscourse which is intricated therein) and provides "each subject" with its "reality," that is, with a system of self-evident truths and significations perceived-accepted-submitted to. (quoted in Thompson 1984: 236)

In this milieu of reification, it is difficult for the reader of the photograph to grasp it as an effect of complex ideological/discursive formations; the symptomatic reading of the historical process is the task of a discursive semantics that would "desyntagmatize" or defetishize what appears normal and natural. The effects of meaning produced by the ideology of individual rights and the discourse of the photographic message (the institution of approved media reporting) can indeed interpellate the reader into a racist subject, one captured by the myth of the Asian "model minority." But is this photograph limited to that imaginary representation of a subject-centered world that elicits the misrecognitions that Palumbo-Liu describes? Or is it one that can also provoke a "dis-identification" with the solitary protagonist and his ironic translation of Malcolm X's message? If all signs and discourses are arenas of class struggle (Hodge and Kress 1988), crisscrossed by relations of power (order and subordination) and solidarity (cohesion and antagonism), then this photograph cannot just be decoded as a coherent message that fixes the viewer into one subject-position. It is actually a complex of contradictory signifiers more or less geared to communicate a hegemonic meaning but still overdetermined enough so as to allow one to articulate it in a counterhegemonic direction and calculate its tactical effectivity within a larger strategy of critical interrogation. If we engage in this task, it will be to refute the charge that such racist media interpellations deprive us of creative, oppositional agency, and that we are not all victims of the regime of commodity fetishism and its ideological apparatuses. But for this to happen, we need to focus more on the racial politics of cultural difference and its capacity to produce racialized subjects/agents necessary for capital accumulation and its political hegemony in the present world system.

DETERRITORIALIZING THE MULTICULTURAL

On the face of Native American resistance and the resurgence of black nationalism as well as Afrocentric separatism, the invocation of America as a "nation of immigrants" may now be deciphered as a symptom of an obsessive nostalgia for a mythical past. What has replaced it is the mantra of pluralism and the ideal of American identity based on the nation's motto *E pluribus unum* (out of many, one). The NEH flyer for "A National Conversation" posits the existence of "what we share as common American values in a nation comprised of many divergent groups and beliefs," a "national purpose." The commonality is supposedly inscribed in "Our country's motto, *E pluribus unum*" which "reflects the traditional belief that there are fundamental qualities that define us as a nation," qualities distilled in the honorific phrase "American pluralism" attached to a national "identity" (NEH 1994: 7). However much we resurrect Melville's plural microcosm in the *Pequod,* or declaim Whitman's paeans to the masses, the social formation of pre–Civil War artisans, farmers, and petty-commodity producers cannot be brought back to resolve the misery of black inhabitants in highly segregated Los Angeles. Nor can the invention of psychic borderlands, whose "inner changes" supposedly prefigure the face of things to come, neutralize the brutality of immigration agents, police, and racist institutions. Concluding his recent multicultural history, Ronald Takaki pontificates: "America's dilemma has been our resistance to ourselves—our denial of our immensely varied selves" and the "fear of our own diversity" (1993: 427). Excellent rhetoric, but impoverished understanding of the complex terrain of antagonisms among classes, ethnicities, races, genders, and so on, that constitutes the U.S. social formation and its contradictory force fields.

This now fashionable celebration of U.S. cultural diversity may be read as an aspect of the postmodern revolt against the Enlightenment universalist paradigm of rationality and progress. It is a rejection of totalizing "metanarratives" that presumably underwrite the relentless homogenization, bureaucratic standardization, and commodification of modern life. Pluralism, heterogeneity, multiplicity, local knowledges, language games of mobile and non-essentialized identities are the buzzwords of polite conversation in the academy and sophisticated gatherings. The fashionable constructivism or contextualism of postmodernists, the philosopher Seyla Benhabib (1996; see also Scott 1992) notes, often leads to the blind alley of cultural relativism and nihilism. But of course these fashions are also mimicked if not surpassed by "the united colors of Benetton," the Body Shop's opportunism regarding indigenous peoples, and the "strategic essentialism" of certain postcolonial celebrities. This trend is less prophetic than nostalgic, an example of retro-pastiche (Jameson), a simulacra or simulation (Baudrillard) that easily occludes one of the lessons of historical capitalism which, according to Immanuel Wallerstein, is the "ethnicization of community life" and the "ethnicization of the world work-force" (1983: 77). In *The Condition of Postmodernity,* the all-encompassing geographer David Harvey has also called attention to something like "combined and uneven development" in the field of culture in which uniformity and streamlining goes along with particularisms and retrogressions. Why is it that in the proliferating discourses on identity and difference, the worldly texture of collective experience and its historical contexts are invariably lost? Instead of pursuing this theme of the political economy of immigration as it articulates with postmodern cultural figuration of difference, I would like to examine one of the most provocative and insightful explorations of what I call the "multicultural imaginary," the Canadian philosopher Charles Taylor's "The Politics of Recognition."

The problem Taylor confronts in his inquiry is as familiar as it is vexatious: how to reconcile the demand of particular groups for recognition of the equal worth of their cultures, their forms of life, with the fundamental principle of liberal democracies: the equal representation of all. What is meant by "recognition"? Taylor traces this need of the individual for recognition of one's authentic identity to the collapse of social hierarchies, the basis of honor, in the transition from the tributary/feudal to the secular and capitalist world. "Democracy has ushered in a politics of equal recognition," he writes, a politics originating from the notion of authenticity argued by Rousseau and Herder: "There is a certain way of being human that is my way" (1994: 30). In short, being human is being true to oneself. Now Taylor of course has no use for theories based on abstract individuals, what Marx calls "Robinsonades," concealing underlying social relations by privileging inwardness, interiority, psychic depth, etc. Taylor insists that human life is "fundamentally dialogical," inextricable from our interaction with "significant others"; therefore, "My own identity crucially depends on my dialogical relations with others" (34).

Pitched on this level of abstraction, the dialogical nature of identity is haphazardly explained. It is conflated with human agency and its "rich human languages of expression." The emphasis on "modes of expression" betrays a formalist conception of mutuality or reciprocity that serves as "the key loci of self-discovery and self-affirmation" (36). The valorization of authenticity underwrites a politics of equal dignity of all citizens, the equalization of rights and entitlements. A dialectical turn occurs in which the politics of difference emerges out of the politics of universal dignity; hence all those deprived and victimized by socioeconomic conditions demand to be treated equally. Dignity, it turns out, is born out of refusal and rebellion; the victims rebelling ask "that we give acknowledgment and status to something that is not universally shared," to something peculiar or specific. It is not clear to me why Taylor says this, why the situation of disadvantage, oppression, or exploitation would be something "peculiar" unless it is viewed from a dominant position that disavows any connection with the plight of minority groups.

We begin to understand why. For halfway through his essay, Taylor switches to a Kantian mode of argument that insinuates an implicit hierarchy of worth, as one will see. Taylor locates the politics of equal dignity as founded "on the idea that all humans are equally worthy of respect," and what commands respect, what occasions dignity, is (follow-ing Kant) "our status as rational agents, capable of directing our lives through principles"—"a universal human potential, a capacity that all humans share" (41). Thus when Saul Bellow is reputed to have said, "When the Zulus produce a Tolstoy we will read him," his error lies in violating the principle that the Zulus also have that potential of becoming worthy. Obviously the "difference-blind" liberalism of such a statement is, as Taylor rightly grants, based on a discriminatory hegemonic judg-ment—an attack that for him "is the cruelest and most upsetting of all."

To resolve this impasse, Rousseau is invoked as the voice of the just and virtuous sensibility: esteem or demand for recognition of one's worth is all right (as contradistinguished from pride or honor) if our society is characterized by the reciprocity and unity of purpose (say, patriotism or nationalism) that makes possible the equality of esteem. Finally Hegel comes to Rousseau's aid with the famous dialectic of master and slave in *The Phenomenology of Mind* whose allegory shows that "the struggle for recognition can find only one satisfactory solution, and that is a regime of reciprocal recognition among equals" (50). Absent this equality, even though not a word about private property or unequal distribution of wealth has been uttered, the wrangling and fighting will continue.

Finally, however, Taylor comes up with another solution: a revised rights-liberalism applied to Quebeckers and aboriginals in Canada who are fighting for the collective goals of autonomy and survival as distinct societies—the common good. Here rights theory clashes with the ethics of virtue, of the good for the community. Taylor has serious reservations about a liberal society neutral on the good life, a neutrality based on the notion of the human agent "as primarily a subject of self-determining or self-expressive choice . . . in the context of the constitutional doctrine of judicial review" (57-58). This procedural liberalism Taylor calls "inhos-pitable to difference because it can't accomodate what the members of distinct societies really aspire to, which is survival" (61). This hospitable variant of the liberal politics of equal respect is ultimately what Taylor endorses, even though at the end he summons to the stage Frantz Fanon as the spokesman of the victims of European colonialism and racial supremacy. But ironically Taylor misrecognizes Fanon and reduces Fanon's ideas to psychological platitude. This trivialization extends to feminism as a question of changing attitudes and self-images. At best, the guardians of the Western heritage, of Western civilization, should at times entertain the presumption that the cultures of other peoples—people of color—have value. But Taylor qualifies and says "I am not sure about the validity of demanding this presumption as a right." Eventually it boils down to a case of individuals expressing like or dislike, of endorsing or rejecting one's taste for this or that manner of performance—a lot of erudition for sanctioning the day's doxa and "business as usual." Meanwhile Taylor cannot miss this opportunity to denounce the neo-Nietzscheans and other social constructionists who would reduce everything to power and counterpower; taking sides is, to him, "hardly a satisfactory solution" (70).

Taylor is not a liberal unless he demonstrates that he is also capable of being skeptical about his own standpoint: "Here is another severe problem with much of the politics of multiculturalism. The peremptory demand for favorable judgments of worth is paradoxically—perhaps one should say tragically—homogenizing. For it implies that we already have the standards to make such judgments. The standards we have, however, are those of North Atlantic civilization. And so the judgments implicitly and unconsciously will cram the others into our categories" (71), which is in effect what he has been doing all along. Finally, he strikes a compromise between the "homogenizing demand for recognition of equal worth" and "the self-immurement within ethnocentric standards" because "There are other cultures, and we have to live together more and more, both on a world scale and commingled in each individual society." So finally he takes the moral high ground and pronounces on the moral dividend accruing to his cautionary tale, a gesture of latitudinarian agnosticism or an *Aufhebung* worthy of a latter-day Hegelian:

> We only need a sense of our own limited part in the whole human story to accept the presumption [that other cultures have worth]. It is only arrogance, or some analogous moral failing, that can deprive us of this. But what the presumption requires of us is not peremptory and inauthentic judgments of equal value, but a willingness to be open to comparative cultural study of the kind that must displace our horizons in the resulting fusions. What it requires above all is an admission that we are very far away from that ultimate horizon from which the relative worth of different cultures might be evident. This would mean breaking with an illusion that still holds many "multiculturalists"—as well as their most bitter opponents—in its grip. (73)

It is not clear whether this pragmatic liberalism deserves a response like the "Theses on Feuerbach," *The Holy Family,* and the earlier

Critique of Hegel's Philosophy of Right. In positing an evolutionary trajectory, Taylor reinforces the cleavage between the two domains constituting what sociologist John Rex (1996) calls the ideal of "egalitarian multiculturalism": the political culture of the public sphere centered on equality, and the private or communal domain of ethnic particularisms. Again, this species of the multicultural Imaginary fails to elude the contagion of commodity fetishism.

Suffice it for me to allude to the criticism of Taylor's views and those of other like-minded communitarians made by Antonio Negri and Michael Hardt in their recent *Labor of Dionysus,* which reads in part:

> The notions of reflective, situated subjectivity and community [the Hegelian notion of *Sittlichkeit*] that these communitarians propose finally lead to the proposition of the State as the fully realized subject. The community conceived on a local level cannot take on a full meaning. Communitarians continually postulate the community as the expression of who we are without giving any particular specifications of this "we." In fact, if one were to try to conceive the community in local terms based on specific commonalities—a community of autoworkers, a community of gay men, even a community of women—we would have to qualify this in Taylor's terms as a "partial community." Such a community cannot assume the role of a fully realized subject, but can only discover (through reflection) its identity in the whole. . . . The State inheres in these arguments as necessity, as the only veritable subject of community, as the full realization of embodied subjectivity. "Es ist der Gang Gottes in der Welt, dass der Staat ist." It is essential to God's march through the world that the State exist. In the final instance, the communitarian preoccupation with the theory of the subject leads to the proposition of the State as the only fully realized and autonomous subject. (1994: 256-57)

One illustration is the trend in Australia where, for example, the state intervenes in revitalizing a racist definition of nation as "imagined community" via the multicultural sensorium: "Multiculturalism is based on a construction of community through a celebration and fossilization of differences, which are then subsumed into an imagined community of national cohesion" (Castles et al 1996: 365). From the multitude thus springs the One coinciding with the state, its military force and its prisons.

ADVENTURES OF THE COMMODITY FORM

One approach to disentangling the aporia of equal recognition of unequal cultures, of assigning comparable worth to a multiplicity of singular and incommensurable forms of life, would be to consider this dilemma as a symptom of the failure to grasp the paradigmatic sociality constituting individuals. This sociality of multiculturalism, however, is historically specific to late capitalism. So it is necessary in the process of ethical and political judgment to grasp the ways in which the concept of value and its forms is theorized in the political economy of commodity production as an epistemological framework in assaying the worth of cultures. The usual point of departure is Marx's comment on the fetishism of commodities in the first book of *Capital:*

> A commodity is therefore a mysterious thing, simply because in it the social character of men's labor appears to them as an objective character stamped upon the product of that labor; because the relation of the producers to the sum total of their own labor is presented to them as a social relation, existing not between themselves, but between the products of their labor. This is the reason why the products of labor become commodities, social things whose qualities are at the same time perceptible and imperceptible by the senses. (Selsam 1970, 276-77)

Commodity fetishism occurs when definite social relations assume "the fantastic form of a relation between things," when products of labor become commodities. What is crucial to elucidate is the "value relation" that in the process of exchange both reveals and hides the human content, the concrete labor embodied in commodities. Marx's analysis of the forms of value may help clarify the antinomies in Taylor's predicament.

Marx begins with the simplest accidental commodity-form instanced in the exchange of any two commodities of given amounts:

x commodity A = [is worth] y commodity B

In effect, if A is worth B, then B expresses the value of A. So then, by analogy for example, if Tolstoy's *Anna Karenina* is worth Achebe's *Things Fall Apart,* then the African novel expresses the value of Tolstoy's work. This is an accidental exchange—no regularity or frequency is implied, given the lack of the political, geographical, and other economic factors to sustain regular trade between two groups, societies, or continents.

In the elementary form of value which comes about when trade becomes a regular practice of various societies, the value of commodity A in the process of exchange is expressed or manifested in commodity B. Commodity A is called "the relative value form" because its value is expressed in B, called the "equivalent form," whose material or corporeal use-value provides the phenomenal form of appearance for the value of A. Here the two sides of the actual exchange process, the relative value form and the equivalent value form, are opposed but united in a contradictory totality. There are different use values in A and B; the only common feature in them is the abstract value that each embodies in their differing use values. Here the various concrete labor that shaped A and B are reduced to abstraction due to capital's social division of labor and the logic of exchange. One commodity that embodies concrete labor is substituted for another commodity. A's value can be manifested only through its reflective mediation in B; B's otherness expresses one single aspect of A, namely, the abstraction to which human labor can be reduced.

It is in this phase of exchange that liberal democracy posits the equality of citizen-subjects mediated through the market and the bourgeois state apparatus. The relative value form of culture A (African Americans) incorporating the expenditure of energies by millions can be apprehended only if submitted to an equation (that parallels exchange); its equivalent form, from Taylor's point of view, would be European culture, which would select an aspect of African American culture that it can embody or express: for example, rational argumentation, male supremacy, etc. In other words, the relative form of African American culture can be appraised or valorized only by the equivalent form (here the dominant system of individual rights) that reveals its value. While value is evidently a social relation, the equivalent form functions enigmatically to hide this contingency by making it appear that it naturally expresses the value of the other. In the primordial stage of exchange, African American culture would simply be worth Western culture in an accidental way: its use value is as good as any other. In this elementary stage, however, we enter a domain in which commodity production is generalized, humans are defined as owners of commodities (labor power) that they can dispose of, and the exchange of commodities predominates. This embraces the historical period from petty commodity production to booty capitalism, soon to be followed by the colonial expansion of Europe in the conquest of territories and the subjugation of peoples (African slaves, aboriginal Indians, etc.) up to the beginning of the Industrial Revolution.

So far Marx posits value not as an eternal or natural form of social production but as the objectification of abstract labor that undergoes a historical metamorphosis. Value is not intrinsic to a single commodity; it reflects the division of labor of independent producers "the social nature of whose labor is only revealed in the act of exchange" (Bottomore 1983: 509). While commodities are embodiments of quantities of labor, their value form derives from a relation: the value of commodity A cannot be identical to its natural self; it acquires objective existence in the physical form of commodity B, which then becomes the value form of A. This expression of equivalence between various commodities demonstrates the specific quality of value-creating labor; the process of exchange reveals the general or common labor that has produced all those commodities.

Concerning the equivalent form of value, Marx identifies its three peculiarities thus: first, commodity B, its material body, objectifies abstract labor in expressing the value of commodity A; second, the concrete labor that produced commodity B becomes the form of appearance of abstract labor so that the particular processes of individual work that fashioned it becomes identical with other kinds of labor; and third, private labor assumes directly the form of social labor. So "while a commodity is both a use value and a value, it only appears in this dual role when its value possesses a form of appearance independent of and distinct from its use value form. This independent form of expression is exchange value" (Bottomore 1983: 510).

Because the elementary form of value does not fully reflect the universality of exchange value, the multiplicity of commodities circulating in the market, we move to the expanded form of value—the analogue to cultural pluralism, or benign multiculturalism. Here commodity A exchanges not only with commodity B but also with commodities C, D, E, ad infinitum; the equivalent form of value is indifferent vis-à-vis the relative form. Here commodity A is configured within a whole world of commodity production, the social totality. At this point we begin to understand that it is not exchange that regulates the magnitude of value but rather the magnitude of the value of commodities that regulates the proportion in which they are exchanged. Since here various useful labors are equalized, the series of representations or equivalent forms of the value of A is limitless, fragmentary, and lacks internal unity.

Eventually a stage is reached when one single commodity is chosen to represent the values of all commodities, setting aside the use values of particular commodities and expressing what is common to all of them; this "universal equivalent" belongs to the general form of value. The natural form of this universal equivalent serves as the value form of all other commodities—that is, exchange value, which erases both abstract labor and the socially necessary labor time that measures it. The form of value then appears in the money form and its quantitative measure. Marx writes: "From the contradiction between the general character of value and its material existence in a particular commodity, etc. . . . arises the category of money." In the transition from the general form to the money form of value as universal equivalent, the determinations of the prior forms of value remain: the contradictory unity and reflexive relations between the relative form and the equivalent form in the simple form, the totality and infinitude brought out in the expanded form, and the mediated character in the general form. Thus, in the general and money forms of value, the relative value form of all commodities are gathered at the same time and expressed in the universal equivalent fixed by custom (money). In this stage, all social relations and with it use values are convertible into money relations. In this context, the price form is a process in which use value, produced by concrete labor, becomes a product of that universal tool controlled by capital: the laborer, labor-power. Price equates an object with all other commodities, its labor with all others, thus rendering it abstract. As the economist Harry Cleaver notes, "The qualitative equality of work has been affirmed and the quantity set socially. Money shows to the commodity that it is a product of abstract labor—a value" (1979, 164).

Anticipating charges of idealism, Marx contends that economic categories are not a priori constructions, they reflect human activities in history. The mode of analyzing the commodity form of value is based on the reality of the process of exchange whereby products of labor are commensurated in capitalism; the process of exchange demonstrates the sociality of production, connects independent producers, and guarantees that the value realized in exchange is the form of appearance of that labor socially necessary to the production of the commodity in question. From this one can elaborate on the law of value (how value is determined by socially necessary labor time) in terms of the categories of capital and its accumulation, the dominance of money relations, and the inversion of social relations of production (commodity fetishism) and its registration in consciousness (ideology).

Viewed from the genealogy of the forms of value summarized here, the multiculturalist Imaginary at first glance remains in the stage of the expanded form of value. Believing in the unrepeatable authenticity of use values embodied in art and other cultural practices, the multiculturalist nonetheless submits to a process of endless substitutions in the hope that this will do away with hierarchy, with domination and subordination. Both the relative forms of value and equivalent forms are shifting, fragmentary, heterogeneous; their contradictory relation obscures their totalizing and mediating effect. Amid this instability, or "bad infinity," Taylor enters the scene and while being appreciative of the range of differences and their dialectical motion, the irreplaceable nature of cultural groups and their right to survival, he doubts if his empathy for those deprived and suffering in the status quo can really be a trustworthy measure of their relative worth. In short, he doubts if a universal equivalent—the fusion of horizons in a hermeneutic transaction—can be found, a symbolic totalizing intuition or act that can genuinely extinguish Eurocentric bias (liberal theory of rights, the Hegelian concept, etc.) and enable parity of all competing parties, groups, cultures.

Unfortunately, this search for a universal equivalent form of value can lead only into the complete reign of commodity fetishism—the money form of value—which equalizes everything in abstraction: the liberal banalities that all cultural groups share common concerns, dreams, anxieties, ideals, etc. We are faced here with the allegory of the Zulu Tolstoy negotiating his identity in the sphere of the Lacanian Imaginary, unaware of the lack that would resolve his crisis into a semblance of Symbolic plenitude.

Meanwhile, the Real insists on the necessity of recognizing that "socially necessary labor time" mystified, perverted, obfuscated by exchange of vernaculars, polyphonic dialogue, interpellation, by ludic speech and "hyperreal" communication. In *Symbolic Economies* (1990), Jean Joseph Goux has traced the history of the connection between exchange value and the symbolic leading to the exclusion of "the surplus of meaning" in capitalist society, this "deficiency of meaning" arising from the reduction of everything into the quantitative universal equivalent, the money form of value. This is the milieu of market liberalism in which free and equal subjects can exchange ideas despite disparities in resources, opportunities, communal notions of the good. Multiculturalism can perhaps thrive here so long as the roots and sources of culture in concrete practices are not submitted to translation or transposition into the value form. But this is inescapable since multiculturalism implies comparison, translation, critical discriminations of all sorts.

But what is at stake in proposing a return to what may probably be dismissed as traditional and old-fashioned thinking?

In the conclusion to his ambitious work now recently published as *American Civilization* (1993a), C. L. R. James envisioned an "integrated humanism" evolving from the multicultural environment of the United States, one that will make politics "an expression of universal man and a totally integrated human existence." Such a belief, almost utopian and even naive, in the capacity of the masses to absorb the whole of civilization and radically transform society is almost impossible for anyone who would ignore the reality of commodity exchange, its contradictory nature, and the possibilities of its overcoming. This humanism of Enlightenment provenance, however, needs to undergo a rigorous critique such as that enunciated by the French theoretician Colette Guillaumin (1995: 57): "[T]he combined forces of atheism, determinism, individualism, democracy and egalitarianism in fact served to justify the system of oppression. . . . By proposing a scheme of immanent physical causality (by race, colour, sex, nature), that system provides an irrefutable justification for the crushing of resourceless classes and peoples, and the legitimacy of the elite" (1995: 57). Partisans of insurrectionary, anti-capitalist multiculturalism can help in the overcoming of liberal, free-market universalism by positing a more radical critique of its own formation and demonstrating a historical sensitivity to the reality of labor, modes of production, and the material underpinnings of culture itself in its largest definition as social transformative praxis.

TRANSCENDING THE STATE/CIVIL SOCIETY DICHOTOMY

I would like to suggest that the aporia between the radically situated and the disembodied subject, between "free and equal others" caught in Taylor's antinomy of plural dignities, is by way of the social ontology found in Marx's *Grundrisse*. This ontology is governed by the historical-materialist critique of alienation and reification in capitalism. While the *Grundrisse* was written in 1857-58 as heuristic notes to the later *Capital*, it departs from premises laid out earlier in the 1843 *Critique of Hegel's Philosophy of the State* and also in the 1844 *Economic and Philosophical Manuscripts* and later on in *The German Ideology* (1845-46). I recapitulate Marx's key observations briefly.

Overall, the controlling framework is the imbrication of humans and social relations; "human" equals "social." "My own existence is a social activity," asserts Marx. Society is not an abstract supraindividual phenomenon but actual relationships with a specific historical form. "Society does not consist of individuals; it expresses the sum of connections and relationships in which individuals find themselves. . . . To be a slave or to be a citizen are social determinations. . . . Man A is not a slave as such. He is a slave within society and because of it" (McLellan 1971: 77). Marx's sixth thesis on Feuerbach states that the individual equals the totality or ensemble of social relations that assume various forms in history.

From this historical-materialist standpoint, the *Grundrisse* describes the genealogy of three forms of society that explains why we don't have to wait for Taylor's utopian moment in which the relative worth of cultures will appear in the fusion of horizons. Marx summarizes the three configurations of society—precapitalist, capitalist, and communist— thus:

> Relations of personal dependence (entirely spontaneous at the outset) are the first social forms, in which human productive capacity develops only to a slight extent and at isolated points. Personal independence founded on objective dependence is the second great form, in which a system of general social metabolism, of universal relations, of all-round needs and universal capacities is formed for the first time. Free individuality, based on the universal development of individuals and on their subordination of their communal, social productivity as their social wealth, is the third stage. The second stage creates the conditions for the third. Patriarchal as well as ancient conditions (feudal, also) thus disintegrate with the development of commerce, of luxury, of money, of exchange value, while modern society arises and grows in the same measure. (1973: 158)

Seen within this first stage of "immediate unity" (exemplified by ancient, classical, and Germanic forms), in which the organic community itself reproduces the individual in his or her specific relation to the community, the notion of "honor" is tied to fixed roles, functions, and statuses ascribed to individuals in the community. Given the traditional culture that imprisons individuals in concrete, particularized, and dependent social relations that appear as natural (landed property and attachment to the soil promote this illusion), this *Gemeinschaft* exhibits a will and self-sufficient unity that precludes any awareness of its lack of freedom,

its restrictive locality, its nonreciprocal regime of loyalties and expectations. Conservative communitarians may long for a return of this milieu
but only at the expense of its conversion into a simulacrum or simulation.

With the appearance of the landless, propertyless worker from the
dispossessed peasantry, we enter the second stage characterized by the
relations of formal equality, by personal independence based on objective
dependence. From undifferentiated unity in the commune, we enter a
world in which ties of personal dependence and distinctions of blood are
exploded to be replaced by mediation through the market, through
exchange of commodities. With the internal/personal relations of precapitalist society replaced by external relations of commodity values,
"indifferent" individuals in capitalism are now reciprocally dependent
on each other through "exchange value," yet this general exchange of
activities and products appear alien to them. Exchange presupposes that
agents are owners of their property (labor power) and are free to engage
in contractual arrangements; individuals recognize each other as proprietors whose wills are incorporated in their commodities. The act of
divesting oneself of one's property defines the legal or juridical person in
this society. When the discourse/practice of exchange constitutes individuals as equal subjects, it also generates the illusion of freedom, as in
"free competition," relative to the preceding stage. Marx points out that
"these objective dependency relations [in capitalism] appear in antithesis
to those of personal dependence in such a way that individuals are now
ruled by abstractions, whereas earlier they depended on one another"
(1973: 164). The universal medium of exchange, money, translates the
abstract quantities of labor time embodied in commodities; such commodities (including labor power) exchange based on the abstraction of
equivalence of value, the objectified form of social relations.

We enter the realm of alienation, the realm of "civil society," from
which the politics of recognition and dignity originates. With the
dissolution of feudal/tributary forms of society, "the various forms of
social connectedness confront the individual as a mere means toward his
private ends, as external necessity" (1973: 83-84). Civil society founded
on free and equal exchange underwrites the theory of the individual as
substantial entity from which collective categories—laws, forms of
society, rights, etc.—were derived. Utilitarian ethics postulated the
existence of separate individuals who calculated the consequences of their
actions, the pleasure or pain they produce. The sovereign individual
postulated by Descartes, Hobbes, and Locke was a conceptual figure or
discursive agency that functioned as the "subject" of reason, knowledge,

and practice. But this assumption of freedom and equality in civil society is the fundamental fallacy promoted by ideologues of today's "civil society" cult (see Serrano 1994; Tandon 1994). Civil-society "harmony" is precisely a function of exchange in which freedom and equality disappear when "value-positing, productive labor" is appropriated by capital and yields surplus value—an activity of objectification and capitalist alienation. For Marx, "the worker necessarily impoverishes himself . . . because the creative power of his labor establishes itself as the power of capital, as an alien power confronting him" (1973: 307).

In this regime of abstract universal social relations in which personal independence coexists with objective dependence (on money or exchange, capital, machinery, etc.), we encounter the contradictions of liberal democracy and pluralist multiculturalism. Difference becomes antagonism here primarily between labor and capital and then, later on, in imperialism, between subjugated races/peoples and the colonizing nations.

Recognition of the equal worth of cultures cannot be possible in a social system founded on relations of commodity exchange and on the reification that Georg Lukács associates with bourgeois culture because the individuals, legally free and equal, who depend on each other in business and everyday transactions are "indifferent" to each other, seeing the other only as an instrument or an external means to their private satisfactions. While, as Marx writes, reciprocity is "a necessary fact, presupposed as natural precondition of exchange . . . it is irrelevant to each of the two subjects in exchange" (1973: 244). In this system of discrete and separate individuals aggregated together in various collectivities, the hegemony (ideological plus political supremacy) of one group over the rest implies the ascendancy of a particular philosophical, ethical, or cultural world view and form of life that subordinates others in a hierarchy that resembles the precapitalist formation—except now it is disguised in the language of democracy and equality. While lip service is paid to the value of diverse interest-groups, lifestyles, and so forth, in a society based on the logic of accumulation, the formal differentiation and abstract universality of the whole operates to reproduce segregation, discrimination, and exclusion. This is inevitable since the instrumental sociality in a system of exchange, the mutual indifference of acquisitive/possessive individuals, blocks what Taylor calls the "universal human potential" of rational agency (Kant) or the unity of purpose expressed in the general will that Rousseau required for equality of esteem.

It seems to me that the appreciation of integral cultures and visions of the good life that they legitimate—the program of critical/resistance multiculturalism—needs to confront alienation and reification in capitalism. It needs to grapple with the problem of how the objective sociality and universality fashioned by living labor can be reappropriated to serve the manifold needs of emergent social individuals. For Marx, capitalism's civilizing influence inheres in developing "the universality and the comprehensiveness of [the individual's] relations and capacities"; and in its "discovery, creation and satisfaction of new needs arising from society itself," from "the diversity of production and the exploitation and exchange of natural and intellectual forces" (1971: 94-95). But not only does capitalist production bring about general alienation, it also engenders that moment when its drive to universality encounters limits in its own nature: "Productive forces and social relationships—the two different sides of the development of the social individual—appear to be, and are, only a means for capital, to enable it to produce from its own cramped base. But in fact they are the material conditions that will shatter this foundation" (1971: 143). Here Marx allows for the relative autonomy of "social relationships," the institutionalized power relations invested in what Habermas calls "the cultural tradition" that normatively regulates responsibilities, rewards, and communication structures through which "subjects interpret both nature and themselves in their environment" (1971: 53).

Only when the power of capital is dissolved and with it the abstract measure of equivalence (labor time) will humans become subjects and recognize each other as such through the concretely differentiated community. This new form of life abolishes the property relation and the division of labor that circumscribed previous forms. Free social individuality, concrete equality, and substantive freedom can be realized only in communism. What will supersede capitalism is an order in which the social activity of individuals become "the organic social body" within which humans reproduce themselves as "social individuals," in which

> the social character of production is presupposed, and participation in the world of products, of consumption, is not mediated by the exchange of mutually independent labours . . . [but] by the social conditions of production within which the individual is active . . . The communal character of production would make the product into a communal, general product from the outset. The exchange which originally takes place in production—which would not be an exchange of exchange-values but of activities, determined by communal needs and communal purposes—would from the outset include the participation of the individual in the communal world of products. (Marx 1973: 171-72)

The development of human powers becomes an end in itself, becomes the wealth of humanity engendered by changes in the forces of production, and this development in turn changes people's relations to their objective conditions—the subject-object dialectic in history (Bologh 1979: 127):

> When the limited bourgeois form is stripped away, what is wealth other than the universality of individual needs, capacities, pleasures, productive forces, etc. created through universal exchange? The full development of human mastery over the forces of nature, those of so-called nature as well as of humanity's own nature? The absolute working-out of his creative potentialities, with no presupposition other than the previous historic development, which makes this totality of development, i.e., the development of all human powers as such the end in itself, not as measured on a predetermined yardstick? Where he does not reproduce himself in one specificity, but produces his totality? Strives not to remain something he has become, but is in the absolute movement of becoming? (Marx 1973, 488)

The form of life freed from the perversion of exchange value is a culture of differentiated unity. In this liberated community, each social individual's needs are those of other humans so that each, in producing for her own needs, is also producing for everyone. Labor as self-realization assumes the form of scientific mastery of the processes of nature as well as its own process as a self-conscious history. In socialized labor, each pursues the universal species-interest not as an abstract aim but as an expression of "self-conscious mastery," that is, a self-conscious form of life in unity with its own posited process of development, its own presupposition. Or, in Marx's words, "the grasping of his own history as a process, and the recognition of nature (equally present as practical power over nature) as his real body" (1973: 542). Now, some might object to the specification of the construction of a single form of social relationship reminiscent of *Gemeinschaft* models of community that ignore heterogeneous needs and desires as a political ideal (Keat 1981: 149-50). What we have here, however, is interaction based on subjective needs, on the mutual enhancement of personal qualities and desires, a domain of personal interaction that would encourage the full development of differences between and within individuals so that everyone attains both subjective and objective independence. The philosopher Carol Gould explains that the universality here is not abstract sameness "but rather a universality in the sense of a fulfillment of the concrete differentiation among individuals . . . a concept of open-ended totality in which the potentialities of the species are fulfilled by the free development of each individual, and where each is free to develop many-sidedly and in cooperation with others" (1978: 26-27)—in short, a concrete and differentiated universality.

If we view culture as a historical form of life, then it is impossible not to engage with Marx's critique of commodity fetishism in under-standing the possibilities and limits of the multicularist Imaginary. For this Imaginary and the play of difference it authorizes subsist within the form of life legitimized by the normalcy or naturalness of exchange—both of material and symbolic values. Liberalism claims neutrality in according equal time to affirmations like "this is how we do things here," and "this is the way I live," and so forth. What needs analysis is the claim of liberal ideology to be pluralist, to exercise equal treatment, to acknowledge and respect differences in the conflicted terrain of civil society. The sociologist Frank Parkin aptly disenchants us about this claim: "Given this fundamental class inequality in the social and economic order, a pluralist or democratic political structure works to the advantage of the dominant class. . . . In the absence of socio-economic preconditions for political equality, pluralism is quite plausibly regarded as a philosophy which tends to reflect the perceptions and interests of a privileged class" (1972: 182). In opposition to the cultural imperialism concealed in procedural majoritarian democracy, philosophers like Iris Marion Young have proposed "group representation" as a principle and mode of implementing an "agenda of building communicatively demo-cratic structures in a society that starts with group-based injustice" (1993: 140; compare Enrique Dussel's idea of "community of life" [1992]). But then, are we resurrecting a version of identity politics here?

I suggest that after criticizing the indeterminacy of the "new social movements" premised on the mystified worship of "civil society," we return to Gramsci's seminal idea of hegemony. Hegemony (rule by a mixture of force and consent via moral-intellectual leadership) involves the process of political struggle that links civil society and state. In elucidating the complex, nuanced mediations between production rela-tions and ideology/culture, Gramsci envisaged the dissolution of civil society—the basis of individualist liberalism—into the superstructure, a process or site of "catharsis." By the latter term, he meant "the passage from the purely economic (egoistic-passional) to the ethico-political moment" (1971: 366), in short, the elaboration of the structure into the superstructure in thought and collective praxis (Bobbio 1979). Collective praxis mediates and interanimates the economic, political, and ideological levels of the social totality. The passage from the objective to the subjective realm, from necessity to freedom, cannot occur if the state is reified as purely coercive (one may ask: what interest motivates the bureaucracy and juridical apparatus to regulate business and private transactions?) and civil society in turn mystified as somehow morally pure, virtuous, and supremely enabling. In fact, the implied glorification of "citizenship" in contemporary civil-society doctrine begs the whole question of how civil society can ever transform political institutions (that is, the state and its tradition of practices) as a separate sphere beyond popular-democratic control. This is the central problem wrestled by Marx in *The Civil War in France* and by Lenin in *State and Revolution*. Moreover, the conquest of hegemony as the result of the struggle between classes/forces in civil society embodying rival ideological principles, competing norms or beliefs that seek to universalize themselves in a "national-popular" discourse combining dominance and directive agency (Urry 1981), is forfeited with the purely moralizing dogma that civil society must be supreme over the state. In effect, despite the proliferation of NGOs in the Philippines and elsewhere, the oppressive status quo is preserved and injustice/inequality renewed as normal everyday routine (see Feffer 1993; Larsen 1995). Ultimately, the market triumphs, private property prevails over all.

SPRINGBOARD FOR INTERVENTION

Critical multiculturalism, as first proposed in the Chicago Cultural Studies Group manifesto of 1990-91, and most provocatively implemented by cultural theorists like Peter McLaren, Henry Giroux, Barbara Harlow, and others, has been theorized to make up for the inadequacies of ethnic-based multiculturalism vitiated by identity politics. The Chicago Group rejects the "romance of authenticity" associated with the demand for recognition of ethnic group identity, considering the "authentic native voice" highly problematic. Its members ask: "What do subalterns have in common except that somehow they are dominated?—a statement so general as to be useless" (1994: 126). Looking back on this document, two of the participants, Lauren Berlant and Michael Warner, continue the trend of bewailing "multicultural" identities "conceived as genetic and iconizing sources of ethnicity, of political validity, and of authenticity." As antithesis to corporate populism, marketized identities, and what they call "postnational" fetishisms of hybridity, the global and postmodern decentered subjectivity, Berlant and Warner conceive of multiculturalism as "a scene of complex and always changing histories that cannot be reduced rhymingly to a face, a postmodern place, or the heritage of an abandoned space" (107). Their version, it seems to me, is a more sophisticated, postmodernist repackaging of liberal pluralism despite their criticism of "the systemic inequities of marketized society." Dreaming of a "self-positioning cultural theory" capable of generating "a strong, transnational, comparative critique," they refuse any Marxist or transformative critique of the dynamics of capitalist reification, of precisely the modalities of late capitalism prefigured in the text of *Grundrisse*. What is bound to result is a "happy family multiculturalism" that, as Cary Nelson contends, aims "to maintain the status quo," "the present uneven distribution of wealth, prestige, and power" (1993: 53). While subscribing to a "resistance post-structuralist approach to meaning and power, the educator Peter McLaren for his part argues for counterhegemonic and collective praxis to attack "the overdetermined structures of race, class, and gender differences" (1995: 137) in the struggle for justice. For McLaren, oppositional agency to injustice in the present system and a politics of transformation can most effectively be articulated in the figure of a "border identity" (inspired by the ideas of Chicana writer Gloria Anzaldua) that is anticapitalist, counterhegemonic, and critically utopian.

With the passage of NAFTA and the New Year's Day uprising of Indian peasants in Chiapas, Mexico, the reality of borders has challenged the incorporative power of the multicultural Imaginary. Class antagonisms are translated into the spatial configuration of nation-state territories linked by "free trade" and immigration, a sociotopological organization of space that reproduces exploitative class and race/ethnic relations. The trope of "borderlands"—border identities, along with the postcolonial rhetoric of "third space of translation" (Bhabha), "shifting multi-place of resistance" (Trinh), speechless subaltern (Spivak), alterity and dialogism, and so on—may capture the affective and transformative potential of what immigration and ethnicity signify for the constitution of metropolitan subjectivity. But however suggestive it is of the decentering processes in flexible, disorganized, global capitalism and its ambivalence, we need to address what Guy Debord calls the "spectacle," the thoroughly mediatized social relation, which seems to be the most nihilistic if not final form of the expropriation and alienation of human sociality itself by the managerial state and corporate business. How can we subvert this spectacularized fate of humanity and recuperate language? How can we mobilize the capacity to speak and enunciate our unrepresentable positions of non-belonging—a devastating political act that all over the planet, for Giorgio Agamben, "unhinges and empties traditions and beliefs, ideologies and religions, identities and communities" (83)?

We might finally locate an answer to that question by looking at one instance of spectacle in which migration of images and representations problematizes the claim of resistance or critical multiculturalism to offer an alternative without going through the detour of the *Grundrisse*. Previously I used the example of Baudrillard's utilization of the Tasaday in his "The Precession of the Simulacra." For this occasion, I take a commentary on neocolonial Filipino society and culture by Arjun Appadurai in his well-known essay "Disjuncture and Difference in the Global Cultural Economy":

> Pico Iyer's own account of the uncanny Philippine affinity for American popular music is rich testimony to the global culture of the "hyper-real," for somehow Philippine renditions of American popular songs are both more widespread in the Philippines and more disturbingly faithful to their originals, than they are in the United States today. An entire nation seems to have learned to mimic Kenny Rogers and the Lennon sisters, like a vast Asian Motown chorus. But Americanization is certainly a pallid term to apply to such a situation, for not only are there more Filipinos singing perfect renditions of some American songs (often from the American past) than there are Americans doing so, there is, of course, the fact that the rest of their lives is not in complete synchrony with the referential world which first gave birth to these songs.
>
> In a further, globalizing twist on what Jameson has recently called "nostalgia for the present," these Filipinos look back to a world they have never lost. This is one of the central ironies of the politics of global cultural flows, especially in the arena of entertainment and leisure. It plays havoc with the hegemony of Eurochronology. American nostalgia feeds on Filipino desire represented as a hyper-competent reproduction. Here we have nostalgia without memory. The paradox, of course, has its explanations, and they are historical; unpacked, they lay bare the story of the American missionization and political rape of the Philippines, one result of which has been the creation of a nation of make-believe Americans, who tolerated for so long a leading lady who played the piano while the slums of Manila expanded and decayed. Perhaps the most radical postmodernists would argue that this is hardly surprising, since in the peculiar chronicities of late capitalism, pastiche and nostalgia are central modes of image production and reception. Americans themselves are hardly in the present

any more as they stumble into the mega-techonologies of the twenty-first
century garbed in the film noir scenarios of the sixties "chills," fifties diners,
forties clothing, thirties houses, twenties dances, and so on ad finitum.
(326)

The observation on the seriality of monadic individualist culture and the
political economy of pastiche and commodified difference are now
received doxa. Appadurai superimposes the postmodern theory of the
"hyper-real" on a historic conjuncture more amply clarified by the
following facts: the nearly total U.S. domination of the music/film/TV
industry in the Philippines; the almost hallucinatory spell of the United
States fantasized as the land of affluence and immigrant success; and the
toleration, nay active complicity, of successive U.S. administrations in
supporting the brutal regime of Cold War ally Ferdinand Marcos and
his "leading lady" against the peaceful and armed resistance of millions
of Filipinos whose "indigenous trajectories of desire and fear," to quote
Appadurai, do not synchronize with global cultural flows. Appadurai also
ignores the heterogeneous temporality of quotidian experience in the
lives of Filipinos neither singing Kenny Rogers songs nor consuming
U.S. goods. The daily construction of their subjectivities and agencies
by modalities of parody, bricolage, and other native resources escape the
postcolonial analyst. Foregoing an inventory of such empirical banalities,
our authority on mimicry and simulation may perform more credibly by
a cognitive mapping of capitalism as the field of alienation (for a recent
example, see Chomsky 1992; 1994)—of labor exploitation, hegemonic
control of ideological State apparatuses, the geopolitical effects of U.S.
military strategy in Asia, and the persistent refeudalizing and recolonizing
of Philippine bodies and minds by the U.S. and its transnational
surrogates. This is not a ploy to rehabilitate a deterministic or reductive
economism in what some call a postrevolutionary and even postcapitalist
world, but simply to recognize and respect—shades of Charles Taylor!—
the substantive, long, and durable history of anticolonial resistance and
popular-democratic insurgency of the Filipino people themselves. Such
a displacement would be a genuine crossing of the border between
periphery and metropolis, the well-nigh insurmountable boundary
between the imperial Self of postcolonial multiculturalism and those
Others, the inscription of whose histories has scarcely begun to unfold.

Revisiting an "Internal Colony": U.S. Asian Cultural Formations and the Metamorphosis of Ethnic Discourse

> *. . . [the Lone Ranger] wore that mask to hide his Asian eyes! . . . And he was lucky Chinaman vengeance on the West . . . I knew the Lone Ranger was the CHINESE AMERICAN BOY of the radio I'd looked for.*
> —Tam Lum, in Frank Chin,
> *The Chickencoop Chinaman*

In the fury and crucible of the sixties, the fable of the American "melting pot" evaporated and a new paradigm gradually replaced it: internal colonialism. One of its eloquent theoreticians was Robert Blauner who, in *Racial Oppression in America* (1972), demarcated the experience of European immigrants from populations of non-Western descent subjugated by a colonizing bureaucratic bloc that monopolized state power. This model has been further refined and elaborated as a "theory of ethnic change" by Michael Hechter in his seminal book, *Internal Colonialism*, to explain the persistence of backwardness in industrial society (in this case, Britain) based on a stratified "cultural division of labor" (1975: 39). Since then, despite sporadic revivals, the concept has fallen into the abyss of chic postmodernist amnesia.

The objections raised against this model deal mainly with supposed exceptions, as in the case of Asians or Puerto Ricans. Let us review first the salient points of this working hypothesis. While classic colonialism conquered and dominated the territories of the peoples of Africa, Asia, and Latin America, European settlers conquered the indigenous inhabitants (North American Indians and Mexicans) of what became the

United States, forcibly enslaved Africans and exploited Asian workers (via state-sanctioned contracts, credit ticket arrangements, and so on). These groups were then reduced to minorities whose cultures, either suppressed or depreciated, gave way to the internalization of the "white supremacist" ethos by castelike subalterns. Spatial demarcations resulted from their subjugation: ghettos, barrios, reservations, and other policed locations controlled by a preponderantly white bureaucracy testify to segregation in residence, education, politics, occupation, and practically all areas of social life. Institutional mechanisms of subordination are more important than control of territory. The structural disadvantage of the internally colonized subjects springs from the logic of their differential incorporation into the U.S. polity, not whether there was actually a process of voluntary or forced entry. The cases of Puerto Rico (still a colony glamorized with the euphemism of "free associated state"), the Philippines, Guam, and to some extent Hawaii and Cuba easily substantiate Blauner's thesis.

When Blauner initiated this "third world perspective," he was careful to emphasize the historical specificity of "internal colonialism" in a settler formation so that its variation from traditional European colonialism could be highlighted. The caveat is important. What distinguishes internal colonialism in the United States is "the more total cultural domination" of people of color, their alienation from a land base, and their numerical size (74-75) all of which are effects of a thoroughgoing institutionalization of white supremacy—not just the ideology— and a complex panoply of racist practices that informs the logic of the prevailing social order. Contrasting this view with the assimilationist model, cultural critic John Liu (1976) underscores the political and economic struggles between the colonizer and the colonized; the latter are not just passive actors but "active participants" in the class war that produces and reproduces the system. What makes internal colonialism of permanent significance is, to my mind, the constitutive linkage established between the periphery and metropolis: "The communities of color in America share essential conditions with third world nations abroad: economic underdevelopment, a heritage of colonialism and neocolonialism, and a lack of real political economy and power" (Blauner: 72). Not only does this method of appraising the plight of the colonized minorities enable us to understand the causes of the 1992 Los Angeles "uprising"; it also helps us understand the dynamics of the new racial politics of fragmentation, ethnic absolutism, and neoliberal individualism. In addition, the model's framework of interaction and interdependency between the transnational corporate interests head-quartered in the United States and the labor/resource markets of Asia, Africa, and Latin America makes possible our comprehension of the salient global trends surveyed by texts like *The New Asian Immigration in Los Angeles and Global Retructuring* (1994) edited by Paul Ong, Edna Bonacich, and Lucie Cheng. From a distance of twenty years since the paradigm was proposed and debated, one may now inquire into what sort of mutations the Asian American "internal colony" has undergone—indeed, whether postcoloniality has overtaken it and decolonization fully installed, thus vindicating "American exceptionalism" beyond our wild-est dreams.

FROM PANETHNICITY TO A NEW DIALOGIC ALLIANCE

In this age of postality (post–Cold War, post–Civil Rights, postcolonial), one would expect that the public perception of Asian Americans—I prefer the term "U.S. Asians" to avoid any hint of successful assimilation or unqualified acculturation—would now be past stereotypes, myths, clichés. Not so. One recent textbook easily splices the narrative of the European "immigrant's quest for the American dream" with the "racial minority's" victimization "by discriminating laws and attitudes" (Dudley 1997: 14). In a revealing analysis of Judge Karlin's sentencing colloquy in the 1992 trial of Du Soon Ja (accused killer of the African American child Natasha Harlins), Neil Gotanda found that old stereotypes are alive and well, fruitfully cohabiting with the new "model minority" doxa. Old paradigms are thriving even as *pax Americana* retools and refurbishes itself. Amid the thoroughgoing reconfiguration of the planet's geopolit-ical/economic map, why this persistence of a racializing syndrome with respect to U.S. Asians?[1]

By the year 2020, the population labeled "Asian Americans" in this country will number 20.2 million. The Asian Pacific population increased from 1.5 million in 1970 to 7.3 million in 1990, with the Filipinos becoming the largest component (more than 2 million, up from 1,406,770 in the 1990 Census Report [Gonzales: 181]) followed by the Indochinese group (Patel 1992). In California, the projection is that Asians will grow from 2.9 million to 8.5 million in 2020. The Filipinos are the majority Asians in California, but they are still considered pariahs: at the University of California in Berkeley, the treatment of Filipinos may be conceived as a symptom of benign "ethnic cleansing." Articulated with manifold interethnic conflicts amid large-scale social crisis, this change is bound to complicate and intensify the multiplication of differences enough to confound taxonomists and the high priests of a normative "common culture."

Given the heterogeneity of the histories, economic stratification, and cultural composition of the post-1965 immigrants and refugees, all talk of Asian pan-ethnicity should now be abandoned as useless and even harmful speculation. Not so long ago, historian Roger Daniels stated the obvious: "The conglomerate image of Asian Americans is a chimera." This is more true today. No longer sharing the common pre–World War II experience of being hounded by exclusion acts, antimiscegenation laws, and other disciplinary apparatuses of racialization, Vietnamese, Kampucheans, and Hmongs have now diverged from the once dominant pattern of settlement, occupation, education, family structure, and other modes of ethnic identification. (It is even more aggravating to reckon with the presence of Thais, Malaysians, Bangladeshis, not to mention distinctive Pacific Islanders.) After 1965, one can no longer postulate a homogeneous "Asian American" bloc without reservations. Fragmentation now characterizes this bloc even as new forms of racism totalize the incompatible subject-positions of each nationality. To use current jargon, the bureaucratic and flattening category "Asian American" (contrived by census and statistics wizards of the state) has been decentered by systemic contingencies. The putatively homogeneous inhabitants of the Asiatic "barred zone" (ascribed by the immigration laws of 1917 and 1924) have been deconstructed beyond repair to the point where today, among postality scholars, a cult of multiple and indeterminate subject-positions is flourishing. However, we have yet to meet a cyborg or borderland denizen of confirmed U.S. Asian genealogy.

Despite such changes, versions of the "melting pot" theory are still recycled to homogenize variegated multitudes. A patriotic dogma of pluralist "common culture" is utilized to deny politically significant mutations and realignments among the citizenry. A monograph of the Population Reference Bureau on *Asian Americans: America's Fastest Growing Minority Group* by William O'Hare and Judy Felt, while acknowledging disparities, lumps its subjects indiscriminately: "While Asian Americans have slightly higher average family incomes than non-Hispanic whites, they also have much higher poverty rates" (O'Hare and Felt 1991: 15). A recent textbook, *Asian Americans* (1995), edited by Pyong Gap Min, for example, has no hesitation predicting that Asians will be easily assimilated in time. While admitting the perception that language barriers still exist and the old stereotypes of disloyal or enemy aliens still affect mainstream perception, Min relies on three factors that will promote rapid assimilation: (1) the presence of well-assimilated, native-born Asian Americans will eliminate the image of the "stranger," (2) multiculturalism or cultural pluralism will promote the toleration of "subcultural differences," and (3) the economic and political power of Asian nation-states will create a positive image in general. In sum, Americanization translates into the promotion of tolerance via consumerist "multiculturalism" backed by the economic power of Japan and the Asian "tigers." These reasons can be canceled by a few arguments whose suasive force has still not been properly registered.

The accommodationist posture typified here refuses to take seriously what I call the Vincent Chin syndrome (see United States Commission on Civil Rights 1992): political demagoguery in times of socioeconomic crisis can shift the target of scapegoating onto any Asian-looking "object" that can reactivate the sedimented persona of the wily, inscrutable, shifty-eyed foreigner in "our" midst. The second reason pertaining to multiculturalism is fallacious since "cultural pluralism" has been around since the attenuation of the Anglo-Saxon supremacy/nativist movement; multiculturalism is now, for the most part, a rehabilitated version of white supremacy, the enshrined co-optative formula for peacefully managing differences among the subalterns (San Juan 1995c). And finally, the process of acculturation of second- or third-generation U.S. Asians has been qualified (by Min himself) as valid only for the cultural, and not the social, dimension. In fact, the sociological data leads to this seemingly paradoxical conclusion: "Although the vast majority of second-generation Asian Americans will lose their native language and cultural tradition, they are likely to maintain a strong ethnic identity and to interact mainly with coethnics" (Min: 279). Acculturation, then, heightens ethnic difference and even fosters separatism.

Given this persistence of the ethnicity paradigm forcefully criticized in the eighties by Michael Omi and Howard Winant in *Racial Formations in the United States,* commentators on the Asian scene still toe the party line of Glazer and Moynihan (1975). As their colleague Werner Sollors (1986) put it, ethnicity is not a matter of descent or lineage, but "of the importance that individuals ascribe to it." Form determines content. In his pathbreaking book cited at the outset, Robert Blauner repudiated the fallacy of subsuming the diverse experiences of subjugation of people of color under the ethnic immigrant model that privileges the teleology of Eurocentric assimilation in defining the character of the U.S. nation-state (see also Takaki 1987). But obviously the lessons have not been learned (Steinberg 1995). Or else the specter of "American exceptional-ism" has a way of being resurrected, especially in periods of crisis and neoconservative resurgence. Pan-ethnicity arises within this conjuncture. It may be construed as one specimen of the ideological recuperation of what I would call the Myrdal complex (the presumed schizoid nature of U.S. democracy preaching equality but institutionalizing exclusionary and oppressive practices) that plagues all utilitarian liberal thought, including its radical and pragmatic variants.[2]

Asian American pan-ethnicity has been promoted by Yen Le Espiritu and others as a historical product of the unity and solidarity of "internally colonized" Asian minorities during the sixties. The pan-Asian framework supposedly arose from the common experience of oppression of Chinese, Japanese, and Filipino workers, students, and middle strata, under-pinned by the ideological conception of "Orientals" in the majoritarian consciousness and institutions (Hamamoto 1994). Espiritu explains the origin of the change: "To define their own image and to claim an American identity, college students of Asian ancestry coined the term Asian American to stand for all of us Americans of Asian descent. . . . While Oriental suggests passivity and acquiescence, Asian American connotes political activism because an Asian American gives a damn about his life, his work, his beliefs, and is willing to do almost anything to help Orientals become Asian Americans" (1996: 57). The first pan-Asian political organization founded in Berkeley in 1969, the Asian American Political Alliance, was mainly composed of students, mostly third- and fourth-generation Asian activists. In the seventies, pan-Asian organizations among social workers, media, public health, and other fields mushroomed, but—as Espiritu herself acknowledges—pan-Asianism "barely touched the Asian ethnic enclaves" (1996: 58). Despite its reflection of a need for principled unity to overcome institutional racism, this version of pan-Asianism concealed the ethnic chauvinisms and class cleavages, hierarchy, and conflicts generated by the operation of U.S. racializing politics or inherited from imperial divide-and-rule policies. The "cultural entrepreneurs" of pan-Asianism turned out to be agents for opportunist electoral politics, lobbyists for middle-class interests, and brokers for the bureaucratic utilitarian, get-rich-quick ethos. This trend accelerated even when Asians (associated with the competitive challenge of the Pacific Rim "tigers") were being collectively perceived as a threat by blacks and other minority groups. These pan-Asianists served as the progenitors of the post-1980s Asian neoconserva-tives who glorify the "model minority" stereotype while opposing affirmative action and social programs for the disadvantaged, thus nurturing the seeds for the Los Angeles explosion of April 1992.

The more profound motivation for pan-Asianism is the historically specific racism of white supremacy toward Asians. As Sucheng Chan noted in her interpretive history: "In their relationship to the host society, well-to-do merchants and poor servants, landowning farmers and propertyless farm workers, exploitative labor contractors and exploited laborers alike were considered inferior to all Euro-Americans, regardless of the internal ethnic and socio-economic divisions among the latter" (187). Instead of valorizing ethnicity or cultural difference per se, we need to concentrate on what Robert Miles (1989) calls the "racialization" process, its ideological and institutional articulations, within the framework of the capitalist world system. For this, a world-systems analysis (see Wallerstein and Balibar 1991) is useful and necessary.[3]

Ethnicization and racism can be properly understood only within the context of the national/international division of social labor. In a suggestive essay, "The Construction of Peoplehood," Wallerstein argued that the varying usages of people, race, nation, and ethnicity stem from their function in expressing political claims whose legitimacy depends on the historical structure of the capitalist world-economy. While "race" concerns the axial division of labor in the world economy (the core-periphery antinomy), nation refers to the political superstructure of this historical system (sovereign states in the interstate system). Wallerstein explains that "ethnic group" is the concept designating "household structures that permit the maintenance of large components of non-waged labour in the accumulation of capital" (79). Given the differential costs of production in the core-periphery system, we have differing internal political structures that serve as the "major sustaining bulwark of the inegalitarian state system that manages and maintains the axial division of labor" today. Race and racism "is the expression, the promoter and the consequence of the geographical concentration associated with the axial division of labour" (179-80). While race/racism and nation/nationalism function as categories that register competing claims for advantage in the capitalist world economy, it is ethnicization conceived as the distinctive cultural socialization of the work force that enables the complex occupational hierarchy of labor (marked by differential allocation of surplus value, class/status antagonisms, etc.) to be legitimized without contradicting the formal equality of citizens before the law in liberal-democratic polities. Wallerstein points out that capitalism gains flexibility in restructuring itself to preserve its legitimacy, hence the unconscionable exploitation of the multicultural work force in the "free trade zones" of Mexico, the Philippines, Malaysia, the Caribbean, and so on. Wallerstein writes: "Ethnicization, or peoplehood, resolves one of the basic contradictions of historical capitalism—its simultaneous thrust for theoretical equality and practical inequality" by exploiting the mentalities of the segmented working populace. In this way, people-based political activity, or the new social movements premised on authentic identities and autonomy of communities, arise because of the contradictions of the system. Ethnicity, then, is not a primordial category that testifies to the virtue of a *laissez-faire* market-centered system but a means utilized to legitimate the contradictions of a plural society premised on racial hierarchy, also sometimes labelled a "*Herrenvolk* democracy*" (Van den Berghe 1967). This is not to imply that we should return to the orthodox Marxist view that dividing workers according to race or ethnicity is a conspiratorial tool by capital to destroy class unity. What I would stress is precisely the need to analyze the racialization of ethnicized class/gendered identities (initially enslaved, conquered, or colonized). In the United States, "whiteness" mediates individual/group conceptions of self, gender, community, and class interest, so that the traditional cost-benefit calculations of economists cannot be valid unless linked "to the self-understanding of workers creating and consenting to whiteness as a culture and political economy of domination" (R. Williams 1995: 307).

In the context of our inquiry, the term "whiteness" alludes to the sociopolitical constitution of the various European cohorts as a hegemonic collectivity coinciding with the history of the formation of the U.S. nation-state as a "settler society." To avoid the trap of multiculturalism as a discourse of formalistically reconciling ethnic differences, we need to recall how the founders of the U.S. nation-state "legitimated and perpetuated . . . the plural society of a racially bifurcated colonist America regulated by the normative code of a racial creed" (Benjamin Ringer, quoted in Janiewski 1995). The "settler society" paradigm (instead of the immigrant model), which sanctioned racially based subordination of nonwhite groups and communities (indigenous, enslaved, conquered), entails the corollary notion of "internal colonialism." The notion of "internal colonialism" involves juridical and state apparatuses that legitimized the exploitation of minorities in segmented labor markets, hierarchical wage scales, residential segregation, and other effects of numerous discriminatory practices by employers and state apparatuses (Stasiulis and Yuval-Davis 1995). Implicitly subscribing to the doctrine of "American exceptionalism" and its associated ethos of laissez-faire multiculturalism, postmodernist racial-formation theory fails to grasp the fundamental fact of institutional racism in the U.S., as well as the reality of North-South contradictions and its replication within the metropoles of North America and Europe—the division between rich white nations versus poor nations comprised of people of color—that exemplifies today the most insidiously dehumanizing form of racism (Rex 1982) sustaining worldwide capital accumulation.

Recent scholarship on the ideological construction of "whiteness" in U.S. history should illuminate also the invention of "Asian American" as a monolithic, standardizing rubric. It is clear that the diverse collectivities classified by official bureaucracy as "Asian American" manifest more discordant features than affinities and commonalities. The argument that they share similar values (Confucian ethics, for example), ascribed "racial" characteristics, and kindred interests in politics, education, social services, and so on, cannot be justified by the historical experiences of the peoples involved, especially those who came after World War II. This does not mean that U.S. Asians did not and do not now engage in coalitions and alliances to support certain causes or cooperate for mutual benefit; examples are numerous. In fact, the insistence on pan-Asianism can only obscure if not obfuscate the enduring problems of underemployment and unequal reward ("glass ceiling"), occupational segregation, underrepresentation, and class polarization obscured by the "model minority" mania that sustains the American dream of success. One need only cite the high rates of poverty among Asian refugees: 26 percent for Vietnamese, 35 percent for Laotians, 43 percent for Cambodians, and 64 percent for the Hmongs (Kitano and Daniels 1995: 179). All studies also show that most Filipinos today find themselves condemned to the secondary labor market—low-wage jobs in the private sector—in spite of higher educational attainment (Nee and Sanders 1985; Cabezas and Kawaguchi 1989; for a general survey, see Ong 1994).

At this point, some conscientious readers might already be ruminating about "model minority," the contemporary version of the "yellow peril" that used to haunt white supremacist America. Lest we be overwhelmed by all the optimistic predictions of impending assimilation/acculturation of U.S. Asians into the larger body politic, I offer as a reminder this concluding observation of the United States Commission on Civil Rights in its 1992 Report:

The root causes of bigotry and violence against Asian Americans are complex. Racial prejudice; misplaced anger caused by wars or economic competition with Asian countries; resentment of the real or perceived success of Asian Americans; and a lack of understanding of the histories, customs, and religions of Asian Americans all play a role in triggering incidents of bigotry and violence. The media have contributed to prejudice by promoting stereotypes of Asian Americans, especially the model minority stereotype; by sometimes highlighting the criminal activities of Asian gangs; and by failing to provide the indepth and balanced coverage that would help the public to understand the diverse Asian American population. Furthermore, the media give little attention to hate crimes against Asian Americans, thereby hindering the formation of a national sense of outrage about bigotry and violence against Asian Americans, a critical ingredient for social change. (1992: 191)

Faced with the racial politics of the eighties and nineties, all talk about fashioning or searching for an "authentic Asian American identity" and "reclaiming" our history can only sound fatuous. More culpable is the view that in order to transcend the Frank Chin–Maxine Hong Kingston misrecognition of each other, U.S. Asian artists should utilize their "ethnic sensibility to describe aspects of the Asian American experience that appeal to a common humanity" (Wei: 357)—a plea for commodifying the exoticized as plain American pie. To conceive of the "Asian American Movement" in terms of its place in the hegemonic scheme of things is to submit to the rules of the game contrived and manipulated by the very forces the egalitarian movement is supposed to overthrow.

A study made in 1991 concluded that the economic success story of U.S. Asians is undermined by two facts: their reward is not commensurate with their educational attainment, and that they have higher poverty rates than non-Hispanic whites (Woo 1989). The myth of the "model minority" persists in obscuring these facts. Because of this, U.S. Asians are collectively perceived as a threat by other minority groups, especially blacks in New York, Washington D.C., and Los Angeles and whites who fear the competitive power of Pacific Rim countries. Asian Americans are thus caught between two antithetical pressures: "On one hand, Asian Americans are lauded as a 'model minority' that is fulfilling the American dream and confirming the image of America as a 'melting pot.' On the other hand, they seem hampered by invisible barriers—a so-called glass ceiling—that keep them from climbing to the top rungs of power" (O'Hare and Felt 1991: 15). What is clearly configuring the dilemma is the contradiction between ideology—the imaginary mode of connecting subjects to reality—and the limits of a racialized political economy, the constraints of transnational, late capitalism.

On the face of these developments, postmodernism enters the scene and proclaims the ontological imperatives of hybridity, multiplicity, and fragmentation as a more viable optic for analyzing the situation. Keith Osajima, for example, proposes a synthetic postmodernism that will combine the virtues of panethnic generalizing with "the multiplicitous nature of our constructed identities" (1995: 83). Ethnic absolutism translates into "identity politics." In general, postmodernists uphold anti-essentialist, fluctuating or ambiguous subject-positions premised on the rejection of "grand metanarratives," rationally constituted agency, and the normative discourse of justice and equality (Stabile 1995). A typical enunciation of this theoretical standpoint may be discerned in Lisa Lowe's thesis: "A multiplicity of social contradictions with different origins converge at different sites within any social formation—the family, education, religion, communications media, sites of capitalist production—and each is uneven and incommensurable, with certain contradictions taking priority over others in response to the material conditions of a given historical moment" (1995: 46). Following the poststructuralist semiotics of Ernesto Laclau and Chantal Mouffe (see the critique of Hunter 1988-89), postmodernists celebrate the alleged dispersal of power into shifting and arbitrary sites of the social field. This move, I submit, effectively disables any long-range collective project of discovering a possible Archimedean point at which the whole system can be dismantled. This is because it does not address the key aspects of the legitimation crisis subtending the production-and-reproduction dynamics of the U.S. formation inter alia: the racializing agencies of "whiteness" in a settler society, the political economy of "internal colonialism," and the continuing injustices and oppression fomented by institutional racism.

Incalculable damage has been inflicted by a postmodernist skepticism that sometimes has claimed to be more revolutionary than the rigorous guidelines of research into internal colonialism, labor segmentation, national self-determination, and so on. This does not mean we don't have the traditional individualistic, aestheticizing trends represented by writers like Garrett Hongo, Gish Jen, and any number of assimilationist would-be celebrities (see Hongo 1995). The ubiquitous troupe of Lotus Blossoms and Gunga Dins, now of course sporting more fashionable trappings, still dominate the traveling roadshows of "Asian American" cultural production today. Probably the most provocative application of Foucaultian and deconstructive tools in analyzing U.S. racial politics is Omi and Winant's aforementioned work (1986). But its inadequacy demonstrated itself in being unable to anticipate the 1992 Los Angeles inter-ethnic conflict between blacks and Korean Americans, nor could it foresee the rise of neoconservatives among Asian Americans (San Juan 1992b). By devaluing the role of ideological state apparatuses and the political economy of labor in globalized capitalism, postmodernist thinking remains trapped in a metaphysics of textualism and an ontology of pragmatic "language games" that only reinforce the unequal division of labor and the unjust hierarchy of power in U.S. society and in the domain of international relations.[4]

One example of postmodernist speculation that substitutes for the now obsolete pan-ethnicity a notion of transnational subjectivity may be cited here. It doesn't require Superman's x-ray vision for us to tell that the paragon of the diasporic subject as a postcolonial "hybrid" often masks the working of a dominant "common culture" premised on differences, not contradictions. Heterogeneity can then be a ruse for recuperative patriotism. The latest version is the theory of "multiple identities" and "fluid" positions of immigrants (for example, Filipino professionals in the eighties and nineties) straddling two nation-states assumed to be of equal status and ranking in the world system; such identities are deemed unique because they allegedly participate in the political economies of both worlds. This is obviously a paradigm based on the dynamics of market exchange-value whereby assorted goods can be made equivalent. Through the mediation of export-import trade and travel, a third abstract entity emerges and circulates between two incommensurable objects or domains, supposedly partaking of both but identical with neither. The artifactual entity is the transnational migrant whose status, however, remains parasitic on the superior nation-state (the United States), belying its claim to autonomy and integrity. I submit that the fatal mistake of the transnational model is analogous to that of pan-ethnicity: despite its gesture of acknowledging political and ideological differences, it assumes the parity of colonized/dominated peoples and the U.S. nation-state in the global ranking of sovereign powers.

Because of the seductive potential of this new theorizing, I would like to comment on Yen Le Espiritu's recent study, *Filipino American Lives* (1995). In it she applies the new conceptual model of transnationalism. When post-1965 second- and third-generation Filipinos (mostly professionals) devise strategies to construct multiple and overlapping identities, thus presumably altering their rank or placing in U.S. society, they succeed (for Espiritu) in resisting the dominant ideology of subordination by race, class, gender, nationality, and so on. While the self-interpretation of Espiritu's informants does contain indices of flux rather than continuity, multilinear lines of narrative rather than one monologic strand, I think this is not due to their overall success in elevating their country and culture of origin to equal status with the United States and its hegemonic norms. This rationale is apologetic and ahistorical. Such idealist subjectivism wreaks havoc on any honest inquiry into the nature of agency and accountability in history. All kinds of fallacious judgments stem from the error of marginalizing the colonial subjugation of the Filipino people by the United States, directly from 1898 to 1946 and indirectly from 1946 to the present (San Juan 1996b; Campomanes 1996).

The resourceful cunning and prudence of Filipino immigrants in trying to survive and flourish in a generally inhospitable environment (San Diego, California, is implicitly assumed to be representative of the whole country) should not be unilaterally construed as a sign of postmodern playfulness and inventiveness. Mindful of the historical relationship between subaltern people and colonizing state, one should interpret Filipino ethnic strategies as symptoms of the colonial trauma and the ordeal of enduring its revival in new forms, this time in the heartland of the imperial power. Because of this, most Filipinos seek assimilation and welcome acculturation; but experiences of racist insult, discrimination, ostracism, and violence disrupt their modes of adaptation and suspend their psyches in a limbo of symbolic ethnicity if not political indeterminacy. This is not a bipolar state oscillating between nostalgic nativism and coercive Europeanization; it is a diasporic predicament born of the division of labor in the world system and the racialization of people of color by capital accumulation (Wolf 1982; Miles 1986).

Without disavowing other limitations of Espiritu's theoretical apparatus and its neglect of contemporary social problems (poverty, teen pregnancy, gang violence, AIDS, drug abuse, and so on) for most Filipinos, I take issue with the positivistic reading of the narratives of Americanization that ignore the symptoms I have alluded to. Espiritu's informants Ruby, Armando, and Elaine, for example, all invoke a distinctive Filipino history that belies Espiritu's claim that Filipino ethnicity lacks "a practiced culture" (1994: 265). It is a truism that for all neocolonized or (to use current jargon) transculturated subjects in the conjuncture of the post-1965 United States, the process of survival involves constant renegotiation of cultural spaces, revision of inherited folkways, simultaneous abrogation and reappropriation of dominant practices, and invention of new patterns of adjustment. All these embody the resistance *habitus* of peoples attempting to transcend subalternity (see Theo Gonzalves' [1995] testing of this hypothesis in his analysis of Pilipino Cultural Night in California). What is crucial is how and why a specific repertoire of practices is enabled by the structures of civil society, the state, and the disposition of the agents themselves. When Filipinos therefore construct the meaning of their lives (whether you label this meaning Filipino American, U.S. Filipino, Americanized Pinoys, the content determines the form), they don't—contrary to Espiritu's claim—simultaneously conform to and resist the hegemonic racializing ideology. This implies a reservoir of free choices that don't exist for most subjugated communities. Indeed the construction of a nascent Filipino identity as a dynamic, complex phenomenon defies both assimilationist and pluralist models when it affirms its antiracist, counterhegemonic antecedent: the long-lived revolutionary opposition of the Filipino people to U.S. imperial domination.[5]

Certain recent developments, particularly the emergence of U.S. Asian neoconservatives (described by Glenn Omatsu [1994]) and the tension between Korean Americans and black communities, direct our focus to the fierce class war waged by the U.S. corporate elite against both the U.S. working masses and their international rivals (Japan, Germany). Meanwhile, the value produced by unpaid labor continues to be expropriated from thousands of Asian and Latino women in the sweatshops of the metropolis and "Third World" borderlands called "free trade zones." I would like to mention here the presence of six million Filipino "contract workers" engaged in domestic and low-paid or demeaning work in the Middle East, Hong Kong, Singapore, Japan, and many European countries.[6]

New post–Cold War realignments compel us to return to a historical materialist analysis of political economy and its overdeterminations in order to grasp the new racial politics of transnationality (Bruin 1996). This has also been described as "Coca-culturalism" which, according to Henry Louis Gates (1996: 60) is "a mode of market penetration that in part alters local environments and in part conforms to them, in a process of mutual adaptation." How mutual is it really? Let me hasten to add that I am not advocating a vulgar Marxist (that is, economistic or mechanical deterministic) approach in understanding race/ethnic relations. What may prove revitalizing for the post-1965 generation is a creative return to the "basics," perhaps a counterfundamentalism that Richard Appelbaum reformulates in these terms:

> Capitalism has always reinforced class divisions with divisions based on race, ethnicity, gender, and other forms of ascription. In any system based to a large degree on the exploitation of one group of people by another, such distinctions provide a useful basis for justifying inequality. Not only does this foster a "divide-and-conquer" ideology among those who otherwise might find common cause, but it also helps to foster a standard of exploitation based on what is accorded the least common denominator—whichever group finds itself at the bottom of the economic heap. (313)

Together with Appelbaum's elucidation of global capitalism's flexibility instanced by the subcontracting modes of manipulating the commodity chains, we can learn from Edna Bonacich's analysis (1996) of how the Los Angeles garment industry deploys multiculturalism to cut production costs and increase surplus value (see Yamato et al 1993: 135). In the light of these reconfigurations, we need not an ethnic politics for moderating the private expropriation of the social surplus but a counterhegemonic strategy that articulates the imperatives of ethnicity, gender, sexuality, place, and so on—the major coordinates of cultural identity—with class-based resistance and other oppositional trends charted within the political economy of racist exploitation and oppression. Such a united-front politics can be viable only within a larger framework of a wide-ranging program targeting the material foundation of iniquitous power and reification in the commodity logic of unequal exchange. This return of the "internal colony," now a multinational assemblage based on "piece work" and casuals, requires linkages with millions around the world who suffer this streamlining of disaggregated, flexible, post-Fordist capitalism.

Think globally, act locally—the slogan has more than timely resonance for those optimists of the will and pessimists of the intellect. With respect to the Asian/Pacific Rim countries whose destinies now seem more closely tied to the vicissitudes of unequal exchange as well as indebtedness to the World Bank-International Monetary Fund, the reconfiguring of corporate capital's strategy in dealing with this area requires more astute analysis of the flow of migrant labor, capital investments, media manipulation, tourism, and so on. There are over a million Filipinos (chiefly women) employed as domestics and low-skilled workers in Hong Kong, Singapore, Japan, Taiwan, Korea, and Malaysia.

Their exploitation is worsened by the racializing process of inferiorization imposed by the Asian nation-states, the Asian "tigers," competing for their share in global capital accumulation. The Western press then reconfigures the Asian as neo-Social Darwinist denizen of booty capitalism in the "New World Order."

All these recent developments inevitably resonate in the image of the Asian—its foreignness, malleability, affinities with the West—that in turn determines a complex tissue of contradictory and variable attitudes toward U.S.-domiciled Asians. Such attitudes can be read from the drift of the following questions: Is Japan always going to be portrayed as the scapegoat for the loss of U.S. jobs? Is China obdurately refusing to conform to Western standards in upholding human rights and opening the country to the seductions of market individualism? What's going to happen to Hong Kong? What about "mail order" brides from the Philippines and Thailand as possible carriers of AIDS virus? Are the Singaporeans that barbaric? How is the Hawaii sovereignty movement going to affect the majoritarian perception of the "natives"? And despite the end of history in this post–Cold War milieu, will the North Koreans continue to be the exemplars of communist "barbarism"? Are the North Koreans hopelessly atavistic and irredeemable?

In effect, given the demographic and sociopolitical rearticulation of U.S. Asian collectivities, we have not even begun to address what Nancy Fraser (1995) calls the redistribution-recognition dilemma, that is, how political-economic justice and cultural justice can be realized together by transformative means instead of refurbishing liberal nostrums so popular among people of color in the mainstream academy. In short, the challenge of a radical democratic critique still needs to be taken up as we confront the disintegration of pan-Asian metaphysics and transcultural discourse amid the post–Cold War realignments of nation-states and North/South power blocs.

A strategy of pacification is being mounted to contain dissidence and disruption from unruly sectors of the U.S. Asian populace as world recession deepens. One indication is the multiculturalist approach deployed by Stanley Karnow and Nancy Yoshihara in a monograph published by the Asia Society in 1992. I juxtapose two passages, the first from the Introduction where the "model minority myth" and a naive Orientalism find renewed life:

> But despite their dissimilarities, Asian Americans share common charac-
> teristics. Whether their backgrounds are Confucian, Buddhist, Hindi,

Muslim, Christian or animist, they tend to adhere to the concept of filial piety, and see achievement as a way to honor their families. Hence their devotion to classic American virtues—hard work, discipline and a willingness to defer instant fulfillment for the sake of future goals. Above all, they make enormous sacrifices to educate their children—a commitment that reflects their esteem for scholarship, supposedly assures success and also raises their own social status.

By national standards, the aggregate accomplishments of Asian Americans are spectacular. [Here follows a listing of statistics whose veracity and implications are at best questionable.] Forever seeking to enshrine the American dream, the news media constantly extol Asian Americans as Horatio Alger heroes. Professor William Petersen, a sociologist at Berkeley, called them the "model minority"—a term, wrote Louis Winnick in *Commentary* recently, that is yesterday's coinage: "By now, Asian Americans have vaulted to a more exalted station—America's trophy population."

Next consider this observation from the section on "Politics":

Apart from Japanese Americans, most Asian Americans are immigrants. Many though not all come from countries with despotic and corrupt regimes, and are either unacquainted with the democratic process or distrust government. Many are riveted more on news from their homelands than on events in America.

The fissure between the patronizing endorsement of the "model minority" archetype and the factual errors compounded with a self-righteous paternalism betrayed by the second quotation is not as wide as it seems. For both stances are symptomatic of the doctrine that Asian immigrants, like all aliens, should be measured against a white supremacist standard, a measure that precisely guarantees the hegemony of capital's "civilizing mission" that is now being challenged by its unruly subalterns in core and periphery. I think that U.S. Asian scholarship, despite the avantgarde triumphalist voice of its postmodernist faction, has not been able to grapple successfully with this old but persistent and even revitalized episteme. This failure vitiates all conversation about revising this invidious immigrant or national paradigms since the ghosts of the past, unless we settle accounts with them, will forever continue to haunt us in our future peregrinations and sabotage all attempts at liberation.

THE VALUE FORMS OF ETHNIC DISCOURSE: ON CURRENT
TRENDS IN ASIAN AMERICAN LITERARY CRITICISM

Given the context of local/global changes articulating the "internal colony" mapped above, what is this thing called in the academy "Asian American studies"?

Despite the decentering of the sociopolitical entity labeled by the official census as "Asian American," a distinctive rhetoric and discourse called "Asian American" seems to be in the process of emerging as a hegemonic qualifier in current academic criticism. But can such a monologic, unitary discourse be sustained as a viable project? Can there be such an ontological category as "Asian American literature"?

In 1973, this ontological question was confronted head on by the "four musketeers," the editors of the now legendary Asian American anthology *Aiiieeeeee!:* Frank Chin, Jeffery Paul Chan, Lawson Inada, and Shawn Wong. Their introduction, "Fifty Years of Our Whole Voice," as well as the separate "Introduction to Filipino American Literature" by Sam Solberg, an Anglo European teacher of Korean at the University of Washington (which replaced the original by Filipino American writers), sought to provide an initial mapping of the ground for an answer. Looking back after "seventeen years," in 1991, the four editors found that their fellow intellectuals/travelers have not cultivated that patch of the backyard seeded earlier by samples of their works, so they supplied their *The Big Aiiieeeee!* In their 1991 preface to the Mentor edition of the first book, Chin *et al* bewailed the fact that there are still no critics: "No one has made the case for an Asian American literary tradition based on the Asian American literature in history" (1991: xxv).[7]

This lack or insufficiency is one of the "discontents" registered by inhabitants of this particular region of the ethnic cosmos. Ghettoized and marginalized, virtually still invisible in spite of the victories of the vanguard party of multiculturalism in the wars of "political correctness," writers, scholars, and critics engaged in the production of knowledge about Asian American culture may have reason to complain when one sees their African American and Chicano counterparts becoming celebrities on talk shows, academic conferences, and other venues. To be sure, *Aiiieeeee!* initiated the identification of "touchstones" and paragons of a singular textuality: for example, Mori, Yamamoto, and Okada, among others. In what is known today as "the politics of recognition," it seems that one can never fully get what one thinks one deserves. In our presumably pluralist but scarcely egalitarian society, all we might get is a compromise. For Ambrose Bierce, a compromise is "such an adjustment of conflicting interests as gives each adversary the satisfaction of thinking he has got what he ought not to have, and is deprived of nothing except what was justly his due" (18). Chin and company refuse the compromise of hyphenation, of dialogism. For them, the melting pot cannot be shattered and second-class citizenship ended by invoking origins in the variegated thickness and self-referentiality of classical Chinese, Indian, and Japanese antiquity.

I would like to frame the following reflections on the emergence of an "Asian American" textuality or imagination with some mundane demographic facts culled from government statistics about the population referred to as "Asian Americans"—after all, there seems to be an artifactual constituency whose borders, though contingent, can be traced in the genealogy of institutions, power relations, and discursive practices.

In 1990, Asians and Pacific Islanders total 7,274 million, 2.9 percent of the U.S. population comprised of 80.3 percent whites, 12.1 percent blacks, and 9 percent Latinos. The three largest of twenty-four ethnic groups in the APA category are the Chinese (1,645,472), Filipino (1,406,770), and the Japanese (847,562), followed by Indians, Koreans, and Vietnamese. Hawaiians number only 211,014. By the year 2000, extrapolations indicate that Filipinos will be the largest (2,070,571), followed by the Chinese (1,683,537), Vietnamese (1,574,385), and Koreans (1,320, 759).

Per capita income of Asian Americans as a whole in 1989 was $13,806, slightly below the national per capita income of $14,143. Because more family members work, the media family income was $41,583 compared to the general median income of $35,225. Does this make Asians a "model minority"? Despite higher educational attainment on the average, 14 percent were classified as living in poverty compared to 13 percent of the total population. The poverty rate for those who arrived in the 1980s was 22 percent compared to those who came before; the highest percentages were those of Hmong (64 percent), Cambodians (43 percent), Laotians (35 percent) and Vietnamese (26 percent). Recently the right-wing pundit Charles Murray, who should know his figures, called Asians the "cognitive elite," which I take it refers to their substantial numbers (particularly Chinese and Asian Indians) in college campuses, but nowhere are APAs in command of conglomerates and their political-bureaucratic extensions.

For the past twenty years, at least since the mid-1960s, APAs have been collectively aggrandized in the mass media as the "model minority" because they are *inter alia* industrious, smarter in math and science, enterprising and polite, family-oriented, and therefore make more money and achieve success quietly. Of late, the qualities of docility and patience may have been permanently exploded by the widely publicized media photographs of Korean merchants waving guns and rifles during the Los Angeles riots. Few Asian Americans are thought to suffer from social problems plaguing other communities; supposedly they have overcome racism and discrimination through hard work and accommodation, without relying on state support. Hence this assimilated "minority," despite a long history as an oppressed and persecuted group, has become successful economically and thus can be considered a model for all other minorities. No longer "inscrutable," at last! Damaging consequences have resulted from this, to cite only a few of them: recent immigrants from Southeast Asia receive limited assistance from the government and charitable agencies. Not only are the economic and social problems of less successful members overlooked, even the relatively successful are victimized by the "glass ceiling," denied affirmative action in various institutions, and exposed to pressures that lead to mental health problems and even teen suicides. Not to be discounted is the fact that this myth of an Asian "superminority" has alienated APAs from the rest of the population, particularly from people of color. It has fueled resentment leading to acts of harassment and violence that have markedly increased in the last decade: from the murder of Vincent Chin in 1982 to the Stockton Schoolyard Massacre in 1989 and the 1992 Los Angeles riots targeting Korean businesses. The 1992 Report of the U.S. Commission on Civil Rights gives us an inventory of the numerous cases of racially motivated bigotry, violence, and hate crimes against Asian Americans in the last few years, not only refuting the "model minority" superstition but also (despite significant progress in the reform of immigration laws and other areas) demonstrating continuity in the tradition of a deeply embedded anti-Asian prejudice and hostility, of mixed fear and loathing of some not quite comprehensible "peril" in our midst.

Allow me to review at this juncture what for many readers may already be common knowledge or received common sense as orientation for my comments on selected critics.

Although the Chinese first arrived in the Hawaii plantations in the 1840s and in the gold mines and railroad sites of the West Coast in the

1850s, it was only during the economic crisis of the 1860s and 1870s that anti-Chinese sentiments erupted, culminating in what I think is an unprecedented politicojuridical event: the passing of the Chinese Exclusion Act of 1882, the first immigration law in U.S. history stigmatizing a specific, racially marked population. In October 1871, about twenty Chinese were massacred in Los Angeles by a white mob who also burned and looted their stores and homes. Similar incidents of lynching, murders, and riots followed in San Francisco, Seattle and Tacoma, Denver, and Rock Springs, Wyoming; in 1887, thirty-one Chinese miners were robbed, murdered, and mutilated in the Sanke River, Oregon, Massacre.

Japanese and Filipinos workers were targeted next by vigilante and bureaucratic racism. Unlike the Chinese and Japanese, Filipinos came here as "nationals" of a subjugated U.S. colony, the Philippines, as a result of the Spanish-American War of 1898 and the subsequent Filipino-American War (1899-1902). Labeled first as "niggers," they were included as part of the "yellow peril" and the "Asiatic hordes" by the 1905 Asiatic Exclusion League of sixty-seven U.S. labor organizations. From 1928 to 1930 and after, Filipinos were attacked in California, Washington, and elsewhere. In 1907-1908, the diplomatic "Gentlemen's Agreement" between the U.S. and Japanese limited the number of workers emigrating from Japan. In 1917, Congress created a "barred zone," another historic landmark, which prohibited natives of China, South and Southeast Asia, the Asian part of Russia, Afghanistan, Iran, part of Arabia, the Pacific and Southeast Asian islands (not owned by the U.S.) from entering the country. Finally the Immigration Act of 1924 added Japan to the list of "barred" peoples and established the "national origins" quota. So all Asians were effectively excluded then (the colonized Filipinos were given "Commonwealth" status in 1935 and an annual quota of fifty)—until World War II when, because of the alliance against Japan, the 1882 Chinese Exclusion Act was repealed. From March 1942 to January 1945, over 100,000 Japanese Americans were rounded up and imprisoned in internment camps—to be vindicated only in 1983 after prolonged court struggles. In 1946, Congress extended the privilege of naturalization to eligible Filipinos and "persons of races indigenous to India," and after the McCarran-Walter Act of 1952 to Japanese and other Asians. While the 1965 Immigration Act abolished the national-origins system and allowed the increase of the Asian population through family reunification, the aftermath of the Vietnam War began a new era of Asian resettlement—refugees and displaced persons from Vietnam, Cambodia, and Laos. Next to Mexicans and the Latino category, APAs are the fastest growing ethnic group today. Nevertheless, despite a few successes, particularly in California and Hawaii, Asian Americans in general do not have significant political representation in proportion to their numbers, nor do they have any real economic power base in U.S. civil society (Kitano and Daniels 1995).[8]

One might object that I have summarized here only the negative and unpleasant features of immigration history, not mentioning the well-nigh irrepressible virtues of survival and resistance that characterize the various communities. This is because I want now to emphasize the pedagogical value of the histories written by Ronald Takaki, *Strangers from a Different Shore* (1989) and Sucheng Chan, *Asian Americans: An Interpretive History* (1991)—both far superior to the run-of-the-mill textbooks that just barely compensate for the damage wrought by Suzie Wong, Charlie Chan, Fu Manchu, Miss Saigon, and other colorful members of the tribe.

The lament of Chin and others on the absence of a historical consciousness or collective memory is no longer tenable. What is decisive, it seems to me, is the way historical and humanistic discourses are fashioned—either to reproduce hegemonic racial politics or subvert it. Since I have already expressed my reservations about Takaki's nostalgic liberalism, which continues to inform his latest work, *A Different Mirror* (1993), in my book *Racial Formations/Critical Transformations,* I want to point out here that it is precisely this mode of undertaking a cognitive mapping of the field that should be avoided. We should oppose it because it deploys again the co-optive immigrant paradigm, the sociological theory of immigration via push/pull factors, that has structured most studies of the problems faced by Asian immigrants in adjusting and conforming to the Anglo-European mold. This paradigm reproduces notions of ambivalence, dual personalities, hybrid or split psyches, and lately borderline personalities disadvantaged in the competition for scarce resources and opportunities. Obviously their life chances are not good. Like the functionalist epistemology used by the reigning authorities like Nathan Glazer and Daniel Moynihan, Brett Melendy, Milton Gordon, and the contributors to the *Harvard Encyclopedia of American Ethnic Groups,* the privileging of a normative ethos that smooths out conflict and occludes the dynamics of world-system crisis can only create malcontents, refugees, displaced persons, deviants and no doubt some dreamers of a better life. In the works of Blauner and Omi and Winant, among others, this immigrant paradigm (though still influential) has since been displaced by the historical-materialist theory of "internal colonialism" in the world-system and the poststructuralist concept of "racial politics." These are alternative modes of constituting the agency of the Asian American subject as interpellated by, and in turn interrogating, the possibilities and limits of change found in the complex realities of the crisis of capital accumulation in the late nineteenth and first half of the twentieth century, and of the movement of bodies that have disturbed the peace of our deeply fissured and fraught geopolitical landscape.

So far, however, the trend begun by Elaine Kim in *Asian American Literature: An Introduction to the Writings and Their Social Contexts* (1982) persists in sustaining this racialized and gendered matrix of delusions. She continues to propagate this doctrine of immigrant adjustment/adaptation to the majority ethos in her recent introduction to Jessica Hagedorn's collection of Asian American short stories, *Charlie Chan is Dead* (1994). In my contribution to Palumbo-Liu's anthology, I have noted that Kim is arguably responsible for reducing the oppositional challenge in writers like Bulosan to a case of psychological ambivalence and cross-cultural misunderstandings. How and why this mode of contextualization can only end in consensual normalization is shown by Lawrence Fuchs's unabashed enlisting of Bulosan's radicalism for a Cold War patriotism in his book *The American Kaleidoscope* (1991).

One would think that at this late hour of the day we have been disabused of this recuperative strategy, the deceptions of this language game. Unfortunately, we find this lack of critical self-reflection on interpretive tools in Shirley Lim and Amy Ling's *Reading the Literatures of Asian America* (1992), with some notable exceptions. I think the more sophisticated use of Victor Turner's "ritual process," Werner Sollors's archetype of "consent and descent," and other models of self-actualization and personal reconciliation cannot compensate for the reduction of shifting, layered, and decentered characters into predefined roles in the marketplace of laissez-faire symbolic exchange. In her tolerant review, Lori Tsang faults Lim for refunctioning outmoded clichés: for Lim, texts like Jon Shirota's *Lucky Come Hawaii,* John Okada's *No-No Boy,* and Carlos Bulosan's *America Is in the Heart* are all "situated within the context of a linear paradigm of self-actualization and identity formation that implies a movement from 'Asian' to 'Asian American,' focusing on immigrant responses to tokenism, marginalization and exoticization in America" (184). I suspect that this doxa of self-accommodation will continue to be influential unless overthrown by massive oppositional response. Despite the gains made in the pathbreaking inquiry into the nexus of race, gender, and sexuality in a handful of essays, one may ask whether the new postmodern tendency in ethnography to transcend the limits of systemic representation by mobilizing genealogy, geography, and history in order to reconcile "self and society, politics and poetry" can really yield any insight into why a text like Kingston's *The Woman Warrior* can easily be purged of any radical potential by being canonized by the MLA ideological apparatus? The desire for recognition, in effect for assimilation into the pluralist hegemonic bloc, turns out to be a self-defeating "civilizing mission" engaged in by the natives themselves. Such a move undercuts the rhetoric of identity, modernist as well as postmodernizing, that pervades current Asian American critical thinking.

Examples of a recolonizing, even refeudalizing, *habitus* (to use Bourdieu's term for generative schemes of social practices) can be illustrated in the three contributions on Asian American writing in the MLA volume *Redefining American Literary History* (1990) edited by A. LaVonne Brown Ruoff and Jerry Ward, Jr. Elsewhere I have commented on how, in a previous MLA volume edited by Houston Baker, *Three American Literatures* (1982), the section on Asian American Literature omits any mention of the Filipino contribution. This omission is repeated again eight years after even when the body of Filipino literary expression and criticism has expanded considerably.

I suggest that we examine the three articles as examples of how the will to belong, to integrate with the dominant class configuration, enacts cultural imperialism via the discourse of rhetorical and generic taxonomy. In "Oral Tradition in Kingston's *China Men*," Linda Ching Sledge aligns her work with folklore research and Walter Ong's advocacy of oral cultures. She argues that the oral tradition of "talk-story" was fully established in ancient Chinese culture, preserving its "traditional wisdom" and the "timeless, stylized realm of heroic history"—paradigms that give "order, purpose, and historical authority" to the biographies of the patriarchs. In short, Kingston's art derives from "a conservative culture like that of Chinese in America" and thus demonstrates "that immigrant culture is a continuation of the ancient oral tradition of the home" (152). This way of legitimizing Kingston is a trivial essentialism that deprives the artist of any originality. It can only reinforce the subordination of works by Asian American writers by judging them as epiphenomenal to the classic Asian icons, a move that Rey Chow has justly criticized as a colonizing strategy aimed to reproduce the hierarchical Eurocentrism of the academy and reinforce the subalternity of "the Rest."

In her "Chinese American Women Writers: The Tradition Behind Maxine Hong Kingston," Amy Ling posits tradition as the practice of women writers of Chinese descent who purveyed Orientalist versions of writing as "an act of self-assertion, self-revelation, and self-preservation." Summarizing the plots and themes of over a dozen books, Ling describes two groups: one "other-directed" goodwill ambassadors like Winnifred Eaton and Helena Kuo, the other introspective and "existential" like Edith Eaton and Han Suyin. Oddly conflating Davis Riesman's simplistic typology with W. E. B. DuBois's intuition of "double consciousness," Ling catalogues her writers in terms not so much of style or technique—good old New Critical methodology—but of hypothetical audience expectations. But the problem is that these expectations never change for her; they are fixed by norms chosen arbitrarily. Ultimately we wonder how such traits that Ling has ascribed to her prototypical authors—"protest, storytelling, nostalgia, and experimentation"—can ever combine to explain the production of a specific cultural practice like *The Woman Warrior* or *China Men*. Aesthetic reception by the elite audience can only guarantee the perpetuation of stereotypes and of canonical orthodoxy.

Finally, in Shirley Lim's "Twelve Asian American Writers: In Search of a Self-Definition," the will to affirm conventionality and demonstrate the normative immigrant reflexes is expressed right in the first paragraph without any twinge of embarrassment at the ingratiating platitudes of Establishment pieties:

> As part of the macrocosm, Asian American writing exhibits the variety of voices, forms, and genres that marks mainstream American literature. At the same time, one finds in it certain inextricably Asian psychological and philosophical perspectives. A strong Confucian patriarchal orientation is a dominant element. (237)

Vitiated by paltry essentialisms and indulgence in the Euro-American immigrant syndrome, Lim's eclectic but mainly formalist readings focusing on "author-controlled narratives" and "authorial presence" can only confirm the prejudice of the editors of *Aiiieeeee!* that there are still no critics of Asian American literature worthy of the subject.

On the face of this complicitous performance, I would like to risk the assertion that surely the texts, always already there, need another community of interpreters sympathetic to the integrity of the authors. Asian American writers deserve critics with an emancipatory vision who will not glorify their art by interring it in the canonical graveyard. The literary historian Eric Sundquist summed up this anxiety of the counterhegemonic archive: "No matter the breadth or diversity of new formulations of the canonical tradition . . . it remains difficult for many readers to overcome their fundamental conception of 'American' literature as solely Anglo-European in inspiration and authorship, to which may then be added an appropriate number of valuable 'ethnic' or 'minority' texts, those that closely correspond to familiar critical and semantic paradigms. Instead, a redefinition of the premises and inherent significance of the central literary documents of American culture is in order" (7). And surely this cannot be done by pursuing the beaten path whose trajectory, as we have sketched earlier, can lead only to reinforcing the tendentious discriminations of the status quo. For one, the object of knowledge still awaiting its moment of theorization has shifted its point of gravity in the altered demography of Asian Americans I have outlined earlier and in the growing inter-ethnic conflicts of post-1965 America. Such mutations in the field of knowledge production cannot be ignored. What is more central, I believe, is the fact that aside from diverse national origins and political genealogies, the shared experience of Chinese, Japanese, and Filipino immigrant workers from the nineteenth century to the middle of the twentieth, after the Delano Grape Strike of 1965 by the last of the Filipino generation of *Manongs,* is no longer a commonality from which to formulate generalizations encompassing all members of the set of "Asian Pacific Americans" (Omi 1989; Hirabayashi and Alquizola 1994). This is also the reason why I think the protocanonical status of works like Okada's *No-No Boy* for Chin, Chan, Inada and Wong, or for that matter Bulosan's *America Is in the Heart,* has now been overtaken by the more "polymorphously perverse" texts of Kingston, David Hwang's *M. Butterfly,* Jessica Hagedorn's *Dogeaters,* or even a quasi-documentary account like Le Ly Hayslip's *When Heaven and Earth Changed Places*—though, I might add, such experimental postmodernist performances may properly be assayed as symptoms of the late-capitalist logic of time-space compression and its mutations of style and idiom.

A hate letter circulated last February to Filipino American students at the University of California law school in Berkeley may indicate why the context for articulating a new, genuinely transformative critical discourse for Asian creative expression in the United States is in order. The unsigned message presumably addressed to the Filipino students reads in part:

Rejoice you crybaby niggers, it's affirmative action month. A town hall meeting will not save you the wetbacks or the chinks. Your failures are hereditary and can't be corrected by these liberals. Look around Boalt Hall besides the few handpicked affirmative action professors this is a quality law school. . . . When I see you in class it bugs the hell out of me because your taking the seat of someone qualified. You belong at Coolie High Law don't you forget. (Ramos, A-14)

The racial politics manifest here cannot distinguish Filipinos from "chinks," "wetbacks," or "niggers." We have at best a postmodern collage, a simulacrum of something that has emerged with Propositions 187 and 209 but has not fully assumed its proper teleology. I won't waste time trying to duplicate the diagnosis of this social malady and its vicissitudes drawn up by Joel Kovel in *White Racism* or David Goldberg in *Racist Culture*.

No doubt, thanks to the indifference of the public to integral differences, the semantics of Asian Pacific American (to use the bureaucratic rubric) identity has become contentious and intractable terrain (Moy 1996). Terms like "coolie," "oriental," "Japs," "Gooks," and so on all evoke oppressive regimes of representation that still persist in the hyphenated census labels. To remedy this, Philip Tajitsu Nash suggests the rubric "Pacific American" which "allows us to start all over without the 'Asiatic hordes'" connotation. From some kind of *tabula rasa,* he adds: "We can define what it is. We can fill it in. We have always been defined by our common victimization" (Yip 1997: 15), so it's about time we determine our nomenclature, define our common attributes of belonging (to which?), and thus control our lives. Easier said than done. While the form of categorization resists instant change, the referent or substance undergoes spontaneous mutations and stages of evolution that fortuitously can be registered by critical discourse more insightful and wide-ranging than the ones I assayed here.

One example of such discourse is the provocative work of Lisa Lowe. In *Immigrant Acts* (1996), she argues that given the monolithic and hermetically sealed narrative of American national culture and the abstract universalist norm of citizenship, we need to valorize Asian American cultural production (contradistinguished from the political practice) as the unique site of disruption, heterogeneity, and alternatives. Culture becomes the locus of "imagining different narratives and critical historiographies, and enacting practices that give rise to new forms of subjectivity and new ways of questioning the government of human life by the national state" (29). Asian American immigrant history thus serves as both symbol and allegory of an Otherness that rejects the state/citizen binary as "the ultimate construction of sociality" (36). Despite its recuperative ambition to rescue the utopian impulses in the homogenized Asian American narratives of oppression and resistance (Asian American alterity is itself parasitic on postulating a EuroAmerican racial formation whose ideals of liberty and equality, both totalizing and exclusivist, underwrite the ethnic, communal narratives themselves), Lowe's argument is fallacious. First, she misreads Gramsci's distinction between state and civil society, privileging the latter as the domain of culture immune from the ironies and ambiguities plaguing the citizen-subject. What results is a vapid formalist culturalism impotent to influence the political wars of position and movement against state ideological apparatuses operating within the expanded or integral state form. Second, Marx's critique is mistakenly conflated with a Hegelian construal of civil society and state in equilibrium, whereas for Marx both domains of bourgeois life are characterized by profound and pervasive alienation and reification based on alienated social labor. In evacuating these key Marxist axioms, Lowe posits culture as free from commodity fetishism, from the fundamental alienation in a capitalist order that fragments the public and private spheres, generating separate categories (citizen, ethnic collective, nation) that mystify thought and the phenomena of everyday life. Third, by fetishizing the cultural moment as already an agency for political mobilization and inflating the literary and aesthetic into political instrumentalities, Lowe abandons the whole process of constructing a social bloc for winning hegemony—the directive moral-intellectual leadership that reinforces domination with consent of the masses—and so allows the system of alienation (racism, sexism, exploitation of labor) to continue.

One can qualify these negative comments by saying that this tactic of "strategic essentialism" is perhaps appropriate to the neoconservatism of the "model minority" ethos and milieu of our time. As a mode of inquiry, however, it ignores the rich and complex legacy of Asian American activism (signified by such names as Karl Yoneda, Har Dayal, Ahn Chang-ho, Philip Vera Cruz, Yuri Kochiyama, and others). Its flaw is revealed by an ironic aphorism uttered by Tam Lum, the protagonist of Frank Chin's powerful play *The Chickencoop Chinaman:* "If you don't have Chinese culture, baby, all you've got is the color of your skin" (1981: 29). The exorbitation of the cultural impoverishes the analytical organon, with its attendant praxis of radical critique, for elucidating precisely the "weak links" of the U.S. racial formation constitutive both of the hegemonic power and its subalterns. Needless to say, the war is conducted on multiple fronts, mediated through determinate contradictions that produce the agencies of inventory, critique, and sublation at specific historical conjunctures.

Meanwhile, I want to propose a synoptic view of the possible stages that a nonconformist critical discourse has to traverse beyond the mode of self-apologetics engaged in by Kim in her pioneering book, replicated and varied by Ling and Lim so far, and now elaborated with criteria indexed to indigenous texts by Sau-ling Wong in her *Reading Asian American Literature*. In Wong's book, one might interject here, we find a hermeneutic apparatus that performs a predictably mechanical permutation of semiotic values revolving around "Necessity" and "Extravagance," notions derived from Kingston and rephrasing the old dualisms between Order and Freedom, System and Chance, etc. Unfortunately, gross reductionism creeps in when this binary formula becomes a ruse to transpose complex social predicaments into psychological anomalies easily domesticated by empiricist sociology and ego-centered psychotherapy. No need then to be afraid of Wong's challenge—if there is one— to the canonical hierarchy.

We have now moved to this point of determining the forms of value through which Asian texts composed in the U.S. milieu have evolved, forms that are designed to capture what I think is the fundamental nature of social relations in a social formation like the United States: the domination of commodity fetishism and its attendant reification of all cultural practice. It is virtually impossible to grasp the intelligibility of any practice of signification without elucidating the "mystery" of commodities on which our whole social existence is based. As Marx explained in *Grundrisse* (1973), the juridical subject of a liberal polity— the "free, autonomous, sovereign individual" citizen—is the individual producer who "divests himself of his property voluntarily" (quoted in Sayer 1987:108). Based on the operations of exchange value in the market, equality and freedom obtain as attributes of humans as owners of commodities (products as well as labor power); on this same basis, where unrequited surplus value is not returned to the worker, inequality prevails. It will also clarify why the difference-blind liberalism of academic multiculturalism finds itself caught in antinomies it cannot resolve without destroying its own condition of possibility.

Why is it that the value of human labor or labor time (as the magnitude of its value) can be grasped only when it is represented in the value of its product, in things or commodities? The alienation of human labor into exchange value occurs in a stage of social development when autonomous private labors proceed independently of one another in fashioning products; such products are commodities that become part of social aggregate labor through the mediation of the market that equalizes the products. This is the logic of capitalism (see Colletti 1972; Cleaver 1979). Products lose their perceptible qualities, their sensory objectivity, when they are transformed into exchangeable commodities, "crystals of social substance," whose value depends on the labor power/labor time expended without regard to the form of its expenditure. Value is a product of abstract human labor that can be measured, equated, interpreted, and critically evaluated.

The value of texts in the field of Asian American cultural production should then be appraised within this political economy of symbolic or ideological exchange involving the parameters of class, gender, and race. While this emergent discipline straddles the boundaries of the traditional disciplines of history, economics, sociology, aesthetics, and psychology, this speculative exercise also derives its rationale from the fact that the literary forms often used—plots of exile and deracination, tropes of self-doubling and self-discovery, metaphors of homecoming and reconciliation—serve as fetishizing agents or vehicles to mystify the real content of the Asian experience: colonial violence, rape, exploitation, and genocidal slaughter, together with the protean resistance of their victims. Before analyzing the cause of this mystification, a process engendered by the dynamics of the accumulation of surplus value and the ideology of individualism underlying the ethnicity/immigrant paradigm, it might be useful to recapitulate in a schematic way the forms of value that Marx traced in the first book of *Capital,* namely accidental or elementary form, extended form, general form with the universal equivalent, and finally the monetary form of value (Goux [1990] discerns three phases in the last form: the fetishized general equivalent, the "symbolic" general equivalent, and the general equivalent as "sign").

The first stage of commodity exchange is marked by barter where value appears essentialized in the concrete or phenomenal appearance of the goods traded. For example, Pardee Lowe's *Father and Glorious Descendants* (1943) can be appreciated for its supply of information about Chinese customary practices and reinforcement of certain stereotypes, a use-value equal to that of any ethnography of "primitive" tribes. The time spent decoding her work can be substituted for time spent reading tourist guides and assorted baedekers introducing alien societies and cultures. When the relative form of value such as those found in Younghill Kang's *East Goes West* (1937) or any of Lin Yutang's works, find their embodiment in the equivalent form of a Western text purveying information in a kindred genre, we operate in the domain of simple exchange.

As contact among groups intensify and trade expands, this simple form soon becomes generalized to the accidental or elementary form of value expressed by the simple equation: x commodity A = y commodity B. The value of commodity A (the use-value embodied in phenomenal form) cannot be manifested (because it has become abstract when it exchanges) without commodity B. Marx writes: "Value as an aspect of the commodity is not expressed in its own use-value, or in its existence as use-value. Value manifests itself when commodities are expressed in other use-values, that is, it manifests itself in the rate at which these other use-values are exchanged for them. A commodity is *ex*change-value only if it is expressed in another, i.e., as a relation" (1973: 205).

To paraphrase: The use-value of a concrete text like Kang's is manifested as exchange-value in the form of the use-value of a corresponding Western text like Fitzgerald's *The Great Gatsby,* the equivalent form of value. The use value (concrete labor) of Fitzgerald's text is the form of manifestation of the relative value (abstract labor contained in it) of Kang's text. Further, the kind of private labor that produced Fitzgerald's text "comes to stand for the social labor of which A must be a result in order to stand in value-relation at all" (Sayer 1987: 26). The labor expended by individuals assumes the form of labor in social form, a process comprising what Pierre Bourdieu (1993) calls "the field of cultural production." Put another way, the abstract social labor that makes two works A and B commensurable is represented by the concrete labor that fashioned B. The translation of value into forms of exchange-value not only inverts but also distorts the actual relations involved; but in all cases, the social and historical element (abstract social labor) is represented by the natural and universal (concrete private labors) that becomes the ground or matrix of commodity fetishism: the canonical as natural/normal.

It is perhaps within this framework that we can appraise a collection like David Hsin-Fu Wand's *Asian-American Heritage* (1974) as a market or warehouse supplying relative forms of value that become translatable into any one of the minority texts—by Ellison, Momaday, etc.—that can supplement the mainstream canon. Wand indulges in the apologetic mode of legitimizing ethnic "minority" writing as one endowed with "universal" appeal because it springs from the "collective unconscious" and is thus concerned with "the human condition of the outsider, the marginal man, or the pariah" (9). By positing the equivalence of two disparate objects, one mystifies the specific value of the objects equated and in the same breath dissolves them into a homogeneous lump.

The premature leap into the universal form bypassing the expanded and general form of value may be illustrated by the success of Amy Tan's *The Joy Luck Club* and its validation of ethnic kinship/ familial ties, a thematic engagement attuned to the neoconservative mood of U.S. society. Its form of expressive-mimetic realism recasts the immigration ordeal into individual problems that can be happily resolved without questioning fundamental norms. Contrast this with Gish Jen's *Typical American* which, despite its caustic and satiric elements, earned kudos from reviewers in the popular media. I hope we can learn something from the dilemma of Ralph Chang, Jen's chief protagonist, whose struggle for social acceptance seems to parody the "inspirational quotes" plastered on the walls of his office, mottos of everyday life in what Henri Lefebvre (1971) calls a "society of bureaucratically controlled consumption":

ALL RICHES BEGIN IN AN IDEA.

DON'T WAIT FOR YOUR SHIP TO COME IN, SWIM OUT TO IT.

FOLLOW THE HERD, YOU END UP A COW.

YOU CAN NEVER HAVE RICHES IN GREAT QUANTITY UNLESS YOU WORK YOURSELF INTO A WHITE HEAT OF DESIRE FOR MONEY. (Jen 1991: 198-99)

What makes the appearance of value enigmatic may be apprehended in the unity of contradictions that make up the commodity. It lies precisely in the fact that the social substance (value) achieves phenomenal expression only in the natural form of the use-value of some other commodity. This becomes evident in the total or expanded form of value when "the value of a single commodity . . . is now expressed in terms of numberless other elements of the world of commodities" so that, given this "interminable series of value equations, it is a matter of indifference under what particular form, or kind, of use-value it appears" (Marx 1967: 62-63). This characterizes the entry of "Asian American" texts into the field of cultural exchange after World War II when the formalist hermeneutics of New Criticism attained hegemony.

As soon as Asian texts multiply, with the appearance of Carlos Bulosan's *America Is in the Heart* (1946), John Okada's *No-No Boy* (1957), Louis Chu's *Eat a Bowl of Tea* (1961), among others, then we graduate to the expanded form of value where any number of these texts can be exchanged for any of the canonical ones by Hemingway, Faulkner, Mailer, and so on. A turning point is reached when a general form of value materializes as soon as the critical texts and commentaries accumulate—indeed, this ordeal of "primitive accumulation" is marked by Chin et al's *Aiiieeeee!* By the time we have Chin's two plays, *The Chickencoop Chinaman* (1972) and *The Year of the Dragon* (1974), we are on the way to realizing a universal form of value that becomes money (universal medium of exchange) in the form of Kingston's *The Woman Warrior* (1977). Commodity fetishism has become fully incarnate when the MLA puts out a handbook on Kingston's masterpiece. Its chief emblem is Elaine Kim's "goodwill" catalogue of merchandise ready to be packaged and shipped, followed by the mainstreaming of the products by way of the division of labor managed by Amy Ling, Shirley Lim, Sau-ling Wong, and other enterprising middlewomen.

Now, one of the peculiarities of the expanded form of value is this. In the elementary form, the role of the equivalent (B) is always played by a single commodity, whereas in the expanded form, all commodities (except the one whose value is being expressed) play this role. Analogously, the value form of, say, Genny Lim's play *Bitter Cane* can be measured by equivalents in the ethnic corpus: by Lorraine Hansberry's *A Raisin in the Sun,* or by any number of plays by Lillian Hellman, Arthur Miller, and Tennessee Williams. The abstract labor that is the hidden substance in these works has been painstakingly calculated, weighed, and indexed by New Critical disciplinary instruments. In the early form, an element of arbitrariness and subjectivity prevails. Here, however, the value of the relative commodity A stays constant throughout its embodiments in several equivalent forms. We discover from this development that "it is not the exchange of commodities which regulates the magnitude of their value; but, on the contrary, that it is the magnitude of their value which controls their exchange-proportions" (Marx 1967: 63). It seems that this is also the juncture at which the multiculturalist imaginary surfaces, given the presence of "a many-colored mosaic" of disparate and independent expressions of value. By reversing the equation, we arrive at the general form of value where diverse forms of relative value A can be translated into one unitary manifestation, this manifestation being a given quantity of money.

We have arrived at last at the final stage of the form of value, the money form. Marx explains: "The value of every commodity is now . . . not only differentiated from its use-value, but from all other use-values generally, and is, by that very fact, expressed as that which is common to all commodities. By this form, commodities are, for the first time, effectively brought into relation with one another as values, or made to appear as exchange values" (1967: 66). Value is now exhibited as not only distinct from the use value of the relative commodity but as common to all commodities; all commodities, as in the expanded and the general forms of value, now have their values expressed in a single or universal equivalent. At this stage, the money commodity becomes the social form in which the value of all commodities is expressed; the social substance, value, is incarnated in a thing, the natural form of the equivalent. Value is now definitely manifested in the bodily form of the universal equivalent, the money form, at which point fetishism becomes consolidated as a way of thinking or judgment in which economic categories are conceived as qualities inherent in the material embodiments of these formal determinants or categories. In short, what are social or historical properties acquired in a historically specific social formation become metamorphosed into what is natural, and what is historical becomes universalized—a double inversion of the natural and social, the universal and historical (for further elaboration, see Meszaros 1995).

Applying this to the job of configuring the field of Asian American knowledge-production, we perceive how the premises laid out by Chin *et al* in their introduction to *Aiiieeeee!*, specifically the valorization of certain key texts as foundational, establish the structure of the general form of value. Use-value contradicts exchange value when the Asian American text refuses the immigrant paradigm, its bifurcation of the ethnic subject-position and gradual incorporation, by privileging certain forms of value as the universal equivalent. This is patently the thrust of the 1991 preface in which Chin *et al* urge critics "to recognize the history, music, and literature in Toshio Mori's voice, the lyrical moment and emotion, our language's instinct for the forms and symbols, gong and rhythms of the heroic tradition of Kwan Kung, the *Romance of the Three Kingdoms,* Sun Tzu, the invincible personal integrity of the Confucian Taoist soldier brandishing his weapons in the first person pronoun (word in Chinese is made of two battleaxes crossed in contention) 'I' alone, 'me' against all time, the soldier, one self-sufficient whole, the basic unit of history with a battleaxe in each hand. That is the 'I' of the Issei and old Nisei generations of Japanese America. That is the 'I' Chinamans landed with in the mid-nineteenth century" (xxxix). This uniform heroic myth, or the quest for one, displaces the bipolarizing logic of the hyphenated sensibilities of Jade Snow Wong, Virginia Lee, Pardee Lowe, and others—a displacement whose metaphor is the spectacle of Fred Eng become a "shrunken Charlie Chan, an image of death," the tourist guide who monumentalizes Chinatown as ethnic enclave, in Chin's *The Year of the Dragon*. Instead of the bricolage engaged by Tam Lum in Act One of *The Chickencoop Chinaman,* the exuberant praise of the demiurgic in Tam's equivalence of Chinaman with the Logos, the play ends with a therapeutic closure: a nostalgic resurrection of the Iron Moonhunter of the Sierra Nevadas that emblematizes the pugnacious will and virility of the nineteenth-century Chinese railroad workers and miners. (Note, however, the caustic and Rabelaisian closure of *The Year of the Dragon,* which somehow escapes the domesticating paraphrase and antiquarian gloss of Dorothy Ritsuko McDonald in her introduction to the two plays.)

The universal form of value then becomes condensed in heroic myth—what Chin *et al* call "the heroic tradition endemic in Chinatowns, Asian language, Asian American writing, and the oral tradition" (xxxviii). The problem with resuscitating the ethnic syndrome here is that, as Colin Greer points out, it also reproduces and revitalizes a brand of laissez-faire individualism, the ethics of do-it-yourself acquisitive and possessive individualism, which ironically also submits to welfare-state divide-and-rule policies. This dogma of individualist competition shrewdly manipulated by neoconservativism is anathema to the agenda of discovering the resources of the self through identifying with the good of the community, through rebuilding the fragments of that community into a self-administering whole.

Recently, however, in *Gunga Din Highway,* particularly in the allegorical reconstruction of "July 4, 1968" by Ulysses Kwan, Chin negates the aforementioned humanist reconstitution of the self and presents us a postmodern pastiche that may be an astute maneuver to undermine commodity fetishism. This is a technique of internal sabotage, a tactic of outwitting the enemy on its own grounds. The danger here involves that surrounding aestheticism, the valorization of sensuous appearance, the form of use-value detached from the object itself, the appearance of use-value (the use form) becoming self-contained—an illusion, a fetish. While exchange-value separates itself from the commodity body and its usefulness as satisfying a specific need, presenting itself as an illusion, the promise of a usefulness that can be appropriated by the consumer, to counter this illusion by another more seductive illusion may not really empower alienated or reified subjects. What is needed is to reclaim the alienated communitarian power inhering in the products of concrete labor, qualitatively different products addressing a variety of social needs (Haug 1986).

We have arrived at an impasse, a turning point. Could it be that in order to thwart the integrative and assimilative power of a vastly sophisticated hegemonic culture, Asian American artists have to take the detour through affirmations of a unique identity through myth, through the rich density of the vernaculars, through an invention of a separatist tradition? Could self-determination be attained only through the mediation of, or passage through, the three forms of value—from the simple exchange or barter of texts with comparable use values, to the expanded form in which concrete use values dissolve into abstract labor in exchange-value, and finally to the universal form? In this passage, as we've seen, a work like *The Woman Warrior* (or for that matter, Joy Kogawa's *Obasan* or Bharati Mukherjee's *Jasmine*) can be converted into a money-form insofar as each embodies a given quantity of labor (hypostatized in the formal/expressive qualities of language and narrative style) that matches the quantity expended in the production of works like, say, Virginia Woolf's *Mrs. Dalloway* or George Eliot's *Middlemarch*. I think this is the epistemology and rhetoric of constructing Asian American history that informs Gary Okihiro's *Margins and Mainstreams*. Unlike Chin and company, Okihiri is empirical and even demythologizing. But in his project of transforming the marginal Asian into a "mainstream" American, his standard of reference is a putative and undefined "American community" (Lowe's nemesis, as noted previously) to which is ascribed the "authorship of the central tenets of democracy," whose "American ideals of independence and national self-determination inspired decolonization and feminist movements among Third World peoples both within and without the United States" (1994: 174). Such large generalizations not only elide social contradictions, in particularly the genocidal catastrophes of the internally colonized peoples that constituted the U.S. nation-state; they also obscure the material conditions of possibility, the alienation and reification entailed by exchange-value and a commodity-centered society, for articulating ideals and principles of democracy enacted in people's lived experiences. Self-determination is foreclosed by prioritizing American liberal democracy as the source of liberation instead of being the power that racialized, surveilled, and exploited bodies with darker or colored skins. In Okihiro's subsumption of Asian American struggles into instances of the ethos of the U.S. national community, we have a complete and final dominance of the money form of value, the money form of course being denominated and authorized by the dominant or hegemonic Euro-Anglocentric bloc that regulates and delimits the production of goods and the circuits of exchange.

I would like to close this chapter with some tactical and strategic speculations. I think it is time now to move beyond Michael Omi and Howard Winant's (1986) inflation of "racial politics" as a transcendent form of political-ethical struggle, a strategy of uniting people of color under the slogans of multiculturalism, difference, and subjectivity. Discursive analysis of neoconservative racist texts can only be a heuristic guide to analysis of lines of antagonistic forces in the pursuit of hegemony, in challenging the power of capital. In this regard, the activist protest against *Miss Saigon* as latter-day purveyor of pop myths to shore up the ruins of Empire is exemplary (see Aguilar-San Juan 1994). In terms of constructing a critical discourse for Asian American cultural production, what is needed is not only a critique of the consensual paradigms I have sketched here. The white supremacist standards legitimizing American literature as a national canon will no longer do— its pluralist or multiculturalist surface is a form of value that preserves material inequality and injustice. Nor will a resort to the tastes and predilections of classical Chinese, Japanese, or Indian literature do unless we fantasize ourselves inhabiting the modes of social/cultural production of the centuries before Christ, the archaic and feudal/tributary social formations that engendered those cultures. I propose that we deploy the concept of "emergent literature," which, according to Wlad Godzich, does not refer to literatures of developing or underdeveloped countries; rather, it refers to "literatures that cannot be readily comprehended within the hegemonic view of literature that has been dominant" (1988: 35) in the current disciplines based on the academic division of labor. We still need to theorize the specificity of the emergence of what we temporarily designate as "Asian American" texts. Our task resembles that of comprehending the postmodern sublime (Kant via Lyotard) whose conception is intuitively accessible but somehow still resists articulation and representation.

Neither American nor Asian, but not in between either inhabiting cyborg-land, the conjuncture or space called "Asian American literature" needs to begin with a critique of current and past formulations, a clearing and demarcation of the ground, which is what I have cursorily attempted to do here. This space will not materialize through neutralizing or distancing stances, nor through hybridity and hyper-real ambivalence; the functional necessity of the "ethnic" text will defy the rationalizing and autonomizing pressure of marketized liberalism together with its racializing motivation. Heterotopia, borderland, *mestizaje* or *metissage* subject-in-process, locations of differential locutions, and so on, may be drawn up as sites of contestation and subversion, and for the recomposition of positional identities. The practice of disjuncture, however, cannot hypostatize such sites into the arena or theater of another if alternative master-narrative. At best, one can configure hypothetical cartographies of struggle without claiming a fixed teleology. In short, Asian American cultural production cannot be legislated into existence based on a master blueprint; nor, conversely, can it be surrendered to absolute contingency. Beyond this, what is required is a wide-ranging historical analysis of the politics of Asian immigration, of the laws regulating the movement of bodies and communities as well as the geopolitical interactions between Asian nations and the United States, an analysis of ideological formations and the determinate forms of value through which cultural practices/products pass as they are encoded and decoded by specific groups.

Contingencies abound, but the stigma persists. Confronting the dilemma of denying the body to validate the spirit, Debra Kang Dean of Okinawan and Korean ancestry confesses: "I am a visible minority who wishes to be asked neither to live in the illusion that it is a fact that makes no difference nor to believe that it is the sole determining factor in my life. My body is the necessary, the essential locus for events" (67). Another testimony is by Geetha Kothari who pleads not to be terrorized by the question "Where are you from?" and counters with the strategic response, "I'm here" (173). Can we escape history and its inscriptions on our bodies? Because it is easy to invoke stratagems of "in-betweeness" and ambivalence, we need a rigorous critique of postcoloniality, difference, versions of Otherness or alterity, intertextuality, hybridity, and so on, notions and rubrics that simply multiply the individualist axioms of liberal normative pluralism in order to mystify the effective subordination and oppression of Asians and other people of color under the pretext that we are all equal and free—except that we as historically specific communities act on the basis of incommensurable values or cultures to which we are all entitled equal recognition. "One in many"/*E pluribus unum*—this, in fact, is the last and final stage of the evolution of the forms of value I have outlined earlier, the multicultural Imaginary now realized in the multinational capitalist world-system in which we are all condemned to struggle.

CHAPTER SIX

Globalization, Dialogic Nation, Diaspora

Liberation from capitalism means liberation from the rule of the economy.

—Georg Lukács

For great changes have taken place [circa 1921] in this respect since the beginning of the twentieth century, namely, millions and hundreds of millions—actually the overwhelming majority of the world's population— are now coming out as an independent and active revolutionary factor. And it should be perfectly clear that in the coming decisive battles of the world revolution, this movement of the majority of the world's population, originally aimed at national liberation, will turn against capitalism and imperialism and will, perhaps, play a much more revolutionary role than we have been led to expect.

—Vladimir Lenin

Only the lessons of reality can teach us to transform reality.
—Bertolt Brecht

In November 1996 the Philippine government hosted the Asia Pacific Economic Cooperation (APEC) forum of eighteen countries in Asia and the Pacific Rim (comprised of 2 billion people, where 56 percent of the world's gross domestic product and 46 percent of the total world exports are produced), geared to establishing a regional commercial bloc with regulatory powers like the World Trade Organization (WTO). APEC is modeled after other free-trade blocs like the European Union and the North American Free Trade Area (NAFTA) designed to speed up WTO trade and investments liberalization timetable. It is also intended to counter the wave of domestic protectionism that accompanied the rise of the Asian "tigers" or NIEs (Newly Industrialized Economies) and the threat of China's full-blown "market socialism." APEC'S chief objective is clear: to ensure and facilitate the regional implementation of the provisions of the General Agreement on Tariffs and Trade (GATT), which benefits the advanced industrial North. Under the aegis of "open regionalism," it aims to abolish international barriers to trade and eliminate restrictions against foreign investments, two steps that will surely devastate the economy, culture, and environment of the poor countries (KMU 1996). APEC is also being used by the United States, as policeman and enforcer of "common market rules" in the Asia-Pacific region (carried out through structural adjustment programs of the World Bank/International Monetary Fund), to regain economic preeminence over Japan (neutralizing U.S. trade deficits), check China's competitive influence, and consolidate U.S. geopolitical hegemony. In consonance with this strategy, the Pentagon has now asserted the operational jurisdiction of its Pacific Command as "highways of trade which are vital to national security," the linchpin for a regional security network based on various U.S.-Japan security cooperation agreements to suppress anti-imperialist national liberation movements and socialist revolutions in the region.

To stage the spectacle of an economic miracle overtaking the Philippines and thus affiliating it with the prosperous NIEs (Hong Kong, Singapore, Taiwan, South Korea), the Ramos government instituted de facto "martial law": at least 30,000 squatter dwellers were evicted from slums lining the major roads, and their homes demolished, and forty thousand troops and police (including the notorious paramilitary Citizens' Armed Forces Geographical Units and Civilian Volunteer Organizations) were deployed to secure the sites of the conference and intimidate peaceful dissenters. Leaders of legal organizations that oppose APEC and Ramos' "Philippines 2000" program have been put on the military's "order of battle," that is, subject to immediate arrest or liquidation. Aside from selective killings and harassment, the Ramos administration continues to engage in flagrant violation of human rights of citizens; a recent example is the bombardment and strafing of civilians in areas where the Moro Islamic Liberation Front enjoys support and the destruction of the indigenous B'laan communities in Kiblawan, Davao del Sur, in southern

Philippines. All these register the genocidal impact of "global restructuring" on the masses for whose welfare the APEC member states are vigorously implementing investment "liberalization," "privatization," "deregulation," and other monopoly-capitalist schemes (Ofreneo 1995).

Engaging over 200,000 participants, nationwide demonstrations and protest forums were held by progressive organizations in Manila and other urban centers with representatives from various countries. One can mention here the Anti-Imperialist World Peasant Summit, the People's Anti-APEC Conference, peasant demonstrations at the Food and Agriculture Organization building, and a people's caravan from Manila to Subic (formerly a major U.S. naval base, the site of the APEC meeting). A "Declaration of the People's Conference against Imperialist Globalization," issued on 23 November by the participants of the Anti-APEC Conference, reads in part:

> We oppose imperialist globalization because the schemes it promotes worsen the uneven development among and within nations, intensify the exploitation of peoples, and deepen inequality and social polarization. They accelerate the concentration of wealth in the handful of imperialist states, their MNCs/TNCs and the billionaire-owners, and drive the majority of nations into deeper impoverishment. These schemes also foster mindless consumerism and trash Western culture that warp, marginalize or efface the cultures of Third World peoples and debase their humanity.
>
> Globalization schemes are wiping out jobs and livelihoods in industry and agriculture, both in industrial and non-industrial countries. Evidence we have seen undoubtedly show that globalization is causing mass layoff of workers via "downsizing," "labor flexibilization," "labor-only contracting" and other management designs; massive landlessness and worsening forms of feudal and capitalist exploitation of peasants and farm workers; displacement, commodification and modern-day slavery of women; eviction of the urban poor; deprivation of indigenous peoples of their ancestral lands and patenting of their human genes; wanton human rights violations and political repression; commodification of migration; razing of the environment; de-industrialization and bankruptcy of small and medium enterprises; cutdown or total absence of state social services; rising costs of consumer goods and services and declining levels of income and standards of living of the majority of the people. They also aim to deprive the toiling masses of their capacity to

organize and effectively fight for their rights and survival and to resist
imperialist domination. (People's Conference 1996: 2)

Like its counterparts the European Union, NAFTA, and WTO,
APEC is supposed to promote above all "regionalization within globalization." What is this globalization scheme really about? Is it actually
meant to usher in a "New World Order" of interchangeable lifestyles,
smooth and felicitous border crossings, abundance of consumer goods,
and rapid communication in cyberspace?

In business, government and the academy, the term "globalization"
seems to offer a magic door to what Marshall McLuhan in 1962 called
the "global village." What we have witnessed in the last decades is the
globalization of markets, now a fashionable theme adopted by international credit and trade institutions of the capitalist nation-states, in
particular the United States. Globalization denotes the putative "internationalization of production" (actually the expansion of speculative
finance capital manifest in the huge foreign debt of "Third World"
countries) as the ideological framework within which TNCs (transnational corporations) can streamline the operations of flexible spatiotemporal business practices, in particular the accelerated turnover of
profits—realization of surplus value—in order to remedy the crisis of
overproduction and surplus capital. There is also a claim that capital's
transcendence of national boundaries will stabilize the internecine rivalry
between Japan, the United States, and Europe. Globalization equals
trade liberalization from which U.S. TNCs would reap enormous
advantages as they exercise monopoly control on open Asian markets,
cheap and docile labor, and immense natural resources. Could this
explain why TNCs have been propagandizing the marvels of modern
telecommunication (such as the Internet), the information highway,
which would convert the planet into one happy global village? APEC
free trade promises to connect all its members (one alleged bonanza is a
laptop for every citizen) as one big consuming family through the
technology of satellite telecommunication. Television ads by AT&T and
GTE, both giant U.S. TNCs, give the impression that these corporations
are bringing the world closer together. Yet while the top eight firms in
this sector earned $290 million in profits in 1995, 90.1 percent of
humankind live in households without telephones.

In general, then, globalization is a recently retooled program of
universal commodification, imperialism for the twenty-first century. It
functions as the paradigm of a supranational process of homogenizing

the world under the political and ideological hegemony of monopoly capitalist states through multilateral agencies (World Bank/IMF, WTO, United Nations) and transnational banks and firms. As noted earlier, one way to solve the periodic crisis of capital accumulation is to restructure the world's uneven development through constant readjustments of state-power relations, finetuning temporary equilibrium between wars "cold" and "hot." Globalization occurs when capital (of select dominant states) maps the productive resources of the world as a total integrated unit and then locates elements of complex production systems at points of greatest cost advantage in terms of costs of labor, materials, transport, and so on.

Activist Janet Bruin of WILPF (Women's International League for Peace and Freedom) contends that the IMF/World Bank structural adjustment programs imposed on ninety countries have accelerated the globalization process that integrates all countries in the global system of capitalist relations. The transfer of resources from South to North, estimated at $432 billion (in the last three years) has chiefly benefited the banks. Such "conditionalities" have been shown "to weaken the State, erode national sovereignty, and compromise the right of peoples to self-determination" (1996: 9). The political and economic crisis of Mexico demonstrates clearly the devastation wrought by the multilateral agencies of globalization. With its patrimony mortgaged to TNCs, Mexico has given birth to an armed liberation movement in Chiapas that vows to institute genuine democracy, dismantle NAFTA, and free the country from global plunder.

Proponents of globalization hold that national borders, nation-states, and nationalism have now become obstacles to Western-oriented development. With the help of neoclassical economic theory, the theory of globalization seeks to break down nation-state barriers to the encroachment of capital—in fact, the most widespread myth is that market forces released by uninhibited trade have made nation/nationality obsolete, residual, or inutile. One may ask: are Japan, Germany, and the United States no longer enjoying nation-state sovereignties? From a radical perspective, David Harvey opposes this myth by asserting that "space-place dialectic is ever a complicated affair, that globalization is really a process of uneven geographical and historical (spatiotemporal) development that creates a variegated terrain of anti-capitalist struggles that need to be synthesized in such a way as to respect the qualities of different 'militant particularisms' (such as those to be found in urban social movements throughout the world) while evolving strong spatial bonds and a global socialist politics of internationalism" (1996: 437). Meanwhile, diverse "militant particularisms" continue to inhabit nation-state territories in which protean forms of class war preponderantly alter and fix borders, frontiers, and sovereignties.

Globalization or spatialization then is a feature of late or transna-tional monopoly capitalism that should be analyzed dialectically. We cannot ignore the political-economic determinants of place construction and representation. Within the uneven geographical development of capitalism, "nation" in the "Third World" involves a construction of place, both territorial-ecological and "imagined communities" (to use Benedict Anderson's now canonical phrase), that does not depend simply on a Lacanian fantasy of enjoyment and desire as its ontological foundation. Rather, this shared community evolves in history with its singular culture, a species of the concrete universal embracing, in Fanon's words, "the whole body of efforts made by a people in the sphere of thought to describe, justify and praise the action through which that people has created and keeps itself in existence" (1963: 233).

Because the problematics of nation and nationalism have always been linked to Europe—its origin ascribed to Protestantism, print capitalism, and linguistic diversity—the derivative nationalism of the "Third World" becomes contentious for Partha Chatterjee (1986) and other postcolonial enthusiasts. In a familiar reflex reaction, Bhabha imputes to the idea of the nation a fatal contingency based on the arbitrary signs and symbols that constitute the template of any national culture. Given the characteristics of homogeneity, literacy and anonym-ity ascribed to the configuration of the bourgeois nation, Bhabha invokes the disjunctive logic of postcoloniality that is always undermined by "ambivalent temporalities," thus belying the organic and holistic theories of culture and community such as those of Fanon and other antibour-geois revolutionaries I shall discuss below. What confirms the reactionary cast of Bhabha's antinationalism, which refuses to discriminate between oppressed and oppressor nations (a plague on both their houses), is his belief that the notion of "the people" ("the nation" as "the many as one") "if pushed too far, may assume something resembling the archaic body of the despotic or totalitarian mass" (1995: 176). Here the discourse of crowd psychology (Le Bon, Joseph De Maistre, Edmund Burke) dove-tails with an anti-Enlightenment nihilism that sees the nation-building agenda of postcolonial regimes as the principal enemy. Meanwhile, globalization administered by aggressive nation-states in the North on behalf of home-based flagship corporations proceeds unquestioned as usual. Ludic postcolonialism such as that exemplified by Bhabha has nothing to say on the role of these national states as instruments of exploitation. It is blind to state machinery as a means of accelerating monopoly capital concentration through the private appropriation of public resources in displacing crisis onto the backs of people of color, in competition and combinations, including the neocolonial utilization of bourgeois client states in colonies, semicolonies, and dependent countries. The nation-state of the industrialized powers is alive but not so well, moribund on the whole and therefore more rapacious, challenged by the national liberation movements and by the revolt of the world's indigenous communities.

Given the absolutist condemnation of national liberation struggles by poststructuralist and postcolonial thinkers, I want to sketch in what follows a Bakhtinian approach to the nation as a mode of collective interpellation. As a type of "fictive ethnicity" (Balibar 1991) around which phantasms of belonging and identity founded on beliefs concerning origin, destiny, and commonality gravitate, the nation can be conceived as a historically and politically constructed place inscribed in the space of late modernity's disaggregated, nonsynchronized globalization. Nationalism then becomes an articulation of permanences within networks of uneven spatiotemporalities. Bakhtin's communicative process as dialogical exchange among interlocutors in specific historic conjunctures will then replace the hybridity/ambivalence binary that reifies borders and supposedly decentered global networks of interdependency and interaction, a binary that faithfully reflects the contradictory tensions of uneven development in the capitalist world-system. Like the dialectical reconnaissances of Freire, Gramsci, and C. L. R. James, Bakhtin's dialogic imagination can bridge seemingly incommensurable heterogeneities without disavowing the vocation of a thoroughgoing social and political transformation across the overlapping and intersecting domains of class, race, gender, and nationality.

ADDRESSING MODALITIES OF THE NATION

Of the most dangerously utilized words in contemporary discourse on culture and politics, "nation" and "nationalism" are salient in the light of the raging ethnonationalist wars in the former Yugoslavia, Northern Ireland, Rwanda, Chechnya, and the territories in which the Kurds are dispersed, to cite only the most publicized. While some predict the demise of the "nation" (more precisely, the bourgeois and neocolonial forms of the nation-state sprung from booty or comprador capitalism), others want "nationalism" arrested, convicted, and buried; both terms, however, are not only alive and well but have acquired urgent multi-accented resonance. Their diasporic presence fortuitously illustrates Bakhtin's concept of words (verbal discourse, speech acts) as social events, not abstract linguistic phenomena or subjective reflexes (1973: 96-100). Condensing the complex social situations that generate their use and constitute their meanings, "nation" and "nationalism" perform in various sites of exchange what Bakhtin would call "double-voiced" functions: they summon forth the partisanship of multiple addressees, releasing heterogeneous impulses with relativizing effects and also circumscribing them in speech genres and chronotopes that somehow map the unfinalizable circuit of communication. I want to explore here how Bakhtin's approach to discourse and its historicity can illuminate the roles/usages that the "nation" assumes when it participates in the shaping of "Third World" utterances of national liberation.

Bakhtin's theories of dialogism, carnivalesque interlocutions, and heteroglossia have thoroughly colored his academic reputation to the extent of converting the corpus of his achievement into its ironic opposite: a monologue on unfinalizability and the infinitude of possible meanings latent in speech acts. Recently, with the publication of *Speech Genres and Other Late Essays* (1986), Bakhtin's sense of a limit to endless semiosis—taming the "delirium" within, as it were—has been called to our attention.

Given the materiality of discourse and its social determinants, we can pose the following heuristic questions: Can the Other (difference) exist without the Same (identity)? Indeed, can heteroglossia occur without an official normative idiom to which stratified voices respond? As Ken Hirschkop would put it, can democratic impulses exist outside a hegemonic order? Aside from valorizing the chronotope of literary forms like the Bildungsroman, the emphasis on speech genres or conventions is salutary. Michael Holquist points to the interface in Bakhtin's theory between the necessity of conventions or patterns and the relative degree of interpretive freedom: "the better we know possible variants of the genres that are appropriate to a given situation, the more choice we have among them" (Bakhtin 1986: xix). Without ground, there is no figure; transgressing frames depends on positing them first.

What kind of speech genre, then, do utterances on nation and nationalism configure? First of all, for Bakhtin, utterance does not correspond to atomized parole but to the act of communication; meaning is produced in the "typical situations" of interlocution that actualize the performative dynamism of language. Dialogism transpires when speech acts of answering coincide with those of anticipation/provocation (Pechey 1987: 67). These situations always involve the loci of speaker, topic of exchange, and addressee. In the speech genre of nationalism (I refer specifically to the "Third World" anti-imperialist kind rooted in the universal principles of democracy and popular sovereignty), the addressee becomes primary insofar as the speaker's attitude to the "other"—a differentiated collective, an actual ethnic group, or an apostrophized and invoked social bloc/alliance—determines the addressivity of the utterance, its constitutive function. Nationalist rhetoric of a Marxist orientation (Lowy 1993) chiefly prefigures the addressee in an imaginary space while at the same time registering its empirical subject-position; the pragmatic axis of this genre then confirms Bakhtin's insight that the sign is the theater par excellence of ideological class struggle.

Central to the ideological class struggle since the rise of European empires has been the "national question": the fact of the colonial oppression of millions of people in Africa, Asia, and Latin America. The representation of this fact and the demystification of the ideology legitimizing it comprise the twin tasks that have so far preoccupied a Bakhtinian/Marxist critique.

The "national question" is fundamentally dialogic and relational in its historical specificity. For example, Marx believed that the proletarian goal of a classless society in England cannot be achieved without the liberation of England's colony, Ireland; likewise, white workers in Europe cannot free themselves from capitalist degradation without emancipating their dark-skinned counterparts everywhere. In a similar vein, Lenin emphasized the progressive character of the national-liberation struggles concurrent with the socialist revolution in Europe. The situation of colonized peoples fighting for self-determination, inflecting the Enlightenment ideas of liberty and equality (as C. L. R. James shows in *The Black Jacobins*), grounds the chronotope of the decolonizing narrative. A polyphony exists between the solidarity of exploited workers in the metropole and subjugated peoples in the periphery, a reciprocity syncopated with the war between the colonizing bourgeoisie and the subaltern natives. What gives universal import to this polyphony is the listener Bakhtin calls "superaddressee," in this case, the hegemonic ethos of "socialist man" (Che Guevara), the utopian figure of the "social individual" under communism envisioned in, for example, Marx's *Critique of the Gotha Program* or *The German Ideology*. This "third party" of the communication circuit can, however, be accessed only through the speech genre of the "nation," a discursive terrain charged with a "heterological" evaluation of the world and cathected with a singular intention (Todorov 1984: 57).

Before drawing the constellation of analogies linking the genre of nationalist discourse and dialogism, I interpolate here a few reminders on Bakhtin's notion of "otherness" that underlies the concept of heterology (that is, the multiplicity of speech genres) as the antithesis to linguistic unification and monologic synchrony.

In their 1929 work *Marxism and the Philosophy of Language,* Bakhtin/Voloshinov elaborated the proposition that social intercourse establishes the possibility of verbal communication and therefore speech performances. The structure of utterances coincides with the transaction among determinate, situated speakers. Not only is the word a two-sided act, "the product of the reciprocal relationship between speaker and listener, addresser and addressee" (86), participating in historical becoming and sociopolitical struggle—a leitmotif developed throughout in "Discourse in the Novel" (see Bakhtin 1981). It is also the "arena of the class struggle" because plural interests converge/diverge within the sign community, generating the "social multiaccentuality of the ideological sign" (23). In the 1952-53 essay "The Problem of Speech Genres," Bakhtin shifts his attention to the explanation of developments in language and literature as revealed by the history of speech genres as they reflect protean changes in social life. Of all speech genres, the dialogue is viewed as "a classic form of speech communication" that entails rejoinders of all kinds and presupposes other (relative to the speaker) participants in the speech communication. In this context, Bakhtin observes that "The very problem of the national and the individual in language is basically a problem of the utterance (after all, only here, in the utterance, is the national language embodied in individual form)" (63).

So far, Bakhtin's theory of the utterance posits the contextuality of the subject, more precisely a community of ideological norms, judgments, and evaluations. This signifies not a plurality of speakers but a chain or configuration of speaking subjects involved in "actively responsive understanding" (68). Intersubjectivity is founded on the principle of alterity and exotopy. "In life . . . we appraise ourselves from the point of view of others," Bakhtin writes. We can never grasp ourselves as a whole; the other is needed to give us a perception of our self as a totality, as a personality "consubstantial with the external world. . . . To be means to be for the other, and through him, for oneself. Man has no internal sovereign territory; he is all and always on the boundary; looking within himself, he looks in the eyes of the other or through the eyes of the other" (Todorov 1984: 97). Life is essentially dialogical—we are always engaged in questioning, listening, answering, agreeing, disagreeing. It requires the protagonists in the dialogue not to be equal but asymmetrical and radically distinct, so as to facilitate what Todorov calls "the objectivation of the I, the erasure of its pseudosingularity" (97). The subject (self, consciousness) is precisely that condition in which the necessity of others is established.

Others (collectivities)—participants in communicative action—are thus needed to actualize the dialogic play of utterance, functioning as the transgredient element needed to realize the moment of socially responsive understanding that validates communication. These others who are addressed can range from the immediate participants to what can be designated as a "third party":

> . . . in addition to this addressee (the second party), the author of the utterance, with a greater or lesser awareness, presupposes a higher superaddressee (third), whose absolutely just responsive understanding is presumed, either in some metaphysical distance or in distant historical time (the loophole addressee). In various ages and with various understandings of the word, this superaddressee and his ideally true responsive understanding assume various ideological expressions (God, absolute truth, the court of dispassionate human conscience, the people, the court of history, and so forth). . . . The aforementioned third party is not any mystical or metaphysical being . . . he is a constitutive aspect of the whole utterance, who, under deeper analysis, can be revealed in it. . . . Karl Marx said that only thought uttered in the word becomes a real thought for another person and only in the same way is it a thought for myself. But this other is not only the immediate other (second addressee); the word moves ever forward in search of responsive understanding. (Bakhtin 1986: 126-27)[1]

Could this "third party" or intermediary participant be the key category that can shed light on how the idea of the nation and its corollary, nationalism, continue to survive despite the forces of universalizing urbanity and the standardizing drive of metropolitan capitalism today?

NOMADIC TRAJECTORIES

When Marx and Engels proclaimed in *The Communist Manifesto* that the working class has no country, they probably expressed more of their own situation of exile and rationalistic aspiration for cosmopolitan solidarity than the lived experience of the proletariat's rootedness in place or locale. Proletarian consciousness then had not yet reached the point of transcending ethnonational boundaries. Consequently the Second International broke up when working-class leaders of various European nation-states opted to support their national bourgeoisie in World War I.

While the bourgeoisie cannot be accused of inventing nationalism to delude the workers, the ideology of nationalism arose with mercantilism in eighteenth-century Europe and the formation of nation-states. The Italian Marxist Gramsci observed the uneven development of the bourgeoisie in late medieval Europe and concluded: "The historical unity of the ruling classes is realized in the State and their history is essentially the history of States or groups of States" (1971: 52; see Arrighi 1993). The power of the sovereign state ruled by a particular bourgeoisie marked the boundaries of internal markets as well as the geopolitical monopoly of available bodies (labor power) and natural resources. Enlightenment thinkers like Rousseau and Kant contemplated the positive value of international solidarity and cooperation among the bourgeois states. Meanwhile, philosophers like Herder and Fichte, followed by Hegel, Mazzini, Acton, and Weber, among others, espoused in various ways the rights of culturally defined collectivities called "nations" against imperial hegemony and its "civilizing" agents. When inflected with liberal or conservative predilections, nationalism acquires either a benign or malignant temper. In "What Is a Nation?" (1882), Ernest Renan rejected Edmund Burke's idea of the nation as founded on religion and tradition. Renan believed that the nation "is a soul, a spiritual principle" that derives from "a common heroic past, great leaders and true glory" confirmed in daily plebiscites (1995: 154). When this idea of nation built on sacrifice is inflected with the racial superiority of its constituents—"a mass psychological vibration predicated upon an intuitive sense of consanguinity" (Connor 1978: 381), modern fascism is born.

"Nation" as a term in verbal transactions focuses on the theme of community or common bonds based on inter alia language, kinship, religion, territory, customs, and so on.[2] Affective ties (many invented or imagined, as Benedict Anderson has shown) can also gravitate around the hypothesis of a common origin or common destiny. Often "the parameters of an imagined community can be specified and legitimated by racism" (Miles 1987: 41). The call for national unity is addressed to those who ascribe to themselves belongingness to certain organic domains that entitle one to membership in the nation. While this impulse toward solidarity leads to an authoritative closure of utterance, to monologic statements, it can also direct us toward a permanent open interrogation that solicits a critical responsiveness. Dialogized (that is, operationalized in a dramatic-narrative stage), it can pose a challenge, an interrogation that demands a response. How is this possible when nationalism ("my nation" demarcated from "yours") implies exclusion and identity premised on affinities, whether real or fantasized? Doesn't nationalism privilege commonalities? Can "nation" be a multiaccentual sign, a double-voiced chronotope that can be deployed in versatile fashion? Can the utterance of "my nation" or "your nation" solicit a free play of into/nation, so to speak?

In the context of the history of "nationalisms" in Europe, the ex-colonized countries of the South (versus the North), and the United States, such questions cannot be answered in the abstract without delimiting the area of reference. Here I propose a specific topic of inquiry. I would like to explore the resonance of Bakhtin's addressivity of utterance vis-à-vis a historical-materialist reading of nationalism and then apply the notion of "third party" and alterity to certain "Third World" articulations of the principle of decolonizing subaltern subjects. The intertextual semantics of "nation" may provide a heuristic guideline to examining the articulation of revolutionary nationalist movements in the "Third World" with the politics of feminism and antiracism in a postmodern milieu (see, for example, Kuumba and Dosunmu 1995).

The Austrian Marxist Otto Bauer defines the nation "as a community of character arising out of a community of fate" (1970: 267). By character he means "national peculiarities" in modes of thought, behavior, temperament, and so on, that compose a distinctive physiognomy. These are differences "in the basic structure of the national mind, intellectual and esthetic taste, and reactions to the same stimuli; differences of which we become aware when we compare the cultural life of the nations, their science and philosophy, their poetry, music, and arts, their political and social life, their customs and way of life" (270). In effect, this character is a "precipitation of past historical processes," not a given biological or genetic inheritance. Since the community of character arises from the common fate of the ruling classes, Bauer argues that the national phenomenon cannot be divorced from the process of integration of the social classes. The "historical nation" arose in capitalism when the governing mercantile classes gained cultural/political hegemony over the masses; while in "unhistorical nations" dominated by alien ruling classes, "it was the very beginning of a national cultural community, a true 'awakening'" (274). Bauer still uses the untenable dichotomy of "historical" and "unhistorical" derived from Marx's prejudice against peoples "without a history" (see Marx 1969). In any case, the discourse of classic Western nationalism is an expansive process that begins with the bourgeoisie and then implicates other classes, so that a socialist project becomes, in the orthodox maxim, "national in form, socialist in content."[3]

According to Bauer, international socialist ideology and tactics cannot help but assume a national form in its development and concrete application. Diverse socialisms are "historical product(s)" of varied national characteristics. Bauer believes that the socialist "task must not be to stamp out national peculiarities but to bring about international unity in national diversity" (275). Although limited to the industrial capitalist societies, Bauer's observation has in effect dialogized the unitary and homogeneous doctrine of "socialism in one country," a move whose resonance can be discerned in the pronouncements of militant anticolonialists like Sun Yat-sen, Jawaharlal Nehru, and Frantz Fanon. The stark limitation of Bauer's theory lies in its blindness to colonial racism. In *Discourse on Colonialism,* Aimé Césaire rightly condemns the "nation" as a "bourgeois phenomenon" insofar as that colonizing nation implements a strategy of white supremacy. The emancipation of the Negro and what the West regards as dark-skinned "barbarians" exceeds the limits of the political class struggle; Marx needs to be completed by providing an answer to the "Negro" or race question (1972: 69-70). What Césaire does is to question the fetishism of "nation," to question its semantic authority, not only by introducing class stratification but also by exposing the racializing subtext in colonialism.

The articulation of "nation" as an anticolonial force against Western imperialism by subjugated peoples necessarily includes the Other (the colonizing master) as one addressee. It is the first stage in overcoming tutelage and gaining autonomy. But this internalization varies according to time and place, thus generating complex genealogies of resistance. For the Chinese nationalist Sun Yat-sen, not only Woodrow Wilson's proposal of "self-determination of peoples" (with its provenance in the French Revolution) but more cogently the example of Lenin's Bolshevik revolution established the stage for repudiating the false cosmopolitanism then deluding China's youth, a cosmopolitanism that is for him only "imperialism and aggression in another guise." In "Three Principles of the People," Sun writes: "We, the wronged races must first recover our position of national freedom and equality before we are fit to discuss cosmopolitanism" (199: 245). Without the national voice, the horizon of addressivity, there cannot be any cosmopolitan utterance since the addressee is no longer conceived as the racial Other but the past civilization of China that has antedated everything in Europe, including communism, except for science. Dialogic understanding, authentic communication, presupposes a recovery of what has been silenced or erased: "Europeans cannot yet discern our ancient civilization, yet many of our race have thought of a political world civilization . . . Because of the loss of our nationalism, our ancient morality and civilization have not been able to manifest themselves and are now even declining" (1995: 246-247). Sun believes that the true spirit of cosmopolitanism, genuine internationalism, can only be built on the foundation of nationalism: "Russia's one hundred fifty million are the foundation of Europe's cosmopolitanism and China's four hundred million are the foundation of Asia's cosmopolitanism" (1995: 247).

In contrast, the Indian leader Nehru seeks to remedy the monologic tradition of India rooted partly in religion, partly in the authority of the exclusivist caste system. Unlike Sun and the influence of a long tradition of popular resistance in China, Nehru seems transfixed by the passivity of the indigenous masses. Nehru calls for a critical rejection of the past and an emulation of the dynamic and scientific outlook of the West. While recognizing the problems of self-destructive change in Europe, Nehru invokes an addressee attuned to "the spirit of the age." Nationalism, from this secularizing perspective, "is essentially a group memory of past achievements, traditions, and experiences" (1995: 250) that intensifies during crisis. This crisis can be resolved by adhering to universal ideals: "a faith in humanity and a belief that there is no race or group that cannot advance and make good in its own way, given the chance to do so," given equal opportunities and freedom.

Acquisition of state power by the comprador bourgeoisie tied to the feudal landlords, however, does not necessarily unify the diverse "nations" within the space of the Indian "nation-state." What renders precarious Nehru's striving for a unified agenda of progress for India is the brute fact of diversity, the centrifugal polyphony of voices and secessionist impulses that British imperialism could barely synchronize. Heteroglossia marks the circumstantial matrix of Indian nationalism that could find temporary focus in resistance against British rule; after independence, the voices of class and ethnic identities shatter the iterable and homophonic closure of nationalism as a political program. Without a socialist orientation, postcolonial nationalism (as in India and elsewhere) replicates in parodic form the emergence of the European bourgeoisie—a mock-intonation of the master's independence.

The dialogic strategy of revolutionary nationalism finds its most impassioned enunciation in Fanon's Manichean vision of the war between natives and settlers in Algeria. Fanon repudiates Leopold Senghor's hybrid African socialism with its easy mix of carnivalesque tropes, cannibalism, and transnational metaphysics of "confederation with France" (1963: 273).[4] In the now classic essay "Concerning Violence," Fanon rejects a postcolonial symbiosis of Self and Other (the postmodern version is Homi Bhabha's "in-betweenness") for a more dialectical narrative of self-emergence. He locates the moment of historical recovery of what is indigenous to a second stage of decolonization after a period of self-hatred and self-denigration. From the stage of being immobilized by colonial subjugation, the native metamorphoses into the world of dances, orgies of possession, rituals of magic—the occult sphere of the community and the unconscious. The nation is born from this mediation: "The native discovers reality and transforms it into the pattern of his customs, into the practice of violence and into his plan for freedom" (1963: 58). The discourse of self-determination finds its institutional embodiments in the practice of violent combat between intransigent forces: the settler and the exploited peasants, workers, and intelligentsia. The "other" then is problematized as pure negativity. The guerilla partisan or combatant who responds to the call of the oppressed "nation" (the "nation" born from this shared experience of domination and resistance) thus enacts the social relations and political practices that comprise the performative dimension of nationalist discourse.

Why is Fanon so enamored by violence, one may ask. Is it a means or an end in itself? Given the Manichean geopolitical arena in which colonialism has paralyzed the natives and fragmented them, it is only collective violent action that can awaken and unify them. The heteroglossia of war destroys the monologic power of the settler state by releasing the petrified others: "The mobilization of the masses, when it arises out of the war of liberation, introduces into each man's consciousness the ideas of a common cause, of a national destiny, and of a collective history" (1963: 93). But violence is not just a cathartic or cleansing force, restoring self-respect to the subaltern. Fanon anticipates that the process of armed struggle will have a more enduring result in the demystification of all state authority, including that of the nationalist bourgeoisie that aspires to supplant the foreign occupier, so that democratic participation of the masses can somehow be insured. The sense of responsibility and the importance of accountability, Fanon hopes, will be lasting pedagogical effects of the mass mobilization that initiates the genesis of the nation at the border between fetishism and demystification:

> Even if the armed struggle has been symbolic and the nation is demobilized through a rapid movement of decolonization, the people have the time to see that the liberation has been the business of each and all and that the leader has no special merit. . . . When the people have taken violent part in the national liberation they will allow no one to set themselves up as "liberators." They show themselves to be jealous of the results of their action and take good care not to place their future, their destiny, or the fate of their country in the hands of a living god. Yesterday they were completely irresponsible; today they mean to understand everything and make all decisions. Illuminated by violence, the consciousness of the people rebels against any pacification. (1963: 94)

Pacification by their native masters, that is, the magicians who will be engaged in imposing a new mystification: the neocolonial or postcolonial state.

Is Fanon's populist utterance here inventing his addressee, a fictional protagonist endowed with an instinct for participatory democracy who will no longer be vulnerable to ideological manipulation? Violence is thus the carnival of the oppressed in the war of national liberation, a process of destruction and renewal, the material body of the people undergoing metamorphosis and radical transformation. Such a revolution embodying the carnival spirit "frees human consciousness, thought, and imagination for new potentialities" (Bakhtin 1965: 49). But is the nation born from this carnival excess fit for the novelistic genre of creative and communal exchange? Is Fanon's populist nationalism a means of defusing class struggle by blurring the antagonism between proletariat and petite bourgeoisie, a rhetorical ploy used by the radicalized middle stratum to establish hegemonic management of internal differences within the emerging nation-state? Is the nation articulated by Fanon's discourse an utterance with sufficient decentering vitality to resist bureaucratic degeneration and systemic incorporation into the seductive Babel/babble of the global marketplace?

Fanon's valorizing of the liberatory act, the process of subversion, is rooted in the context of the Manichean universe of perpetual antagonism—the key chronotope of a plot of reversal and recognition. In "Discourse in Life and Discourse in Art," Bakhtin emphasized the inscription of context or lived situation in the structure and import of the utterance. In life, utterance becomes "an objective social enthymeme," a milieu of social/pragmatic evaluations shared by the community—also called "choral support"—that enables the "I" to "realize itself verbally only on the basis of 'we'" (1989: 600). Exotopy or outsidedness is the condition of possibility of inner speech, the vehicle of another's utterance. What links the verbal discourse and the extraverbal purview in utterance is intonation, the border between the said and unsaid. What is useful for our inquiry here is Bakhtin's concept of the "third participant," the hero of the verbal production, hovering between speaker and listener.

In Fanon's discourse on the making of the nation, we discover this "third participant" as the gap that opens up in the spontaneous explosion of Manichean violence, when the vanguard leadership of the anticolonial struggle displaces the masters (settlers) and closes the debate between the native intellectual and the metropolitan addressee. In fact, this erasure of the emergent nation/people seems enacted in the closure of Fanon's text "Concerning Violence" when the task of "introducing mankind" into the world becomes a joint collective project of Europeans and "Third World" subalterns. The nation/people agency of decolonization becomes the implied omitted premise in a global social revolution that elides the moment of national self-determination. In "The Pitfalls of National Consciousness," Fanon (1963) recognizes the inadequacy of the nationalist soliloquy performed by the underdeveloped native "middle class," essentially a comprador parasitic stratum tied ideologically and economically to the former colonizer. He stresses political education and participation of every citizen in order to prevent the cult of the leader, elitist Bonapartism and military caciquism: "Nationalism is not a political doctrine, nor a program." What is it then? Fanon calls for the elevation of the masses "from national consciousness to political and social consciousness"; however, unless social consciousness proceeds through the moment of nationalism, it will degenerate into "primitive tribalism" (203-04).

As though anticipating objections, Fanon asserts this controlling insight: "But if nationalism is not made explicit, if it is not enriched and deepened by a very rapid transformation into a consciousness of social and political needs, in other words into humanism, it leads up a blind alley. . . . The national government, if it wants to be national, ought to govern by the people and for the people" (204-05). It is clear now that this "third participant," the emergent community of the nation/people, to borrow Bakhtin's phrasing, "has not yet assumed full and definitive shape; the intonation has demarcated a definite place for the hero but his semantic equivalent has not been supplied and he remains nameless" (602).

The sheer "otherness" of its goal informs the dynamism of the revolutionary nationalist project. Because of this, semantic referentiality gives way to illocutionary pragmatic tendencies in thought and social practice. The performative dimension in utterance preponderates over the constative in Fanon's discourse in "On National Culture." The resonance of Fanon's intonation verges toward apostrophe, with the second participant (the addressee) as witness and ally, as if magically invoking/evoking the missing, prefigured locutionary "hero." But this hero is not an abstraction. Fanon constantly reiterates the constitution of "nation" by popular action: "The living expression of the nation is the moving consciousness of the whole of the people," the "coherent, enlightened action" of men and women, which implies "the assumption of responsibility on the historical scale" (1963: 204), a locutionary gesture reminiscent of Amilcar Cabral, Che Guevara, and Fidel Castro. Fanon dissociates himself from populism when he elucidates the link between culture and nation:

> A national culture is not a folklore, nor an abstract populism that believes it can discover the people's true nature. It is not made up of the inert dregs of gratuitous actions, that is to say actions which are less and less attached to the ever-present reality of the people. A national culture is the whole body of efforts made by a people in the sphere of thought to describe, justify, and praise the action through which that people has created itself and keeps itself in existence. A national culture in underdeveloped countries should therefore take its place at the very heart of the struggle for freedom which these countries are carrying on. (1963: 233)

The struggle for sovereignty and independence proceeds through the struggle of the masses for building the institutions of participatory democracy. Born in the "concerted process" of struggling for liberation and equality, the nation as the locus of the mobilized masses serves as the framework in which the renaissance of culture and the democratic state can occur. It is also "national liberation" that enables the culturally defined people to play its role in global/international affairs. In this light, one can appreciate Amilcar Cabral's whole philosophy of national liberation as essentially Fanonian: "the liberation of the process of development of national productive forces" for Cabral is essentially an "act of culture" (1973: 43; see also Davidson 1986).

In Fanon's address to militants, it is ultimately the "third partici-pant"—the nation-people—that enables dialogue to escape the mimetic circuit of speaker-listener, becoming the synecdoche for the circumstan-tial grounding of the idea of "nation" in historical specificity. This avoids essentialism and the perils of identity politics by preventing the fetish of textuality, even intertextuality, from foreclosing the conversation on the uses of the nation-form. Here the nationalist discourse becomes novel-ized, as it were, politicizing culture and interpellating the complicities of power and discursive-institutional forms (see Hirschkop 1989).

If the "nation" for Fanon is defined by the actors of revolutionary violence, for the Cuban revolutionaries Che Guevara and Fidel Castro, what is at stake is the transformation of the ethos of a whole community in which the nascent "third participant" appears as the heroic masses of Cuba and (via synecdoche and metonymy) of Latin America. This subject-position addressed by the Cuban texts acquires paradoxically concrete and also utopian attributes when inserted into the site of the nation as a community of sacrifice and self-fulfillment. The self-transforming agent in Fanon's text then finds its proper multi-accented intonation, as it were, in the historically anchored but also prophetic stance of the nation-based transnational protagonists envisioned by Che and Fidel.

In the famous letter to Carlos Quijano, editor of *Marcha* (an independent radical weekly published in Montevideo, Uruguay) in 1965 entitled "Notes on Man and Socialism in Cuba," Che exemplifies the politicization of translinguistics. The dialogization of the orthodox nation-centered discourse is carried out by reversing the anticommunist charge that the socialist state subordinates the individual: humans are, for Che, the "basic factor." But this mobilization of the individual from the inert mass molded by centuries of subaltern domination can be achieved only by the inculcation of the "heroic attitude in daily life" (1972: 325). This is the task of the vanguard party epitomized by Fidel Castro who, in his exchanges with the people, personifies the "close dialectical unity between the individual and the mass, in which the mass, as an aggregate of individuals, is interconnected with its leaders" (326). The mutualities condensed in the speaking subject (temporarily occu-pied here by Che) dissolves the gap between leaders and led. Contrasted with the subordination of humans to the capitalist "law of value" mystified as absolute freedom, the socialist narrative manifests itself as a pedagogical novelization: socialism is a transitional stage from the dominance of market relationships and class divisions to the beginning of rehumanization when socialist man reaches "total consciousness of his social function, which is equivalent to his full realization as a human being, once the chains of alienation are broken" (329).

Three points need to be underscored in Che's reflections: First, the chronotope of nation mutates into the chronotope of a borderline or threshold site. We notice the transitory and liminal nature of socialist reconstruction of the old dependent formation in which the "Other" of capitalist alienation acts as the centrifugal force against the sociopolitical project of socialist hegemony. In this discursive economy, the synchronic regularity of the "law of value" is disrupted by the diachronic intervention of the "heroic" sacrifice that displaces the "beaten track of material interest." Second, we witness an analogue of Bakhtin's theory of sign-production in Che's constant reference to the "quality of incompleteness, of being an unfinished product" (326) that characterizes the individual in socialism as a dual entity: unique person as well as member of society. This accords with Bakhtin's notion of exotopy: "I cannot do without the other; I must find myself in the other, finding the other in me (mutual reflection and perception). . . . I receive my name from the other, and this name exists for the other (to name oneself is to engage in usurpation)" (Todorov 1984: 97). From Che's perspective, the inchoate individual-in-process "educates himself" to his "social duty" as mover of society, part of a collective agent of change: "In this period of the building of socialism we can see the new man being born. His image is not yet completely finished—it never could be—since the process goes forward hand in hand with the development of new economic forms" (328). Third, Che's language is saturated with the rhythm of hope, invested with an obsession for beginnings. Cesaire's memorable line seems to have Che in mind: "The work of man is only just beginning" (Cesaire 1969: 85). We perceive here an affinity with the neo-Kantian principle of ethical participation in the realization of a "concrete ought," "my own actively answerable deed" (Bakhtin 1993: 57) that instances the categorical imperative when Che moves from the utopian argument of creating "the man of the twenty-first century" to the thematic topos of Cuba as a "vanguard nation" of the Americas:

> The individual in our country knows that the illustrious epoch in which it was determined that he live is one of sacrifice; he is familiar with sacrifice. The first came to know it in the Sierra Maestra and wherever else they fought; afterwards all of Cuba came to know it. Cuba is the vanguard of the Americas and must make sacrifices because it occupies the post of

advance guard, because it shows the road to full freedom to the masses of Latin America. . . .

In these circumstances one must have a great deal of humanity and a strong sense of justice and truth in order not to fall into extreme dogmatism and cold scholasticism, into an isolation from the masses. We must strive every day so that this love of living humanity will be transformed into actual deeds, into acts that serve as examples, as a moving force. . . . The revolution is made through man, but man must forge his revolutionary spirit day by day. . . .

We know that sacrifices lie before us and that we must pay a price for the heroic act of being a vanguard nation. . . . Each and every one of us must pay his exact quota of sacrifice, conscious that he will get his reward in the satisfaction of fulfilling a duty, conscious that he will advance with all toward the image of the new man dimly visible on the horizon. (Guevara 1972: 334-35)

The "superaddressee" as communist society-in-the-making, a future immanent in the present, becomes more visible in Fidel's "Words to the Intellectuals," remarks delivered to a 1961 meeting of Cuban intellectuals and artists in Havana after hearing diverse viewpoints on cultural policy for the Revolution. The formula he introduced—"Within the Revolution, everything; against the Revolution, nothing"—may sound extremely abstract and ambiguous, but later on Fidel spells out its practical antisectarian and antidogmatic implications (see Retamar 1989). His self-identification as a Cuban comes only at the end when he explains the reason why intellectuals would want to collaborate in the Revolution: to be witness to a world-historical happening. Cuba as an event, less than a national entity, becomes a locus for the privilege of testifying to and witnessing an unprecedented reordering of global priorities:

Something happened to me, for example, when I read about the Cuban War of Independence. I was sorry that I hadn't been born in that period and that I hadn't been a fighter for independence and that I hadn't lived at that epic time. All of us have read the chronicles of our War of Independence with deep-felt emotion, and we envied the intellectuals and artists and fighters and leaders of that time. However, to us has fallen the privilege of living now and being witnesses to a Revolution, to a Revolution whose force is now developing beyond the bounds of our country, whose political and moral influence is making imperialism on this continent tremble and totter. And this has made the Cuban Revolution the most important event of this century for Latin America, the most important event since the wars of independence of the nineteenth century; in truth, the redemption of man is new, for what were those wars of independence but the replacement of colonial domination by the domination of exploiting classes in all those countries?

And it has fallen to us to live in the time of a great historical event. . . . And we Cubans are its creators, knowing that the more we work the more the Revolution will be an unquenchable flame, the more it will be called upon to play a transcendent role in history. (Castro 1972: 296-97)

Orthodox, tradition-bound nationalism is thus reconfigured and modified by Fidel and Che when the formal rhetoric of dialogism, the acknowledgement of multiple ideological tendencies within the national space, is articulated with the project of forging a socialist nation-based hegemony against global capital (see Guevara 1962: 454-67). Like Che's exhortation to the cadres of the vanguard nation to sacrifice for the liberation of a whole continent, Fidel deploys Cuba and its historic defeat of U.S. imperialist power in its national territory as the springboard for emancipatory intervention in South America. The socialist project begins with national liberation—the vernacular utterance that frees itself from the official discursive economy—but transcends national boundaries, given capital's worldwide reach. Intonation of Cuba's example becomes an "othering of the nation-self" insofar as the emotional-volitional tone that surrounds the semantics of decolonization reveals a utopian, not an ethnocentric, intention. What is intended is the "third participant," masses in motion epitomized by the communist militant. We anticipate the advent of the superaddressee that preserves the virtue of the particular (national culture), elevates, and then incorporates it into another speech genre whose key terms are popular sovereignty, equality, and justice.

THE WEAPON OF "PRACTICAL CONSCIOUSNESS"

Finally, I want to cite here an example of how Bakhtin's idea of "reported speech," what I would call a specimen of intercontextual communication, can also shed light on the discourse of "Third World" nationalism as an attempt to displace the racist, "civilizing" nationalism of the West.

This is a species of creative production, the alterization of the bourgeois cogito, the imperial Self. I have in mind the context of the Filipino-American War (1899-1902) in which the United States military forces, after claiming friendship with General Emilio Aguinaldo, president of the first Philippine Republic, waged a brutal and savage war against the Filipino insurgents. This "insurrection," as the U.S. colonial authorities designated it, met a fierce campaign of suppression that ultimately led to the death of at least a million natives and over eight thousand American soldiers—historians call it America's "First Vietnam."[5]

During the early phase of the war, the leading Filipino intellectual and adviser to General Aguinaldo, Apolinario Mabini, responded to a manifesto signed by American Commissioners Jacob Gould Schurman, George Dewey, Elwell S. Otis, Charles Denby, Dean C. Worcester, and John R. MacArthur. Mabini described this Commission as one named by President McKinley "in order that the United States might fulfill her obligations under the Treaty of Paris, which transferred sovereignty over the Philippines from Spain to the United States." After quoting the stated intention of the Commission to introduce political, judicial, and economic reforms with the threat that those who refuse to submit will encounter the "ravages" of its armed forces, Mabini responds:

> In order to be believed in it did not hesitate to employ lies and shameless enough to say that my Government was the one which issued a challenge [to the Americans], this action being the result of the Filipino's ignorance of the goodwill and fraternal feelings of the Commission's greedy President, although in reality the whole world knows that it is President McKinley who actually gives the order to compel the American opposition senators to ratify the Treaty of Paris which transferred the Philippines to the United States. . . . What a spectacle it is to see that at the end of the century called enlightened and civilized, a people who know how to love their sovereignty and proud of their sense of justice now would use their accumulated force to wrest from a weak people the very rights which in their case they believe to be inherent in natural law! (1974: 230-31, translated from the original Tagalog by Teodoro Agoncillo)

From the linear style of speech reporting, Mabini shifts to what Bakhtin calls "pictorial" (1986: 120). The reporter infiltrates the reported statement with authorial retort and commentary, obliterating the boundaries between the reporting context and the reported speech. The author's positional staging of anger, sarcasm, disbelief, and resignation orchestrates the intonation of the quoted passage. Mabini quotes the American manifesto's claim of U.S. sovereignty as "compatible with reason and with our [Filipino] freedom" only to mock it by introducing McKinley's greed and in particular the refusal of the signatories to the Treaty of Paris to hear the representatives of the Filipinos "in accordance with reason and with international law." This critique of U.S. hypocrisy alludes to a "third participant" that Mabini summons, U.S. citizens and lawmakers who are sympathetic to the Filipino aspiration for independence and who opposed ratification of the Treaty of Paris and U.S. annexation of the Philippine Islands. In any case, the marks of pictorial reporting in most cases, for Bakhtin, indicates "a severe debilitation of both the authoritarian and the rationalistic dogmatism of utterance" (1986: 121).

At the end, however, Mabini invokes the addressee of this national utterance—the insurgent nation/people—now no longer tyrannized by Spanish arrogance but by "race prejudice, which is deep, cruel, and implacable in the North American Anglo-Saxon" (233). Like Sun Yat-sen, Césaire, and other radical democrats, Mabini counterpoints racism with rational Enlightenment humanism, but he quickly moves to a Fanonian moment of allusion. Mabini's text begins with the protocol of reporting information and the other's claim to truth, proceeds to an agonistic critique and interrogation of what is reported, and ends with a performative gesture: an apostrophe to the listener/audience, a call to arms and to sacrifice. If utterance is language infused with life via "addressivity" (Clark and Holquist: 217), the discourse of revolutionary nationalism that sublates the nation-identity into that of the people or masses exemplifies a genre that bridges the distance between the carnivalesque heteroglossia of Rabelais, its utopian futurism (Bakhtin 1965: 33), and the polyphonic vertigo of Dostoevsky.

In sum, what the kind of revolutionary nationalism espoused by Che Guevara, Fidel Castro, Aimé Césaire, and others all enact is the summoning forth, the evocation, of the "third party" whose testimony is the ongoing process of transformation marking the passage from the realm of Necessity (nation belongs here) to the realm of Freedom. The perils of fetishism and essentialism are thus thwarted by the unfinalizable, exotopic determination of the project. To grasp what long-range impact this decolonizing nationalism may have in the post–Cold War era, at the threshold of the twenty-first century, requires a series of concrete conjunctural analysis (for the case of Irish nationalism, see Crowley and Deane; for a cognitive mapping of nation-oriented movements, see Harvey). Despite the transcultural and transnational globalization being trumpeted as signaling the "end of history," the dialogue of nations will continue and national identifications survive well into the third millenium. The genealogist of this trend, Anthony D. Smith, assures us that nationalism as a mode of collective identity will persist for various reasons, among them "the need for collective immortality and dignity, the power of ethno-history, the role of new class structures and the domination of inter-state systems in the modern world" (1991: 176). In this inter-state configuration, the Filipino diaspora explodes as a poignant cry of the nation aborted once more, quarantined, disseminated in the wilderness of bazaars, the voices of OCWs drowned by the hawkers and money-changers. At any rate, the intonation and signifying of the "nation," now transcoded by the revolutionary masses in the speech genre of anti-imperialist militants, promises to be a rich field in which to explore further Bakhtin's seminal proposition of the sign as the battlefield of multiple social forces, sensibilities, and ideologies.

ENGENDERING DISSEMINATION

It is a long way since the Spanish-American War at the turn of the century, the collapse of the old empires, and the dawn of *pax Americana*. As we move to the threshold of the next millenium, we encounter the phenomenon of transnational capitalist class practices informed by the ubiquitous culture-ideology of consumerism (Sklair 1991). But transnationalism, as we have ascertained, is deceptive since one does not easily leap across and beyond nations or national frontiers—unless in fantasy or metaphysical speculation. Nonetheless, the reality of a kind of cosmopolitan outlook beyond primordial attachments has been celebrated by artists like Guillermo Gomez Peña as the occasion for "a new internationalism ex centris . . . for new hybrid identities and metiers constantly metamorphosing in a polysemantic border culture. . . . We walk amid the rubble of the Tower of Babel of our American postmodernity" (quoted in McLaren 1995). This "border" cartography imagined by many Latino and some Caribbean intellectuals reveals its true nature in the example of Los Angeles, the archetypal postmodernist city, in which (as Appelbaum [1996] and Bonacich [1996] have indubitably demonstrated) the sharper conflicts articulating class, gender, race, and nationality generate the contours, gaps, and zones of combat all deciphered by the cash nexus and profit accumulation. Underneath the veil of a hallucinatory multicultural Disneyland of consumption, we discover the logic of the "transportation" (to revive a quaint expression), surveillance, exploitation, and mutilation of bodies chiefly from the South.

This logic has ravaged also the psyches and bodies of Filipina women workers in export-processing zones, TNC subsidiary corporations, and overseas domestic quarters. In the Philippines, women succumb to an ascendant regime of labor market flexibility: job subcontracting, agency hiring, denial of fringe benefits and other protections afforded by unions, and other measures to intensify the rate of the production of surplus value. While the flows of foreign investment, mass media products, and information accelerate, the flow of the return to the workers and enlargement of their share of the social wealth have slowed down considerably or halted. But what I want to foreground here amid the praise for transcultural circulation of commodities and images in cyberspace and satellites is the unprecedented growth of the export of Filipino "warm bodies"—the Overseas Contract Workers.

In the transnational restructuring of state-power relations after the demise of the Soviet Union, the Philippines has been compelled to experience a late-capitalist diaspora of its citizens. A new sociopolitical category, Overseas Contract Workers (OCWs), has become the arena of hegemonic contestation. In 1995, we find about 7 million Filipinos (of a population of about 70 million) scattered around the markets of 135 nation-states (about 2,000 are deployed every day); they are extolled as new heroes, *bagong bayani,* constituting the negativity or alterity of capitalist hegemony—not yet a wandering proletarian vanguard but a potentially destabilizing leverage against the mantras of technocratic growth and prosperity.

While migration is a common worldwide trend in the socioeconomic interaction among countries, the background to the dynamics of contemporary labor diasporas is sketched by Milton Esman: "Demographic pressures—low birthrates in affluent countries, explosive population growth in nearby Third World countries, the availability of safe and cheap transportation, strong continuing demand in rich countries for low cost, docile labor—together have sustained powerful incentives and opportunities for large-scale migratory movement from impoverished Third World countries to affluent industrial and postindustrial economies" (1992: 34). What is missing in such antiseptic description is the dialectic between neocolonies and imperial metropoles (Vickers 1993). As Robert Miles pointed out, "labor migration accentuated the process of uneven development of the world capitalist economy" (1986: 60), thus perpetuating the unequal division of labor and lopsided redistribution of social wealth. In short, the industrialized North grew richer at the expense of the underdeveloped South; the gap between center and periphery widened.

In the Philippine case, the massive and swift growth of migrant labor during the Marcos regime and after (from 12,501 in 1975 to 719, 602 in 1994; Tujan 1995) signaled the complete breakdown of national sovereignty. It indicated also the deterioration of formerly cohesive extended families amid the deterioration of the economy (Eviota 1992; Aguilar 1995), a process exacerbated by the structural adjustment program of the IMF/World Bank. Impoverishment of the majority of Filipinos has driven many to desperation, even using illegal means to go abroad. Globalization thus becomes literal: to take advantage of petro-dollar-funded development projects in Saudi Arabia and other Middle Eastern states, the Marcos dictatorship organized and facilitated the labor subcontracting and recruitment of Filipino workers for overseas placement. Recruitment agencies multiplied and diversified, at first deploying highly paid professional and technical workers in the mid-seventies and then shifting to mass-recruited production workers in the eighties up to the present. Why this expenditure of state resources? The answer is simple: the amount of OCWs remittances (about $10.05 billion from 1990-94) have made the economy viable and the comprador elite solvent, the clearest sign of a government in distress (Aguilar 1997a).

The play of value (use, exchange, surplus) is inscribed in the symbolic economy of self-replicating migrant worker narratives. In the *Grundrisse,* Marx emphasized that "society does not consist of individuals; it expresses the sum of connections and relationships in which individuals find themselves . . . [Thus] to be a slave or to be a citizen are social determinations." Likewise, to be a Filipina migrant laborer in the domestic sphere today is to be determined in a geopolitical hierarchy in which the fact of being located as (1) Filipino, (2) female, (3) worker, and (4) domestic/household slave produces texts/narratives that can be read simultaneously as symptoms of a new global political economy of accumulation and as allegories of resistance. In transnational capitalism, the productive consumption of labor power as the prime commodity (abstract, quantitatively comparable) that is exchanged has been marked by gender, sexuality, region/locality, and nationality in order to reduce the labor needed to reproduce it and therefore maximize surplus value (unpaid labor). What is "socially necessary" becomes politically defined: Third World women are paid subsistence wages, even starved as virtual slaves, denied basic rights, abused, raped, and even killed. Female domestic and sexual labor-power yields a use-value (a product) whose marketprice as commodity is depreciated because of its property as (1) female, and (2) as subaltern impoverished nationality (Filipina, Sri Lankan, Indian, Bangladeshi). The unequal division of international labor and the abundant supply of such cheap "Third World" labor in the world market, as well as the hegemonic pressures of the centers of finance capital, all converge to reverse the equalizing and liberating power of abstract exchange value (money as "universal social property") and make the expropriated use-value reinforce tributary or semifeudal patriarchal relations.

In the classic narrative plot of accumulation and mastery (progress), $M1 \longrightarrow C \longrightarrow M2$, exchange value grows by consuming labor-power. But for the stories recounted by migrant female domestic workers (contracted overseas labor), the plot evokes the order of simple or petty commodity production: $C \longrightarrow M \longrightarrow C$. Consequently, the fetishism of exchange-value is destroyed by the constant and immediate conversion of money into consumer goods. The textuality of servitude and death in the policed domestic sphere dissolves with the purchasing power of whatever wage is received: "the power that each individual exercises over others' activity or over social wealth exists in her as the owner of exchange values, money" (Marx 1971: 66). Orgies of consumption, spectacles of expenditure, and other extravagant displays all aim to celebrate use-value and overcome by spasmodic shopping sprees, by an evocation of utopian finality, the death drive prefigured in the postmodern sublime whose text is nothing but the infinite circulation of signifiers of difference— circulation in itself. This is the farce that redoubles tragic lives. Such female narratives of diaspora and return may be parables of subversive energies attempting to transform the market and the commodity form into signs of the triumph of use-value per se, commodities valorized as aesthetic objects and as instruments to negate their exchange value. At the very least, when Filipina women either strike back (like Lorna Laraquel, who killed her employer, a member of the Kuwaiti royal family, in 1992 [Maglipon 1990]) or escape from their multiple confinements, their narratives begin to interrupt the flow of warm bodies into the market and signal a crisis in the postmodern traffic of differences that matter.

Recruited by agencies for work in the Middle East, Hong Kong, Japan, Singapore, and many European countries, 80 percent of the OCWs are women exploited, harassed, mutilated, raped, and killed in a way unprecedented in modern history. Most of them work as domestic helpers or as semiskilled labor in low-paying, hazardous jobs (entertainers) that eventually drive them to prostitution. Others have taken the refuge of being "mail order" brides, a kind of lifetime indenture or peonage. Hundreds have suffered brutalities and privations of all kinds, with many returning to the Philippines in coffins. It is estimated that there are two thousand Filipino OCWs in jail abroad, with one hundred of them facing the death penalty (Center for Women's Resources 1996). The most recent cases of Flor Contemplacion (hanged in Singapore) and the sentencing of Sarah Balabagan for killing the employer who tried to rape her (she was released in 1996) have aroused national indignation and a storm of protests.

The enigmatic lacunae of Flor Contemplacion and Sarah Balabagan's narratives testify to the ruthless march of globalization. They afford a grisly antithesis to the postcolonial cliches of exile, the unhomely, and diaspora in which intellectuals like Said, Bhabha, and Gilroy have wagered their polymorphous prestiges (Tadiar 1993). Flor Contemplacion's agony—twenty-two months in detention before execution on 17 March 1995—was neither metaphor nor trope; her confession was forced under torture by prison officials of that police state. No one advised her of her rights. Apart from the ineptitude of lawyers assigned to her and the apathy of Philippine diplomatic officials, she was, even if guilty, "not given the protection necessarily afforded by law to an accused as a basic human right" (Beltran and Rodriguez 1996: 69). She was not allowed to take the defense of "diminished responsibility." According to medical testimony, Contemplacion was suffering from epileptic symptoms (dismissed as "slight migraine" by court doctors) when she supposedly killed a child and fellow co-worker. Her history of illness was absent from the court records. From the age of twelve to twenty-five, she was subject to high fevers, headaches, nausea, shivering and shaking of the body. When she was twenty-five, "after the birth of her first child, she woke up one morning with a severe headache, shivering and nauseated. She opened her eyes and saw lightning pass by. At the same time, she felt strangely strong, saw people floating in the air, who were shrinking in size. She also felt rage and anger" (Beltran and Rodriguez 1996: 56). The Gancayco Commission that reviewed her case concluded that Flor Contemplacion was the victim of an affluent society that had ceased to be humane and caring, concerned more with economic than human rights. In the age of the refugee, displaced person, masses of uprooted people, Flor Contemplacion exposes the subliminal aesthetic distancing of the nomadic hybrid as a gratuitous cover for elite indifference.

Sarah Balabagan, one of the twenty-one thousand OCWs in the United Arab Emirate (UAE), was not executed like Contemplacion but "only" punished with one hundred strokes of the cane, in addition to being imprisoned for one year and obligated to pay blood money (US$40,000) to the family of the rapist. The tables had been turned: the rapist needs restitution. Balabagan was fifteen years old when she arrived at the UAE—indeed she was a minor, a child, which should not have been allowed if international standards against the trafficking and slavery of children were followed. On 6 June 1995, she was jailed for seven years for killing her eighty-five-year-old employer who raped her. She was ordered to pay $40,000 because she was deemed guilty of "abusing her right to self-defense" by stabbing her assailant thirty-four times (Beltran and Rodriguez 1996: 61). When a violent demonstration ensued in the Philippines, the president of the UAE ordered another trial in which Balabagan was found guilty of premeditated murder and sentenced to death. After President Ramos appealed for clemency, her sentence was reduced. The last news report dealing with her return home may be a seriocomic denouement under the postmodernist gaze: Sarah Balabagan's life will be the subject of a commercial film that will make her an instant celebrity, unlike previous OCWs who returned home in coffins, among them, Maricris Sioson, Cecilia Gelio-Agan, Jocelyn Guanezo, and others; bodies severely damaged and mutilated by their Japanese patrons (Beltran and De Dios 1992).

In retrospect, the numerous victims of this diaspora now function as the addressees of the nation, subaltern speech mortgaged to the traffic in still warm if docile bodies. In *The Black Atlantic,* Paul Gilroy elevates the "ontological rupture of the middle passage," the pain and degradation of slavery, as the central paradigm of modernity characterized by diasporic double consciousness and ethnicity as an "infinite process of identity construction" (1993: 223). But this hermeneutics of mutation, hybridity, and intermixture ignores the facts of contemporary history (Dayan 1995), the terror of late modern export/import of millions of women of color not found in the novels of Toni Morrison and Richard Wright. Globalized trade in OCWs certainly incorporate the contamination and complicity so prized by postcolonial critics, but their aestheticization of unevenness and nonsynchronicity leads to a metaphysics of what Herbert Marcuse once called "repressive desublimation." One cannot help but suspect that the postcolonial sublime flourishes in the wreckage and misery of global capitalism.

Women of color are now chattel goods in jet-propelled slaveships, caught by the "violence of speed [that] has become both the location and the law, the world's destiny and its destination" (Virilio 1977: 151). No longer can we accurately analogize this diaspora to the Jewish or African precedents. In this itinerary of deterritorialization, who are the interlocutors that can suture the signifiers of pain to the signifieds of simulacra and bytes in the electronic media? Who can chart the dematerialized flows of their anguish and dreams that finally congeal in battered cadavers? What listener in the transcendental realm of Lyotard's *differend* can restore the lives of tortured victims like Gloria Ferlin (murdered in Lebanon), Angelina Palaming, Norma Barroga and Myrna Andrade (slain in Singapore), and Regina Loyola (killed in Hong Kong), just to cite the most recent incidents? Indeed, who can speak or negotiate for these identities no longer unstable, beyond the aura of the uncanny and the *unheimlich,* irrecuperable from their transcendental finitude? Where can one discover the differential subject/object position bereft of countermemory, of the delirious other within, of the "displaced shadow space" that marks subaltern heterogeneity? These questions sound, to be sure, like mock-pastiches assembled from postcolonial and postmodernist wreckage of discourses that litter the graves of OCWs in their global odyssey. If they are counterfeits, where are the original stigmata of suffering, loss, defeat? If they are ventriloquistic, artificial and contrived, where are the authentic voices, the autochtonous signatures, the privileged seals of truth and authorized representation?

CHAPTER SEVEN

Beyond Postcolonial Theory:
The Mass Line in C. L. R. James's Works

One of the many facets of the career of Mzee C. L. R. James is precisely the awareness that African freedom will not be won without building on the positive elements in the history of Mankind.

—Walter Rodney

C. L. R. James is a great West Indian of complex spirit ... a unique Marxist thinker whose dialectic is attuned, it seems to me, to necessity for individual originality as much as it is involved in analyses of historical process in the life of the people or the body-politic.

—Wilson Harris

Migrating from the academic periphery to the center, the current orthodoxy of postcolonial studies has advanced to the point at which certain doctrines concerning hybridity, syncretism, ambivalence, and so on, mimic ironically what they are supposed to denounce: the master discourses of hegemonic Europe and North America. To rectify this tendency, the authors of the influential textbook *The Empire Writes Back* proclaim that imperial suppressions work "through as well as upon individuals and societies" and transcend "the egregious classification of 'First' and 'Third' World," thus claiming all space/time as its field of investigation. In *The Post-Colonial Studies Reader,* the same authors— Bill Ashcroft, Gareth Griffiths, and Helen Tiffin—proceed to revise the old "civilizing mission" of the West by mandating the desideratum of concentrating on lineages. Consequently, the study of settler colony cultures becomes paradigmatic: "Settler colonies, precisely because their filiative metaphors of connection problematise the idea of resistance as a simple binarism, articulate the ambivalent, complex and processual nature of all imperial relations" (1995: 3-4).[1] Following the poststructuralist tenets of Derrida, Foucault, and Lyotard, the discursive practices of the colonizer are assumed to limit opposition peremptorily so that all resistance is fated to be complicit in domination, and all we can hope for is what postcolonial guru Homi Bhabha (1995) calls the "Third Space of enunciation," the "in-between" of Derrida's *ecriture,* of translation and interstitial negotiation, the "discontinuous intertextual temporality of cultural difference."[2]

I want to argue here that to the disjuncture between postcolonial undecidability, ethnic/nationalist essentialism, and what Paul Gilroy (1992) hypothesizes as a "black Atlantic" transcendence of boundaries can be counterposed the practice of the diasporic thinker C. L. R. James. His is neither a third way nor a reconciliation of opposites. His body of work illustrates how the political and artistic engagements of a decolonizing subject can refunction the master discourse of "dialectical materialism" without being complicit in restoring or recuperating domination. Such a discourse (the legacy of the European Enlightenment from Spinoza and Hegel to Marx, Engels, Lenin, and Trotsky) is not just enunciated by the subaltern but remolded to speak to/about circumstances and protagonists beyond those addressed by its originary theoreticians. What James accomplished is not just the invention of a counterdiscourse, a dialogic performance, suitable for "flexible" accumulation. It is a reaffirmation of the theme of "universality" against Cold War bipolarity and the pervasive fragmentation and reification of life in late capitalism. In the wake of the demise of Soviet "state capitalism" and globalized capitalism's commodification of the whole planet (Magdoff 1992), James's reconstruction of the materialist dialectic valorizes three motifs in his analysis of culture and society: contradiction as the basis of historical motion, the agency of the masses as creative and transformative force, and the practice of freedom as the embodiment of universality. Of these three, the agency of the masses and how it negates the need for mediation (by the party, bureaucrats, etc.) becomes pivotal to James's cultural politics. It informs the narrative of complex dynamic forces in *The Black Jacobins* (1938). It enables James to avoid the perils of economism, class reductionism, voluntarism/sectarianism, and empirical determinism when he reflects on the Cold War conjuncture in the posthumously published *American Civilization* (1995).

The question of mass agency is linked to a controlling principle that governs James's project of subverting state capitalism whether Stalinist or liberal: the centrality of movement in everything, in particular the dialectical transition from the old to the new. Transcontinental imperialism cannot be overcome without grasping motion in space and time. Disjunctions or distances in space becomes intelligible when the process of becoming (the ec-stases of human temporality) is reinscribed in the historicist organon that James distills in a sentence: "We can orient for the future only by comprehension of the present in the light of the past" (1994: 168). It took him almost half a century to realize this diasporic orientation in his life and thought, that "it is not quality of goods and utility which matter, but movement; not where you are or what you have, but where you have come from, where you are going, and the rate at which you are getting there" (Henry and Buhle 1992: 39).

Before examining this principle of becoming and the themes of universality and contradiction in James's texts, a biographical parenthesis may be useful. A product of British Caribbean colonial education, James's love of English literature and his devotion to cricket as an art combined with his involvement in Trinidad's organized labor movement. His first book, *The Life of Captain Cipriani* (1932), also laid claim to the foundations of West Indian nationalism in the interwar period. When he moved in 1932 to England, he was exposed to the Trotskyist movement and became an independent socialist critical of Stalinism and the Comintern, as shown in his book *World Revolution* (1938). In essence, his critique of authoritarian forms of rule centered on the notion of a vanguard party that would substitute for the revolutionary creative energies of the people and of the popular forces of the left around the world. What complicates James's Trotskyism is his pan-Africanism: his collaboration with George Padmore, Paul Robeson, and the Guyanese activist Ras Makonnen linked him to a historical process begun by W. E. B. DuBois and the Pan-African Congress and by Marcus Garvey; through this James exerted influence on Jomo Kenyatta and Kwame Nkrumah. James's play *Toussaint L'Ouverture* was sponsored by the League for the Protection of Ethiopia.

Transported to the metropolis, the West Indian colonial subject discovers the African subtext in the palimpsest of world proletarian revolution. James's book *The Black Jacobins* (1938) demonstrates his historical-materialist breadth of vision by connecting the French Revolution and the slave uprising in Haiti with the history of the Central

African peoples on which the Atlantic slave trade depended. The Trotskyist concept of Bonapartism is applied to L'Ouverture, according to Stuart Hall, so that the Haitian revolution is read "as a mass uprising in which the leader became trapped in bureaucracy and was slowly transformed into a self-effacing dictator who capitulated, contained, and defused the popular revolution" (1992: 9). Hall's description is not entirely correct; the Haitian masses completed the war of independence by destroying all the whites in the island.[3]

Imprisoned in Ellis Island at the height of McCarthyism in 1953, James completed his study of Herman Melville, *Mariners, Renegades and Castaways*. He read *Moby Dick* as an allegory of power relations, and expounded on how the ship symbolized the social relations of production at a certain period of U.S. history. Like his later work *Beyond a Boundary,* where cricket assumes the status of an emblematic game in which nature is reshaped into a dramatic artifice and given historical substance by the anti-imperialist struggle, *Mariners* can be read as a postcolonial discourse in which complicity and resistance dovetail. On the other hand, James's obsessive concern with the tension between leadership, intellectuals, and masses (between Ahab, Ishmael, and the crew of the *Pequod*) derives from his preoccupation with historical motion, universality, and contradiction. In his engagement with American popular culture, with sports, carnival and West Indian politics, James applied a totalizing intellect to discern how a cultural practice crystallized the manifold historical forces at work in any given period. Whether it was the rise of the bourgeoisie during Shakespeare's time, or the emergence of new productive forces at the moment when Melville and Whitman wrote or when Picasso painted *Guernica;* or the appearance of new mobilized energies of whole peoples, as in Haiti or the Gold Coast of Africa, James had an intuitive sense of the triangular play between historical moment, masses, and artist/intellectual. One might say that he privileged the totality of the revolutionary process of change, the sublation of the old into the new. He valued above all the resourceful, spontaneous, and creative force of the masses, the political energies of the working people, of a collective power mobilized during periods of crisis—this, I think, is the kernel of James's dialectical materialism. Was this simply appropriated from the Hegelian-Marxist tradition? Is the privileging of mass agency (reminiscent of Rosa Luxemburg's critique of centralized, bureaucratic leadership) a mere abrogation of Hegelian statism and vulgar Marxist technicist instrumentalism?

THE INCARNATION OF DIALECTICS

Such questions can be understood better if we see their rearticulation in James's magisterial review of world history in the 1947 essay, "Dialectical Materialism and the Fate of Humanity," and its foregrounding of the telos of universality. Here James rearticulates Hegelianized Marxian themes toward what I would call a "mass line" orientation, which would later on find its historical crucible and incarnation in the 1962 discourse, "From Toussaint L'Ouverture to Fidel Castro."

Echoing *The Communist Manifesto,* the 1947 essay begins with the collapse of capitalist civilization and the bankruptcy of bourgeois thought, humanity finally freed from illusions and faced now with "the real conditions of life." Not only do Nazi Germany and Stalinist Russia personify barbarism, but so do the victorious Allies presumably safeguarding the legacy of Western civilization. Dialectics enables James to grasp the fundamental contradiction between the abundant "possibilities of living" and the increasing "terror of mass annihilation" with the onset of the Cold War. Illustrating the law of the change from quantity to quality, James evokes the antithesis to counterrevolutionary barbarism: "the readiness for sacrifice, the democratic instincts and creative power of the great masses of the people" (1992: 159). Philosophy has not only become worldly but the world faced by either barbarism or socialism has become philosophical—that is, humanity posits freedom and happiness as conceivable only in the integrity of its struggle to transcend its subjection to nature and achieve a truly concrete universality. Such universality is prefigured in Marx's notion of "species-being" in the *Economic and Philosophical Manuscripts of 1844.*

James reviews the worldwide failure to realize the potential of "species-being" from the time of Christianity to the Protestant Reformation. He holds that the dialectic of concrete and abstract embedded in the logical principle of universality has been short-circuited by Hegel's idea of "mediation." These mediations are symptoms of the failure to grasp truth as the whole: not only in human actions but also in people's needs and aspirations. It was Marx who succeeded in theorizing absence and negativity by a historical-materialist method, that is, by resolving the problem of mediation with the intervention of praxis. For Marx, James asserts, "these concrete revolutionary stages are the work of the great masses of the people forever seeking the concretion of universality as the development of the productive forces creates the objective circumstances and the subjective desires which move them" (1992: 166).

Productive forces—are we then caught in a productivist trope or paradigm? No, because James reinscribes development within the orbit of social praxis moving between abstract possibility and concrete necessity. In tracing the development of Western civilization from primitive Christianity through Renaissance humanism to the rise of merchant capitalism, he focuses on slave revolts, peasant insurrections, the agitation of free workers in the medieval guilds, all of which culminated in the establishment of humanism and the national state of the absolute monarchy: "mediations of the mass proletarian desire for universality no longer in heaven but on earth." This triumph of bourgeois liberalism, however, only sharpened the contradictions in the "mass quest for universality in action and in life," for James "the moving force of history" (1992: 170). Discerning the contradiction between abstract and concrete in the English Civil War and the French Revolution, James underscores the rupture that suspends the need for mediation (the vanguard party, elite, charismatic intellectuals): "If out of the individual's responsibility for his own salvation, there had leapt democracy, out of his political freedom, there leapt communism" (1992: 171).

The last mediation to be surpassed is the Hegelian State, Weberian bureaucracy, and the illusion of pluralist/liberal representative democracy under the aegis of capital. James exposes here Hegel's limitations and the teleological idealism of Absolute Spirit. He opts for Marx's mode of conceptualizing the "objective movement" in the process of production, an approach that is not "productivist" in the positivistic sense but one that coincides with "the quest for universality in the need for the free and full development of all the inherent and acquired characteristics of the individual in productive and intellectual labour." Such a process of socialized labor would also abolish the fateful division between manual and intellectual labor, the theoretical foundation of postcolonial notions of interjacency, hybridity, etc. James is uncompromising in affirming that "the quest for universality, embodied in the masses, constituting the great mass of the nation, forbids any mediation" (1992: 173-74). Does this then imply that the subject can no longer be viewed as an effect of difference, whether linguistic or ontological?

Difference as contradiction still exists amid globalization, but the point is to rearticulate it within a differentiated concrete totality. James cites a passage from Marx and Engels's *The German Ideology*, written a hundred years ago: "Only with this universal development of productive forces is a universal intercourse between men established which produces in all nations simultaneously the phenomenon of the 'propertyless' mass (universal competition), makes each nation dependent on the revolutions of the others, and finally has put world-historical, empirically universal individuals in place of local ones" (1992: 179). If revolutionary politics, for James, requires linking the "needs of the objective situation" with the state of development of the masses, what is needed to renew the "vast wreck of the modern world" is the "total mobilization of all forces in society."

Facing the vast wreckage of imperialism fifteen years after, James, in "From Toussaint to Fidel Castro," pursues the antinomy between concrete universality and its geopolitical mediations in the specific region of the Caribbean.[4] Here Castro's revolution epitomizes the "ultimate stage of a Caribbean quest for national identity" (1992: 296). The two poles of the antithesis in Caribbean history, the sugar plantation and Negro slavery, become figures in a constellation (to use Walter Benjamin's term) for the traditional colonial order and for modernity respectively. The Haitian revolution was a mediation whose ambivalence disappeared in 1914 when the U.S. invasion ushered in the need for "Negritude," a moment in the quest for universality. The rediscovery of Vodun in Haiti marked Negritude as a peculiar West Indian contribution, one supplemented by the invention of *Cubanidad* after the Platt Amendment subordinated Cuba to U.S. supremacy. In the interwar period, James presents four figures whose mediations embodied the struggle of the West Indian masses for independence: Marcus Garvey, George Padmore, Aimé Césaire, and Arthur Cipriani. It was Césaire's poem *Cahier d'un retour au pays natal* (1939) that exploded the axiom of linear, uniform evolution and introduced the dialectical leap: "that salvation for the West Indies lies in Africa, the original home and ancestry of the West Indian people" (1992: 302).[5] Marx's vision of the beginning of the "real history of humanity" is expressed in Césaire as the convergence of African and Western worlds and the past and future of mankind, this convergence springing from (in James's words) "the self-generated and independent being and motion" of the Africans themselves.

While James credits "Negritude" as the key mediation between Africa and the West Indian masses, Africa itself (contingently personified in the persons of Nkrumah, Kenyatta, Lumumba, Nyerere, and others) becomes integrated into West Indian life through the vehicle of mass communication: "There was therefore in West Indian society an inherent antagonism between the consciousness of the black masses and the reality of their lives, inherent in that it was constantly produced and reproduced not by agitators but by the very conditions of the society itself. It is the modern media of mass communication which have made essence into existence" (1992: 307). In effect, it is finance capitalism and the world market that provide the conditions of possibility for the West Indian national community to emerge, for West Indian artists like George Lamming and Wilson Harris to accept "complete responsibility for the West Indies." James concludes by celebrating popular culture as the incarnation of the new things. In James's planetary view, West Indians, emerging from "the pass and fell incensed points/Of mighty opposites" that define the Cold War, will contribute to the comity of nations: "In dance, in the innovation in musical instruments, in popular ballad singing unrivalled anywhere in the world, the mass of the people are not seeking a national identity, they are expressing one" (1992: 314). By counterpointing Western imperial barbarism with the rebellious subjectivity of the colonies in Africa and the Caribbean, James rediscovers the germinal Marxist concept of the "people" immanent in "empirically universal individuals."

Contrary to Sylvia Wynter's claim that James's poiesis is exhaustively distilled by a multicultural Caliban who rejects the nationalitarian paradigm or nation model, James himself posits the historical specificity of West Indian revolutions (symbolized by Toussaint, Castro, the struggle against the Chaguaramas U.S. base in Trinidad) as necessary for comprehending the notion of universality. I would argue that the articulation of West Indian identity with global capitalism—eloquently enunciated in the 1966 lecture "The Making of the Caribbean People"—is the move James makes to recover the national-popular (to borrow Gramsci's terminology) from its subsumption in elite vanguardism and the putative "labor-centric categories of orthodox Marxism."[6] But to delegitimate capital accumulation and its privileging of instrumental rationality over the autonomy of the body, we need to inquire not only into disciplinary regimes of power/knowledge but also more crucially into commodity-fetishism and the ideological apparatus of reification and postcolonial mystification. I think it is untenable to ascribe to James the epistemological presuppositions of Foucault and poststructuralist thought in general. Bourgeois power based on consumption and circulation of goods doesn't spring primarily from the head/body opposition, just as the tension between the categories of race and class cannot be so easily dissolved by the mediations of jazz, calypso, and the reggae of Rastafarianism. Mass consumerism cannot so facilely displace the labor-centered paradigm Wynter rejects, despite the consensus on the protean virtues of James's intelligence and the "pluridefined social totem pole" of Trinidad.

Engaging with Heideggerian deconstruction and the translations of alterity in response to the normative texts of Eurocentric "Orientalism," critics like Bhabha, Gayatri Spivak, and their followers all privilege the peculiar intimacy between colonizer and colonized. It is instructive to counterpose James's unabashed totalizing of ethnic difference and contingent diversity immanent in his historiographical practice. I do not mean by this the counterdiscourse of "marvellous realism" (originally broached by the Cuban novelist Alejo Carpentier as "real maravilloso" in *El Reine de este Mundo*) proposed by Jacques Stephen Alexis, Michael Dash, and others, or the creolized *différend* of Commonwealth artists. Rather, the deconstruction of European master-narratives is performed through shifting the concern on limits—how human freedom in making history is "limited by the necessities of environment and conjuncture of circumstances."

TRIANGULATING NEW WORLDS

At this juncture, I would like to call attention to an interview of James in the mid-seventies in which the crucial themes of mass agency and universality are staged conjuncturally. James the historian conceived of his role as studying the struggle of classes (a political, not an economistic, category), which is indivisible with the mass movements—"the emotions, activities, and experiences of the great mass of the population"— from an international perspective. Just as the sliding of signifiers cannot go on forever, the power of the individual, no matter how great, is strictly limited. *The Black Jacobins* opened the field of inquiry into the subsumption of individuals into race/class within imperialism. James's point of departure in analyzing the Haitian revolution was his belief that "the center of the Black revolution was Africa, not the Caribbean" (1983: 267). A certain "native" intransigence saved James from succumbing to the temptation of "parliamentarism"; his association with George Padmore and his activities in the International African Service Bureau enabled him to make connections with African nationalists. Anti-imperialist solidarity allowed him to appreciate Césaire's "Negritude" as "not only a revolt against assimilation, but a poetical assertion of an African civilization" (1983: 270), analogous to the emancipatory projects of Marcus Garvey and Frantz Fanon.

What James stresses in the African context is not the antiracist or separatist cultural nationalism of the natives but rather the way British capitalism introduced slavery in the sugar plantations and how it brought its own "gravediggers" into its heartland. He insists that it is not economic relations that generate social movements but "the relations between classes," so that West Indians living in Britain attack bourgeois society not because they are West Indians but because this particular society "trained them to act in the most advanced possible way." In short, black people in the imperialist metropole have "succeeded in posing the question of the revolution" (1983: 272-73). James can unreservedly take this stance because of his conviction that the Haitian Revolution played a "decisive" role in the destruction of mercantilism and the abolition of the capitalist slave trade. He compares his task of demonstrating the role blacks played in the creation of modern Europe with DuBois' endeavor to show how black people helped create modern America. In prophesying that capitalism was coming to an end, James might have exceeded the limits of his vocation as historian.

But I think the lesson he was trying to communicate is that the postcolonial strategy of deconstructing subjectivity concedes too much to the schematism of ideological texts and neglects the dynamics of transition whose understanding hinges on an analytic method that he derives from Marx's *Capital:* "We learned that when something new takes place, if you want to understand it, you must begin from the highest peak of the previous form" (1983: 271). I think this presupposes again the problem of working through and beyond mediations in order to grasp the imperative of universality. This is the methodological axiom underlying James's prolegomenon to his study of American civilization, the 1944 essay entitled "The American People in 'One World': An Essay in Dialectical Materialism."

Is James guilty of a populist/demagogic fetishizing of the masses and thus instigating a cult of anarchic spontaneity? I do not think so. In *The Black Jacobins,* James describes the "remarkable liveliness of intellect and vivacity of spirit" that characterized the slaves in the eighteenth century. But without the leadership of those "who have been able to profit by the cultural advantages of the system" (such as Toussaint, Christophe, Dessalines), their revolt would have suffered the same fate as the Mackandal rebellion and other aborted uprisings. James analyzes not so much the economic status of slaves and plantation aristocrats but rather the changing alignment and disposition of various forces in Haiti at the time before the outbreak of the French Revolution. What he was unfolding was a plot of education in which the slaves learned "how liberty and equality were won or lost" (1963: 82) through mistakes, failures, and the ineluctable pressure of circumstances. James takes into account not just the racial conflicts but the specific maneuvers in which participants registered the limits and possibilities of their actions: "Political treachery is not a monopoly of the white race, and this abominable betrayal so soon after the insurrections shows that political leadership is a matter of programme, strategy and tactics, and not the colour of those who lead it" (1963: 106). Overall James charted the oscillating, complex interactions between leaders and masses, between black slaves and mulattos and their French masters, between the colonial administrators and the bureaucrats in Paris; this triangulation becomes the midwife to the birth of the people, the praxis of universality.

What I want to highlight here is James's all-sided, tactfully calculated, dramatic representation of Toussaint's character, its weakness and strength, in Chapter XI of *The Black Jacobins*. The class or socioeconomic determinants of Toussaint's personality are drawn with nuanced deliberation, taking care neither to glorify nor understate. After examining Toussaint's correspondence, James offers his judgment: Toussaint's "vision of precisely what is required is unerring, his taste is faultless, and the constantly varying approach is always suffused with revolutionary passion, a large humanity and a never-failing distinction" (1963: 253). But this seemingly static portrait and attributes are then set into motion when Toussaint makes the wrong judgment to execute Moise, his nephew and leader of several insurrections, for his sympathy with the black slaves in the North Province. Toussaint's rationale then was to assure the French plantatocracy and Bonaparte that he would keep the blacks and mulattos in line. James sharpens the contrast between Moise and Toussaint by transcribing their voices. Moise first:

> Whatever my old uncle may do, I cannot bring myself to be the executioner of my colour. It is always in the interests of the metropolis that he scolds me; but these interests are those of the whites, and I shall only love them when they have given me back the eye that they made me lose in battle. (1963: 275)

Toussaint replies to a notable creole of San Domingo:

> I took up arms for the freedom of my colour, which France alone proclaimed, but which she has no right to nullify. Our liberty is no longer in her hands: it is in our own. We will defend it or perish. (1963: 281)

James notes the "strange duality" starkly displayed here, the loyalty to France coexisting with the assertion of autonomy and self-sufficiency—an emblem of the law of "uneven and combined development."

But in the following remarks, we see James again grappling with the drive for universality and how the strategy for national liberation of the colonized has to somehow mediate between class, ethnicity (emergent nationality), and race. James praises Toussaint's long-range perspective: he is "one of those few men for whom power is a means to an end, the development of civilization, the betterment of his fellow creatures," a power committed to realizing the full potential of species-being. And yet his disregard of the masses and their level of consciousness, his authoritarian and aristocratic habitus, his failure to critique the abstract universality of the ideals of the French bourgeois revolution, his naivete about Napoleon—all constitute a flaw not tragic enough but still lethal in its consequence:

> [Toussaint] could not admit to himself and to his people that it was easier to find decency, gratitude, justice, and humanity in a cage of starving tigers than in the councils of imperialism. . . . It was in method, and not in principle, that Toussaint failed. The race question is subsidiary to the class question in politics, and to think of imperialism in terms of race is disastrous. But to neglect the racial factor as merely incidental is an error only less grave than to make it fundamental. (1963: 282-83)

But the irony is that in the last chapter of *The Black Jacobins,* entitled "The War of Independence," the error became Toussaint's grave. This statement of Toussaint's habit from hindsight becomes double-edged: "in the hour of danger Toussaint, uninstructed as he was, could find the language and accent of Diderot, Rousseau and Raynal, of Mirabeau, Robespierre and Danton" (1963: 198). That constituted both his virtue and his blindness—his blindness to what was emergent, growing, fighting to be born. Only by seizing race, nationality, and class as "unity of opposites" and rallying the masses of black people (including the mulattos) against the slaveowners and the French Empire could Dessalines and Christophe succeed in liberating the country. And for that it was necessary that Toussaint, the hybrid transcultural mediation, be removed from the scene.

At this juncture, we see that the allegory of *The Black Jacobins* functions as the residual subtext of both the two aforementioned essays whose purpose is to show the quest for universality immanent in historical experience. Within James's Marxist framework, "universality" can be concretized only in communism won by a permanent world revolution. While it is true that James (like most postcolonial intellectuals) worked

within the Western cultural orbit and expressed the adversarial consciousness of subjugated people of color, it is not quite correct to say, as Edward
Said does, that James unqualifiedly identified Europe as his own world,
even if James himself stated that "fundamentally we are a people whose
literacy and aesthetic past is rooted in Western European civilization"
(quoted in Said 1993: 248). James precisely urged their antinomic
conjunction; the symbiosis or synergesis of the West Indian and European
was, for James, always fraught and contentious, without any guaranteed
closure. And contrary to Said's allegation that James "saw the central
pattern of politics and history in linear terms" (253), one has to emphasize
the interruptions and returns, a syncopation of unpredictable breaks that
precisely rendered unnecessary the mediations by enigmatic, free-floating
signifiers or the iron cage of administrators.

A turning point in James's cultural politics occurred when he broke
away from the mainstream American Trotskyist movement in 1950 and,
together with Raya Dunayevskaya and Grace Lee, formed the Johnson-
Forest Tendency. From James's experience in the independence movement of Trinidad, the struggles of African Americans in the southern
states and in the factories of Detroit evolved the Tendency's emphasis on
workers' self-activity; their autonomous rank-and-file revolts made the
prerequisite of a vanguard party superfluous. In *State Capitalism and
World Revolution*, James considered the Ford assembly line as "the
prototype of production relations in fascist Germany and Stalinist Russia"
(Cleaver 1979: 46). The Soviet Union was not just a degenerate worker's
state but thoroughly state capitalist, its bureaucracy nothing else but
"American bureaucracy carried to its ultimate and logical conclusion."

Linking his vision of mass insurrection in Haiti that overtook any
conscious design of the leaders or intellectuals to a quasi-anarchosyndicalist
trend, James substituted the "disciplined spontaneity" of workers for the
mediation of a vanguard party: "The proletariat always breaks up the old
organization by impulse, a leap. . . . The new organization, the new
organism will begin with spontaneity, i.e., free creative activity, as its
necessity" (Cleaver 1979: 47). This was a drastic revision of the fundamental proposition found in *Notes on Dialectics:* "The Universal of socialism is
the free proletariat" (1980: 152). In a letter to Constance Webb in 1944
while he was studying Hegel, James wrote: "The Marxist prepares the
workers subjectively for what history prepares them objectively" (1996b:
148). In *Modern Politics* ten years later, James again privileged the self-
activity of the "great masses of people," participatory radical democracy in
action (1960: 42). The sociologist Kevin Anderson points out that in the

1948 study of Hegel, James synthesized Lenin's ideas on organization and the "spontaneous activity and self-movement" or "free creative activity of the proletariat" within their own mass formations (1995, 200-01). Universality, in James's hermeneutics, epitomizes the kernel of dialectics, the interpenetration of opposites, multileveled contradictions as the impetus of historical motion (Ollman1993). The search for universality begins and ends with the collective praxis of the people, popular energies unified and harnessed to explode commodity-fetishism and the legitimacy of unequal property/power relations (on "universality" from a critical-realist perspective, see Bhaskar 1993).

By the end of World War II, James traced the genealogy of United States imperialism from its beginning, the break with the "triangular trade of mercantilism," through its intervention in Asia and Latin America, up to its victory against fascist barbarism. The profoundly synthesizing reach of the essay "The American People in 'One World'" (1944) affords us a foretaste of the prescience invested in the 1947 discourse on "Dialectical Materialism." It also foreshadows what James speculated as the impending apocalypse of world capitalism rehearsed in the 1962 Appendix to *The Black Jacobins,* which juxtaposes the figures of Toussaint and Fidel Castro embedded in the tradition of capital's "gravediggers." I would like to quote a lengthy passage from this 1944 essay to illustrate the antipostcolonial unequivocality typical of James's intellect:

> American imperialism there becomes the chief bulwark of the capitalist system as a whole. . . . The colossal power of American imperialism is the apex of a process—the rise, maturity and decline of the capitalist world market. In the eighteenth century, "our country," in the triumph of its industrial bourgeoisie, released the great political potentialities of the European proletariat, the mortal enemy of the European bourgeoisie. Today "our country" can release nothing. Driven by the contradictions of its own capitalistic development and of capitalism as a whole, it is now the enemy of hundreds of millions of people everywhere. The appearance of liberator of peoples is a necessary disguise for the essential reality of American imperialism, epitome of decadent capitalism, mobilized for the defense of privilege and property against a world crying to be free.
>
> The laws of dialectics are to be traced not in metaphysical abstractions such as 168 years of "our country," but in economic development and the rise, maturity, and decline of different social classes within the expansion and construction of the capitalist world market.

The greatest progressive force in the eighteenth century, the nationalism of "our country," is in the twentieth century the greatest of obstacles to social progress. In accordance with a fundamental dialectical law, the progressive "nationalism" of eighteenth-century America is transformed into its opposite, the reactionary "internationalism" of American imperialism. . . . American imperialism cannot escape its entanglements in foreign class struggles even if it would. . . . In our compact world, successful revolt in any area will sound the tocsin for the center more violently than the American revolutions of the eighteenth and nineteenth century shook metropolitan Europe. And the social crisis in America must bring onto the scene the American proletariat. (1994: 175-76)

The submerged narrative line of this essay follows the twists and turns found in the 1938 masterpiece, *The Black Jacobins*. I would like to emphasize three paramount theses enunciated here. First, the rise of the world market converts the whole world into an arena of revolutionary struggle so that the challenge in the periphery immediately registers in the metropolitan center. Second, the mode of imperial accumulation has generated the American proletariat that inherits the international revolutionary tradition and also utilizes "the great American tradition of the past" in the struggle for socialism. Third, the agencies of transformative politics aim for concrete specific objects that eventually generate worldwide repercussions: "The farmers, mechanics and artisans, the workers and Negro slaves, pursued strictly immediate and concrete aims and made world history" (1994, 177). The cunning of Reason becomes immanent in quotidian events, rendering even defeats and reversals stepping-stones in the oppressed people's quest for universality, i.e., for freedom and happiness.

The universality we confront daily in the twentieth century is that of the world market, which has compressed time/space through mass communications and technological innovations in travel. For James, however, that signifies the universality of commodity-fetishism and the totalitarian state. All the same, the phenomenon is constituted by multiple contradictions. James's unfinished project, *American Civilization,* is precisely the endeavor to anatomize the universality known as United States imperialism, its essence (only grasped through theoretical practice) and appearances, the phenomenology of everyday life.

The fundamental thrust of *American Civilization* is "the creation of an integral human being." This is predicated on the idea of the good life associated with freedom and happiness as revolutionary goals. Closely identified with African Americans and women as social forces, those goals have been compromised, mocked, postponed, sidetracked, or even negated by capitalist "mass production" and its drift toward barbarism. The original ideals of liberty, pursuit of happiness, and free individuality have now been shipwrecked in the economic and social realities of the Depression in the thirties and the relentless barbarism of the Cold War.

In assessing the impotence of American intellectuals, James arrived at the only force that can resist the worldwide barbarism: "the instinctive rebelliousness and creative force of the modern masses" (1993a: 226). Unlike Weber and the resort to charismatic leaders, James pits the masses against a world-system of bureaucratic state structures. What climaxes James's analytic of the contradiction between aspirations and realities is the chapter on "Popular Arts and Modern Society," in which modern film, newspaper, comic strip, jazz, and radio are seen as "an expression of mass response to society, crises, and the nature and limitations of that response" (1993a: 122). This contradiction is embodied in the figure of the gangster, "the persistent symbol of the national past which has no meaning—the past in which energy, determination, bravery were certain to get a man somewhere in the line of opportunity . . . [The] gangster who displays all the old heroic qualities in the only way he can display them, is the derisive symbol of the contrast between ideals and reality" (1993: 127). The rage and violence one finds in popular film constitute an index of "the mass exposing . . . its desire to smash the impasse in which it finds itself"—in short, a cathartic release of the repression of the masses by a disciplinary, surveillance system, what Henri Lefebvre (1971) calls the "bureaucratic society of controlled consumption."

In 1960, James turned to the dynamics of the revolution in the Gold Coast of Africa and reinstated the conceptual primacy of the term "people" in the lexicon of socialist political theory (1971: 133; on James's views on Ghana's Nkrumah, see Marable 1986). Thus when he invokes the American "people" in his brand of reception-aesthetics, James returns to the guiding insight of *The Black Jacobins* derived from Lenin and Michelet in which the dialectic between leaders and masses is calibrated with astute realism. The dialectical method is premised on the "concrete analysis" of material conditions that determine the limits and possibilities of action. James's analysis of popular association and mass organizing together with their symbolic expression is thus able to imbue the "national-popular" striving for revolutionary hegemony with the intractable "thickness" of historicity.

But historicism in *American Civilization* is neither antiquarian nor monumental because it is oriented to present imperatives and agendas. It acquires a prophetic thrust when James underscores its utopian telos: happiness. What distinguishes his socioanalytic of the American character is an abundant faith in its potential: "[The American people] combine an excessive individualism, a sense of the primary value of their own individual personality, with an equally remarkable need, desire and capacity for social cooperative action" (1993: 273). Because this volatile, aggressive individualism has been suppressed by technocratic corporate statism, a profound social crisis has ripened: anger and fear "irresistibly explode in private life." Such explosions are registered not in refined intellectual exchanges but in popular culture. The twin drive for autonomy and for association, for asserting a distinctive personality and for "intimate communion with his fellows," cannot be fulfilled within the regime of commodity-fetishism or mass consumerism, hence the crisis and its symptoms in gangster movies, in the private lives of women, blacks, and intellectuals.

In *Mariners, Renegades and Castaways* (1953), James pointed out how Melville captured in Ahab's predicament the crisis of transition, the tension between the masses "seeking a new basis for a sense of community" and the eruption of "the most boundlessly egotistical individual personalities" in the political arena (130). But as always, James finds a resolution to all this crisis in his argument about the overriding importance of "the struggle for happiness" and for self-fulfillment in social reciprocity.[7] By "happiness" is meant the integration between individual personality and the larger community, the synthesis of public commitment and private interest—in short, the political life defined and elaborated by James in *Modern Politics* (1960) and *Every Cook Can Govern* (1956).

The theoretical framework deployed in this ambitious cognitive mapping of the United States as a "civilization," its contradictory trends and aleatory tendencies, is what we have already encountered in *The Black Jacobins*. It is an invention of the diasporic sensibility that apprehends the manifold links between national and the international, the local and global, the singular and the universal. I designate it the triangulation of universality in the capitalist world-system.[8] One illustration can be adduced here. In the last chapter of *The Black Jacobins*, James traced the race war and carnage in Haiti as due to "the greed of the French bourgeoisie" (355). From this he concludes that in contrast to nineteenth-century Haiti, the "blacks in Africa [in mid-twentieth century] are more advanced" in their pursuit of freedom:

From the people heaving in action will come the leaders; not the isolated blacks at Guys' Hospital or the Sorbonne, the dabblers in surrealisme or the lawyers, but the quiet recruits in a black police force, the sergeant in the French native army or British police, familiarising himself with military tactics and strategy, reading a stray pamphlet of Lenin or Trotsky as Toussaint read the Abbe Raynal. (1963: 377)

What sutures the diverse materials in *The Black Jacobins, American Civilization,* and *Mariners, Renegades and Castaways* is a singular theme of universality, this time cognized as the spontaneous, self-directed, inexhaustible power of the masses.

James reworked his Eurocentric education and redefined his identity as "a Man of the Caribbean" by triangulating the regions that configured the African diaspora: Africa, the Caribbean, and Europe.[9] Colonialism and the slave trade established the necessity of the Caribbean as a vital, irreplaceable link in primitive capital accumulation. With his adventurous intuition, James could encompass distant points in space that would otherwise remain isolated fragments, enabling him to render not syncretic pastiches or bricolage of semiotic utopia but the actual process of decolonization: "All problems today, particularly the emancipation of the underdeveloped countries, are matters in which the world in general is involved; and at the centre of African emancipation, particularly in the development of ideas and international strategy, are the urban blacks of America" (1992: 376). This passion of the islander for cognitive and geopolitical mapping—an index of the masses' self-activity and drive for collective self-representation—explains why he considers "Negroes" as Americans, not a separate ethnic community, whose combined segregation and integration epitomize the national crisis, the "modern Americanism, a profoundly social passion of frustration and violence" that distinguishes the United States in the midst of the Cold War.

SOCIALISM OR BARBARIC CAPITALIST RACISM

A decisive turn in James's itinerary as an authentic dialectical-materialist thinker occurred in his re-examination of the "Negro question" or the articulation of the categories of race and class in social critique. He had already confronted the race-class nexus in the early thirties in united-front campaigns in support of Abyssinian resistance to Italian imperialism and the campaign for West Indian self-government. Before he returned to the United States by way of New Orleans after his fateful meeting with Trotsky in Mexico in 1939, James invariably subsumed the fact of "racism" in the master-code of class struggle. The encounter with "race"—the recent volume *C. L. R. James on the "Negro Question"* edited by Scott McLemee documents this fateful encounter—reconfigured his whole way of thinking and generated the praxis of what became the "mass line" in "Third World" people's war in Vietnam, Nicaragua, the Philippines, and elsewhere.

In 1938, towards the end of *The Black Jacobins,* C. L. R James reflected on the dialectic between the categories of race and class that framed his narrative of the first black slave uprising in the world: "The race question is subsidiary to the class question in politics, and to think of imperialism in terms of race is disastrous. But to neglect the racial factor as merely incidental is an error only less grave than to make it fundamental" (1963: 283). The reason for the internationalist focus on the class question, according to Paul Buhle (1988), lies in the Trotskyist principle of transcending national specifics for the sake of a grand epic of solidarity between the European proletariat and the "black Jacobins" of the colonies.

James at that time had never paid attention to the condition of the African Americans in the United States, but before his trip he had already been involved in the pan-African movement in England, particularly in the campaign for Abyssinian independence against European imperialism. And yet this concern of people of color for national self-determination of African colonies, and later of Caribbean societies, allegedly did not change his view that the class question predominates over the race question. In a useful review, Tony Martin reiterated this position: "Even when accepting the applicability of Lenin's ideas on national minorities to the movement for self-determination among Afro-Americans, for example, or when appearing to condone the rhetoric of Black Power, he has never deviated from his view that race is subordinate to class" (1972: 186).

Is it correct to affirm the argument that James never deviated from his 1938 conviction of the priority of class over race? I contend that it is not correct. In the aforementioned collection of writings by James on the "Negro Question" (1996), Scott McLemee also concurs with the idea that James's final word on the race/class antithesis may be found in the resolution James authored for the Socialist Workers' Party Convention of 1948. The document entitled "The Revolutionary Answer to the Negro Problem in the United States" indeed synthesizes scattered thoughts and reflections on the situation of African Americans in the United States that James expressed in voluminous writings. But this synthesis does not indicate the easy, automatic subsumption of race into class. In fact, the trajectory of the argument here implies a move toward a concrete dialectic negotiation of the claims of these two categories.

What is striking here, compared to his previous writings on the "Negro question," is James's insistence that the vitality and validity of the independent Negro struggle for democratic right "is in itself a constituent part of the struggle for socialism." It has deep historic roots that entitle it to autonomous and integral identity. While James emphasizes that blacks "approach the conclusions of Marxism," the problematic aspect is the relation between the organized labor movement and the African American demand for equality. James denies that this is "merely a class question," even though he states that what is involved is "a question of the reorganization of the whole agricultural system" of the country. He invokes Lenin to resolve this impasse: Lenin says "that the dialectic of history is such that small independent nations, small nationalities, which are powerless . . . in this struggle against imperialism nevertheless can act as one of the ferments, one of the bacilli, which can bring onto the scene the real power against imperialism—the socialist proletariat" (182). So the black struggle can become the catalyst for the emergence of the socialist proletariat. But it does not mean that because the oppressed minorities, or nationalities, are powerless, therefore the proletariat has got to lead them and that "they cannot do anything until the proletariat actually comes forward to lead them. [Lenin] says exactly the opposite is the case" (182).

James reviews history and concludes: "Such is the situation of the masses of the Negro people and their readiness to revolt at the slightest opportunity, that as far back as the Civil War, in relation to the American bourgeoisie, they formed a force which initiated and stimulated and acted as a ferment" (183). The metaphor of ferment or bacilli is revealing but loaded also with dissonant connotations. But if the function of the oppressed nationalities is to initiate the proletariat into the scene by their agitation and resistance, are they therefore to be incorporated into the revolutionary proletariat and forfeit their autonomy? The evidence of black participation in the War of Independence and more crucially in the Civil War, as well as in the Populist movement, all demonstrate the need for a leadership that will not betray their cause. Except for the Garvey movement, all previous social movements failed to acknowledge their demand for emancipation from "capitalist humiliation and from capitalist oppression" (184).

James then posits the independent character of the African American struggle within the social crisis of the political formation. But this independence is distinguished for being attuned to the progressive forces at any historical conjuncture. Before it was the bourgeoisie and now it is the proletariat. Based on their response to the CIO (Congress of Industrial Organizations) organizing efforts, James concludes that "the Negro movement logically and historically and concretely is headed for the proletariat" (185). This movement of the blacks "toward the revolutionary forces" is, James notes, "stronger today than ever before" in the context of the decay of capitalism and the resurgence of the labor movement (185). James observes that "a substantial number of Negroes" have been placed in "a position of primacy in the struggle against capitalism," but this place in the vanguard of the proletarian movement coincides with their position in the Negro community—a decisive intersection or confluence of the democratic and anticapitalist impulses. James does not collapse the two. He reserves an integral place for the bacilli in his concluding, prophetic statement: "Let us not forget that in the Negro people, there sleep and are now awakening passions of a violence exceeding, perhaps, as far as these things can be compared, anything among the tremendous forces that capitalism has created. . . . [A]lthough their social force may not be able to compare with the social force of a corresponding number of organized workers, the hatred of bourgeois society and the readiness to destroy it when the opportunity should present itself, rests among them to a degree greater than in any other section of the population in the United States" (187).

It is in this light that James can be justly regarded as the innovative theoretician of black self-emancipation. The African American scholar Sundiata Cha-Jua (1996) historicizes James's exploration of the race-class nexus that led to the crafting of a "neo-Marxist diasporan historiography" and proposes the view that "what began as a progressive project to fill theoretical gaps in Marxism regarding race, by the late 1940s had evolved into a theory recognizing the autonomous activity of all socially con- structed groups, by the late 1950s ended as a renouncement of the proletariat's historical agency." There is no doubt that James abandoned a sclerotic vanguardism after 1958 and became preoccupied with the problem of mass agency, although I think his populist strain did not completely displace a class analysis, as evidenced by talks like "Black Power" (1967), "Black Studies and the Contemporary Student" (1969), and "Black People in the Urban Areas of the United States" (1970). The praxis of popular-democratic radical transformation for him still pivoted around the slogan "socialism or barbarism" (Glaberman 1995).

POWER TO THE PEOPLE

James's rich and complex body of work cannot of course be reduced to the topic of black self-emancipation or antipostcoloniality. But this is one way of estimating its worth, its usefulness for the exploited and oppressed. It is also part of a project of shaping an epistemology of the revolutionary subject, of collective agency. "Knowing one's self" is, in Gramsci's famous phrase, an affair of trying to sort out the infinity of traces deposited in us by a historical process that unfortunately forgot to supply us with an inventory. Such traces are not just discursive palimpsests or tropological language games, as postcolonial theory insists. Knowing C. L. R. James is a matter of constructing the inventory of engagements that he has partly provided in *Beyond a Boundary, Mariners, Renegades and Castaways, American Civilization,* and voluminous tracts and essays. There is much in James's geopolitical hermeneutics of cricket that reveals the trajectory of his quest for universality; but the indigenization of cricket could have been realized only through the mediation of a rich and complex Marxist tradition (albeit from the Trotskyist archive), through American literature exemplified by the prophetic art of Melville, and through a series of antiimperialist struggles in Africa and Asia, including the African American insurrections of the sixties and seventies.

James was one of the first Marxist-Leninists to appreciate the symptomatic value of mass media culture. But his dialectical brand of cultural criticism can be reappropriated by the fashionable trend in Cultural Studies only at the risk of positivist vulgarization. In an astute essay, Neil Larsen demonstrates that for James it is the "negativity" in popular culture, the promises of freedom and happiness that it intimates but cannot supply, its transgressive meanings that need appraisal, not its formal popularity; this negativity "makes popular culture into a potentially 'popular art,' that makes it a progressive moment relative to the elite culture whose negation it posits" (1996: 99). This application of a "negative dialectics" to mass culture actually originates from the moment James in exile experienced the discordance between the schemas of received theory and the recalcitrance of lived experience.

In a sense, James's exile conforms to Said's contrapuntal version of it: "Exile is predicated on the existence of, love for, and a real bond with one's native place; the universal truth of exile is not that one has lost that love or home, but that inherent in each is an unexpected, unwelcome loss" (1993: 336). Such unwelcome loss is not James's but the hegemonic elite in the United States and other oppositional activists in the American hemisphere who never recognized or acknowledged his substantial contribution to the critical assessment of what he calls "American civilization."

When he was about to write his book on Melville, James was sent to Ellis Island in June 1952. He compared the immigration quarters there to Melville's *Pequod*, microcosm of world civilization; he was an alien, however, and told that he "could always leave and go to Trinidad, where I was born, and drink my papaya juice" (1985: 146). But it was not this contemptible treatment that James sought to register in the memoirs of his captivity; rather, it was his encounter with M, a Communist Party member, whose instructive help may have neutralized his residual Trotskyism;[10] and the numerous prisoners, sailors, and members of an entire diasporic assemblage whose comprehension of global events was enabled and sustained by their aboriginal roots, their nativist loyalties. This brief incarceration exhibits not postcolonial aporia, liminal indeterminacy, or even creolized signification but rather the cunning and versatility of a praxis-oriented (in contrast to pragmatic) imagination that can sum up heterogenous materials in a way capable of moving and inducing action:

> This then is the crowning irony of the little cross-section of the whole world that is Ellis Island. That while the United States Department of Justice is grimly pursuing a venomous anti-alien policy, and in the course of doing so disrupting and demoralizing its own employees desperately trying to live up to their principles, the despised aliens, however fiercely nationalistic, are profoundly conscious of themselves as citizens of the world. (1985: 161-62)

Provisionally I suggest that James's belief in permanent world revolution ultimately committed him to a radical-popular democracy almost anarchic and utopian in temper and motivation. Not so much a DuBoisean "double consciousness" but an unabashedly totalizing reconnaissance of polarities and their nexus of mutations characterizes James application of historical materialism. Like Fanon, he did not dispense with the nation or nationalitarian longings as a moment in the liberation struggle. He was of course a victim of the Cold War. But what made him transcend this victimage is the narrative of his itinerary as diasporic intellectual, from the time of his departure from the West Indies in 1932 to his political and scholarly engagements while in Britain, to his grass-roots work in the United States, and finally to August 1952 and his indictment as a writer equal to Lenin and Marx as founders of revolutionary organizations—the government's main brief.

In summing up his lifework in *Beyond a Boundary,* James invoked the anticipatory figure of Shakespeare's antihero in *The Tempest:* "To establish his own identity, Caliban, after three centuries, must himself pioneer into regions Caesar never knew" (1993b: 166). James was a pioneering revolutionary writer, indeed, who preoccupied himself with the inescapable choice confronting humanity—between socialist humanism/universalism or Eurocentric capitalist barbarism—whether in diasporic motion (immigrants, refugees, "castaways") or in entrenched fortresslike habitats. Caribbean scholars today attribute this concern to his Trinidad background, to a peculiar West Indian cosmopolitanism, its unique mode of cultural resistance (cricket, carnival, calypso, and reggae), its gift of looking outward, the genius of its passion for universality.

Whatever the weight of primordial influences, the fact is that it was Marxism, at first with a Trotskyite orientation and later with a diasporic or "Third World" inflection, that was always susceptible to global happenings (for example, the emergence of "workers" councils in the Hungarian revolution), that allowed James to articulate his intellectual and moral responsibility toward the West Indian community with what Hazel Carby calls "historical readings of the international significance of cultural production." When he made the dialectical leap from the doctrinaire idea of "proletarian literature" (Carby 1988: 42) to the notion of "revolutionary literature" that coalesced individual, class, and national dimensions, James had already superseded the postcolonial obsession with difference and its "politics of recognition" (see Taylor 1994) and transvalued this phase of the "Unhappy Consciousness" for the strategic tasks of worldwide popular emancipation. And for us engaged in those tasks, that is what makes the necessary difference.

CHAPTER EIGHT

Imagining the End of Empire: Emergencies and Breakthroughs

I hope I have said enough to make it clear that I am abandoning neither Marxism nor communism but only the use which some people have made of them, which I deplore. I wish to see Marxism and communism serving the black peoples, not the black peoples serving Marxism and communism. The doctrine and the movement should exist for the sake of the people, not the people for the good of the doctrine and the movement. And, of course, this principle does not apply only to communists. And if I were a Christian or a Muslim, I would say the same thing: every doctrine is worthless unless it is rethought by and for us and adapted to our own needs. . . . This is why we must insist upon a veritable Copernican revolution in order to break with the European habit, which is deeply rooted in every party and group from extreme right to extreme left, of acting on our behalf—of deciding for us, thinking for us and, in short, denying us the right of initiative which I have already mentioned—the right, in fact, to personality.
—Aimé Césaire, *Lettre à Maurice Thorez* (1957)

Against the background of the continuing U.S.-led war against Iraq (with Libya and Iran looming behind) and the unprecedented upheavals in regions formerly known as the Soviet Union and Yugoslavia rapidly making obsolete any ongoing academic pontification, reflections on the twin fates of freedom and progress in dependent formations are bound to assume greater urgency and resonance than before. In particular, what is the fate of culture in these contested territories? There is an obvious reason for the renewed salience of the territories of people of color (also known as "the South," "developing countries," or in business parlance, "emerging markets"): it is that the bulk (at least two-thirds) of the world's population inhabiting the periphery exerts an incalculable force on sovereign nation-states and transnational corporate-policy decisions in the industrialized metropolis that now comprises three centers: the European Community, Japan and its satellites, and North America. The logic of capital requires a hierarchical division of labor throughout the world that constantly reproduces its own condition of existence. In a world system dominated by the messiahs of the "free market" hard on the tracks of fleeing Kurds, Palestinians, and millions of refugees from Eastern Europe and elsewhere, the inauguration of a "New World Order" opens up the space for rethinking cherished beliefs and received notions rendered anachronistic by the precipitous turn of events.

In both the Middle East and Eastern Europe, the talismanic shibboleth of "democracy" broadcast by the Western media claims to promise nothing short of absolute redemption. "Free World" triumphalism for now—despite quandaries in Somalia and Haiti—preempts all dissent, criticism, refusal.[1] Meanwhile, in El Salvador, South Africa, the Philippines, and other presumed democratic polities, the problems of *inter alia* poverty, social injustice, military brutality, ecological disasters, and so on continue to confound the technocratic experts of the International Monetary Fund and the World Bank. The new status quo is volatile and unpredictable. But as everyone knows, the worry of Western governments concerns not the plight of impoverished citizens but rather the gigantic debt of countries like Brazil, Mexico, Argentina, and a dozen others in Africa and Asia; debts whose foreclosure might precipitate a global financial crisis worse—in the minds of the corporate elite—than a nuclear war. We hear this uncanny whispering behind: Never question the legitimacy of this new dispensation, for it's the same old thing—unequal exchange on a world scale—lest you unleash the barbarism of Prospero and Ariel against Caliban's hordes. In such a scenario, the significations of "postcolonial" literature and "postmodern" art, including the rubric "Third World," again become the site of struggle for redefinition, revaluation, and reappropriation (Buchanan 1974).

In retrospect, Peter Worsley's inaugural text *The Third World* (1964) is one of the first cognitive mappings of the world system—its differential political economies, its "actual infinity," as it were—that privileged the Third World as a challenge to both late capitalism and communism. He quotes Frantz Fanon's assertion that the Third World's singular task

"consists in reintroducing Man into the world, man in his totality" (275).
Peter Weiss concurs by rejecting the derogatory connotation of "Third"
and insists that by reintroducing "human dignity," these exploited and
poor countries are really the actually developed ones (quoted in Gugelberger 1991: 522). In short, to echo the fabled inversion, the last is really
first. What is at stake here, however, is not the revival of Renaissance
humanism or biblical eschatology but the concept of a world society in
which problems of poverty, ecology, genocide, and human rights
implicate every human across nation-state boundaries. This idea of a
planetary ethics has long been anticipated by Marxist thought and its
stress on the centrality of labor as life/species activity, work that fashions
the world as an expression of self-conscious, universalizing species-
power. But it would not have been possible without the sequence of
events that signaled the advent of a late-modern "givenness" some years
after the onset of the Cold War: Ghana's independence (1957), Fidel
Castro's victory in Cuba (1959), Lumumba's murder (1961), the
vicissitudes of the Algerian revolution (1957-62), and the instructive
lessons of U.S. involvement in Indo-China following the stalemate in
the Korean peninsula.

    After the 1973 military coup in Chile against the socialist Allende,
the U.S. debacle in Vietnam, and the maturing of crises in South Africa
and in Central America, the quest for an internationalist ethics moved
to a qualitatively new stage. The phrases "national liberation struggle"
and "people's war" began to acquire substantive weight in academic
exchange. The anthropologist Sidney Mintz reminds us of the original
problematique, the interdiscursive field of our inquiry: "the uneven and
multiplex relationship between the capitalist heartland and the societies
and peoples on which that heartland has fed" (377). To demystify "third
worldism" as contrived by the New Left, Mintz introduces Wallerstein's
"theme of a worldwide capitalism transcending national and continental
boundaries and encompassing forms of labor in no way reducible to a
single proletarian model." In another context, Samir Amin introduces
plurality within the "concrete universal" of liberation: "A development
that is not merely development of underdevelopment will therefore be
both national, popular-democratic, and socialist, by virtue of the world
project of which it forms part" (1985: 383). Across the spectrum of usages
and references, the term "Third World" releases its force as an operational
and situational signifier rather than an analytic ontological category; thus
we see the ironic unfolding of its heterogeneity in Gerard Chaliand's
Revolution in the Third World, contemporaneous with Mintz's essay, in

which disillusionment with Utopia (now synonymous with all those transitional experiments Chaliand used to extol) becomes a pretext for valorizing the key "Western" ideas of freedom and equality.

THE PERSONA AS POLITICAL

It seems that the messianic vision of Fanon's *The Wretched of the Earth* has become simply a Third World Imaginary, an erstwhile heresy now reduced to superstition. Before the waning of third worldism into the eclectic cosmopolitanism of postcoloniality, I want to enter a personal digression here to frame my subsequent remarks. In June 1981, I organized a seminar on "Revolutionary Third World Culture: Theory and Literature" for the Inter-University Centre of Postgraduate Studies in Dubrovnik, Yugoslavia, an extension of my years of teaching Third World cultural practices at the University of Connecticut, Brooklyn College, and other institutions. Two years before, at about the time when the Sandinistas (FSLN) overthrew the Somoza dynasty, I wrote an essay on "Third World" revolutionary literature (published in *Social Praxis);* its abstract contained these initial propositions:

> In the specific historic juncture of the late seventies, culture in the Third World has increasingly asserted itself as a form of ideological practice structurally determined by the class struggle. Literature is defined as an instance of concrete political practice which reflects the dynamic process of the national democratic revolution in the developing countries. (San Juan 1976: 19)

In 1983, two years after the seminar in Yugoslavia and just after the invasion of Grenada by U.S. Marines, I attended a conference on "Marxism and the Interpretation of Culture" at the University of Illinois, Urbana-Champaign. A group of participants in Professor Stuart Hall's class distributed a one-page leaflet entitled "Third World Intervention" whose intent and thrust can be discerned in these passages:

> Given the new international division of labor, and given this era of the multinational economy (which characterizes the postmodern), is it any longer possible to limit questions of culture and Marxism to culture defined within the framework of the nation-state or within the framework of the western world? The second related question regards the adequacy or applicability of theories generated in and for the first world context to

the third world scene. . . . The third world is always an implicit part of first world cultural production.

The project of anthropology, which is the locus of cultural studies par excellence in the U.S., has been to describe, codify, and systematize cultures on the margins of Western civilization. Not only has ethnographic representation entailed an imposition of synchronicity upon these other societies whereby transformation can only be seen as initiated from the outside. It also displaces the question of domination into an issue of relativized cultural logics of difference. But the ideological project of anthropological practice succeeds in assigning to those other cultures a symbolic meaning within the dominant ideological discourse of the West, a meaning of alterity which is constitutive in the construction of the identity of the subject in the West, which entails a certain deformation of the colonial subject as well.

The Third World Study Group responsible for this manifesto also speculated whether the international division of labor has not also entailed the "international division of the subject," rendering the category of "nation" suspect in the context of the dynamics of international capital and also the idea of exploitation as chiefly derivative of the capital-labor class contradiction. This instance of dissent may be taken as emblematic of the unequal distribution of interpretive power in the academy. Order is guaranteed by the "excluded middle," in this case the "absent" or "erased" labor of subjugated nationalities. In an ironic twist, the protest against unwarranted generalization by Eurocentric discourse refunctioned the poststructuralist "exorbitation" of discourse attributed to Derrida, Foucault, Lacan, and others, so that what it aimed ostensibly to deny at the start is reaffirmed in the end.

It is perhaps at this juncture that we can appreciate Aijaz Ahmad's *In Theory* (1992) as a salutary polemical intervention, clarifying in its exposition of the historical background the ambiguities and ironies of the new counterhegemonic trend. Problematizing the ethos of its adherents, Ahmad attacks the poststructuralist skepticism of postcolonial theorists, their avant-gardist stance of irony, and their rhetorics of migrancy. His rejection of nationalism (of the bourgeois comprador or *desarrollista* brand) posited as the determinate opposite of imperialism is based on a prior calculation of its role "in the determinate socialist project"; hence the struggle is not against "nations and states as such, but for different articulations of class, nation, and state" (11). While condemning reactionary "third-worldist nationalism," Ahmad does not dismiss (as do the epigones of Baudrillard and Lyotard) "the historical reality of the sedimentations which do in fact give particular collectivities of people real civilizational identities" (11). In this approach he is in solidarity with partisan intellectuals situated in disparate cultures such as Aimé Césaire, Amilcar Cabral, Ngugi Wa Thiong'o, Tan Malaka, Sultan Galiev, Hanafi Muzzafar, Nicolas Guillen, Walter Rodney, and many more unpublicized "others." He also recognizes how "the tendential law of global accumulation" produces not greater homogenization but "greater differentiation among its various national units," hence his rejection of Fredric Jameson's hypothesis of "national allegory" (which I discuss later). Ahmad's prudent qualifications, however, do not save him from a certain leftist monumentality that has no patience with alliance or populist politics practiced in, say, South Africa today; nor do we find much latitude there for calculating and harnessing to our advantage the oppositional effects of what Ernst Bloch calls "nonsynchronicities" in the interstices of middle-strata quotidian existence. Ahmad may yet prove to be a nostalgic "postcolonial" in spite of himself.

In general I agree with Ahmad and others (for example, Mukherjee 1990) in their view that theory from the metropolis cannot escape the "specter" of insurgent "natives," of anti-imperialist resistance. But neither can we in the Third World escape its contagion. The question is: how do we negotiate the complex linkages of this ideological conjuncture and use the "weak links" of the enemy? In my judgment, the only dialectical way of mediating the capitalist world system and historically specific national formations as we examine concrete processes of cultural production is to deploy Gramsci's concept of the "national-popular," which I attempt in my books *From Nation to People, Allegories of Resistance,* and *The Philippine Temptation.* Following Otto Bauer's (1970) insight that "in each country, the socialist ideology merges with its peculiar cultural tradition and becomes nationally differentiated" (274-75), Gramsci emphasizes the circumstantiality of aesthetic form and cultural practice in general as shaped by varied audiences and generic conventions (117-19), local knowledges, ethnic self-construals, and other contingencies. The philosophical justification for discerning the force of a specific "national" concern and a popular orientation lies in Gramsci's historical-materialist understanding of aesthetic praxis:

> If one cannot think of the individual apart from society, and thus if one cannot think of any individual who is not historically conditioned, it is obvious that every individual, including the artist and all his activities,

cannot be thought of apart from society, a specific society. Hence the artist does not write or paint—that is, he does not externalize his phantasms—just for his own recollection, to be able to relive the moment of creation. He is an artist only insofar as he externalizes, objectifies and historicizes his phantasms. Every artist-individual, though, is such in a more or less broad and comprehensive way, he is "historical" or "social" to a greater or lesser degree. (1985: 112)

The historicity of the forms of individual consciousness, the social contradictions immanent in the language of the psyche, the dynamic interconnections of social existence registered in the flows of desire and flux of lived experience—all these axioms found in Gramsci can be used to explain the collectivist impulse behind artistic representation. In the peripheral hinterlands, this impulse is very much alive. It has escaped complete dissolution by the leveling "realism" of exchange-value in the marketplace. And so far as one can calculate from this distance, the force of reification has not yet sublimated or transmogrified its inhabitants into free-floating signifiers or aleatory simulacra.

Given this unashamedly totalizing (but not essentializing) framework, we can now appreciate Jameson's cogently argued hypothesis that when a dialectical hermeneutic or method of metacommentary is deployed on a typical "Third World" narrative (for example, Lu Hsun's "Diary of a Madman" and Sembene's *Xala*), the text emerges as a kind of national allegory. Jameson writes: "Third-world texts, even those which are seemingly private and invested with a properly libidinal dynamic, necessarily project a political dimension in the form of national allegory: the story of the private individual destiny is always an allegory of the embattled situation of the public third-world culture and society" (1986: 69). Note that his formulation assumes that in the West the public-private split tends to reduce everything into subjectivist or psychologized phenomena, while the radical disparity of the "Third World" lies in its uneven, unsynchronized milieu in which subjectivity is grounded and refigured by its social context, where the metonymy/syntax of personal lived experience ultimately finds intelligible expression in the paradigmatic axis of the community (see also Beverley and Zimmerman 1990). In the "Third World" narrative of quotidian existence, the artist is necessarily a political intellectual since the forms of artistic expression assume political valence in all the moments of its production, circulation, and reception.[2]

It might be instructive to point out two complementary tasks fulfilled by Jameson's approach in the light of displacing the empiricist hybridity ascribed to "postcolonial" texts. While this transcoding hermeneutic reveals how a cultural artifact performs a specific ideological vocation, its instrumental function, it also seeks to measure its utopian power "as the symbolic affirmation of a specific historical and class form of collective unity" (1981: 291). This anticipatory or prefigurative mission of "Third World" cultural practice is tied with the collective and reintegrative impulse, the popular memory, of masses crushed by the juggernaut of imperial market forces (Jameson 1976). To recover the memory of those silenced and "disappeared," the negativity of their difference from consumer society requires critical labor that demystifies atomizing, fragmented appearances and exposes the deceptive pluralism of the "liberal" consensus. This liberatory hermeneutic thus goes beyond the prejudiced horizon of readers/audiences and ludic zones of indeterminacy, passing critical judgment on transitory social arrangements from the perspective of mankind's struggle for freedom, justice, and happiness for all.

REVISITING THE DREAM OF WORLD REVOLUTION

At this point I can think of no better illustration of what Jameson is saying about the necessarily ethicopolitical function of the third-world intellectual than C. L. R. James and his massive life-long engagement in the cultural and political transformation of three continents. One can easily demonstrate how, for example, James's early story "Triumph" exemplifies the Caribbean allegory of conscientization originating from the intersection of sexuality, economics, and the resistance against patriarchy. Suffice it to consider here briefly his dramatization of the nonsynchronic and overdetermined process of Haiti's slave revolution, *The Black Jacobins*. The subtle choreography of moods, attitudes, and actions displayed by the major protagonists of the drama—Toussaint, Dessalines, and Moise—is plotted primarily to reveal the complex sensorium in which the colonial habitus operates and the uneven alignment of diverse ideological agencies in any transitional conjuncture. The defeat of the symbol of autonomy and of becoming-human, Moise, and the eclipse of the masses (symbolized by the displacement of voodoo by European music/dance) signal the way in which the force of historical necessity limits the influence of European radicalism (bourgeois individualism); they also signal how the deformation of the Bolshevik revolution by Stalin's authoritarian *diktat* translates into James's quest for a new historic agency in the form of the colonized, oppressed people of color in the "Third World." Nationalitarian allegory metamorphoses into a world-system parable. A note in the staging of the play betokens James's prefigurative sensibility: "Crowds say little but their presence is felt powerfully at all critical moments" (1992: 68). Certain key texts may be alluded to here as effectively demonstrating James's overarching principle that the masses of workers-peasants with their organized spontaneous energies create the decisive breaks in history (for example, the destruction of mercantilism by the slave revolt): "From Toussaint L'Ouverture to Fidel Castro," "The People of the Gold Coast," and the uncompromising testament of his faith, "Dialectical Materialism and the Fate of Humanity." Because James perceived the paradoxical and contradictory effects of capital, its progressive and regressive pressures on specific communities that triggered the astute responses of all classes and types, he was fully appreciative not only of the totalizing regime of commodity exchange in which the socialist project is the only alternative but also of the concrete sites where resistance is born. Thus by attending to the configuration of events in specific arenas of struggle and its interplay with the concrete mechanisms of the world system, James embodied in his lifework the allegorizing imagination, catholicity, and rigor that distinguish Marxism as a revolutionary praxis, the name of an intractable heterogeneous desire.

Under the aegis of allegory, synecdoche writ large, the "Third World" presents itself as a complex of narratives juxtaposing movements of disenfranchisement and of empowerment, of ruptures and convergences. In the light of varying temporalities, "nation" is only one term for reinscribing the fusion between agency and structure; other categories are race, class, ethnicity, religion, and their permutations—all loci for the strategic affirmation of a creative "Third World" subjectivity. The moment/process called "nation" is easily conflated or subsumed in that of class, gender, and other categories. How is it that Fanon's inaugural project of the nationalitarian conquest of identity has been disparaged and disavowed by postcolonial intellectualism?

One answer lies in the worldwide hegemony of poststructuralist ideology that valorizes the primacy of exchange, pastiche, fragmentation, textuality, and difference as touchstones of critique and understanding. Repudiating myths of origin (for example, Wole Soyinka's invocation of "universal verities" contained in the world view or "self-apprehension" of indigenous peoples) via techniques of abrogation and appropriation, the Australian authors of the influential textbook *The Empire Writes Back* proclaim that only syncretism, hybridity, and counterdiscourse can express the authentic essence of postcolonial literatures. But who authorizes this new doctrine? And what kind of rationality or will-to-power underwrites its portentous agendas? We are now indeed far removed from the time when a skillfully nuanced historicizing approach to cultural practices such as that illustrated by Umberto Melloti's *Marx and The Third World* is still a viable option. After criticizing the Eurocentric discourse of "Asiatic despotism" as well as the distortions of "bureaucratic collectivism" in transitional formations, Melotti proceeds to demarcate "Third World" civilizational uniqueness as an integral part of "world society":

> The different structure of the Third World has given birth to other no less important values, such as the communal ethic, the concept of a proper balance between man and nature, and the integration of the social and natural worlds, but it has never interpreted them in a truly liberating sense and has frequently carried them to a repressive conclusion. But today we are more than ever one world, and the synthesis of those values through truly socialist relations will finally permit the supersession of bourgeois individualism and repressive collectivism alike by a society where, as summed up in Marx's phrase, "The free development of each is the premise of the free development of all." (1977: 157)

ON THE EVE OF STORMS

At the threshold of the twenty-first century, we arrive at the crossroads of tradition and modernity in the far-flung margins of the empire. Obviously this trope of a journey insinuates a metanarrative biased against fixity and stasis, a "totalizing" figure suspect to postcolonial thinkers. But what is the alternative? Mapping the contours of the recent past may help prefigure the shape of what's to come in the controversy over the internationalization of critical (poststructuralist) theory (McClintock 1994). The impasse of technocratic development in the Third World in the last twenty-five years, since the two UNCTAD (United Nations Conference on Trade and Development) sessions in 1964 and 1968, returns us to the ineluctable questions that defy any premature forecasting of "the end of history" as touted by neoconservative pundits, among them: Is the Enlightenment project of winning human freedom from Necessity a ruse for imperial hegemony over people of color? Is the discourse of progress a mask for oppression? Is Marxism, inheritor of Enlightenment ideals, complicit with the discourse of modernization now rebaptized as "transculturation"? What original humane culture can the "natives" in the periphery offer to counter the fetishism of simulacra, pastiche, spectacle? Culture for the sake of whom, in the name of what?

We know from the historical record that the uneven and combined development of the Third World is the consequence of the lopsided and hierarchical division of international labor as well as the accumulation of capital by the industrial powers through plunder, slave trade, direct expropriation of resources and surplus value in the colonies from the sixteenth century up to the present (Wolf 1982, Rodney 1982, Weisskopf 1972). In *Theories of Development and Underdevelopment,* Ronald Chilcote surveyed the archive of analytic instruments and concepts used to explain the asymmetry of power, wealth, and status between the industrialized countries of Europe and the poor, underdeveloped societies of Asia (excluding Japan, of course), Africa, and Latin America. In the last three decades of research, diffusionist modernization theories gave way to developmentalist, dependency, and world-system theories, followed by a mode-of-production approach. What Chilcote finds lacking is the close integration of theory with actual social history that links imperialism to the histories of the exploited classes and their struggles. In response, James Petras (1981) calls for investigating the operations of the hegemonic imperial state (the worldwide network facilitating the process of capital accumulation), redefinition of political economy centered on exploitation and not development, and class/state relationships on both internal and international levels. I find this reorientation timely in the wake of the globalized retooling of the hierarchical division of international labor (Schaeffer 1997), the use of NAFTA and GATT by corporate/state organs, and the rearticulation of class with identity politics (associated with ethnicity, race, gender, sexuality, religion, among others) that make notions of global citizenship and solidarity opportunist traps if not slogans for Benetton and Coca-Cola.

Notwithstanding the periodic realignments of nation-states in this post–Cold War epoch, we still persist in the reign of sameness-with-difference: commodity exchange for the sake of profit/surplus value. But the growth of productive forces and people's critical responses have altered the systemic forms of capital accumulation. From market to transnational capitalism, the pattern of imperialist exploitation of the world's labor and resources has undergone a series of mutations. When the prescription of import-substitution carried out in the fifties and sixties failed to usher in sustained, independent growth, the elite of the dependent countries resorted to export-oriented industrialization administered by the National Security State. The result? A rich harvest of massive human rights violations by U.S.-backed authoritarian regimes, systematic corruption of cultures, degradation of work through "warm body exports" (migrant labor), and unrelenting pauperization of the masses. In the Free Trade Zones where the global assembly line generates superprofits out of cheap labor, total surveillance and draconian prohibitions prevail. Western monopoly of knowledge/information and the means of communication (mass media) become more crucial (see Schiller 1889). Empirical evidence and all kinds of testimony demonstrate that the cult of the Gross National Product institutionalized by the disciples of W. W. Rostow's *The Stages of Economic Growth* and the Chicago school of monetary economics, among others, has brought with it only rampant unemployment, widespread poverty, cycles of repression and stagnation, cultures and environments destroyed, for people of color whose underdevelopment is reproduced daily by such formulas meant to maintain archaic patronage systems and "trickle-down" philanthropy (Alavi and Shanin 1982, Woddis 1972, Amin 1977). Meanwhile, IMF/World Bank structural adjustments or conditionalities serve only to reinforce dependency. The plight of Argentina or Chile might well foreshadow the future of the Asian NICs (Newly Industrialized Countries).

In this life-and-death agon for millions, the literary conceits of undecidability and indeterminacy offer neither catharsis nor denouement, only mock-heroic distractions. Long before the failure of the reformist UN "Programme of Action on the Establishment of a New International Economic Order," Denis Goulet, in his provocative work *The Cruel Choice* (1975), had already proposed that the philosophy of development involves not just democracy in the political realm but "the basic questions about the quality of life in society, the relationship between goods and the good, and human control over change processes." In an incisive assessment of mainstream modernization theory, Timothy Luke (1990) criticized it for metrocentrism, discursive ethnocentricity, chronocentricity, and technocentricity: "'Technology,' 'industrialization,' and 'rationality' serve as mystifications that obscure a political struggle by typing it as a predetermined process, that turns a violent process into an automatic natural behavior, and that renders a self-serving economic activity into a historical certainty" (236; see also Leys 1982). Further, academic experts on modernization employed a structural-functionalist paradigm to cancel out conflict and privilege a stable authority, conformity to the status quo, and a pragmatic psychologizing of politics and society (Gendzier 1979). What is at stake is the question of responsibility and accountability for the goals and procedures of social change.

Wrestling with the theme of transition and development in underdeveloped revolutionary societies, Richard Fagen, Carmen Diana Deere, and Jose Luis Corragio (1986) focus not only on growth and equity but also on democratic political practice. Key to this is mass participation and its meaningful institutionalization as a central mediating link between citizens and agencies of governance. In dealing with schemes of progress imposed by organizations like the IMF/World Bank, then, we need to confront the key issue of self-determination in the realm of civil society and the public sphere: who decides and ultimately determines the goals, means, and trajectory of any development program? Can the indigenous elite who inherited the colonial state be relied upon to mobilize the masses, articulate their aspirations, and redistribute wealth/power? In short: Is the path of material progress for former colonies via dependent capitalism or popular-democratic (socialist) revolution?

There is no doubt that this mode of critical inquiry challenges conventional wisdom and official paradigms. Its criterion of social practice unsettles postcolonial ambivalence and Manichean delirium. It repudiates the bureaucratic syndrome concerned with "who gets what when" and with the economics of scarcity and supply-and-demand. In practically all orthodox thinking on modernization, private ownership of the means of production (land, technology, etc.) and "efficient resource allocation and enhanced productivity" through foreign investment and marketing strategies of elite sectors function as axiomatic givens, received "common sense." By privileging private interests and instrumental/utilitarian solutions, the explanatory model of neoclassical economics fails to take into account the historical contexts of class, ethnicity, gender, and other sectoral conflicts. It elides the centuries-long dispute over land. It evades the question of citizen participation in political-economic decisions, a context in which (as the Philippine case demonstrates so clearly [O'Brien 1990; Canlas, Miranda and Putzel 1988; Boyce 1993)[3] ownership of land is only one factor embroiled in the larger issue of oligarchic monopoly of wealth and power maintained by hierarchical structures, institutions, and mentalities left over from the past. Top-down bureaucratic planning ignores the overriding force of the international division of labor in the removal of economic surplus by foreign capital, a phenomenon that Paul Baran, in his classic study *The*

Political Economy of Growth (1957), has thoroughly analyzed. Baran concludes that

> It is the economic strangulation of the colonial and dependent countries by the imperialist powers that stymied the development of indigenous industrial capitalism, thus preventing the overthrow of the feudal-mercantile order and assuring the rule of the comprador administrations. It is the preservation of these subservient governments, stifling economic and social development and suppressing all popular movements for social and national liberation, that makes possible at the present time the continued foreign exploitation of underdeveloped countries and their domination by the imperialist powers. (1982: 203-04)

It is not surprising to discover once again that neoliberal empiricism and its post-Fordist descendants cannot envisage what is really at stake in such a life-or-death matter as land reform or grass-roots democracy in contested zones.

One last marker of geopolitical import need be rehearsed here. The centrality of transnational corporations in structuring power relations among nations and peoples needs no elaborate argument. Considering how today 600 of these corporations produce 25 percent of everything made in the world and account for 80 to 90 percent of the exports of the U.S., Japan, Britain, and Canada, no substantive appraisal of programs for democratic change can be conducted without interrogating the role and impact of such entities in the social, political, and cultural transformation of the Third World (Fitt *et al* 1980). This is precisely what Armand Mattelart has accomplished in his book *Transnationals and the Third World* (1983). Mattelart analyzes the logistics and ideological apparatuses engaged in the production of cultural commodities for the world market and reveals how the ethos of Western business practice, legitimized by such notions as security, freedom, efficiency, and so forth, are normalized in Third World societies through the virtually unconstrained operations of the Western-managed knowledge or consciousness industry.[4] Can the postcolonial intellect dismantle this set-up? Fed to this recuperative machine of the conglomerates, the now archetypal romance of decentered alterity can only be one more consumer item for Baudrillard and Lyotard's indefatigable shopper.

The prospect, however, need not be dismaying. It can be considered an occasion for intoning the mantra of certain fellow-travelers: "pessimism of the mind, optimism of the will." Against the long duration of colonial reification and fragmentation fostered by metropolitan High Culture, virtually the "prehistory" of people of color, Third World activists inspired by Fanon, Mao, Che Guevarra, Malcolm X, and others, have mounted offensives against the Orientalizing will-to-power of the Western Self. One can cite here Aimé Césaire's eloquent *Discourse on Colonialism;* the testimonios of Rigoberta Menchu and other indigenous witnesses from South America, Africa, and Oceania; *Song of Ariran,* the magnificent allegory of a revolutionary coming-of-age by the Korean Kim San; and film-texts from the Philippines like *The Perfumed Nightmare* by Kidlat Tahimik and *Orapronobis* by Lino Brocka, not to mention the rich exemplary achievement of Cuban cinema.

In a revisionary move sometime in the early eighties, I proposed that national allegories composed in the midst of authoritarian or military fascist regimes be designated "emergency writing" after Walter Benjamin's ever timely exhortation: "The tradition of the oppressed teaches us that the 'state of emergency' in which we live is not the exception but the rule. We must attain to a conception of history that is in keeping with this insight. Then we shall clearly realize that it is our task to bring about a real state of emergency" (1969: 257). And so, instead of the rubrics "postcolonial" or "subaltern," the resonance of "emergency" corresponds more to the structure of feeling enunciated in the works of Ngugi, Darwish, Dalton, and others in their beleaguered and besieged positions.

TWO STEPS FORWARD, ONE STEP BACKWARD

Symptomatic of the attenuation of Third World resistance in the eighties is the rise of postcolonial textualism. In contrast to the countercanonical archive cited above, this new speculative trend inaugurated by Edward Said's pathbreaking *Orientalism* (and its much more committed sequel, *Culture and Imperialism*) focuses on one singular task: the demystifying interrogation of Eurocentric discourse. It seeks to dismantle the truth-claims of this discourse by exposing how its epistemic violence has fashioned the marginal, negative, subaltern Other. The problematic within which postcolonial critics like Homi Bhabha, Gayatri Spivak, Trinh Minh-ha, and their disciples operate is defined by what Ahmad calls "the main cultural tropes of bourgeois humanism" (1992: 36): the exorbitation of discourse; the poststructuralist epistemology of the unstable, schizoid and polyvocal subject; the constitution of knowledge/power by language, by difference, aporia, and so on (Bhabha 1992;

Spivak 1991). Such maneuvers to transcend the fate of marginality bear all the stigmata of their social-historical determinations. Where is the "Other" situated in this play of Symbolic and Imaginary registers? Benita Parry has charged postcolonial deconstructionists of erasing "the voice of the native" and limiting "native resistance to devices circumventing and interrogating colonial authority," thereby discounting the salience of "enabling socioeconomic and political institutions and other forms of social praxis" (1987: 43). Thus the "posting" of reality coincides if not sanctions the metaphysics of the West's infamous "civilizing mission" (see Callinicos 1989). Meanwhile, the social theoretician Jorge Larrain assays the conservative neo-liberal politics of postmodernism as a defense of the interests of the ruling class, upholding "the supremacy of the blind forces of the market" (1995: 288).

European scholars of emergent and "new literatures" are also wary of postcolonial sophistry. The German critic Frank Schulze-Engler (1993) has inventoried the inadequacies of this trend. He explains how Bhabha, Spivak, and others have consistently ignored the fact that "it is the interaction of communicating people that constitutes the world for language" and in so doing they cannot account for 'subjectivity' or 'agency' except in a highly instrumental or strategic sense." The result is "epistemological necrophilia." In this carnival of shifting positionalities, amid this ludic heteroglossia inconceivable even from the standpoint of the arch-dialogist Bakhtin, the postcolonial intelligence is unable to discriminate the specific modernities found in the settler colonies (one model of a postcolonial society proposed by *The Empire Writes Back* is the United States!), the invaded/occupied domains, and assorted neocolonies. It cannot imagine such an unthinkable event as New Zealand becoming the nation of Aotearoa (see During 1987; Slemon 1987), or the new order envisaged by the Brazilian Worker's Party, described by its spokesperson, Luiz da Silva, as "a new society founded on the values of liberty and social justice" (1993); or the commitment of Hawaiian Haunani-Kay Trask in fighting for Papahanaumoku, the Earth Mother. Could it be that these intellectuals, as Henry Louis Gates (1994) insinuates, are only sophisticated narcissists acting out the predicament of exile and dislocation? Or are they the new heroines/avatars of an apocalyptic judgment looming in the horizon?

We in the "Third World" certainly hope for change, not for utopia but for the chance to be in control of our lives. This can happen only under conditions not of our own making, in the shadow of "forms of life" inherited from the past. While my recent works, in particular

Reading the West/Writing the East and *From the Masses, to the Masses,*
evoke, in response to the circumstantial imperatives of the 1970s and
early 1980s, a conjuncture that will not be replicated again after the
demise of "actually existing socialism," I believe that the examples of Ho
Chi Minh, Ngugi, Dalton, Cardenal, Turki, and many others (the rich
tradition of oral performances have been only alluded to here) possess a
catalyzing usefulness and relevance for present and future generations.
The reason for this is that the ground or substratum of manifold
experience allegorized by their art persists in the "Third World," manifest
in the nightmare of exploited and alienated labor, of sexism and racist
oppression, and latent in the gratifications of the postmodern Sublime.
The historic agency of native actors/protagonists and the sensuous
particularities of their resistance demand to be witnessed, not just
represented, inscribed in that space once circumscribed by the colonial
episteme, and now multiply determined by global exchange, a stage in
which social identity has become world-historical in its constitution. It
is in the context of an evolving planetary horizon of cultural politics that
Neil Lazarus contends that postcolonial intellectuals disavow their
comprador ventriloquism and instead try to revitalize the category of
universality—nationalitarian, radical, liberationist—"from which it is
possible to assume the burden of speaking for all humanity" (1993: 52).

We are then finally faced with the dilemma of discriminating among
native informant, ethnographic construct, subaltern mimicry, and/or
genuine historical agent of insurrectionary practice. We are in search of the
collective speaking subject, a figure that refers to specific communities,
variegated and no longer anonymous "identity groups," with all their
incommensurable genealogies and dissonant traditions. They comprise the
quanta of energy in the unsynchronized force field of the "national
popular." They are not unitary or monadic subjects of a metaphysical
nationalism sprung from Hegel's brain and privileging the telos of self-
realization (Eagleton 1990). They materialize in a contradictory unity of
classes and groups locked in conflict but in permanent motion (which is
what "dialectic" signifies), in the uneven disarticulated sites labeled (for
convenience's sake) the "Third World." In those sites, what proves
efficacious is a dialectical approach which subverts the containment
strategy of idealist metaphysics and enables Eqbal Ahmad (1981) and
Samir Amin (1989), among others, to discern the resonance of autoch-
thonous or aboriginal subtexts in dependent milieus, to hear a multiplicity
of voices running against the grain. It also enables us to acknowledge the
originality of the Palestinian *intifada,* its virtue as the "moral and mobiliz-

able force of coordinated, intelligent, courageous human action" (El Masri 1990: 5). This dialectical method of allegorizing the resistance of the subjugated is our antithesis/substitute for postcolonial scholasticism.

In July 1993, a gathering of left and progressive organizations around the world known as the Sao Paolo Foro released a declaration that makes obsolete previous UN programs. The founding vision is enunciated in this affirmation: "We urge . . . the creation and implementation of development models which, expressing the interests and organized power of mass movements, move toward sustained and independent, environmentally balanced economic growth with equitable distribution of wealth, in the framework of strengthening democracy in all areas" (Pizarro 1993: 22). Daniel Ortega of the Sandinista party in Nicaragua counseled that while integration of national economies is needed, "policies must be according to our own circumstances in our own countries." This is a view shared by Cuauhtemoc Cardenas, leader of the Revolutionary Democratic Party of Mexico, for whom policies "must be rooted in our own country's history and culture." We apprehend here not a totalizing unity but a contradictory or dialogical synthesis that heralds the advent of a new epoch for the impoverished majority of our planet. We are just beginning to witness the emergence of Third World peoples as historic agents in the shaping of their own ethnic, racial, and national histories salvaged from the hubris of Manichean politics and the specular abyss of *différance*. Amid the revolt in the hinterlands, metropolitan elites with their monopoly of knowledge and apparatuses of ideological hegemony continue to uphold and impose their supremacy over a planet where exchange-value and the commodification of everything still govern our sensibilities, stultify our imagination, and limit the pleasure of use-values in our everyday lives.

Historical materialism affords us insight into the present crisis of revolutionary movements in the "Third World." Changes there will come from a convergence of popular initiatives, the mediating force of the indigenous intellectuals (in the large sense defined by Gramsci) both traditional and organic, and the solidarity of progressive forces across nation-state, linguistic, and religious/ethnic borderlines. This is perhaps the moment to suggest how the absence of a democratizing impulse in mainstream development thought (soon to be absorbed in the new discipline of Cultural Studies), a characteristic of the ideology of competitive accumulation in the global marketplace, can be traced to two foundations of capitalism as a world-system that Immanuel Wallerstein (1983: 75-93) denominates as racism and universalism. While racism functions as a worldwide mechanism to control the direct producers by hierarchical and differential distribution of wealth (see also Sivanandan), universalism proclaims truth (in the mind of the ascendant European bourgeoisie) to inhere in technical and instrumental rationality, hence the slogan of progress and modernization justifying the predatory effects of Western cultural imperialism. Opposing technocratic modernization sponsored by transnational conglomerates are diverse nationalisms, ethnic revivals, and a diverse coalition of communities and regions bound to be sacrificed in the name of free enterprise and consumer satisfaction. What is called for in any democratizing mandate, in any counterhegemonic project today, is critical anatomy or diagnosis of the contemporary resurgence of ethnically based or religion-oriented nationalisms and, in particular, of sharp racial antagonisms overdetermined by *ressentiment,* unaddressed grievances, and assorted libidinal investments that are currently renegotiating the boundaries of First World/Third World transactions.

The revolutionary power of native agency absent in postcolonial discourse may be encountered in the current transvaluation of traditional beliefs and archaic practices. From the perspective of liberation theology (as enunciated particularly by Asian and Latin American activists), the radically democratic aspiration of people of color in both metropolis and periphery is in essence a struggle for liberation, a process of self-empowerment. This endeavor problematizes the construction of subaltern agents in neocolonial society and releases social energies otherwise channeled to profit-making and other wasteful pursuits. This process of transition involves difficult choices, antinomies, zigzags and detours, vexing ambiguities and paradoxes (Fagen 1986). Refusing to be seduced by the material rewards of technocratic/instrumental reason, the conscientized masses will have to choose between two competing principles: competitive bureaucratic efficiency or participatory social justice. While the rhetoric of this choice is oppositional, disjunctive, and even utopian, the emancipatory thrust of grass-roots organizing among workers and peasants in many developing countries is unequivocal. Meanwhile, in the industrialized nations, both fetishisms of technology and of untamed nature (advocated by some ecology groups) rule out the attainment of antiracist social justice and the shaping of new alternative forms of life, collective goals that Raymond Williams (1983a: 175-217) foresees as the real challenge of the twenty-first century. The spirit of national-popular liberation celebrated by "Third World" allegories encompasses both order and freedom, discipline and social justice. What is at stake in this initiative of reconceptualizing popular agency and foregrounding the transgressive potential of the national-popular imagination? Precisely the answer to the questions introduced earlier: Growth for whom? Progress for what?

Opposing the chauvinist elitism of Western planners and advisers, *The People's Development Agenda* (1990: 3-4) drawn up by the Council for People's Development in the Philippines presents an alternative (for a background, see Sison 1986; Chapman 1987; Davis 1989). It sums up the lessons of half a century of mass struggles for popular democracy and national liberation: development "refers to the struggle to advance the socioeconomic rights of the poor majority, to strengthen their capacity to gain control of production resources, to improve their capability to meet basic needs, and to create the means towards their sustained development. It is an integral part of the process of transferring political and socioeconomic power from the elite to the majority who are poor" (3-4). This Filipino desideratum of "democratic participation of the people in development processes" is not parochial since it echoes the sentiment of Third World self-determination crystallized in "The Pastoral Letter from the Third World" issued by fifteen Latin American bishops headed by Dom Helder Camara in 1968. It takes up the message of the Cocoyoc (Mexico) Declaration formulated in 1974 by the participants of the "Symposium on Models of Resources Utilization: A Strategy for the Environment and Development" organized by UNCTAD and UNPE (United Programs for the Environment). This declaration affirms the primacy of self-reliance even as it valorizes the solidarity of peoples: "reliance on the capacity of people themselves to invent and generate new resources and techniques . . . to take a measure of command over the economy, and to generate their own way of life" (Galtung, O'Brien and Preiswerk 1980: 24). It upholds production for equitable use, not for profit or power, to satisfy basic human needs (which includes self-fulfillment, participation, conviviality). It also calls for affirming the first principle of human dignity, "namely that human beings as well as their culture need to be treated by others with due respect, for their own sakes and on their own terms" (25). Surpassing the demand for formal civil rights, this principle of reciprocity/integrity rejects outright the canonical methodology of technocratic development and assigns priority to the task of preserving and enriching indigenous, national/popular culture as "an integral whole of accumulated resources, both material and nonmaterial, which they [the Calibans of transnational capital] utilize, transform and transmit in order to satisfy their needs, assert their identity and give meaning to their lives." (Mattelart 1983: 25).

THE JOURNEY BEGINS

A decade after the UN call for a New International Economic Order, Samir Amin (1985) reprised the major contradiction in the world-system arena: "between the pressures of globalization (or 'transnationalization') imposed by the predominance of capital, and the aspirations of working classes, peoples and nations for some autonomous space." To remedy the disarticulating effects of the new "electronic revolution" resulting in drastic time-space compression (Harvey 1989) and various forms of coercive displacements (Bello 1987; Klare and Kornbluh 1989), constituencies in the Third World have invented an arsenal of novel techniques of resistance, transgression, and self-recovery. Unity of opposites thus gives way to antagonism and subject-formation. Witness (to cite only the most well-known instances) the 1986 "People Power" insurrection in the Philippines, the student rebellions in South Korea, the revival of revolutionary opposition in Brazil after decades of military rule, and the inexhaustible resourcefulness of Mandela's African National Congress faced with the vicious terrorism of the apartheid State. Sparks of hope in the wasteland of the global megamall? Perhaps. Petra Kelly, the murdered leader of the German Green Party, confessed once that "those in the Third World confront violence and structural violence much more directly then we [Westerners] do, so they are more radical in their whole analysis" (1993: 139). This intervention of new historical subjects—the spiritually dispossessed "hewers of wood and drawers of water" carving out a zone of nomadic, perverse energies that then explode and circulate across the East-West ideological divide—is a protean and self-renewing movement that may bridge the gulf between North and South, between rich and poor nations, between the past and the future.

Of late some activists in the United States have put out the claim that the Brundtland UN Report of 1987 on Environment and Development focusing on the theme of "sustainable development" can serve as a basis for a political-ethical alliance between North and South. Resource depletion, environmental injury, burgeoning human populations, oppression—these are surely urgent concerns with universal appeal. But can the project of participatory democracy and self-reliance survive the "New World Order" born from a war propelled by racist exterminism and commercial greed? There are in fact several wars raging today in every continent (one can cite offhand those in East Timor, in Kurdistan, in the Philippines). With the demise of Soviet and East European "socialism" as a counterbalance to the domination of the transcendental commodity and the omnipotent market, increased rivalry among the European states, the U.S., and Japan is bound to complicate interstate relations, notwithstanding the establishment of free trade linkages and respective spheres of influence. Local surrogate wars (targeting recalcitrant states such as Iran, North Korea, or Cuba, who are alleged by the U.S. State Department to be sponsors of "terrorism") will be tomorrow's scenarios. Some observers (for example, Petras 1991) predict that the compradorization of Eastern Europe and the refeudalization of other regions as a result of the weakening and fragmentation of state structures will open up new markets of cheap labor and capital. This will occur in the wake of revitalized racisms and ethnocentrisms, along with the recrudescence of sexist, chauvinist, and religious intolerance of all sorts. Writing on "the future of Maoism," Samir Amin (1981) predicted that if the national autocentric path of development via delinking from the capitalist world system is not adopted by dependent societies, then compradorization (as in the Newly Industrialized Countries, and in "postrevolutionary" countries like Nicaragua, Tanzania, and Zimbabwe) is bound to result.

What is the alternative? After a judicious reconnaissance of the impacts that resistance intellectuals (like Ruth First, Ghassan Kanafani, Roque Dalton) produced in the interregnum between World War II and *glasnost,* Barbara Harlow points to "the new geographies of struggle" representing "the transformations and reversals that have resulted from the peripeties of the historic move—political, discursive, critical—from interrogation and assassination to negotiation" (1996: 153). Resistance literature shifts its center of gravity from guerilla diaries and *testimonios* to human rights reporting and the memorabilia of victims demanding commissions of truth for their vindication. Interrogation, assassination, negotiation, revelation—is this the new rite of passage for repairing the damaged hubris of postcolonial lives?

Let us listen to a partisan voice from the "second world." In a recent lecture delivered at Tribhuvan University, Kathmandu, Nepal, Sam Noumoff, director of the Center for Developing Area Studies at McGill University, sketched the dismal prospect of development in the Third World: greater penetration of these societies by the transnational market's control of the production process (knowledge-intensive industries), loss of leverage with the decline of the need for raw materials, decrease of agricultural earnings due to Western protectionism, the traps of the "green revolution" and debt (this last, administered by the IMF/World Bank, prevents indigenous capital formation), export-led growth insuring permanent dependency through import of capital-intensive technology, the rule of comparative advantage freezing the Third World in a dual economy, and so on. As countermeasures, Noumoff suggested regional cooperation in research to break the technological monopoly of the North, integrated training in joint ventures to break the multinational corporations' marketing monopoly, and internal diffusion of technology throughout society, among others. In retrospect, Noumoff's proposal evokes the ideal of self-reliance affirmed by the 1974 Cocoyoc Declaration, the theme of empowerment in the Filipino "people's agenda," and the prophetic passion of the Latin American theology of liberation: "One must institute a program which uses as a measure of development the most deprived in the society. The measure of a developed society is not how the best live; the measure of a society is what is the state of the poorest person, and one must start there" (Noumoff 1991: 18).

A beginning then has to be made from the rubble of predatory modernization. Self-sustained local development displaces capitalist profit-making and transfers power into the hands of the community. It makes humans the aim of social production in the way Marx envisioned it: "In fact, when the narrow bourgeois form has been peeled away, what is wealth if not the universality of needs, capacities, enjoyments, productive powers, etc., of individuals, produced in universal exchange? What, if not the full development of human control over the forces of nature—those of his own nature as well as those of so-called 'nature'?" (1964: 84). Only in conceiving wealth as the "universality of needs and powers," I think, can we effect a breakthrough from the emergencies of domination and exploitation afflicting the planet. Only through popular-democratic revolutions will the antinomy of postcolonial democracy and capitalist modernization inscribed in the history of the world system be transmuted (by those whom Fanon designated as "the wretched of the earth") into the protracted process of liberation and empowerment of the majority—workers, women, peasants, the poor in general—that will also guarantee the preservation of the earth's biosphere. Against the Leviathan of commodification marching on the ruins of Baghdad and the Kremlin, one can oppose the solidarity of peoples of color, their history of creativity and resourcefulness, their heterogeneous cultures of resistance, their commitment to the dignity and freedom of specific communities as the best hope of humankind's survival and regeneration in the next millennium.

NOTES

INTRODUCTION

1. Of enormous significance are the issues elucidated and resolved by Ebert (1996) on contemporary feminism and Giroux (1995) and Larrain (1995) on national/postmodern identity. On multiculturalism and cultural studies in general, the most helpful are Jameson (1995) and Balibar (1995). I recommend their voluminous writings on a wide range of topics. On an in-depth critique of poststructuralist theory which informs postcolonial ruminations, see Zavarzadeh and Morton (1991).

2. One concern is the origin of this new discipline in studies on Commonwealth Literature of the British Empire. Aside from the two anthologies on postcolonial texts already cited, another collection edited by Rajan and Mohanram (1995) verifies the suspicion that postcolonialism privileges India, Australia, Canada, and other ex-British possessions. An NEH 1996 Summer Seminar devoted to this topic in fact considers London the metropolis not only of the colonial world but also of the postcolonial one. According to the organizers, "With the end of Empire, Britain's encounter with the world has entered a new phase in which the population of the world, particularly of those countries formerly colonized by Britain, has moved to Britain," hence London is the "perfect site for a seminar on post-colonial literature" (Jussawalla and Dasenbrock 1996). What about Miami, where ex-colonial subjects (of the empire once called *pax Americana*) from Asia, Latin America, and Africa have gathered recently? Or why not Los Angeles, the capital of the "Third World" (by media consensus)?

    With the appropriation of the equally nascent field of "cultural studies" by Australians, Canadians, and other Commonwealth settlers resentful of British and American hegemony, postcolonial studies seem destined to become a terrain of contestation by warring disciplinarians from settler regions. In that case, the horrors of Western imperialism will be replayed—this time on the backs of postcolonized victims everywhere.

3. The term is used by Edward Said who, in an interview with Michael Sprinker and Jennifer Wicke, judges any Marxist ontology or epistemology as "extraordinarily insufficient" (1992). Notwithstanding Said's substantial contribution to a nonconformist academic competence and secularist reflexivity, I find his limitations much more severe than the anarchism of Chomsky with which he claims affinity. Unlike Said, Chomsky confronts capitalist institutions head-on without voluntarist micropolitics getting in the way. In contrast to Said's coy anti-Marxism, Stuart Hall's application of Marx's method presents a more

fertilizing and serviceable example, despite his apparent conversion to a merely discursive articulation theory (tied to Laclau and Mouffe), because he deals with the institutions and concrete practices of racism within specific historical formations. Hall's sense of place, or misplacement, and repertoires of cultural positions where identities are enunciated, is rooted in the reality of the black diaspora in Britain: "Since migration has turned out to be the world-historical event of late modernity, the classic postmodern experience turns out to be the diasporic experience" (1996: 490). Precisely because Hall emphasizes the structural determinants of historical belonging, what he calls "real structural properties," he cannot be associated with a ludic, performative postcolonialism obsessed with dismantling the intelligibility of Western modernity. Hall's Marxism (or its articulatory version, if you like) is a critical take on the postcolonial metaphysics of hybridity and liminality whose sterile formalism and aestheticism can only reinforce the status quo.

CHAPTER ONE

1. I would endorse here the qualified review of postcolonial theory vis-à-vis Establishment disciplinary canon by Apter (1995).

2. For a comparison/contrast to Bhabha's approach to racism, see Kovel (1984). For the communicative rationality of Fanon's anti-psychoanalytic stance, see Gendzier (1979; 1985).

3. But Fanon's "ethical universal" is not the same as Appiah's notion of postcolonial humanism, which embraces a mystical transnational in-between, what remains after rejecting the modernist binarism of Self and Other, "a unitary Africa over against a monolithic West" (1995: 124).

4. For an excellent analysis of ethnography as critique of assimilation, see Portillo (1995); for Menchu's rhetoric of resistance, see Sommer (1993).

5. For examples of *testimonio* by Filipina women, see Wynne (1979). For an example of collective feminist expression, see Arriola (1989).

6. Compare the notion of "emergent writing" suggested by Godzich (1988).

CHAPTER TWO

1. When I first broached in the sixties this idea of the decline of English as a literary medium for expressive cultural forms, I was attacked by the American New Critic Leonard Casper and his Filipino disciples. Should Filipino literature continue to be judged by the imperial master's criteria? Casper's entry on Filipino poetics in the Princeton *Encyclopedia of Poetry and Poetics* (1965) is typical of such procedure when it denigrated the vernacular while seeming to judge Filipino poets objectively in English, oblivious of its own discriminatory reductiveness. And Casper's recent revision of the entry compounds his doctrinaire selectiveness.

2. As witnessed by the volume *Cultures of United States Imperialism* (1993), edited by Amy Kaplan and Donald Pease, to cite one example.

3. Lest I be accused of chauvinism or xenophobia, I hasten to state here the obvious caveat. I don't subscribe to the view that accounts by Filipino historians, sociologists, anthropologists, and critics are more authentic and trustworthy just because they are by "natives" or "insiders." That would be patently false both on empirical and theoretical grounds. Not so long ago, numerous Filipino intellectuals claiming nationalist credentials openly worked for CIA/Cold War outfits like the Congress for Cultural Freedom, "Operations Brotherhood" in Vietnam, US-AID, Philippine Rural Reconstruction Movement, and many others later fostered by the Marcos dictatorship.

4. Recent work by American social scientists such as Putzel (1992) and Boyce (1993) are just two examples of excellent, painstaking analysis of the political economy of the Philippine social formation that provides a wider and deeper comprehension of what is going on than the previous texts I have cited. An earlier monograph by Robert Stauffer entitled *The Marcos Regime: Failure of Transnational Developmentalism and Hegemony-Building from Above and Outside* (1985) is a brilliant model of concrete analysis that I would recommend for those disgusted by academic subservience to "conventional wisdom." For similar studies, see Gill (1993).

5. One can even venture the scandalous proposition that a book originally written for popular consumption, Joseph B. Smith's *Portrait of a Cold Warrior* (1976), affords us a survey of the Filipino comprador oligarchy and its elite representatives more textured and plausible than tomes of statistical analysis turned out by RAND experts and researchers for Congressional committees. Even the enemy can be granted to possess a degree of realism sufficient to manipulate players that would produce results. Their realism is the pragmatic calculation of those in power, those determined to preserve the status quo. On the other hand, those resolved to alter that situation—one deemed unjust, painful, and inhumane by the world's conscience—would have more reason to be clear-eyed, sensitive, and cognizant of as many factors and forces in play, and on guard lest illusions of success or utopia waylay them. That of course is not always the case. Nevertheless the views of Filipino protagonists (such as those included in the anthology by de Dios et al [1988]) cannot be dismissed as unreliable simply because they are partisan, committed to popular democracy, nationalist and egalitarian. What study of social phenomena does not proceed from a certain framework or set of informing assumptions?

6. Karnow's narrative reflects, of course, the hegemonic outlook, even though it claims to represent the genuine Filipino ethos by quoting prestigious politicians and invoking the authority of selected indigenous informants. A claim of impartiality or liberal latitude is thus subtly insinuated. Everyone knows, of course, that not a few subjects of the Empire have volunteered to attest to the

authority of their tutors and legitimize such production of knowledge about themselves, in exchange for recognition of their status. Analysts of the colonial syndrome and its equivocal metamorphosis like Edward Said, C. L. R. James, Albert Memmi, and others have testified to this paradoxical symbiosis.

7. On modernization theory in general, see Martin and Kandal (1989), Gendzier (1985), and Escobar (1995).

8. Despite the decades that have passed since the foundational texts of Forbes, Hayden, and Taylor, not to speak of the operations of an entire range of ideological apparatuses like schools, census, periodic elections, mass media, sports, and so on, we find their categories and repertoire of tropes and syllogisms still operational in whole or in part in such representative texts as Steinberg (1982), Bresnan (1986), and Buss (1987). A plethora of books on the February 1986 insurrection has tried to exploit the commercial opportunity opened by those transitional events—another testimony to the commodifying reach of capitalist mass communication. Most of these works, however, are flawed by the uncritical or naive acceptance of the narrow functionalist and empiricist paradigm that claims to represent the "truth" about the dense, multilayered, complex experience of millions of workers and peasants victimized by putative "special relations" binding the United States and the Philippines.

9. In diametrical opposition to the sentimental and racist patronage of the commentators I have cited earlier, it is an immense relief and joy to find splendid accounts of recent cultural developments like Eugene Van Erven's *The Playful Revolution* (1992) on the evolution of grass-roots theater, the theater of liberation network, in the Philippines; Fredric Jameson's infinitely suggestive and provocative reading of Kidlat Tahimik's *The Perfumed Nightmare* in *The Geopolitical Aesthetic* (1992); and Mary Bresnahan's pioneering study on the virtues of the vernacular for crosscultural communication, *Finding Our Feet* (1991). With the current revaluation and revision of Establishment canons and the emergence of "Cultural Studies" with a world-system orientation, we hope that the parochialism and chauvinism of Eggan, Netzorg, and their ilk can be permanently consigned to the museum of colonial artifacts without much loss for a new generation of students and scholars.

10. To cite a recent example: this hybrid or split physiognomy is ascribed to the writing of a "postcolonial" Filipino woman poet in this description from the publisher's blurb: "The *manananggal,* a supernatural character in Filipino folklore, flies at night seeking prey, her winged upper torso casting shadows from the moonlit sky while the lower part of her body waits patiently below" (from the Fall and Winter 1995-96 Book Catalogue of the Ohio State University Press).

11. This tradition of revolt as dramatized in literary texts and other discursive performances has been inventoried and rehearsed in my *Toward a People's Literature, Only By Struggle,* and *From People to Nation.*

12. An example of how this ideology of postmodern chic versatility is played out may be illustrated by a tourist guidebook that enacts a virtual commodification of the Filipino "essence" as one mixing Mexican, Peruvian, Argentinian, and "all the other indios of Madre Espana's former colonies" given to, among others, "the pursuit of all fads and fashions with avid enjoyment" (Mayuga and Yuson 1980; see also Francia 1993) The Filipino's hard act of "sudden shifts from Utopian optimism to moody fatalism" is neither unique nor inimitable. Peoples displaced or transported across borders—slaves, refugees, emigres, fugitives, exiles—and forced to live by cannibalizing cultures and carnivalizing them as well, may be said to exhibit this contrariness, this mirage of protean gracefulness. This is one contemporary version of what some Filipinos have become as a result of the struggle to endure colonial domination and still retain their humanity. But it is definitely not a version that expresses the clamor of millions of workers and peasants for justice and dignity. (For a somewhat nuanced guidebook into the complexity of U.S.-Philippine cultural interactions that improves on Mayuga and Yuson, see Gochenour 1990.)

13. In my *Crisis in the Philippines* (published in 1986 but written before the 1986 February uprising) as well as subsequent works—*Writing and National Liberation, Allegories of Resistance,* and *The Philippine Temptation,* I have attempted to outline those possibilities for renewal in the face of the dogmatisms of the past, skepticism and cynicism of the present, and uncertainties of the future.

14. In this context, I know only of one progressive American writer who succeeded in capturing this irrepressible Filipino desire for liberation. In his quasi-documentary novel *Fortress in the Rice,* Benjamin Appel transcribes the "structure of feeling" that animated the Huk rebellion:

> For blowing around that bowl of rice there was a sighing wind made up of the whispers, the laments, the passions of generations. A wind that had blown across the rice provinces for half a century. The wind of freedom. Luis Taruc had called it. For who had fought with the Katipuneros against the Spaniards in 1896 but the peasants? Who were the Colorums, years later, swearing that Jose Rizal would return like a second Christ to divide the land? Who the Sakdals of the 1930s, believing that Japan would send her fleets to Manila to liberate her brother Asiatics from the mestizo landlords? A wind of many names, a wind that would never stop. For who could stop the wind could stop the soul of man. (77)

CHAPTER THREE

1. According to Lynne Lawner, Gramsci's analysis of the relation between North and South in Italy is applicable to "colonial and underdeveloped countries and to ethnically and socially subordinate minorities" (129).

2. One may ask: Does the peasantry not have its unique physiognomy or world view? The French sociologist Georges Gurvitch has summed up the peasant cognitive system thus: "Except in unusual circumstances, therefore, the political knowledge of the peasant class is characterized by cautiousness, suspicion, a tendency toward ambiguity, and, contrary to what one might have supposed, this class is little inclined to the mythological element characteristic of the political knowledge of other social classes" (1971: 94).

3. Freire's world view has, I am sure, been influenced by Jean-Paul Sartre, whose concept of project captures the dialectics of learning in conscientization. According to Sartre: "The project, as the subjective surpassing of objectivity toward objectivity, and stretched between the objective conditions of the environment and the objective structures of the field of possibles, represents in itself the moving unity of subjectivity and objectivity, those cardinal determinants of activity. The subjective appears then as a necessary moment in the objective process. . . . Only the project, as a mediation between two moments of objectivity, can account for history; that is, for human creativity" (1968: 99, 101). Opposing cultural and other determinisms, Sartre argues that the project harbors a "double simultaneous relationship. In relation to the given, the praxis is negativity; what is always involved is the negation of a negation. In relation to the object aimed at, praxis is positivity, but this positivity opens unto the 'non-existent,' to what has not yet been" (1968: 92).

CHAPTER FIVE

1. In a fit of exasperation, Russell Leong, editor of *AmerAsia Journal,* sent an e-mail circular to all his colleagues concerning the "current rap about redefining, throwing away, or retheorizing the term Asian American into diasporic this or that": "Asian American is a tenacious word, born out of struggle, fire, darkness and color. It means that America is not white, particularly, but that Asians, as well as Native Americans, Latinos, and African Americans are politically, culturally, and economically of the United States. For even as we are disenfranchised, separated, and discriminated against, at the same time our bodies, our labor and our intelligence are exploited, as our cultures and communities are appropriated. Thus the strength of the term, 'Asian American,' lies in its power to point out the contradictions that characterize America at the end of the 20th century—a society whose popular rhetoric is one of inclusion, but whose primary history has been one of continued exclusion." We applaud the reiteration of self-evident truths, but the signification of the term "American" and its supererogatory claim to exclude all others in the continent, not just within the U.S. nation-state, is not so easily amenable to arbitrary definition nor periodic negotiation. It drags with it a whole massive history of what we want to reject: exploitation, racist violence, exclusion and oppression.

2. Enamored of the fashionable Foucaultian view of multiple power/discourse formations, Howard Winant endorses a "radicalized pluralism" (1994: 107) as the antidote to virulent institutional racism of the nineties. Meanwhile, U.S. Filipinos continue to repeat the mistake (see Jacinto and Syquia 1995) of blaming the victim's culture while subscribing to the Glazer/Moynihan thesis that it's the immigrant's normative values, not the freedom and opportunities of market society, that perpetuate marginality and even the "underclass" status.

3. In line with the assault against Eurocentrism and following the model of Afrocentrism, its mirror opposite, Paul Wong and colleagues (1995) have suggested "Asiacentrism" as an alternative paradigm in academic studies. The attempt is bold and pathbreaking but open to objections. One objection is that it valorizes selected commonalities and downplays substantive differences, sidetracking historical specificity for a project of reversing the past. This trend is immanent also in the indiscriminate "culturalism" that, for example, reduces the Korean-black conflict to a matter of cultural differences (Karnow and Yoshihara 1992).

4. I think the most positive offshoot of the postmodern trend is Critical Race Theory (CRT). CRT intends to expose the political and ideological function of law and legal rules. By applying hermeneutic methodology to specific legal cases, Neil Gotanda (1995), for example, demonstrates the historical contingency of court rulings. He also shows how legal judgments embed racializing narratives that conjoin national-state boundaries, immigration practices, and colonial/imperialist patterns of domination. At best, he discloses the contradiction and instability that are the conditions of possibility for liberal law's efficacy. For his part, Robert Chang (1995) believes that CRT will be revitalized by going through its "Asian American Moment" in which the violence and disenfranchisement of Asian Americans (through law, model minority myth, etc.) can become paradigmatic cases for deconstructing the positivistic neutrality of liberal law and evince its irreconcilability with any program of realizing participatory democracy and social justice.

5. Filipino Americans still muse over the vexed topic of U.S.-Philippines relations, a "dark romance" sprung from the problematic results of the Philippine revolution of 1896-98 and the "insurrection" (as U.S. official historians put it) against U.S. aggression. I take this as a symptom of the Myrdal disease. A little review of history should cure if not alleviate the symptom. After and before the anti-Filipino riot of Watsonville in January 1930, Filipinos carried weapons with them, even while they told their folks back home: "Everyone treated me good" (see Johnson 1989: 14). Racial and national discrimination of Filipinos as wards or "nationals" (neither citizens nor aliens) is distilled in the antimiscegenation laws against them (declared unconstitutional in 1948 but not revoked until 1967). In 1926, Filipinos were declared "not Mongolians" but Malays predisposed to running amuck! Still they were "persons of mixed blood" covered

by the California Civil Code as subjects prohibited from marrying white persons (Quinsaat et al 1976).

6. About 6 million Filipinos comprise the Overseas Contract Workers diaspora consisting chiefly of Filipina women recruited by labor agencies in the Middle East and in Europe, making the Philippines a remittance economy based on the dollars sent by these workers to their families back home. Given the scattering of the Filipino nationality around the world—particles of brain drained but also the flesh of "hospitality" entertainers in Japan and elsewhere—the neo- (not post-) colonial plight of the people has worsened. This demands a new materialist analysis. The "identity politics" of Commonwealth postcoloniality needs the categories of peoplehood, a historicized concept of nation, class struggle, sexuality, and gender in order to make sense of the Filipino predicament in the United States. To avoid the postcolonial "blackmail," Filipinos need to redefine their communities and their trajectories in the ongoing social transformation as a force either for preserving the status quo or for accelerating the movements for popular democracy.

7. Three women critics have contributed substantially to the elaboration of an "Asian American" critical discourse: Elaine Kim, Amy Ling, and Shirley Lim. One may cite here as notable accomplishments Lim's MLA handbook for Kingston's *The Woman Warrior,* the anthology of criticism edited by Ling and Lim and, most recently, Sau-Lin Wong's book *Reading Asian American Literature.*

8. One might object that I have summarized here only the negative and unpleasant features of immigration history, not mentioning the well-nigh irrepressible virtues of survival and resistance that characterize the various communities. This is because I want now to emphasize the value of the histories written by Ronald Takaki, *Strangers from A Different Shore* (1989) and Sucheng Chan, *Asian Americans: An Interpretive History* (1991)—both far superior to textbooks by Harry Kitano and Roger Daniels and by others.

CHAPTER SIX

1. In notes written in 1970-71, Bakhtin noted that "In life as the object of thought (abstract thought), man in general exists and a third party exists, but in the most vital experience of life only I, thou, and he exists" (1986: 44).

2. It is instructive to note the contrast between "nation" and sovereign state since a population like the Kurds may qualify as a nation (shared language, experience, for example) and aspire to a state (Kurdistan), but do not at present control a sovereign space. George Demko reminds us of several nations in this predicament: "There are Armenians, Sikhs, Basques, Singhalese, Inuits, Tamils, Palestinians, and Biafrans, to name a few. Some have states but many do not. Many—such as the nations within Russia, the United States, and the People's

Republic of China—share sovereign states. Almost every sovereign state, or country, is multinational, in that it includes more than one nation. Sweden has Lapps, Japan has Ainus. The only state that comes close in a true sense to being a single nation-state is Iceland" (44).

3. On the problems surrounding this orthodox formulation, see the liberal analysis of Connor. Connor cites Mao Tsetung's version of this dualism in a document of 1938: "Communists are internationalists, but we can put Marxism into practice only when it is integrated with the specific characteristics of our country and acquires a definite national form. The great strength of Marxism-Leninism lies precisely in its integration with the concrete revolutionary practice of all countries" (1984: 546). So far, I think the best Marxist exposition of the "national question" is that by Lowy, "Marxism and the National Question" (1978).

4. Senghor was one of the initiators of the artistic movement called "Negritude," which tried to blend "Africanity" and "Westernization" as part of a modernizing trend (Davidson 1982: 178). On Senghor as a specimen of African Bonapartism, D. Fogel writes: "The national bourgeoisie, of virtually all political stripes, is deathly afraid of the development of 'disunifying' social class differentiation and the irreconcilable class struggle which it generates. Senegal's longtime president Leopold Senghor, Africa's foremost neocolonial puppet of France, urged his fellow African heads of state at a 1979 U.N. food conference to 'reread Marx and Engels' and adapt it to the realities of the black [sic] continent" (1992: 165).

5. See Francisco (1987), Schirmer and Shalom (1987), San Juan (1986; 1996b), and De Dios et al (1988).

CHAPTER SEVEN

1. Following this tenet, the "postcolonial" nation-states of Australia, Canada, and the United States function as the vanguards in postcolonial knowledge-production, in theory and in practice! Are we witnessing the return of the old imperial "civilizing mission"? Other dire consequences follow, to be sure.

2. For a recent critique of postcolonial orthodoxy personified by Bhabha, see Parry (1994), Callinicos (1995), Larsen (1995b), Ahmad (1995a), and Dirlik (1997).

3. From 1938 to 1953, James lived in the United States and became involved in the debates of American Trotkyism as well as black cultural life. It was at this stage of his career that he began seriously to rethink the category of race. His conversation with Trotsky, I think, proved to James that Trotskyism and classical Marxism subordinated the black struggle (and by extension anti-colonial struggles) to the class question. In 1941, James (together with Raya Dunayevskaya) formed the Johnson-Forest Tendency; beginning with his book *State Capitalism and World Revolution* (1986), in which James argued that the

Soviet Union was a state capitalist system with a party bureaucracy that served as an instrument of capital accumulation, James parted with fundamentalist Trotskyism and moved to the last period of his life marked by his deportation from the United States in 1953.

4. The accent on praxis should answer the fallacious attempt to rescue James from Bolshevik/Trotskyist contamination by first setting up the straw figure of vulgar "Marxist" determinism/economism and then ascribing to James a culturalist post-Marxism that I think he would be the first to disavow. See, for example, Robinson (1992).

5. One can compare to James's global assessment a typical academic exercise in this genre written in the seventies, George L. Beckford, "The Anglophone Caribbean: Change and Continuity," *Masks* 1.1 (Fall 1975): 53-61.

6. By this James of course doesn't mean the literal return of the descendants of former slaves to Africa. Césaire glorified the colonized subjects who, "possessed/ by the pulse of things/indifferent to mastering but taking the chances of the world," are challenged to "conquer all/the violence entrenched in the recesses of his passion."

7. See Wynter (1992).

8. As James enunciates it in one letter, "The American character does not reconcile itself to [the European acceptance of the dominance of the unknown over the known], for it is dominated by the idea of the Illumination, with its perspective of life, liberty and the pursuit of happiness" (1992: 278). Instead of "internal moral axes" to which they must conform as Europeans do, the average American, he thinks, "wants to know and feel that his life, from day to day, from hour to hour, has been substantially altered and that the pursuit of happiness is now realisable" (1992: 280).

9. In the last chapter of *The Black Jacobins,* James traces the race war and carnage in Haiti as due to "the greed of the French bourgeoisie." From this he concludes that in contrast to nineteenth-century Haiti, the "blacks in Africa [in mid-twentieth century] are more advanced" in their pursuit of freedom, as demonstrated by such figures as Amilcar Cabral, Agostinho Neto, Nelson Mandela, and many others.

10. In the sixties, James remarked that Trinidad doesn't have the native languages or ways of life found in Ceylon or India: "We are Western, [but] have yet to separate what is ours from what is Western, a very difficult task" (quoted in Buhle 1988: 159).

11. Buhle, in his biography, considers this section of *Mariners, Renegades, and Castaways* James's apologia for social life under capitalism.

> From his arrival in October 1938 on invitation by the Socialist Workers Party to his deportation in 1953, a fifteen-year sojourn whose richness and impact still remain to be appreciated, James embodied in his American

period the conjuncture of accidence and necessity, of contingency and determinism, that motivates the synoptic, pedagogical insights of his Melville study.

CHAPTER EIGHT

1. A recent article in *Newsweek* (9 September 1991) entitled "How the West Can Win the New World Order" (33) registers this Establishment triumphalism in a mass media style. For an example of a recent radical response to globalizing trends, see the articles in the first volume of *Red Orange* (Nowlan 1996).

2. To validate this thesis, one need only consult Wlad Godzich's (1988) ingenious commentary on a short story by Angolan writer Manuel Rui as part of his argument for the recognition of "emergent literature" as constitutive of the field of comparative literature.

3. A succinct background to the problems of land reform and social inequality, and to the prospect of popular democracy in the Philippines, may be found in Canlas et al (1988). See also Sison (1986), Aguilar (1997a; 1997b), and BAYAN International (1994).

4. For a brilliant specimen of deconstructive analysis dealing with asymmetrical North/South encounters, and also epitomizing the dialectic of an exploitative modernity and popular resistance, see Buck-Morss (1987). For a substantial survey of spatial geopolitics in globalized, postmodern capitalism, see Featherstone, Lash and Robertson (1995).

BIBLIOGRAPHY

Abaya, Hernando. 1984. *The Making of a Subversive*. Quezon City: New Day Publishers.

Achebe, Chinua. 1988. *Hopes and Impediments: Selected Essays*. New York: Anchor Books.

Agamben, Giorgio. 1993. *The Coming Community*. Minneapolis: University of Minnesota Press.

Aguilar, Delia. 1988. *The Feminist Challenge*. Manila: Asian Social Institute.

———. 1993. "Engendering the Philippine Revolution: An Interview with Vicvic." *Monthly Review* (September): 25-37.

———. 1995. "Gender, Nation, Colonialism: Lessons from the Philippines." In *Women, Gender and Development*. Eds. Lynn Duggan et al. London: Zed Books.

———. 1997a. "Behind the Prosperous Facades." *Against The Current* (March-April): 17-20.

———. 1997b. "Gender, Nation, Colonialism: Lessons from the Philippines." In *Women, Gender and Development*. Ed. Lynn Duggan et al. London: Zed Books.

Aguilar-San Juan, Karin. 1994. *The State of Asian America*. Boston: South End Press.

Ahmad, Aijaz. 1992. *In Theory: Classes, Nations, Literatures*. London: Verso.

———. 1995a. "The Politics of Literary Postcoloniality," *Race and Class* 36.3: 1-20.

———. 1995b. "Post-Colonialism: What's In a Name?" In *Late Imperial Culture*. Ed. Roman de la Campa, E. Ann Kaplan, and Michael Sprinker. London: Verso.

Ahmad, Eqbal. 1981. "The Contemporary Crisis of the Third World." *Monthly Review* 32: 1-11.

———. 1982. *Political Culture and Foreign Policy: Notes on American Interventions in the Third World*. Washington, DC: Institute for Policy Studies.

Alavi, Hamza. 1965. "Peasants and Revolution." In *Socialist Register 1965*. New York: Monthly Review Press.

———. 1973. "The State in post-colonial societies: Pakistan and Bangladesh." *Imperialism and Revolution in South Asia*. Ed. Kathleen Gough and Hari Sharma. New York: Monthly Review Press.

Alavi, Hamza and Theodor Shanin, eds. 1982. *Introduction to the Sociology of Developing Societies*. New York: Monthly Review Press.

Alcoff, Linda. 1991-92. "The Problem of Speaking for Others." *Cultural Critique*: 5-29.

Alea, Tomas. 1990. *Memories of Underdevelopment*. New Brunswick and London: Rutgers University Press.

Alexis, Jacques Stepen. 1995. "Of the Marvellous Realism of the Haitians." In *The Post-colonial Studies Reader*. Eds. Bill Ashcroft, Gareth Griffiths, and Helen Tiffin. New York: Routledge.

Allen, James S. 1993. *The Philippine Left on the Eve of World War II*. Minneapolis: MEP Press.

Althusser, Louis. 1969. *For Marx*. New York: Pantheon Books.

———. 1971. *Lenin and Philosophy and Other Essays*. London: New Left Books.

Amariglio, Jack and Antonio Callari. 1983. *The Theory of Commodity Fetishism and the Social Constitution of Individuals*. Discussion Paper #1. Amherst: Association for Economic and Social Analysis.

American Assembly. 1994. *Threatened Peoples, Threatened Borders: World Migration and U.S. Policy*. New York: Columbia University.

Amin, Samir. 1977. *Imperialism and Unequal Development*. New York: Monthly Review Press.

———. 1981. *The Future of Maoism*. New York: Monthly Review Press.

———. 1985. "The Crisis, the Third World, and North-South, East-West Relations." In Stephen Resnick and Richard Wolff, eds., *Rethinking Marxism*. New York: Autonomedia.

———. 1989. *Eurocentrism*. New York: Monthly Review Press.

———. 1994. *Re-Reading the Postwar Period: An Intellectual Itinerary*. New York: Monthly Review Press.

Amnesty International. 1992. *The Killing Goes On*. New York: Amnesty International USA.

Amuta, Chidi. 1996. "The Materialism of Cultural Nationalism: Achebe's *Things Fall Apart* and *Arrow of God*." In *Marxist Literary Theory*. Eds. Terry Eagleton and Drew Milne. Oxford: Blackwell.

Anderson, Benedict. 1983. *Imagined Communities: Reflections on the Origin and Spread of Nationalism*. London: Verso.

———. 1995. "Cacique Democracy in the Philippines: Origins and Dreams." In *Discrepant Histories*. Ed. Vicente Rafael. Philadelphia: Temple University Press.

Anderson, Bridget. 1993. *Britain's Secret Slaves*. London: Anti-Slavery International.

Anderson, Kevin. 1995. *Lenin, Hegel, and Western Marxism: A Critical Study*. Urbana and Chicago: University of Illinois Press.

Anderson, Warwick. 1995. "'Where Every Prospect Pleases and Only Man is Vile': Laboratory Medicine as Colonial Discourse." *Discrepant Histories*. Philadelphia: Temple University Press.

Appadurai, Arjun. 1994. "Disjuncture and Difference in the Global Cultural Economy." In *Colonial Discourse and Post-Colonial Theory*, edited by Patrick Williams and Laura Chrisman, pp. 324-39. New York: Columbia University Press.

Appel, Benjamin. 1951. *Fortress in the Rice*. New York: Bobbs-Merrill.

Appelbaum, Richard P. 1996. "Multiculturalism and Flexibility: Some New Directions in Global Capitalism." *Mapping Multiculturalism*. Ed. Avery Gordon and Christopher Newfield. Minneapolis: University of Minnesota Press.

Appiah, Kwame Anthony. 1992. *In My Father's House: Africa in the Philosophy of Culture*. London: Methuen.

———. 1995. "The Postcolonial and the Postmodern." In *The Post-colonial Studies Reader*. Ed. Bill Ashcroft, Gareth Griffiths, and Helen Tiffin. New York: Routledge.

Apter, Emily. 1995. "Comparative Exile: Competing Margins in the History of Comparative Literature." In *Comparative Literature in the Age of Multiculturalism*. Ed. Charles Bernheimer. New York: MLA.

Arrighi, Giovanni. 1993. "The Three Hegemonies of Historical Capitalism." In *Gramsci, Historical Materialism and International Relations*. Ed. Stephen Gill. Cambridge: Cambridge University Press.

Arriola, Fe Capellan. 1989. *Si Maria, Nena, Gabriela atbp*. Manila: Gabriela and Institute of Women's Studies, St. Scholastica.

Arthur, C. J. 1986. *Dialectics of Labour*. London: Basil Blackwell.

Ashcroft, Bill, Gareth Griffiths, and Helen Tiffin. 1989. *The Empire Writes Back: Theory and Practice in Post-colonial Literatures*. New York: Routledge.

———, eds. 1995. *The Post-colonial Studies Reader*. London: Routledge.

Asian Women United of California, ed. 1989. *Making Waves*. Boston: Beacon Press.

Axelos, Kostas. 1976. *Alienation, Praxis, and Techne in the Thought of Karl Marx*. Tr. Ronald Bruzina. Austin, Texas: University of Texas Press.

Baker, Houston, ed. 1982. *Three American Literatures*. New York: MLA.

Bakhtin, Mikhail M. 1965. *Rabelais and His World*. Tr. Helen Iswolsky. Cambridge, Ma.: MIT Press.

———. 1973. *Freudianism: A Marxist Critique*. New York: Academic Press.

———. 1981. *The Dialogic Imagination*. Ed. Michael Holquist. Austin, TX: University of Texas Press.

———. 1984. *Problems of Dostoevsky's Poetics*. Ed. Caryl Emerson. Minneapolis: University of Minnesota Press.

———. 1986. *Speech Genres and Other Late Essays*. Ed. Caryl Emerson and Michael Holquist. Tr. Vern McGee. Austin, Texas: University of Texas Press.

———. 1993. *Toward a Philosophy of the Act*. Ed. Michael Holquist and Vadim Liapunov. Austin: University of Texas Press.

Bakhtin, Mikhail and V. N. Voloshinov. 1989. "Discourse in Life and Discourse in Art." *Literary Criticism and Theory*. Eds. Robert Con Davis and Laurie Finke. New York: Longman. 594-613.

Balibar, Etienne. 1991. "The Nation Form: History and Ideology." In *Race, Nation, Class: Ambiguous Identities* by Etienne Balibar and Immanuel Wallerstein. London: Verso.

———. 1995. "Culture and Identity (Working Notes)." In *The Identity in Question*. Ed. John Rajchman. New York: Routledge.

Balibar, Etienne and Immanuel Wallerstein. 1991. *Race, Nation, Class: Ambiguous Identities*. London: Verso.

Banton, Michael. 1987. *Racial Theories*. Cambridge: Cambridge University Press.

Baran, Paul. 1982. "A Morphology of Backwardness." In *Introduction to the Sociology of "Developing Societies."* Eds. Hamza Alavi and Theodor Shanin. New York: Monthly Review Press.

Barratt Brown, Michael. 1982. "Developing Societies as Part of an International Political Economy." In *Introduction to the Sociology of "Developing Societies."* New York: Monthly Review Press.

Barros, Maria Lorena. 1975-76. "Three Poems: Sampaguita, Ipil, Yesterday I Had a Talk." *Collegian Folio:* 12; also in Pahayag (January 1977): 7.

Barthes, Roland. 1972. *Mythologies.* New York: Hill and Wang.

Baudrillard, Jean. 1984. "The Precession of Simulacra. In *Art After Modernism.* Ed. Brian Wallis. New York: The New Museum of Contemporary Art.

Bauer, Otto. 1970. "National Character and the Idea of the Nation." In *Essential Works of Socialism.* Ed. Irving Howe. New York: Bantam Books.

BAYAN International. 1995. *The Truth About the Ramos Regime.* Los Angeles: Philippine Peasant Support Network.

Bello, Walden. 1987. *Creating the Third Force: U.S.-Sponsored Low Intensity Conflict in the Philippines.* San Francisco, CA: Institute for Food and Development Policy.

Beltran, Ruby P. and Aurora Javata de Dios, eds. 1992. *Filipino Women Overseas Contract Workers . . . At What Cost?* Manila: Goodwill Trading Co., Inc.

Beltran, Ruby P. and Gloria Rodriguez, eds. 1996. *Filipino Women Migrant Workers: At the Crossroads and Beyond Beijing.* Quezon City: Giraffe Books.

Benhabib, Seyla. 1996. "The Intellectual Challenge of Multiculturalism and Teaching the Canon." In *Field Work: Sites in Literary and Cultural Studies.* Ed. Marjorie Garber, Paul Franklin, and Rebecca Walkowitz. New York: Routledge.

Benjamin, Walter. 1969. *Illuminations.* New York: Schocken.

Bennis, Phyllis and Michael Moushabeck, eds. 1993. *Altered States: A Reader in the New World Order.* New York: Olive Branch Press.

Berlant, Lauren and William Warner. 1994. "Introduction to 'Critical Multiculturalism." In *Multiculturalism* edited by David Goldberg, pp. 102-113. Oxford: Basil Blackwell.

Berreman, Gerald. 1990. "The Incredible 'Tasaday': Deconstructing the Myth of the 'Stone-Age' People." *Cultural Survival Quarterly* 15: 3-25.

Beveridge, Albert. 1987 [1990]. "Our Philippine Policy." In *The Philippines Reader.* Eds. D. B. Schirmer and Stephen Shalom. Boston: South End Press.

Beverley, John. 1989. "The Margin at the Center: On Testimonio (Testimonial Narrative)." *Modern Fiction Studies* 35.1 (Spring): 11-28.

Beverley, John and Marc Zimmerman. 1990. *Literature and Politics in the Central American Revolutions.* Austin: University of Texas Press.

Bhabha, Homi. 1990. *Nation and Narration.* New York: Routledge.

——— 1992. "Postcolonial Criticism." In *Redrawing the Boundaries.* Eds. Stephen Greenblatt and Giles Gunn. New York: Modern Language Association of America.

———. 1994a. "Remembering Fanon: Self, Psyche and the Colonial Condition." *Colonial Discourse and Post-Colonial Theory: A Reader.* Eds. Patrick Williams and Laura Chrisman. New York: Columbia University Press.

———. 1994b. *The Location of Culture.* New York: Routledge.

————. 1995. "Cultural Diversity and Cultural Differences." *The Post-colonial Studies Reader*. Eds. Bill Ashcroft, Gareth Griffiths, and Helen Tiffin. New York: Routledge.

Bhaskar, Roy. 1993. *Dialectic: The Pulse of Freedom*. London: Verso.

Bierce, Ambrose. 1958 [1906]. *The Devil's Dictionary*. New York: Dover Publications.

Birch, A.H. 1971. *Representation*. New York: Praeger Publishers.

Blaisdell, Kekuni. 1994. "Stolen Islands." *Breakthrough* 18.1 (Spring): 47-49.

Blauner, Robert. 1972. *Racial Oppression in America*. New York: Harper and Row.

Bloch, Ernst. 1970. *A Philosophy of the Future*. New York: Herder and Herder.

Bobbio, Norberto. 1979. "Gramsci and the Conception of Civil Society." In *Gramsci and Marxist Theory*. Ed. Chantal Mouffe. London: Routledge and Kegan Paul.

Bologh, Roslyn Wallach. 1979. *Dialectical phenomenology: Marx's method*. London: Routledge and Kegan Paul.

Bonacich, Edna. 1996. "The Class Question in Global Capitalism." *Mapping Multiculturalism*. Minneapolis: University of Minnesota Press.

Bottomore, Tom, ed. 1983. *A Dictionary of Marxist Thought*. Cambridge, MA: Harvard University Press.

Bourdieu, Pierre. 1993. *The Field of Cultural Production*. New York: Columbia University Press.

Bouvier, Leon and Robert Gardner. 1986. *Immigration to the U.S.: The Unfinished Story*. Washington, DC: Population Reference Bureau.

Boyce, James K. 1993. *The Philippines: The Political Economy of Growth and Impoverishment in the Marcos Era*. Honolulu: University of Hawaii Press.

Brecher, Jeremy, John Brown Childs, and Jill Cutler, eds. 1993. *Global Visions: Beyond the New World Order*. Boston: South End Press.

Bresnan, John, ed. 1986. *Crisis in the Philippines: The Marcos Era and Beyond*. Princeton, NJ: Princeton University Press.

Bresnahan, Mary. 1991. *Finding Our Feet: Understanding Crosscultural Discourse*. New York: University Press of America.

Brewer, Anthony. 1980. *Marxist Theories of Imperialism: A Critical Survey*. London: Routledge and Kegan Paul.

Bruin, Janet. 1996. *Root Causes of the Global Crisis*. Manila, Philippines: Institute of Political Economy.

Brydon, Diana. 1995. "The White Unit Speaks." *The Post-colonial Studies Reader*. New York: Routledge.

Buci-Glucksmann, Christine. 1979. "State, transition and passive revolution." In *Gramsci and Marxist Theory*. Ed. Chantal Mouffe. London: Routledge and Kegan Paul.

Buchanan, Keith. 1974. "Reflections on a 'Dirty Word.'" *Dissent* 31 (Summer): 25-31. Reprinted in *Radical Geography* edited by Richard Peet. 1977. Chicago: Maaroufa Press.

Buck-Morss, Susan. 1987. "Semiotic Boundaries and the Politics of Meaning: Modernity on Tour—A Village in Transition." In *New Ways of Knowing* by Marcus Raskin and Herbert Bernstein. New Jersey: Rowman and Littlefield.

Buhle, Paul. 1988. *C. L. R. James: The Artist as Revolutionary*. London: Verso.

Bush, Ray, Gordon Johnston, and David Coates, eds. 1987. *The World Order: Socialist Perspectives*. London: Polity Press.

Buss, Claude A. 1987. *Cory Aquino and the People of the Philippines*. Stanford: Stanford Alumni Association.

Cabezas, Amado and Gary Kawaguchi. 1989. "Race, Gender, and Class for Filipino Americans." *A Look Beyond the Model Minority Image*. Ed. Grace Yun. New York: Minority Rights Group Inc.

Cabral, Amilcar. 1973. *Return to the Source: Selected Speeches*. New York: Monthly Review Press.

Caldwell, Malcolm. 1970. "Problems of Socialism in Southeast Asia." In *Imperialism and Underdevelopment*. Ed. Robert I. Rhodes. New York: Monthly Review Press. 376-403.

Callari, Antonio, Stephen Cullenberg, and Carole Biewener, eds. *Marxism in the Postmodern Age*. 1995. New York: Guilford Press.

Callinicos, Alex. 1976. *Althusser's Marxism*. London: Pluto Press.

———. 1989. *Against Postmodernism: A Marxist Critique*. New York: St. Martin's Press.

———. 1995. "Wonders Taken for Signs: Homi Bhabha's Postcolonialism." *Postality: Marxism and Postmodernism*. Ed. Masud Zavarzadeh, Teresa Ebert, and Donald Morton. Washington, DC: Maisonneuve Press.

Cammett, John. 1967. *Antonio Gramsci and the Origins of Italian Communism*. Stanford: Stanford University Press.

Campomanes, Oscar. 1996. "The New Empire's Forgetful and Forgotten Citizens: Unrepresentability and Unassimilability in Filipino-American Postcoloni-alities." *Critical Mass* 2.2 (Spring): 145-200.

Canlas, Mamerto, Mariano Miranda Jr., and James Putzel. 1988. *Land, Poverty and Politics in the Philippines*. London: Catholic Institute for International Relations.

Capulong, Romeo. 1986. *U.S. Intervention Still the Main Problem of the Filipino People after Marcos*. New York: PhilCir Educational Services Program.

Carby, Hazel. 1988. "Proletarian or Revolutionary Literature: C.L.R. James and the Politics of Trinidad Renaissance," *South Atlantic Quarterly* 87.1 (Winter): 39-52.

Cashmore, E. Ellis. 1984. *Dictionary of Race and Ethnic Relations*. 2nd ed. London: Routledge.

Casper, Leonard. 1965. "Philippine Poetry." In *Encyclopedia of Poetry and Poetics*, edited by Alex Preminger. Princeton: Princeton University Press.

Castles, Steven et al. 1996. "Australia: Multi-Ethnic Community Without Nation-alism?" In *Ethnicity*. Eds. John Hutchinson and Anthony Smith. New York: Oxford University Press.

Castro, Fidel. 1972. "Words to the Intellectuals." In *Radical Perspectives in the Arts*. Baltimore: Penguin Books.

Catholic Institute for International Relations. 1989. *Comment: The Philippines*. London: CIIR.

———. 1992. *Politics and Military Power*. London: CIIR.

Caws, Mary Ann and Christopher Prendergast, eds. 1994. *The HarperCollins World Reader*. New York: HarperCollins.

Césaire, Aimé. 1957. "Lettre a Maurice Thorez." In *Studies in the Theory of Imperialism*. Eds. Roger Owen and Bob Sutcliffe. London: Longman, 1972.

Césaire, Aimé. 1969. *Return to My Native Land*. Tr. John Berger and Anna Bostock. Baltimore: Penguin Books.

———. 1972. *Discourse on Colonialism*. New York: Monthly Review Press.

Center for Women's Resources. 1996. *Philippines 2000 in the Year 1995*. Quezon City: Center for Women's Resources.

Chaliand, Gerard. 1978. *Revolution in the Third World*. New York: Penguin Books.

Chan, Sucheng. 1991. *Asian Americans*. Boston: Twayne Publishers.

Chang, Robert S. 1995. "Toward an Asian American legal Scholarship: Critical Race Theory, Post-Structuralism, and Narrative Space." In *Critical Race Theory: The Cutting Edge*. Ed. Richard Delgador. Philadelphia: Temple University Press.

Chapman, William. 1987. *Inside the Philippine Revolution*. New York: Norton.

Chatterjee, Partha. 1993. *The Nation and Its Fragments*. Princeton: Princeton University Press.

Chicago Cultural Studies Group. 1994. "Critical Multiculturalism." In *Multiculturalism*. Oxford: Basil Blackwell Ltd.

Chilcote, Ronald. 1984. *Theories of Development and Underdevelopment*. Boulder and London: Westview Press.

Childers, Joseph and Gary Hentzi, eds. 1995. *The Columbia Dictionary of Modern Literary and Cultural Criticism*. New York: Columbia University Press.

Chin, Frank. 1981. *The Chickencoop Chinaman and The Year of the Dragon: Two Plays*. Seattle: University of Washington Press.

———. 1994. "Gunga Din Highway." In *Asian American Voices*. Minneapolis: Coffee House Press.

Chin, Frank, Jeffery Paul Chan, Lawson Inada, and Shawn Wong, eds. 1991. *Aiiieeeee!* New York: Mentor.

Chomsky, Noam. 1978-1992. *What Uncle Sam Really Wants*. Berkeley, CA: Odonian Press.

———. 1979. *Towards a New Cold War*. New York: Pantheon.

———. 1989. *Necessary Illusions: Thought Control in Democratic Societies*. Boston: South End Press.

———. 1994. "Time bombs." *In These Times* (February 21): 14-17.

Chow, Rey. 1993. *Writing Diaspora*. Bloomington: Indiana University Press.

Cirese, Alberto Maria. 1982. "Gramsci's Observations on Folklore." *Approaches to Gramsci*. Ed. Anne Showstack Sassoon. London: Writers and Readers.

Clark, Katerina and Michael Holquist. 1984. *Mikhail Bakhtin*. Cambridge, Mass: Harvard University Press.

Cleaver, Harry. 1979. *Reading Capital Politically*. Austin: University of Texas Press.

Cohen, G. A. 1989. "Reconsidering Historical Materialism." In *Marxist Theory*. Ed. Alex Callinicos. New York: Oxford University Press.

Colletti, Lucio. 1972. *From Rousseau to Lenin*. New York: New Left Books.

Connor, Walker. 1978. "A nation is a nation, is a state, is an ethnic group is a . . ." *Ethnic and Racial Studies* 1.4 (October): 378-400.

———. 1984. *The National Question in Marxist-Leninist Theory and Strategy.* Princeton, NJ: Princeton University Press.

Constantino, Renato. 1975. *A History of the Philippines.* New York: Monthly Review Press.

———. 1978. *Neocolonial Identity and Counter-Consciousness.* New York: M. E. Sharpe, Inc.

Council for People's Development. 1990. *The People's Development Agenda.* Manila: Council for People's Development.

Coward, Rosalind and John Ellis. 1977. *Language and Materialism.* New York: Routledge.

Crowley, Tony. 1989. "Bakhtin and the history of the language." In *Bakhtin and Cultural Theory.* Eds. Ken Hirschkop and David Shepherd. New York: Manchester University Press.

Dahbour, Omar and Micheline R. Ishay, eds. 1995. *The Nationalism Reader.* New Jersey: Humanities Press.

Daniels, Roger and Harry Kitano. 1970. *American Racism: Exploration of the Nature of Prejudice.* Englewood Cliffs, NJ: Prentice-Hall.

Davidson, Basil. 1978. *Let Freedom Come.* Boston: Little, Brown and Co.

———. 1982. "Ideology and Identity: An Approach from History." *Introduction to the Sociology of "Developing Societies."* Ed. Hamza Alavi and Theodor Shanin. New York: Monthly Review Press.

———. 1986. "On revolutionary nationalism: the legacy of Cabral." *Race and Class* 27: 21-45.

Davis, Leonard. 1989. *Revolutionary Struggle in the Philippines.* London: Macmillan.

Davis, Mike. 1985. "Urban Renaissance and the Spirit of Postmodernism." *New Left Review* 151 (May-June): 106-111.

———. 1987. "From Fordism to Reaganism: The Crisis of American Hegemony in the 1980s." In *The World Order: Socialist Perspectives.* Eds. Ray Bush, Gordon Johnston, and David Coates. London: Polity Press.

Dayan, Joan. 1995. "Paul Gilroy's Slaves, Ships, and Routes: The Middle Passage as Metaphor." Paper given at the African Literature Association, Columbus, Ohio, on 16 March 1995. Forthcoming in Kamau Brathwaite and Timothy Reiss, *Sisyphus and Eldorado: Magical and Other Realisms in Caribbean Literatures.*

Dean, Debra Kang. 1995. "Telling Differences." In *Under Western Eyes.* Ed. Garrett Hongo. New York: Anchor Books.

Deane, Seamus. 1987. "Imperialism/Nationalism." In *Critical Terms for Literary Study.* Eds. Frank Lentricchia and Thomas McLaughlin. Chicago: University of Chicago Press.

De Beauvoir, Simone. 1952. *The Second Sex.* New York: Knopf.

De Dios, Aurora Javate, Petronilo Daroy, and Lorna Kalaw-Tirol, eds. 1988. *Dictatorship and Revolution: Roots of People's Power.* Quezon City: Conspectus.

De la Torre, Ed. 1986. *Touching Ground, Taking Root.* London: CIIR/British Council of Churches.

Delgado, Richard, ed. 1995. *Critical Race Theory.* Philadelphia: Temple University Press.

Demko, George J. 1992. *Why in the World: Adventures in Geography.* New York: Anchor Books.

Derrida, Jacques. 1976. *Of Grammatology.* Translated by Gayatri Spivak. Baltimore: Johns Hopkins University Press.

———. 1991. "Eating Well, or the Calculation of the Subject: An Interview with Jacques Derrida." In *Who Comes After the Subject?* Eds. Eduardo Cadava, Peter Connor, and Jean-Luc Nancy. New York: Routledge.

Diokno, Jose W. 1987. *A Nation for Our Children.* Quezon City: Claretian Publications.

Dirlik, Arif. 1994a. *After the Revolution.* Hanover and London: Wesleyan University Press.

———. 1994b. "The Postcolonial Aura: Third World Criticism in the Age of Global Capitalism." *Critical Inquiry* 20 (Winter): 328-56.

———. 1997. *The Postcolonial Aura.* Boulder, Co.: Westview Press.

Domhoff, G. William. 1969. "Who Made American Foreign Policy, 1945-1963." *Corporations and the Cold War.* Ed. David Horowitz. New York: Monthly Review Press.

Doty, Roxanne Lunn. 1996. *Imperial Encounters.* Minneapolis: University of Minnesota Press.

Doyo, Ma. Ceres. 1993. *Journalist in Her Country.* Manila: Anvil Publishing Co.

Dudley, William, ed. 1997. *Asian Americans: Opposing Viewpoints.* San Diego, CA: Greenhaven Press, Inc.

Dunayevskaya, Raya. 1981. *Rosa Luxemburg, Women's Liberation, and Marx's Philosophy of Revolution.* New Jersey: Humanities Press.

During, Simon. 1987. "Postmodernism or Postcolonialism Today." *Landfall* 39.3: 366-80.

Dussel, Enrique. 1992. "Theology and Economy: The Theological Paradigm of Communicative Action and the Paradigm of the Community of Life as a Theology of Liberation." In *Development and Democratization in the Third World: Myths, Hopes, and Realities.* Ed. Kenneth Bauzon. Washington, DC: Crane Russak.

Eagleton, Terry. 1990. "Nationalism: Irony and Commitment." In *Nationalism, Colonialism, and Literature.* Ed. Seamus Deane. Minneapolis: University of Minnesota Press.

———. 1991. *Ideology.* London: Verso.

Ebert, Teresa. 1996. "Towards Red Feminism." *Against the Current* (November-December): 27-31.

Eggan, Fred. 1991. "The Philippines in the Twentieth Century: A Study in Contrasts." *Reviews in Anthropology* 20: 13-23.

El Masri, Rafik. 1990. "Intifada—Present and Future." *Tricontinental* 129: 4-20.

El Saadawi, Nawal. 1975. *Woman at Point Zero.* Tr. Sherif Hetata. London: Zed Books Ltd.

———. 1985. "Politics—United Kingdom." In *Women: A World Report*. Ed. New Internationalist. New York: Oxford University Press.

———. 1994. "Memoirs of a Female Physician." In *The HarperCollins World Reader*. Ed. Mary Ann Caws and Christopher Prendergast. New York: HarperCollins.

Enriquez, Virgilio. 1992. *From Colonial to Liberation Psychology*. Quezon City: University of the Philippines Press.

Epstein, Barbara. 1996. "Radical Democracy and Cultural Politics." In *Radical Democracy*. Ed. David Trend. New York and London: Routledge.

Escobar, Arturo. 1995. *Encountering Development: The Making and Unmaking of the Third World*. Princeton: Princeton University Press.

Esman, Milton J. 1992. "The Political Fallout of International Migration." *Diaspora* 2 (Spring): 3-42.

Espiritu, Yen Le. 1994. "The Intersection of Race, Ethnicity, and Class: The Multiple Identities of Second-Generation Filipinos." *Identities:* 249-273.

———. 1995. *Filipino American Lives*. Philadelphia: Temple University Press.

———. 1996. "Asian American Panethnicity." In *The Meaning of Difference*. Ed. Karen Rosenblum and Toni-Michelle Travis. New York: McGraw-Hill.

Evasco, Marjorie et al, eds. 1990. *Women's Springbook*. Quezon City: Women's Resource and Research Center.

Eviota, Elizabeth. 1992. *The Political Economy of Gender*. London: Zed Books Ltd.

Fabian, Johannes. 1990. "Presence and Representation: The Other and Anthropological Writing." *Critical Inquiry* 16 (Summer): 753-772.

Fagen, Richard R. 1986. "The Politics of Transition." In *Transition and Development*. Eds. Richard Fagen, Carmen Diana Deere, and Jose Luis Coraggio. New York: Monthly Review Press.

Fagen, Richard R., Carmen Diana Deere, and Jose Luis Corragio, eds. 1986. *Transition and Development*. New York: Monthly Review Press.

Fanon, Frantz. 1963. *The Wretched of the Earth*. Tr. Constance Farrington. New York: Grove Press.

———. *Black Skin, White Masks*. 1967. New York: Grove Press.

Featherstone, Mike. 1990. "Global Culture: An Introduction." In *Global Culture*. Ed. Mike Featherstone. London: Sage Publications.

———. 1991. *Consumer Culture and Postmodernism*. London: Sage.

Featherstone, Mike, Scott Lash, and Roland Robertson, eds. 1995. *Global Modernities*. London: Sage Publications.

Feffer, John. 1993. "The Lessons for 1989." In *Global Visions*. Ed. Jeremy Brecher, John Brown Childs, and Jill Cutler. Boston: South End Press.

Fernandez, Ronald. 1994. *Prisoners of Colonialism*. Monroe, Maine: Common Courage Press.

Figueroa, Hector. 1997. "Does globalization matter?" *In These Times* 21.10 (March 31-April 13): 16-18.

Fitt, Yann, Alexandre Faire, and Jean-Pierre Vigier. 1980. *The World Economic Crisis*. London: Zed Press.

Flaubert, Gustave. 1954. *The Dictionary of Accepted Ideas*. Tr. Jacques Barzun. New York: New Directions.

Fogel, D. 1982. *Africa in Struggle.* Seattle: ISM Press.

Francia, Luis, ed. 1993. *Brown River, White Ocean.* Brunswick, NJ: Rutgers University Press.

Francisco, Luzviminda. 1987. "The Philippine-American War." In *The Philippines Reader.* Ed. Daniel B. Schirmer and Stephen Shalom. Boston: South End Press.

Francisco, Luzviminda and Jonathan Fast. 1985. *Conspiracy for Empire.* Manila: Foundation for Nationalist Studies.

Franco, Jean. 1967. *The Modern Culture of Latin America.* Baltimore, MD: Penguin Books.

Franklin, Bruce. 1986. *War Stars.* New York: Oxford University Press.

Fraser, Nancy. 1995. "From Redistribution to Recognition? Dilemmas of Justice in a 'Post-Socialist' Age." *New Left Review* 212 (July-August 1995): 68-93.

———. 1996. "Equality, Difference, and Radical Democracy: The United States Feminist Debates Revisited." *Radical Democracy.* Ed. David Trend. New York: Routledge.

Freire, Paulo. 1970. *Cultural Action for Freedom.* Cambridge, MA: Harvard Educational Review and Center for the Study of Development and Social Change.

———. 1972. *Pedagogy of the Oppressed.* New York: Herder and Herder.

———. 1985. *The Politics of Education.* Tr. Donaldo Macedo. South Hadley, MA: Bergin & Garvey Publishers Inc.

———. 1987. "Letter to North-American Teachers." In *Freire for the Classroom.* Ed. Ira Shor. Portsmouth, NH: Heinemann.

———. 1996. *Letters to Cristina: Reflections on My Life and Work.* New York: Routledge.

Friedman, Jonathon. 1990. "Being in the World: Globalization and Localization." In *Global Culture.* Ed. Mike Featherstone. London: Sage.

Friend, Theodore. 1986. "Philippine-American Tensions in History." In *Crisis in the Philippines.* Ed. John Bresnan. Princeton: Princeton University Press.

———. 1989. "Latin Ghosts Haunt An Asian Nation." *Heritage* 3.4 (December): 4.

Freud, Sigmund. 1989. *The Freud Reader.* Ed. Peter Gay. New York: W.W. Norton.

Fuchs, Lawrence. 1991. *The American Kaleidoscope.* Hanover, N.H.: University Press of New England.

Fusco, Coco. 1995. *English Is Broken Here.* New York: The New Press.

Gabel, Joseph. 1978. *False Consciousness.* New York: Harper Torchbooks

Galeano, Eduardo. 1973. *Open Veins of Latin America.* New York: Monthly Review Press.

Galtung, J., P. O'Brien, and R. Preiswerk, eds. 1980. "The Cocoyoc Declaration." In *Self-Reliance: A Strategy for Development.* London: Bogle-L'Ouverture Publishers.

Gates, Henry Louis, Jr. 1994. "Critical Fanonism." In *Contemporary Literary Criticism.* Eds. Robert Con Davis and Ronald Schleifer. New York: Longman.

Gendzier, Irene. 1973. *Frantz Fanon.* New York: Grove Press.

———. 1979. "A Critique of Modernization Theory." Lecture delivered at Brooklyn College, May 7-8, 1979. 33 pages.

————. 1985. *Managing Political Change: Social Scientists and the Third World.* Boulder: Westview Press.

Gilbert, Tony and Pierre Joris. 1981. *Global Interference.* London: Liberation.

Gill, Stephen, ed. 1993. *Gramsci, Historical Materialism and International Relations.* Cambridge, Ma.: Cambridge University Press.

Gilroy, Paul. 1992. "Cultural Studies and Ethnic Absolutism." *Cultural Studies.* Ed. Lawrence Grossberg, Cary Nelson, and Paula Treichler. New York: Routledge.

————. 1993. *The Black Atlantic.* Cambridge, Mass.: Harvard University Press.

Giroux, Henry A. 1995. "National Identity and the Politics of Multiculturalism." *College Literature* 22.2 (June 1995): 42-57.

Glaberman, Martin. 1995. "The Marxism of C.L.R. James." In *C.L.R. James: His Intellectual Legacies.* Eds. Selwyn Cudjoe and William Cain. Amherst: University of Massachusetts Press.

Gochenour, Theodore. 1990. *Considering Filipinos.* Yarmouth, ME: Intercultural Press, Inc.

Godzich, Wlad. 1988. "Emergent Literature and the Field of Comparative Literature." In *The Comparative Perspective on Literature.* Eds. Clayton Koelb and Susan Noakes. Ithaca: Cornell University Press.

Goldberg, David Theo. 1994. *Multiculturalism.* New York: Blackwell.

————. 1993. *Racist Culture.* New York: Blackwell.

Gonzales, Juan L., Jr. 1993. *Racial and Ethnic Groups in America.* Dubuque, Iowa: Kendall/Hunt Publishing Co.

Gonzalves, Theo. 1995. " 'The Show Must Go On: Production Notes on the Filipino Cultural Night." *Critical Mass* 2.2 (Spring): 129-144.

Gotanda, Neil. 1995. "Critical Legal Studies, Critical Race Theory and Asian American Studies." *Amerasia Journal* 21.1 & 2(1995): 127-36.

————. 1996. "Multiculturalism and Racial Stratification." *Mapping Multiculturalism.* Minneapolis: University of Minnesota Press.

Gould, Carol. 1978. *Marx's Social Ontology.* Cambridge, Ma.: MIT Press.

Goulet, Denis. *The Cruel Choice.* New York: Atheneum, 1975.

Goux, Jean-Joseph. 1990. *Symbolic Economies: After Marx and Freud.* Ithaca: Cornell University Press.

Gramsci, Antonio. 1957. *The Modern Prince and other writings.* Tr. Louis Marks. New York: International Publishers.

————. 1971. *Selections from the Prison Notebooks.* New York: International Publishers.

———— 1975. *History, Philosophy, and Culture in the Young Gramsci.* Ed. Pedro Cavalcanti and Paul Piccone. Saint Louis: Telos Press.

————. 1977a. *Selections from Political Writings 1910-1920.* Ed. Quintin Hoare. New York: International Publishers.

————. 1977b. *Selections from Political Writings 1920-1926.* New York: International Publishers.

————. 1978. "From 'In Search of the Educational Principle.'" In *Studies in Socialist Pedagogy.* Eds. Theodore Mills Norton and Bertell Ollman. New York: Monthly Review Press.

———. 1985. *Selections from Cultural Writings.* Tr. William Boelhower. Cambridge, Mass: Harvard University Press.

———. 1995. *The Southern Question.* Tr. Pasquale Verdicchio. West Lafayette, Ind.: Bordighera Incorporated, 1995.

Greene, Felix. 1970. *The Enemy: What Every American Should Know About Imperialism.* New York: Random House.

Greer, Colin. 1984. "The Ethnic Question." In *The 60s Without Apology.* Eds. Sohnya Sayres et al, pp. 119-136. Minneapolis: University of Minnesota Press.

Greider, William. 1997. "One World Ready or Not." *Rolling Stone* (February): 37-41.

Grossberg, Lawrence. 1996. "Identity and Cultural Studies: Is That All there Is?" In *Questions of Cultural Identity.* Eds. Stuart Hall and Paul du Gay. London: Sage.

Guevara, Che. 1962. "Notes for the Study of the Ideology of the Cuban Revolution." In C. Wright Mills, *The Marxists.* New York: Dell Publishing Co.

———. 1972. "Notes on Man and Socialism in Cuba." In *On Revolution.* Ed. William Lutz and Harry Brent. Cambridge, Ma.: Winthrop Publishers, Inc.

Gugelberger, Georg. 1991. "Decolonizing the Canon: Considerations of Third World Literature." *New Literary History* 22 (Summer): 505-24.

———. 1994. "Postcolonial Cultural Studies." *The Johns Hopkins Guide to Literary Theory and Criticism.* Baltimore: The Johns Hopkins University Press.

Guillaumin, Colette. 1995. *Racism, Sexism, Power and Ideology.* London: Routledge.

Gurvitch, Georges. 1971. *The Social Frameworks of Knowledge.* New York: Harper Torchbooks.

Habermas, Jurgen. 1971. *Knowledge and Human Interests.* Boston: Beacon Press.

Hacker, Andrew. 1961. *Political Theory: Philosophy, Ideology, Science.* New York: The MacMillan Co.

Hadjor, Kofi. 1993. *Dictionary of Third World Terms.* New York: Penguin Books.

Hagedorn, Jessica. 1993. *Charlie Chan is Dead.* New York: Penguin Books.

Hall, Stuart. 1980. "Race, Articulation and Societies Structured in Dominance." In *Sociological Theories: Race and Colonialism.* Ed. UNESCO. Paris: UNESCO.

———. 1992a. "The Question of Cultural Identity." In *Modernity and Its Futures.* Eds. Stuart Hall, David Held, and Tony McGrew. London: Polity Press.

———. 1992b. "C.L.R. James: A Portrait." In *C.L.R. James's Caribbean.* Eds. Henry Paget and Paul Buhle. Durham: Duke University Press.

———. 1996. *Stuart Hall: Critical Dialogues in Cultural Studies.* Eds. David Morley and Kuan-Hsing Chen. London and New York: Routledge.

Hamamoto, Darrell Y. 1994. *Monitored Peril: Asian Americans and the Politics of TV Representation.* Minneapolis: University of Minnesota Press.

Harlow, Barbara. 1987. *Resistance Literature.* New York: Methuen.

———. 1996. *After Lives.* London and New York: Verso.

Harris, Wilson. 1985. "Adversarial Contexts and Creativity." *New Left Review* 154 (Nov.-Dec.): 124-128.

Harvey, David. 1989. *The Condition of Postmodernity.* Oxford: Basil Blackwell.

————. 1996. *Justice, Nature and the Geography of Difference.* Cambridge, Ma.: Blackwell.

Haug, W. F. 1986. *Critique of Commodity Aesthetics.* Minneapolis: University of Minnesota Press.

Hawkins, Janet. 1994. "Confronting a 'Culture of Lies.'" *Harvard Magazine* 97.1 (September-October): 49-57.

Hayslip, Le Ly and Jay Wurts. 1989. *When Heaven and Earth Changed Places.* New York: Plume Book.

Hechter, Michael. 1975. *Internal Colonialism.* Berkeley: University of California Press.

Hegel, Friedrich. 1967. *Hegel's Philosophy of Right.* Tr. T. M. Knox. London: Oxford University Press.

Henry, Paget and Paul Buhle, eds. 1992. *C. L. R. James's Caribbean.* Durham, NC: Duke University Press.

Hidalgo, Cristina Pantoja and Priscelina Legasto, eds. 1993. *Philippine Post-colonial Studies.* Quezon City: University of the Philippines Press.

Hirabayashi, Lane and Marilyn Alquizola. 1994. "Asian American Studies: Revaluating for the 1990s." In *The State of Asian America.* Ed. Karin Aguilar-San Juan. Boston: South End Press.

Hirschkop, Ken. 1986. "Bakhtin, Discourse and Democracy," *New Left Review* 160 (Nov.-Dec.): 92-111.

————. 1989. "Introduction." In *Bakhtin and Cultural Theory.* Ed. Ken Hirschkop and David Shepherd. Manchester: Manchester University Press.

Hirst, Paul. 1979. *On Law and Ideology.* London: Macmillan.

Hodge, Robert and Gunther Kress. 1988. *Social Semiotics.* Ithaca: Cornell University Press.

Hofstadter, Richard. 1967. *The Paranoid Style in American Politics and Other Essays.* New York: Vintage.

Hongo, Garrett, ed. 1995. *Under Western Eyes.* New York: Anchor Books.

Hunter, Allen. 1988-89. "Post-Marxism and the New Social Movements." *Theory and Society* 17.6: 885-900.

Hutcheon, Linda. 1989. *The Politics of Postmodernism.* New York: Routledge.

————. 1995. "Colonialism and the Postcolonial Condition: Complexities Abounding," *PMLA* 110.1 (January): 7-16.

IDAC (Institute of Cultural Action). 1974. *Freire/Illich: The Pedagogical Debate.* Geneva, Switzerland: Institute of Cultural Action.

————. 1975. *Freire/Illich: The Oppression of Pedagogy and the Pedagogy of the Oppressed.* Geneva, Switzerland: Institute of Cultural Action.

————. 1975-76. *Guinea-Bissau: Reinventing Education.* Geneva, Switzerland: Institute of Cultural Action.

Jacinto, Jaime Antonio and Luis Malay Syquia. 1995. *Lakbay: Journey of the People of the Philippines.* San Francisco: Zellerbach Family Fund.

Jacoby, Russell. 1995. "Marginal Returns: The Trouble with Postcolonial Theory," *Lingua Franca* (September-October): 30-37.

Jalee, Pierre. 1977. *How Capitalism Works.* New York: Monthly Review Press.

James, C. L. R. 1960. *Modern Politics.* Port of Spain, Trinidad: PNM Publishing Co.

——. 1963. *The Black Jacobins.* New York: Vintage Books.

——. 1971. "Colonialism and National Liberation in Africa: The Gold Coast Revolution." In *National Liberation: Revolution in the Third World.* Eds. Norman Miller and Roderick Aya. New York: The Free Press.

——. 1980a. *Spheres of Existence.* Westport, CT: Lawrence Hill and Co.

——. 1980b. *Notes on Dialectics: Hegel, Marx, Lenin.* Westport, CT: Lawrence, Hill and Co.

——. 1983. "Interview." In *Visions of History.* Ed. MARHO [The Radical Historians Organization]. New York: Pantheon Books.

——. 1985. *Mariners, Renegades and Castaways.* London: Allison and Busby.

——. 1986. *Every Cook Can Govern and What's Happening Every Day: 1985 Conversations.* Ed. Jan Hillegas. Jackson, MS: New Mississippi Inc.

——. 1986. (1950). *State Capitalism and World Revolution.* Chicago: Charles Kerr Publishing Co.

——. 1992. *The C.L.R. James Reader.* Oxford: Blackwell.

——. 1993a. *American Civilization.* Oxford: Blackwell.

——. 1993b. *Beyond a Boundary.* Durham, NC: Duke University Press.

——. 1994. *C.L.R. James and Revolutionary Marxism.* Eds. Scott McLemee and Paul LeBlanc. Atlantic Highlands, NJ: Humanities Press.

——. 1996a. *On the "Negro Question."* Ed. Scott McLemee. Jackson, Miss.: University Press of Mississippi.

——. 1996b. *Special Delivery: The Letters of C.L.R. James to Constance Webb, 1939-1948.* Ed. Anna Grimshaw. Cambridge, Ma.: Blackwell.

Jameson, Fredric. 1976. "Collective Art in the Age of Cultural Imperialism." *Alcheringa* 2: 108-111.

——. 1981. *The Political Unconscious.* Ithaca: Cornell University Press.

——. 1986. "Third-World Literature in the Era of Multinational Capitalism." *Social Text* 15:65-88.

——. 1988. "Cognitive Mapping." In *Marxism and the Interpretation of Culture.* Eds. Cary Nelson and Lawrence Grossberg. Urbana and Chicago: University of Illinois Press.

——. 1992. *The Geopolitical Aesthetic: Cinema and Space in the World System.* Bloomington: Indiana University Press.

——. 1995. "On *Cultural Studies.*" In *The Identity in Question.* Ed. John Rajchman. New York: Routledge.

Janiewski, Dolores. 1995. "Gendering, Racializing and Classifying: Settler Colonization in the United States, 1590-1990." In *Unsettling Settler Societies.* Ed. Daiva Stasiulis and Nira Yuval-Davis. London: Sage Publications.

Jen, Gish. 1991. *Typical American.* New York: Plume.

Johnson, Lawrence. 1989. "The Migration Waves of Filipinos." *Philippine-American Journal* 1.2 (Winter): 13-15.

Jones, Gareth Stedman. 1970. "The Specificity of U.S. Imperialism." *New Left Review* (March-April): 1-23.

Jussawalla, Feroza and Reed Way Dasenbrock. 1996. *Announcement for NEH Seminar.* Las Cruces: New Mexico State University.

Justiniani, Victoria. 1987. "Makibaka Statement," *The Manila Chronicle* (22 February): 10.

Kagan, Leigh and Richard. 1971. "Oh Say Can you See? American Cultural Blinders on China." In *America's Asia: Dissenting Essays on Asian-American Relations.* New York: Vintage Books.

Kaplan, Amy and Donald Pease, eds. 1993. *Cultures of United States Imperialism.* Durham: Duke University Press.

Karnow, Stanley. 1989. *In Our Image: America's Empire in the Philippines.* New York: Random House.

Karnow, Stanley and Nancy Yoshihara. 1992. *Asian Americans in Transition.* New York: The Asia Society.

Katrak, Ketu. 1989. "Decolonizing Culture: Toward a Theory for Postcolonial Women's Texts." *Modern Fiction Studies* 35.1: 157-79.

———. 1995. "Decolonizing Culture: Toward a Theory for Post-colonial Women's Texts." *The Post-colonial Studies Reader.* Ed. Bill Ashcroft, Gareth Griffiths and Helen Tiffin. New York: Routledge.

Keat, Russell. 1981. "Individualism and Community in Socialist Thought." In *Issues in Marxist Philosophy.* Vol. IV. Eds. John Mepham and David-Hillel Ruben. Sussex: Harvester Press.

Kelly, Petra. 1993. "A Very Bad Way to Enter the Next Century." In *Global Visions: Beyond the New World Order.* Eds. Jeremy Brecher, John Brown Childs, and Jill Cutler. Boston: South End Press.

Kerkvliet, Benedict J. 1977. *The Huk Rebellion.* Berkeley: University of California Press.

———. 1990. *Everyday Politics in the Philippines.* Berkeley: University of California Press.

——— and Resil Mojares. 1991. *From Marcos to Aquino.* Quezon City: Ateneo de Manila University Press.

Khare, R. S. 1992. "The Other's Double—The Anthropologist's Bracketed Self: Notes on Cultural Representation and Privileged Discourse." *New Literary History* 23: 1-23.

Kim, Elaine. 1982. *Asian American Literature: An Introduction to the Writings and Their Social Contexts.* Philadelphia: Temple University Press.

Kitano, Harry and Roger Daniels. 1995. *Asian Americans.* 2nd ed. Englewood Cliffs, NJ: Prentice Hall.

Klare, Michael T. and Peter Kornbluh, eds. 1988. *Low Intensity Warfare.* Quezon City: Ken Incorporated.

KMU (Kilusang Mayo Uno). 1996. "The business of APEC." *Correspondence* (July-August): 10.

Kolko, Gabriel. 1963. *The Triumph of Conservatism.* New York: Harper.

———. 1976. *Main Currents in Modern American History.* New York: Pantheon Books.

Komite ng Sambayanang Pilipino. 1981. *Philippines: Repression and Resistance.* Utrecht: KSP and Permanent People's Tribunal.

Korsch, Karl. 1990. "Independence comes to the Philippines." *Midweek* (6 June): 40-42.

Kothari, Geeta. 1995. "Where Are You From?" In *Under Western Eyes*. Ed. Garrett Hongo. New York: Anchor Books.

Kovel, Joel. 1984. *White Racism: A Psychohistory*. New York: Columbia University Press.

Kuumba, M. Bahati and Ona Alston Dosunmu. 1995. "Women in National Liberation Struggles in the Third World." In *The National Question*. Ed. Berch Berberogly. Philadelphia: Temple University Press.

Labor/Community Strategy Center. 1994. *Derechos Humanos para los Immigrantes / Immigrant Rights and Wrongs*. Los Angeles: Labor/Community Strategy Center.

Lacan, Jacques. 1977. *Ecrits: A Selection*. Tr. Alan Sheridan. London: Tavistock.

———. 1978. "The Subject and the Other: Alienation." In *Four Fundamental Concepts*. Ed. Jacques-Alain Miller. New York: Norton.

Laclau, Ernesto and Chantal Mouffe. 1985. *Hegemony and Socialist Strategy*. London: Verso.

Lam, Maivan. 1994. "Feeling Foreign in Feminism." *Signs:* 865-92.

Larrain, Jorge. 1995. "Identity, the Other, and Postmodernism." In *Post-ality: Marxism and Postmodernism*. Eds. Mas'ud Zavarzadeh, Teresa Ebert, and Donald Morton. Washington, DC: Maissoneuve Press.

Larsen, Neil. 1995a. *Reading North by South*. Minneapolis: University of Minnesota Press.

———. 1995b. "DetermiNation: Postcolonialism, Poststructuralism and the Problem of Ideology." *Dispositio/n* 20.47: 1-19.

———. 1996. "Negativities of the Popular: C. L. R. James and the Limits of 'Cultural Studies.'" In *Rethinking James*. Ed. Grant Farred. Cambridge, Ma.: Blackwell.

Lawner, Lynne, tr. 1973. *Antonio Gramsci: Letters from Prison*. New York: Harper and Row.

Lazarus, Neil. 1992. "Cricket and National Culture in the Writings of C.L.R. James." In *C L R James's Caribbean*. Eds. Henry Paget and Paul Buhle. Durham: Duke University Press.

———. 1993. "National Consciousness and the Specificity of (Post)Colonial Intellectualism." Unpublished typescript.

Lefebvre, Henri. 1968. *Dialectical Materialism*. Tr. John Sturrock. London: Jonathan Cape.

———. 1971. *Everyday Life in the Modern World*. New York: Harper Torchbooks.

———. 1991. *The Production of Space*. Tr. Donald Nicholson Smith. Oxford: Blackwell.

Lenin, Vladimir. 1939. *Imperialism: The Last Stage of Capitalism*. New York: International Publishers.

———. 1968. *National Liberation, Socialism and Imperialism*. New York: International Publishers.

Leys, Colin. 1982. "Samuel Huntington and the End of Classical Modernization Theory." In *Introduction to the Sociology of "Developing Societies."* Eds. Hamza Alavi and Theodor Shanin. New York: Monthly Review Press.

Lim, Genny. 1993. "Bitter Cane." In *The Politics of Life*. Ed. Velina Houston. Philadelphia: Temple University Press.

Lim, Shirley. 1990. "Twelve Asian American Writers: In Search of a Self-Definition." In *Redefining American Literary History*. Eds. A. L. Brown Ruoff and Jerry Ward. New York: MLA.

Lim, Shirley Geok-lin and Amy Ling, eds. 1992. *Reading the Literatures of Asian America*. Philadelphia: Temple University Press.

Liu, John. 1976. "Towards an Understanding of the Internal Colonial Model." In *Counterpoint*. Ed. Emma Gee. Los Angeles: UCLA Asian American Studies Center.

Longxi, Zhang. 1988. "The Myth of the Other: China in the Eyes of the West." *Critical Inquiry* 15: 108-131.

Lowe, Lisa. 1995. "On Contemporary Asian American Projects." *Amerasia Journal* 21. 1 & 2: 41-54.

———. 1996. *Immigrant Acts*. Durham: Duke University Press.

Lowy, Michael. 1978. "Marxism and the National Question." In *Revolution and Class Struggle*. Ed. Robin Blackburn. Sussex: The Harvester Press.

———. 1993. "Why Nationalism?" In *The Socialist Register 1993*. Eds. Ralph Miliband and Leo Panitch. London: The Merlin Press.

Luce, Edward. 1996. "The Philippines: Manila chalks up several tiger stripes." *Financial Times,* 18 September, p. I.

Lukács, Georg. 1971. *History and Class Consciousness*. Tr. Rodney Livingston. London: Merlin Press.

Luke, Timothy. 1990. *Social Theory and Modernity*. Newbury Park: Sage Publications.

Mabini, Apolinario. 1974. [1989.] "The Struggle for Freedom." In *Filipino Nationalism*. Ed. Teodoro A. Agoncillo. Quezon City: R. P. Garcia Publishing Co.

Magdoff, Harry. 1992. *Globalization: To What End?* New York: Monthly Review Press.

Maglipon, Jo-Ann Q. 1990. *The Filipina Migrant: Braving the Exile*. Hong Kong: Mission for Filipina Migrant Workers.

Maksoud, Clovis. 1993. "Redefining Non-Alignment: The Global South in the New Global Equation." In *Altered States: A Reader in the New World Order*. Eds. Phyllis Bennis and Michael Moushabeck. New York: Olive Branch Press. 28-37.

Mandel, Ernest. 1979. *Introduction to Marxism*. London: Links.

———. 1995. "The Relevance of Marxist Theory for Understanding the Present World Crisis." In *Marxism in the Postmodern Age*. Ed. Antonio Callari, Stephen Cullenberg, and Carole Biewener. New York: Guilford Press.

Marable, Manning. 1986. "The Fall of Kwame Nkrumah." In *C. L. R. James: His Life and Work*. Ed. Paul Buhle. London: Allison & Busby.

Martin, Michael and Terry Kandal, eds. 1989. *Studies of Development and Change in the Modern World*. New York: Oxford University Press.

Martin, Tony. 1972. "C.L.R. James and the Race/Class Question." *Race* XIV.2: 183-193.

Marx, Karl. 1959. "Theses on Feuerbach." In *Basic Writings on Politics and Philosophy by Karl Marx and Friedrich Engels*. Ed. Lewis Feuer. New York: Anchor Books.

———. 1964. *Pre-Capitalist Economic Formations*. New York: International Publishers.

———. 1967. *Capital*. London: Lawrence and Wishart.

———. 1968. "Critique of the Gotha Programme. In *Selected Works* by Karl Marx and Frederick Engels. New York: International Publishers.

———. 1969. *On Colonialism and Modernization*. Ed. Shlomo Avineri. New York: Anchor Books.

———. 1971. *Marx's Grundrisse*. Ed. David McLellan. New York: Macmillan.

———. 1973. *Grundrisse*. Tr. Martin Nicolaus. New York: Vintage Books.

———. 1975a. *Early Writings*. New York: Vintage Books.

———. 1975b. *Texts on Method*. Tr. and ed. Terrell Carver. New York: Barnes and Noble.

Marx, Karl and Friedrich Engels. 1964. *The German Ideology*. Tr. S. Rayazanskaya. Moscow: Progress Publishers.

Mattelart, Armand. 1983. *Transnationals and the Third World*. Massachussetts: Bergin & Garvey.

May, Glenn Anthony. 1996. *Inventing a Hero*. Madison: University of Wisconsin Center for Southeast Asian Studies, and Manila, Philippines: New Day Press.

Mayer, Arno J. 1971. *Dynamics of Counterrevolution in Europe, 1870-1956*. New York: Harper Torchbooks.

Mayuga, Sylvia and Alfred Yuson. 1980. "In the Wrong Waters." In *Philippines*. Ed. Hans Johannes Hoefer. Hong Kong: Apa Productions.

McClintock, Anne. 1994. "The Angel of Progress: Pitfalls of the Term 'Postcolonialism.'" In *Colonial Discourse and Post-colonial Theory: A Reader*. Eds. Patrick Williams and Laura Chrisman. New York: Columbia University Press.

McLaren, Peter. 1995. *Critical Pedagogy and Predatory Culture*. New York: Routledge.

———. 1997. *Revolutionary Multiculturalism*. Boulder: Westview Press.

McLellan, David. 1971. *Marx's Grundrisse*. London: McMillan.

McWilliams, Carey. 1964. *Brothers Under the Skin*. Boston: Little, Brown, and Co.

———. 1973. "Introduction" In *America Is in the Heart* by Carlos Bulosan. Seattle: University of Washington Press.

Medvedev, P. N. and Mikhail Bakhtin. 1978. *The Formal Method in Literary Scholarship*. Tr. Albert Wehrle. Baltimore: The Johns Hopkins Press.

Medel-Anonuevo, Carolyn. 1990. "Women Abroad." *Midweek* (21 March): 20-22.

Meillassoux, Claude. 1993. "Toward a Theory of the 'Social Corps.'" In *The Curtain Rises: Rethinking Culture, Ideology, and the State in Eastern Europe*. Ed. Hermine De Soto and David Anderson. New Jersey: Humanities Press.

Melotti, Umberto. 1977. *Marx and the Third World*. London: Macmillan.

Memmi, Albert. 1965. *The Colonizer and the Colonized*. Boston: Beacon Press.

———. 1968. *Dominated Man*. Boston: Beacon Press.

Menchu, Rigoberta. 1984. *I, Rigoberta Menchu*. Ed. Elisabeth Burgos-Debray. New York: Verso.

Meszaros, Istvan. 1970. *Marx's Theory of Alienation*. London: Merlin Press.

———. 1995. *Beyond Capital*. London: Monthly Review Press.

Miles, Robert. 1986. "Labour Migration, Racism and Capital Accumulation in Western Europe since 1945: an overview." *Capital and Class* 28 (Spring): 49-86.

———. 1987. "Recent Marxist theories of nationalism and the issue of racism." *The British Journal of Sociology* 38 (March): 24-43.

———. 1989. *Racism*. London: Routledge.

Min, Pyong Gap, ed. 1995. *Asian Americans: Contemporary Trends and Issues*. Thousand Oaks: Sage Publications.

Mintz, Sidney. 1976. "On the Concept of a Third World." *Dialectical Anthropology* 1: 377-82.

Mishra, Vijay and Bob Hodge. 1994. "What is Post(-) colonialism?" *Colonial Discourse and Post-Colonial Theory: A Reader*. Ed. Patrick Williams and Laura Chrisman. New York: Columbia University Press.

Mocnik, Rastko. 1993. "Ideology and Fantasy." In *The Althusserian Legacy*. Eds. E. Ann Kaplan and Michael Sprinker. London: Verso.

Moy, James. 1996. "Fierce Visibility: Anglo-American Desire Constructing Asian Sexuality." In *Nationalism and Sexuality: Crises of Identity*. Eds. Yiorgos Kalogeras and Domna Pastourmatzi. Thessaloniki, Greece: Hellenic Association of American Studies.

Mukherjee, Arun. 1990. "Whose Post-Colonialism and Whose Postmodernism?" *World Literature Written in English* 30: 1-9.

Nabudere, Dan. 1977. *The Political Economy of Imperialism*. London: Zed Press.

National Endowment for the Humanities. 1994. *A National Conversation: On American Pluralism and Identity*. Washington, DC: NEH Division of Public Programs.

Nee, Victor and Jimy Sanders. 1985. "The Road to Parity: Determinants of the Socio-economic Achievements of Asian Americans." *Ethnic and Racial Studies* 8.1 (January): 75-93.

Negri, Tony and Michael Hardt. 1994. *Labor of Dionysus*. Minneapolis: University of Minnesota Press.

Nehru, Jawaharlal. 1995. "The Discovery of India." *The Nationalism Reader*. New Jersey: Humanities Press. 248-254.

Nelson, Cary. 1993. "Multiculturalism Without Guarantees: From Anthologies to the Social Text." *Journal of the Midwest Modern Language Association* 26.1 (Spring): 47-57.

Ngugi wa Thiong'o. 1993. *Moving the Centre: The Struggle for Cultural Freedoms*. London: James Currey.

Noumoff, Sam J. 1991. "The New International Order as an Impediment to Third World Development." Lecture delivered at the Centre for Nepal and Asian Studies, Tribhuvan University, Kathmandu, Nepal, 11 June. 20 pp.

———. 1996. "Democratic Rights, Resistance and Civil Society." Unpublished lecture delivered to the Central Party School of the Communist Party of

China and the Foreign Ministry Training Institute in Havana, Cuba, in Summer 1996. 7 pp.

Nowlan, Bob, ed. 1996. *Red Orange* [May issue]. Tempe, Arizona: Red Orange Education and Media Action Center.

O'Brien, Thomas. 1990. *Crisis and Instability: The Philippines Enters the Nineties.* Davao City: Philippine International Forum.

Ofreneo, Rene. 1995. *Globalization and the Filipino Working Masses.* Quezon City: Foundation for Nationalist Studies.

O'Hare, William P. and Judy Felt. 1991. *Asian Americans: America's Fastest Growing Minority Group.* Washington, DC: Population Reference Burea Inc.

Okihiro, Gary. 1994. *Margins and Mainstreams.* Seattle: University of Washington Press.

Ollman, Bertell. 1993. *Dialectical Investigations.* New York: Routledge.

Omatsu, Glenn. 1994. "The 'Four Prisons' and the Movements of Liberation: Asian American Activism from the 1960s to the 1990s." In *The State of Asian America.* Ed. Karin Aguilar-San Juan. Boston: South End Press.

Omi, Michael. 1989. "'Elegant Chaos': Postmodern Asian American Identity." In *Asian Americans: Collages of Identities.* Ed. Lee C. Lee. Ithaca: Asian American Studies Program, Cornell University.

——— and Howard Winant. 1986. *Racial Formations in the United States.* New York: Routledge, Kegan and Paul.

Ong, Paul, ed. 1994. *The State of Asian Pacific America: Economic Diversity, Issues and Policies.* Los Angeles: LEAP Asian Pacific American Public Policy institute and UCLA Asian American Studies Center.

Ong, Paul, Edna Bonacich, and Lucie Cheng. 1994. *The New Asian Immigration in Los Angeles and Global Restructuring.* Philadelphia: Temple University Press.

Osajima, Keith. 1995. "Postmodern Possibilities: Theoretical and Political Directions for Asian American Studies." *Amerasia Journal* 21. 1 & 2: 79-88.

Palumbo-Liu, David. 1994. "Los Angeles, Asians, and Perverse Ventriloquisms: On the Functions of Asian America in the Recent American Imaginary." *Public Culture* (Winter 1994): 365-84.

———, ed. 1995. *The Ethnic Canon.* Minneapolis: University of Minnesota Press.

Paredes, Ruby, ed. 1988. *Philippine Colonial Democracy.* Monograph Series 32, Yale University Southeast Asia Studies. New Haven: Yale Center for International and Area Studies.

Parenti, Michael. 1989. *The Sword and the Dollar.* New York: St. Martin's Press.

———. 1994. *Land of Idols.* New York: St. Martin's Press.

———. 1995. *Against Empire.* San Francisco: City Lights Books.

Parkin, Frank. 1972. *Class Inequality and Political Order.* London: Granada Paladin.

Parry, Benita. 1987. "Problems in Current Theories of Colonial Discourse." *The Oxford Literary Review* 9: 27-58.

———. 1994. "Signs of Our Times: Discussion of Homi Bhabha's *The Location of Culture.*" *Third Text:* 5-24.

Patel, Dinker. 1992. "Asian Americans: A Growing Force." In *Race and Ethnic Relations 92/93.* Ed. John Kromkowski. Guilford, Conn.: Dushkin Publishing Co.

Pechey, Graham. 1987. "On the Borders of Bakhtin: Dialogization, Decolonization." *The Oxford Literary Review* 9: 1-2: 59-84.

Peck, David and John Maitino, eds. 1995. *Teaching American Ethnic Literatures.* Albuquerque: University of New Mexico Press.

People's Conference Against Imperialist Globalization. 1996. "Declaration of the People's Conference Against Imperialist Globalization." http://www.geocities.com/~cpp-ndf/natsit10.htm/ (18 December)

Pe-pua, Rogelia. 1989. *Sikolohiyang Pilipino: Teorya, Metodo at Gamit.* Quezon City: University of the Philippines Press.

Petras, James. 1981. "Dependency and World System Theory: A Critique and New Directions." *Latin American Perspectives* 7 (Summer and Fall): 148-55.

———. 1991. "World Transformations: The Challenges for the Left." *Against the Current* 34 (September-October 1991): 17-22.

———. 1993. "Cultural Imperialism in the Late 20th Century." *Journal of Contemporary Asia* 23.2: 139-48.

Pineda-Ofreneo, Rosalinda and Rene Ofreneo. 1995. "Globalization and Filipino Women Workers." *Philippine Labor Review* 19.1 (January-June): 1-34.

Pizarro, Rafael. 1993. "The regrouping of the Latin American left." *Corresponder* 2 (August-September): 28, 22.

Portillo, Ma. Josefina Saldana. 1995. "Re-Guarding Myself: Menchu's Autobiographical Renderings of the Authentic Other," *Socialist Review* 24.1-2: 85-114.

Pozzolini, A. 1970. *Antonio Gramsci: An Introduction to his thought.* London: Pluto Press.

Prairie Fire Organizing Committee. 1989. "Interview with Makibaka," *Breakthrough* 13.1 (Spring): 22-31.

Putzel, James. 1992. *A Captive Land.* New York: Monthly Review Press.

Quinsaat, Jesse et al, eds. 1976. "Anti-Miscegenation Laws and the Filipino." In *Letters in Exile.* Los Angeles: UCLA Asian American Studies Center.

Rafael, Vicente, ed. 1995. *Discrepant Histories: Translocal Essays on Filipino Culture.* Philadelphia: Temple University Press.

Rajan, Gita and Radhika Mohanram, eds. 1995. *Postcolonial Discourse and Changing Cultural Contexts.* Westport, Conn.: Greenwood Press.

Ramos, Corin. 1995. "Racism stirs up West, East Coast Campuses." *Philippine News* (March 1-7): 1, A-14.

Reimers, David. 1992. *Still the Golden Door: The Third World Comes to America.* New York: Columbia University Press.

Renan, Ernest. 1995. "What Is a Nation?" In *The Nationalism Reader.* Eds. Omar Dahbour and Micheline R. Ishay. New Jersey: Humanities Press.

Resnick, Stephen and Richard Wolff. 1987. *Knowledge and Class.* Chicago: University of Chicago Press.

Retamar, Roberto Fernandez. 1989. *Caliban and Other Essays.* Minneapolis: University of Minnesota Press.

Rex, John. 1982. "Racism and the Structure of Colonial Societies." In *Racism and Colonialism: Essays on Ideology and Social Structure*. Ed. Robert Ross. The Hague: Martinus Nijhoff.

———. 1996. "Multiculturalism in Europe." In *Ethnicity*. Eds. John Hutchinson and Anthony Smith. New York: Oxford University Press.

Rice-Sayre, Laura. 1986. "Witnessing History: Diplomacy Versus Testimony." In *Testimonio y Literatura*. Ed. Rene Jara and Hernan Vidal. Minneapolis: Institute for the Study of Ideologies and Literature.

Richardson, Jim. 1989. "Introduction." *The Philippines*. Oxford: Clio Press.

Richards, Glen. 1995. "C. L. R. James on Black Self-Determination in the United States and the Caribbean." In *C. L. R. James: His Intellectual Legacies*. Ed. Selwyn Cudjoe and William Cain. Amherst: University of Massachusetts Press.

Robbins, Bruce. 1993. *Secular Vocations*. New York: Verso.

Robinson, Cedric. 1992. "C. L. R. James and the World System, " *Race and Class* 34.2: 49-62.

Rodil, B.R. 1993. "The Lumad and Moro of Mindanao." In *Minority Rights Group Intervention Report*. London: Minority Rights Group.

Rodney, Walter. 1982. *How Europe Underdeveloped Africa*. Washington, DC: Howard University Press.

Rosaldo, Renato. 1994. "Social justice and the crisis of national communities." In *Colonial Discourse/Postcolonial Theory*. Ed. Francis Barker, Peter Hulme and Margaret Iversen. New York: St. Martin's Press.

Rossi-Landi, Ferruccio. 1990. *Marxism and Ideology*. New York: Oxford University Press.

Ruoff, A. LaVonne Brown and Jerry Ward, Jr., eds. 1990. *Redefining American Literary History*. New York: MLA.

Said, Edward. 1978. *Orientalism*. New York: Vintage.

———. 1992. Interview with Jennifer Wicke and Michael Sprinker. In *Edward Said: A Critical Reader*. Ed. Michael Sprinker. Oxford: Blackwell.

———. 1993. *Culture and Imperialism*. New York: Alfred A. Knopf.

Salman, Michael. 1995. "Nothing Without Labor: Penology, Discipline and Independence in the Philippines Under United States Rule." In *Discrepant Histories*. Ed. Vicente Rafael. Philadelphia: Temple University Press.

San, Kim and Nym Wales. 1941. *Song of Ariran*. San Francisco: Ramparts Press.

San Juan, E. 1976. "Literature and Revolution in the Third World." *Social Praxis* 6: 19-34.

———. 1984. *Toward a People's Literature: Essays in the Dialectics of Praxis and Contradiction*. Quezon City: University of the Philippines Press.

———. 1986. *Crisis in the Philippines: The Making of a Revolution*. South Hadley, MA: Bergin and Garvey.

———. 1990. *From People to Nation: Essays in Cultural Politics*. Manila: Asian Social Institute, Inc.

———. 1991. *Writing and National Liberation*. Quezon City: University of the Philippines Press.

———. 1992a. *Reading the West/Writing the East*. New York: Peter Lang, Inc.

———. 1992b. *Racial Formations/Critical Transformations*. Atlantic Highlands, NJ: Humanities Press.

———. 1994a. *Allegories of Resistance*. Quezon City: University of the Philippines Press.

———. 1994b. *From the Masses to the Masses: Third World Literature and Revolution*. Minneapolis: Marxist Educational Press.

———. 1995a. "On the Limits of Postcolonial Theory: Trespassing Letters from the Third World." *Ariel* 26.3 (July) : 89-116.

———. 1995b. "From the 'Boondocks' to the 'Belly of the Beast': What We Can Learn from the Life-History of a Filipino Worker-Intellectual." *Mediations* 19.1 (Spring): 76-91.

———. 1995c. "Multiculturalism and the Challenge of World Cultural Studies." In *Hegemony and Strategies of Transgression*. Albany: State University of New York Press.

———. 1996a. "Configuring the Filipino Diaspora in the United States." In *Race and Ethnic Relations 96/97*. Ed. John A. Kromkowski. 6th ed. Guilford, Conn.: Dushkin Publishing Group/Brown and Benchmark Publishers.

———. 1996b. *The Philippine Temptation: Dialectics of Philippines-United States Literary Relations*. Philadelphia: Temple University Press.

Sangari, Kumkum. 1987. "The Politics of the Possible." *Cultural Critique* 7: 157-86.

———. 1995. "The Politics of the Possible." In *The Post-Colonial Studies Reader*. Eds. Bill Ashcroft, Gareth Griffiths, and Helen Tiffin. London: Routledge.

Sanjines, Jorge and the Ukamau Group. 1989. In *Theory and Practice of a Cinema with the People*. Willimantic, CT: Curbstone Press.

Sartre, Jean-Paul. 1968. *Search for a Method*. Tr. Hazel Barnes. New York: Vintage.

Sassoon, Anne Showstack. 1980. *Gramsci's Politics*. New York: St. Martin's Press.

———. 1983. "Civil Society." In *A Dictionary of Marxist Thought*. Ed. Tom Bottomore. Cambridge, MA: Harvard University Press.

Sayer, Derek. 1983. *Marx's Method*. Sussex: The Harvester Press.

———. 1987. *The Violence of Abstraction*. London: Blackwell.

Schaeffer, Robert K. 1997. *Understanding Globalization*. Lanham, Md: Rowman and Littlefield Publishers.

Schiller, Herbert. 1989. *Culture, Inc.* New York: Oxford University Press.

Schirmer, Daniel B. 1995. *Military Access: The Pentagon vs. the Philippine Constitution*. Boston: Friends of the Filipino People.

———. 1996. *Sexual Abuse and the U.S. Military Presence: The Philippines and Japan*. Durham, NC: Friends of the Filipino People.

Schirmer, Daniel B. and Stephen Shalom, eds. 1987. *The Philippines Reader*. Boston: South End Press.

Schulze-Engler, Frank. 1993. "Universalism with a Difference: The Politics of Post-Colonial Theory." Paper read at Karl-Franzens University, Graz, 18 May.

Schwarz, Roberto. 1992. *Misplaced Ideas: Essays on Brazilian Culture*. London and New York: Verso.

Scott, James. 1976. *The Moral Economy of the Peasant*. New Haven: Yale University Press.

Scott, Joan W. 1992. "Multiculturalism and the Politics of Identity." *October* 61 (Summer): 12-19.

Scott, William Henry. 1993. *Of Igorots and Independence.* Baguio City: ERA.

Selsam, Howard and Harry Martel, eds. 1963. *Marx, Engels, Lenin: Reader in Marxist Philosophy.* New York: International Publishers.

Selsam, Howard, David Goldway, and Harry Martel, eds. 1970. *Dynamics of Social Change: A Reader in Marxist Social Science.* New York: International Publishers.

Senghor, Leopold Sedar. 1995. "On African Socialism." In *The Nationalism Reader.* New Jersey: Humanities Press.

Serrano, Isagani. 1994. "Civil Society in the Asia-Pacific Region." In *Citizens: Strengthening Global Civic Society.* Ed. Miguel Darcy de Oliviera and Rajesh Tandon. Washington, DC: Civicus

Shalom, Stephen Rosskamm. 1993. *Imperial Alibis.* Boston: South End Press.

Shanin, Theodor. 1971. "Peasantry as a Political Factor." In *Peasants and Peasant Societies.* Ed. Theodor Shanin. New York: Penguin Books.

Silko, Leslie Marmon. 1980. "Stories and Their Tellers—A Conversation with Leslie Marmon Silko." In *The Third Woman.* Ed. Dexter Fisher. Boston: Houghton Mifflin Co.

———. 1991. *Almanac of the Dead.* New York: Penguin Books.

———. 1994. "Fences Against Freedom." *Hungry Mind Review* 31 (Fall): 9, 20, 58-59.

Silva, Luiz da. 1993. "The Transformations Must Be Deep and Global." In *Global Visions.* Ed. Jeremy Brecher et al. Boston: South End Press.

Sison, Jose Maria. 1986. *Philippine Crisis and Revolution. Ten Lectures.* Delivered at the Asian Center, University of the Philippines, Quezon City. April-May.

Sivanandan, A. 1982. *A Different Hunger.* London: Pluto Press.

Sklair, Leslie. 1991. *Sociology of the Global System.* Baltimore: The Johns Hopkins University Press.

Slemon, Stephen. 1987. "Monuments of Empire: Allegory/Counter-Discourse/Post-Colonial Writing." *Kunapipi* 9: 1-16.

Smith, Anthony. 1991. *National Identity.* Reno: University of Nevada Press.

Smith, Joseph. 1976. *Portrait of a Cold Warrior.* New York: Ballantine Books.

Smith, Neil and Cindi Katz. 1993. "Grounding Metaphor: Towards a Spatialized Politics." In *Place and the Politics of Identity.* Eds. Michael Keith and Steve Pile. London and New York: Routledge.

Soja, Edward and Barbara Hooper. 1993. "The Spaces that Difference Makes: Some Notes on the Geographical Margins of the New Cultural Politics." In *Place and the Politics of Identity.* London and New York: Routledge.

Solomon, Mark. 1994. "Reflections on the Global Economy." *Dialogue and Initiative* 9 (Summer): 28-32.

Sollors, Werner. 1986. *Beyond Ethnicity: Consent and Descent in American Culture.* New York: Oxford University Press.

Sommer, Doris. 1993. "Resisting the Heat: Menchu, Morrison, and Incompetent Readers." In *Cultures of United States Imperialism.* Eds. Amy Kaplan and Donald Pease. Durham: Duke University Press.

Spinoza, Benedict. 1995 (1883). *Ethics: Works of Spinoza.* Tr. R. H. M. Elwes. New York: Dover Publications.

Spivak, Gayatri Chakravorty. 1985. "Three Women's Texts and a Critique of Imperialism." *Critical Inquiry* 12.1: 43-61.

————. 1987. *In Other Worlds.* New York: Routledge.

————. 1988. "Can the Subaltern Speak?" In *Marxism and the Interpretation of Culture.* Edited by Cary Nelson and Lawrence Grossberg. Urbana and Chicago: University of Illinois Press.

————. 1991. *The Post-Colonial Critic: Interviews, Strategies, Dialogues.* New York: Routledge.

————. 1996. *The Spivak Reader.* Edited by Donna Landry and Gerald MacLean. New York: Routledge.

Sprinker, Michael. 1995. "Introduction." In *Late Imperial Culture.* Eds. Roman de la Campa, E. Ann Kaplan and Michael Sprinker. New York: Verso.

Stabile, Carole. 1995. "Postmodernism, Feminism, and Marx: Notes from the Abyss." *Monthly Review* (July/August): 89-107.

Stanley, Peter. 1974. *A Nation in the Making: The Philippines and the United States, 1899-1921.* Cambridge, Ma.: Harvard University Press.

Stasiulis, Daiva and Nira Yuval-Davis, eds. 1995. *Unsettling Settler Societies.* London: Sage Publications.

Stauffer, Robert B. 1985. *The Marcos Regime: Failure of Transnational Developmentalism and Hegemony-Building from Above and Outside.* Research Monograph No. 23. Sydney, Australia: Transnational Corporations Research Project.

————. 1987. "Review of Peter Stanley, Reappraising an Empire." *Journal of Asian and African Studies* 12, 1-2: 102-04.

————. 1990. "Philippine Democracy: Contradictions of Third World Redemocratization." University of Hawaii: Philippine Studies Colloqium, May 4, 1990.

Steinberg, David Joel. 1982. *The Philippines: A Singular and a Plural Place.* Boulder, CO: Westview Press.

Steinberg, Stephen. 1995. *Turning Back.* Boston: Beacon Press.

Stratton, Jon and Ien Ang. 1996. "On the impossibility of a global cultural studies in an 'international frame.'" In *Stuart Hall: Critical Dialogues in Cultural Studies.* London and New York: Routledge.

Sturtevant, David. 1976. *Popular Uprisings in the Philippines 1840-1940.* Ithaca: Cornell University Press.

Sun Yat-sen. 1995. "Three Principles of the People." In *The Nationalism Reader.* New Jersey: Humanities Press. 240-247.

Sundiata, Cha Jua. 1996. " 'The Interpretation of History is a Class Question'? C. L. R. James and the Making of a Neo-Marxist Diasporan Historiography." Unpublished paper. 54 pp.

Sundquist, Eric. 1993. *To Wake the Nations: Race In the Making of American Literature.* Cambridge, Ma.: Harvard University Press.

Sussman, Gerald. 1992. "What 'Hearts of Darkness' Left Out." *Guardian* (29 April): 19.

Szeftel, Morris. 1987. "The Crisis in the Third World." In *The World Order: Socialist Perspectives*. Eds. Ray Bush, Gordon Johnston, and David Coates. New York: Polity Press.

Tadiar, Neferti Xina M. 1993. "Sexual Economies in the Asia-Pacific Community." In *What Is in a Rim?* Ed. Arif Dirlik. Boulder: Westview Press.

Takaki, Ronald. 1987. "Reflections on Racial Patterns in America." In *From Different Shores*. Ed. Ronald Takaki. New York: Oxford University Press.

———. 1989. *Strangers from a Different Shore*. Boston: Little, Brown and Co.

———. 1993. *A Different Mirror*. Boston: Little, Brown and Co.

Tan, Amy. 1989. *The Joy Luck Club*. New York: G. P. Putnam's Sons.

Tandon, Rajesh. 1994. "Civil Society, the State and the Role of NGOs." In *Civil Society in the Asia-Pacific Region*. Ed. Isagani Serrano. Washington, DC: Civicus.

Tarr, Peter. 1989. "Learning to Love Imperialism." *The Nation* (5 June): 779-84.

Taruc, Luis. 1953. *Born of the People*. New York: International Publishers.

Tatum, Chuck. 1992. "Paraliterature." In *Handbook of Latin American Literature*. Ed. David William Foster. New York: Garland Publishing.

Taylor, Charles. 1994. *Multiculturalism: Examining the Politics of Recognition*. Princeton: Princeton University Press.

———. 1994. "The Politics of Recognition." In *Multiculturalism: A Critical Reader*. Ed. David Goldberg. Cambridge: Blackwell.

Terkel, Studs. 1992. *Race*. New York: The New Press.

Todorov, Tzvetan. 1984. *Mikhail Bakhtin: The Dialogical Principle*. Minneapolis: University of Minnesota Press.

Tomlinson, John. 1991. *Cultural Imperialism: A Critical Introduction*. Baltimore: The Johns Hopkins University Press.

Trinh Minh-ha. 1989. *Woman, Native, Other: Writing Postcoloniality and Feminism*. Bloomington: Indiana University Press.

Tujan, Antonio Jr. 1995. "The Crisis of Philippine Labor Migration." *Ibon Special Release* (May): 1-15.

———. 1996. "The Philippine Crisis Rages On." *Institute of Political Economy* (January): 1-18.

Turki, Fawaz. 1978. *Tel Zaatar Was the Hill of Thyme*. Washington, DC: Free Palestine Press.

Turner, Bryan S. 1994. *Orientalism, Postmodernism, and Globalism*. New York: Routledge.

Twain, Mark. 1992. "Thirty Thousand Killed a Million." *The Atlantic Monthly* (April): 52-65.

United States Commission on Civil Rights. 1992. *Civil Rights Issues Facing Asian Americans in the 1990s*. Washington, DC: United States Commission on Civil Rights.

Urry, John. 1981. *The Anatomy of Capitalist Societies*. Atlantic Highlands, NJ: Humanities Press.

Van den Berghe, Pierre. 1967. *Race and Racism*. New York: John Wiley and Sons, Inc.

Van Dijk, Teun. 1993. *Elite Discourse and Racism*. Newbury Park: Sage Publications.

Van Erven, Eugene. 1992. *The Playful Revolution.* Bloomington: University of Indiana Press.

Vickers, Jeanne. 1993. *Women and the World Economic Crisis.* London: Zed Books.

Vidal, Gore. 1986-92. *The Decline and Fall of the American Empire.* Berkeley: Odonian Press.

Vilas, Carlos. 1992-93. "Latin American Populism: A Structural Approach." *Science and Society* 56.4: 389-420.

Virilio, Paul. 1977. *Speed and Politics.* Tr. Mark Polizzotti. New York: Semiotext(e).

Voloshinov, V. N. and Mikhail Bakhtin. 1986. *Marxism and the Philosophy of Language.* Tr. Ladislaw Matejka and I. R. Titunik. Cambridge, Ma.: Harvard University Press.

Wallerstein, Immanuel. 1983. *Historical Capitalism.* New York: Verso.

———. 1991. "The Construction of Peoplehood: Racism, Nationalism, Ethnicity." In *Race, Nation, Class* by Etienne Balibar and Immanuel Wallerstein. New York: Verso.

Wand, David Hsin-Fu, ed. 1974. *Asian-American Heritage.* New York: Washington Square Press.

Wei, William. 1996. "Reclaiming the Past and Constructing a Collective Culture." In *Multicultural Experiences, Multicultural Theories.* Ed. Mary F. Rogers. New York: McGraw Hill.

Weisskopf, Thomas. 1972. "Capitalism and Underdevelopment in the Modern World." In *The Capitalist System.* Englewood Cliffs, NJ: Prentice Hall.

Wilden, Anthony. 1972. *System and Structure.* London: Tavistock Publications.

Williams, Raymond. 1977. *Marxism and Literature.* New York: Oxford University Press.

———. 1983a. *The Year 2000.* New York: Pantheon Books.

———. 1983b. *Keywords.* New York: Oxford University Press.

Williams, Rhonda M. 1995. "Consenting to Whiteness: Reflections on Race and Marxian Theories of Discrimination." In *Marxism in the Postmodern Age.* Eds. Antonio Callari, Stephen Cullenberg, and Carole Biewener. New York: The Guilford Press.

Williams, William Appleman. 1962. *The Tragedy of American Diplomacy.* New York: Dell Publishing Co.

Wilson, Rob and Arif Dirlik. 1995. *Asia/Pacific As Space of Cultural Production.* Durham, NC: Duke University Press.

Winant, Howard. 1994. *Racial Conditions: Politics, Theory, Comparisons.* Minneapolis: University of Minnesota Press.

Woddis, Jack. 1972. *Introduction to Neo-Colonialism.* New York: International Publishers.

Wolf, Eric. 1966. *Peasants.* Englewood Cliffs, NJ: Prentice Hall.

———. 1971. "Peasant Rebellion and Revolution." In *National Liberation: Revolution in the Third World.* Eds. Norman Miller and Roderick Aya. New York: The Free Press.

———. 1982. *Europe and the People Without History.* Berkeley: University of California Press.

Wolfenstein, Eugene Victor. 1993. *Psychoanalytic Marxism*. New York: Guilford Press.

Wong, Paul, Meera Manvi, and Takeo Hirota Wong. 1995. "Asiacentrism and Asian American Studies?" *Amerasia Journal* 21. 1 & 2: 137-48.

Wong, Sau-lin. 1993. *Reading Asian American Literature: From Necessity to Extravagance*. Princeton: Princeton University Press.

Woo, Deborah. 1989. "The Gap Between Striving and Achieving: The Case of Asian American Women." In *Making Waves. Asian Women United of California*. Boston: Beacon Press.

Wood, Ellen Meiksins. 1995. "What is the 'Postmodern' Agenda? An Introduction." *Monthly Review* (July-August): 1-12.

———.1997. "A Reply to A. Sivanandan." *Monthly Review 9.* (February): 21-32.

Worsley, Peter. 1964. *The Third World*. Chicago: University of Chicago Press.

Wynne, Alison. 1979. *No Time for Crying*. Hong Kong: Resource Center for Philippine Concerns.

Wynter, Sylvia. 1992. "Beyond the Categories of the Master Conception: The Counterdoctrine of the Jamesian Poiesis." In *C. L. R. James's Caribbean*. Eds. Henry Paget and Paul Buhle. Durham: Duke University Press.

Yamato, Alexander et al, eds. 1993. *Asian Americans in the United States*. Vol. 1. Iowa: Kendall/Hunt Publishing Company.

Yip, Alethea. 1997. "One or the Other." *Asianweek* (3 January): 14-15.

Young, Iris Marion. 1993. "Justice and Communicative Democracy." In *Radical Philosophy*. Ed. Roger Gottlieb. Philadelphia: Temple University Press.

Zahar, Renate. 1974. *Frantz Fanon: Colonialism and Alienation*. New York: Monthly Review Press.

Zavarzadeh, Mas'ud and Donald Morton. 1991. *Theory (Post)Modernity Opposition*. Washington, DC: Maisonneuve Press.

Zinn, Howard. 1992. *The Twentieth Century*. New York: Harper and Row.

INDEX

Abu-Jamal, Mumia, 13, 83
Accumulation, 3, 57, 69, 81, 117, 133, 163, 167, 170, 177, 199, 222-23, 256; logic of, 147 primitive, 4, 15, 187
Achebe, Chinua, 15, 139
Aesthetics, 14, 34, 40, 59, 69, 73, 75, 165, 178-79, 189, 223-25, 242
Africa, 12, 27, 28, 156, 229, 233, 235, 245
African Americans, 139, 142, 244, 247-48
Agamben, Giorgio, 153
Agency, 1, 7-9, 25, 37, 42, 49-51, 58, 65, 81, 85, 97, 98, 103, 108, 118, 121, 130, 133-35, 146-47, 152, 154, 165, 167-68, 177, 183, 230, 235, 249, 258-59, 266, 270
Ahmad, Aijaz, 5, 6, 30, 43, 255-56, 265
Ahmad, Eqbal, 68, 267
Alavi, Hamza, 23, 100
Alcoff, Linda, 101
Alexis, Jacques Stephen, 235
Algeria, 27, 210, 253
Alienation, 11, 36, 71, 130, 144, 148, 152, 154, 158, 180, 190, 215
Allegory, 24, 37, 40, 42, 57, 72, 109, 123, 143, 146-47, 156, 222, 230, 238, 256-57, 259, 265, 267, 269; national, 5, 50
Allende, Salvador, 253, 262
Almanac of the Dead (Silko), 103, 108
Alterity, 26, 51-52, 84, 111, 120, 152, 181, 192, 204, 218, 221, 225, 235, 255, 264. See also Other
Althusser, Louis, 57, 119, 120-22, 125, 132, 166
Ambivalence, 10, 22, 27, 30, 42, 47, 86, 176-77, 192, 227, 262
Americanization, 11, 58, 65, 153, 159, 167, 220
Amin, Samir, 98, 253, 267, 271-72
Amnesty International, 32, 77
Anarchism, 7, 29, 118
Anderson, Benedict, 200, 206
Anderson, Kevin, 238
Appadurai, Arjun, 153-54
Applebaum, Richard, 169
Aquino, Corazon, 43, 60, 66, 76, 79, 80
Arbenz, Jacobo, 32
Arendt, Hannah, 26

Art, 38, 49, 51, 143, 250, 257; Greek, 40, 173
Ashcroft, Bill, 7, 39, 227
Asia Pacific Economic Cooperation (APEC), 196
Asian Americans, 155-93
Asiatic "barred zone," 115, 158, 175
Assimilation, 156-59, 163-68, 163-74, 190, 227
Bakhtin, Mikhail, 15, 26-27, 39, 84-85, 201-205, 212, 215, 219-20, 266. See also Dialogue; Speech-act
Balabagan, Sarah, 224-25
Baran, Paul, 263-64
Barros, Maria Lorena, 29-30, 43-52
Barthes, Roland, 26, 129
Baudrillard, Jean, 31, 34, 74-75, 134, 153, 256, 264
Bauer, Otto, 78, 207-208, 256
"Benevolent Assimilation," 61, 68
Benjamin, Walter, 49, 103, 233, 265
Berlant, Lauren, 151-52
Bhabha, Homi, 2, 6-7, 22, 25-28, 50, 56, 108, 152, 200-201, 210, 224, 228, 235, 265-66
Bierce, Ambrose, 173
Black Skin, White Masks (Fanon), 27-28
Blauner, Robert, 155-56, 159, 176
Bloc, 51, 87, 90, 94, 98, 121, 181. See also Gramsci; Hegemony
Bloch, Ernst, 18, 256
Body, 1, 12, 29, 50, 131, 149, 177, 189, 191-92, 234
Bonacich, Edna, 157, 169
Bonapartism, 23, 212, 230
Bonifacio, Andres, 69
Border crossing, 2, 26, 109, 111, 152, 176, 192, 220
Bourdieu, Pierre, 185
Bourgeoisie, 16, 23, 91-92, 128, 206, 208-10, 218, 234, 238, 258, 269
Braithwaite, Edward, 39
Brazil, 104, 106, 266, 271
Brecht, Bertolt, 74, 195
Brocka, Lino, 78, 265
Bruin, Janet, 199
Bulosan, Carlos, 177, 180, 187

Burgos-Debray, Elizabeth, 37
Cabral, Amilcar, 57, 100, 213, 256
Callinicos, Alex, 7, 27
Camara, Dom Helder, 270
Canada, 29, 136
Capital, 1, 15, 54-55, 108, 114, 117, 120, 141, 147-48, 200-201, 217, 252, 271
Capitalism, 1, 3, 5, 17-18, 22, 30, 36, 43, 52, 61, 70, 76, 92, 94-95, 99, 116, 121, 130, 144, 146, 154, 161, 169-70, 180, 184, 205, 222, 225, 236, 253, 263, 268; booty, 139; late, 6, 9, 14, 23, 57, 59, 77, 113, 118, 126-27, 139, 152, 165; mercantile, 5, 207, 236; monopoly, 197, 221-23, 228, 234, 273; post-Fordist, 8, 166; state, 42, 229-30
Cardenal, Ernesto, 49, 267
Cardenas, Cuauhtemoc, 268
Caribbean, 28, 39, 40-42, 50, 233, 235, 244, 250, 258
Carpentier, Alejo, 235
Carter, Jimmy, 32
Castoriadis, Cornelius, 15
Castro, Fidel, 8, 213-17, 219, 233-34, 240, 253
Center/periphery, 1, 24, 25, 33, 41, 156, 161, 171, 222
Central Intelligence Agency (CIA), 32, 33, 66
Césaire, Aimé, 41, 208, 215, 219, 233, 235, 251, 256, 265
Cha-jua, Sundiata, 247
Chaliand, Gerard, 253-54
Chan, Sucheng, 161, 176
Change, 4, 18, 22, 27, 47, 51-52, 58, 87, 107, 111, 149, 155, 215. See also Class struggle; Crisis; Transformation
Chatterjee, Partha, 86, 200
Chilcote, Ronald, 261
Chin, Frank, 155, 164, 172, 181, 187-89
Chin, Vincent, 159, 174
China, 3, 17, 99, 101, 115, 196; cultural revolution in, 43
Chinese Americans, 173-75
Chinese Exclusion Act (1882), 114, 116, 175
Chow, Rey, 178
Cirese, Alberto Maria, 97
Citizenship, 24, 88, 115, 128, 135, 139, 150, 161, 181, 183, 261, 263
Civil society, 11, 44-45, 76, 78, 92, 98, 100, 112, 128, 130, 146-47, 168, 176, 150-51, 181, 227, 263

"Civilizing mission," 13, 15, 29, 54, 56, 61, 68, 72, 95, 136, 144, 171, 178, 217, 231-32, 255, 266
Class, 27, 41, 44, 73, 84, 87-89, 91-92, 94, 96, 102, 106-107, 115, 130, 140, 160, 178, 207, 214, 220, 271
Class struggle, 4, 11, 17, 27, 89, 96, 100, 119, 122-23, 133-34, 152, 156, 161, 163, 168-69, 200, 203, 208, 211, 235, 241, 245, 254
Cleaver, Harry, 141
Clinton, Bill, 77
Cold War, 1, 10, 12, 24, 37, 39, 42-43, 54, 64, 77, 80, 154, 168, 170, 177, 228, 231, 234, 244, 249, 253, 261
Colonialism, 1, 5, 9, 15, 21, 23, 31, 40-42, 44, 51, 66, 71, 75, 98, 136, 139, 155-56, 167, 178, 203, 206, 208, 210, 217, 227, 233-34, 244, 264, 266-67
Commodification, 18, 25, 47, 52, 73-74, 78, 81, 110, 134, 139, 146, 164, 169, 184, 197-98, 221, 228, 264, 268, 272-73
Commodity fetishism, 11, 72, 75, 118, 126-29, 133, 138-39, 141, 143, 150, 181, 183-89, 234, 240-43
Communism, 47, 57, 90, 97, 99, 109, 148, 203, 209, 216-17, 232, 238, 249, 251
Communist Party of the Philippines (CPP), 43, 46
Communitarians, 138, 146
Community, 10, 15, 17, 22, 36, 38, 47, 49, 50-51, 59, 68, 78, 81, 86, 88, 96, 100-101, 107, 111, 118, 120, 138, 144, 146-50, 162, 168, 176, 190, 192, 200, 204, 206, 210, 212, 214, 257, 267, 269, 273
Comprador, 54, 57, 59, 72, 78-79, 202, 209, 212, 221, 264, 272
Compromise, 2, 64, 68-69, 173, 177
Conrad, Joseph, 42, 73
Conscientization, 45, 70, 104-108, 258
Consumerism, 8, 10, 30, 52, 72, 78, 118, 159, 186, 197, 220, 234, 241
Contemplacion, Flor, 224
Contradiction, 7, 16, 22, 28-30, 40, 57, 70, 99, 107, 110, 117-18, 139, 141, 162, 183, 186, 190, 210, 228-31, 240, 257, 271
Coppola, Francis Ford, 73
Counterrevolution, 3, 9, 65, 68, 79, 94, 96, 101
Crisis, 3, 8, 16, 57, 104, 113, 160, 176-77, 244, 252

Critique, 7, 8, 13, 17, 24, 30, 49-51, 56, 70-71, 80, 86, 90, 95, 103-104, 107, 144, 150, 170, 181, 183, 191-92, 229, 257
Cuba, 37, 49, 156, 214-17, 233, 253, 265
Cultural studies, 1, 11, 21, 131, 168, 255
Culture, 18, 28, 24, 26, 30, 42, 45, 51, 63, 72, 83, 88, 95, 101-105, 125, 139, 143-44, 147, 156, 160, 178, 213, 251, 268; common, 118, 131, 158, 166; late imperial, 15, 52; minority, 10, 115; popular-democratic, 36; public, 11; wars, 1, 11, 55
da Silva, Luiz, 266
Dalton, Roque, 265, 267, 272
Daniels, Roger, 158
Darwish, Mahmoud, 265
Dash, Michael, 235
Davidson, Basil, 52
Davis, Mike, 4
de Beauvoir, Simone, 84
Debord, Guy, 152
Decolonization, 5, 18, 22, 59, 85, 101, 157, 207, 210-12, 217, 219, 228, 244
Deconstruction, 2, 14, 26, 27, 56, 85-86, 119, 129, 235, 266
Deleuze, Gilles and Felix Guattari, 124, 226
Democracy, 38, 40, 65, 69, 70-71, 78-81, 91, 104, 106, 113, 135, 147, 150, 190, 203, 232, 247, 252, 264, 269; *Herrenvolk,* 161; radical, 46, 154, 170, 213, 239, 249, 263, 270-71
Dependency, 17, 24, 63, 68, 92, 98, 146-47, 157, 261-62, 272-73
Derrida, Jacques, 26, 57, 85, 108, 228, 255
Descartes, Rene, 146
Desire, 1, 27, 39, 50, 76, 84, 123, 257
Development, uneven, 3, 5, 9, 12, 14, 31, 44, 58, 69, 94, 98, 110, 134, 151, 199-201, 206, 221, 237, 253, 261-63, 270, 272; organic, 96; sustainable, 271
Dewey, Admiral George, 60, 72
Dialectic, 10, 26, 28, 36, 39, 41, 52, 58, 72, 98-99, 104-105, 107, 120-21, 126, 131, 135, 149, 200, 214, 221, 229, 231, 233, 238-40, 242, 245-46, 248, 256, 267
Dialogue, 26, 31, 33, 84, 104-105, 125, 135, 143, 148, 173, 202-203, 205, 207, 209, 214, 217, 225, 268
Diaspora, 2, 7, 9, 11, 25, 51, 59, 112, 166-67, 220-21, 224-26, 229, 244, 247, 249

Difference, 1, 6-7, 9, 16, 23-26, 28, 39, 49, 52, 55, 58, 84, 86, 120, 129, 133-34, 138, 147, 149, 151-52, 158-59, 161, 228, 232, 255, 258, 265; cult of, 29; cultural, 6, 12; linguistic, 25; logic of, 34; politics of, 7
Dirlik, Arif, 1, 14, 30
Discourse, 1, 21, 25-26, 33, 39, 101, 124-25, 131-32, 172, 183, 202, 226; imperial, 7, 65; master, 108; racialist, 119; technocratic, 68; theological, 125
Dostoevsky, Fyodor, 31, 219
DuBois, W. E. B., 179, 229, 236, 249
Dunayevskaya, Raya, 238
Dussel, Enrique, 150
East Timor, 13, 72, 272
Economy, 88, 100, 118, 122, 161; political, 88, 120, 122, 129, 132, 139, 154, 162, 166, 168, 252, 261; racialized, 165; symbolic, 63, 184, 222
Education, 24, 50, 66, 70, 90-91, 94, 97, 104-108, 121, 125; banking, 105; plot of, 36, 236
Egypt, 101, 103
Eisenhower, Dwight, 32
El Saadawi, Nawal, 101-103
El Salvador, 252
Elite, 23-24, 36, 59, 76, 79, 80, 85, 129, 144, 179, 224, 249, 270; cognitive, 173
Ellis, C.P., 123
Emerson, Ralph Waldo, 56
Empiricism, 117, 122, 258, 264
Engels, Friedrich, 110, 205, 228
Environment, 30, 43, 76, 99, 269
Epistemology, 30, 42, 107, 190, 265; functionalist, 176
Equality, 12, 38-39, 130, 136, 138, 147, 165, 213, 217, 254; gender, 44, 51, 54, 103, 148, 183
Escobar, Arturo, 13, 83, 100
Espiritu, Yen Le, 160, 166
Essentialism, 2, 8, 12, 25, 28, 57, 71, 108, 119-20, 122, 126, 134, 143, 178, 181, 214, 219, 228; anti-, 79, 86
Ethics, 1, 9, 12, 18, 22, 39, 40, 43, 75, 98, 100, 106, 136, 146, 150, 189, 215, 253, 260
Ethiopia (Abyssinia), 229, 244-45
Ethnicity, 4, 6, 11, 16-17, 38, 41, 43, 72, 101, 115-18, 129, 134, 137-38, 152, 155-57, 159, 160-69, 176, 180, 189, 192, 201, 206, 225, 269

Ethnography, 31, 35, 37, 74, 178, 184, 255
Ethos, 1, 10, 38, 67, 69, 163, 176, 191, 264
Eurocentrism, 12, 22, 25, 28-29, 41, 56, 80, 109-10, 131, 143, 159, 178, 244, 255, 260, 265
European Enlightenment, 2, 18, 22, 27, 42, 52, 54-56, 95, 134, 144, 203, 206, 219, 228, 260
Evolution, 63, 66, 138, 192
Exchange, 10, 33, 49, 57-58, 100, 127-28, 130, 139, 141, 144; ludic, 11; unequal, 33, 72, 146-48, 150, 169, 177, 184-85, 187, 201, 252, 259, 261, 267, 273
Exile, 7, 25, 35, 184, 206, 224, 248, 266
Existentialism, 28, 51
Experience, 25, 27, 50; lived, 37, 104, 190, 248, 257
Exploitation, 3-4, 33, 37, 43, 45, 57, 89, 100, 103, 111, 119, 121, 130, 152, 162, 169, 181, 197, 201, 221, 261, 273
Family, 36-37, 41, 45, 88, 121, 186
Fanon, Frantz, 17, 26-28, 30, 50, 70, 100, 103, 136, 200, 208, 210-14, 219, 235, 249, 252, 254, 259, 265, 273
Fantasy, 84, 123-34, 131
Fascism, 33, 66, 68, 88, 91, 94, 96, 118, 206, 230-31, 262, 272
Faulkner, William, 56
Feminism, 44, 50, 52, 136
Fetishism, 2, 9, 22, 58, 74, 129, 130-32, 151, 181, 184, 188-89, 208, 211, 219, 223, 261
Feudalism, 5, 11, 47, 65, 88, 93-94, 135, 144, 146, 178, 191, 209, 223, 272
Feuerbach, Ludwig, 144
Filipino American Lives (Espiritu), 166
Filipino-American War (1899-1902), 15, 43, 61, 75, 175, 218
Filipinos, 44-45, 55, 69, 71, 116, 154, 157, 163, 167-69, 175, 180; knowledge of, 14
First, Ruth, 272
Fitzgerald, F. Scott, 185
Flaubert, Gustave, 125
Forbes, William Cameron, 64
Foucault, Michel, 26, 57, 63, 108, 110-11, 119, 143, 166, 228, 234, 255
Franklin, Bruce, 62
Fraser, Nancy, 12, 170
Free trade zones, 72, 162, 168, 221, 262
Freedom, 9, 18, 28, 38, 70, 95, 98, 104, 110, 122, 144, 146-47, 151, 183, 219,

228, 235, 241-42, 244, 251, 258, 269, 273
Freire, Paulo, 14, 45, 70, 72, 103, 104-108, 201; self-criticism, 105
Freud, Sigmund, 84, 129
Functionalism, 63, 121, 176, 262
Fusco, Coco, 5
Galeano, Eduardo, 31
Garcia Marquez, Gabriel, 17
Garvey, Marcus, 229, 233, 235, 246
Gates, Henry Louis, 168, 266
Genocide, 12-13, 31-32, 62, 111, 184, 190, 253
Geopolitics, 26, 50, 64, 69, 86, 129, 154, 157, 177, 192, 196, 222, 264
Ghana, 23, 253
Giddens, Anthony, 129
Gilroy, Paul, 17, 224-25, 228
Giroux, Henry, 151
Glazer, Nathan, 159, 176
Globalization, 1, 4, 11, 15-17, 54-55, 72, 154, 172, 198, 201, 219, 222, 224, 271
Gobineau, Arturo de, 128
Godoy, Julio, 32
Godzich, Wlad, 191
Goethe, Johann Wolfgang, 55
Goldberg, David Theo, 69, 119-20, 181
Gotanda, Neil, 157
Gould, Carol, 149
Goulet, Denis, 262
Goux, Jean-Joseph, 143, 184
Gramsci, Antonio, 23, 50, 57, 70, 86-100, 104, 107-108, 150, 181, 201, 206, 234, 248, 256-57, 268
Greer, Colin, 115
Grenada, 254
Grundrisse (Marx), 152-53, 222
Guatemala, 31-33, 34, 37, 38
Guerilla insurgency, 47, 60, 77, 86, 154
Guevara, Che, 57, 213-15, 219, 265
Gugelberger, Georg, 21, 25
Guha, Ranajit, 26, 86
Guillen, Nicolas, 256
Gulf War, 13, 31
Habermas, Jurgen, 148
Hagedorn, Jessica, 177, 180
Haiti, 42, 72, 118, 229-30, 233, 235-36, 239, 243, 252, 258
Hall, Stuart, 119, 230, 254
Hansberry, Lorraine, 187
Hardt, Michael, 138
Harlins, Natasha, 157
Harlow, Barbara, 37, 151, 272
Harris, Wilson, 18, 39, 41, 227, 234

Hart-Celler Act (1965), 115
Harvey, David, 134, 199
Hawaii, 72, 156, 170, 174
Hayslip, Le Ly, 180
Hechter, Michael, 155
Hegel, Friedrich, 27-28, 84, 136-37, 143, 206, 228, 230-32, 239, 250, 267
Hegemony, 1, 6-7, 14, 22, 24, 33, 39-40, 54, 59, 63, 67, 78, 87, 91, 94-99, 101, 108, 118, 133, 136, 147, 150-51, 154, 162, 164, 171, 176, 181, 183, 187, 190-91, 199, 202, 207, 215, 217, 221, 227, 268; counter-, 13, 23, 30, 81, 168-69, 180, 242, 269
Heidegger, Martin, 235
Hellman, Lillian, 187
Herder, Johann G., 135, 206
Hermeneutics, 28, 74, 101, 143, 179, 184, 187, 225, 240, 248, 257-58
Heterogeneity, 5, 21, 71, 116, 156, 158, 166, 202, 209, 225
Hikmet, Nazim, 17
Hirschkop, Ken, 202
Hirst, Paul, 121
Historical materialism, 10, 16, 23, 74, 86, 107, 111, 144, 168, 176-77, 228-31, 240, 249, 256, 259, 268
Historicity, 23, 27, 42, 64, 70, 73, 88, 90, 104, 110, 112, 202, 229, 243, 247, 257, 260
History, 1, 3, 6, 8, 10, 14, 18, 22, 27-29, 39, 50, 52, 57-58, 83, 86-87, 90, 93, 95, 98, 106-11, 116, 129, 149, 154, 161, 163-64, 192, 214, 216-17, 220, 232, 235, 242, 256, 273
Ho Chi Minh, 56, 267
Hobbes, Thomas, 3, 11, 54, 146
Hodge, Bob, 24
Humanism, 29, 36, 52, 83, 106, 122, 144, 176, 212, 219, 232, 250, 253, 265
Hungarian revolution, 250
Hutcheon, Linda, 21, 25
Hwang, David Henry, 180
Hybridity, 10, 16, 29, 41, 59, 70-71, 109, 151, 165-66, 176, 192, 224-25, 227, 258-59
Idealism, 9-10, 18, 22, 52, 56, 63, 141, 266-67
Identification, 2, 26, 124, 132-33, 158
Identity, 1, 6-7, 9, 11, 15, 21-22, 27, 30, 40, 49, 71, 92, 95, 114-15, 120, 133-35, 159, 162, 164, 166, 169, 178, 190, 271; politics of, 12, 43, 150-51, 165,

214, 225-26, 255-56, 259, 267; post-modern, 12, 79
Ideology, 6-8, 10, 12, 14, 23-24, 27-30, 40, 43, 68, 84, 91-92, 96-97, 107, 111, 117-18, 121-22, 124-26, 128, 132-33, 141, 150, 154, 156, 169, 165, 167-68, 178, 192, 203, 254-55, 258, 264, 268
Imagination, 22, 49, 59, 103, 131, 249, 259, 270
Immigration, 1, 7, 11, 25, 113-18, 132, 134-35, 152, 155, 157, 159, 166, 169, 171, 175-76, 179-81, 184, 186, 188, 221-22, 255, 262
Imperialism, 3, 5, 11-13, 19-30, 38, 57, 65-66, 68, 75, 78, 81, 86, 150, 154, 197-98, 203, 208-209, 217-18, 220, 228-29, 233-35, 244-45, 255, 260-61, 264, 269; neo-, 24
Indeterminacy, 2, 7, 15, 23-25, 107, 258, 262
India, 99, 209
Indigenes, 29, 33, 77, 155, 201, 259
Individualism, 1-2, 9-12, 39, 41, 70, 78, 88, 121, 130, 133, 144, 147-49, 154, 170, 184, 189, 192, 242 43, 260; lais-sez-faire, 115
Indochina, 43, 253
Industrial revolution, 140
Inequality, 11, 13, 55, 57, 76, 106, 115, 143, 150-52, 162, 169, 183, 191, 197
Injustice, 2, 37, 39, 55, 106, 115, 150, 191
Intellectuals, 3, 51, 54, 66, 92, 95-96, 250, 258, 267-68, 272; collective, 95; organic, 80, 94, 97
Internal colony, 14, 59, 81, 112, 155-93, 162, 165, 169, 172, 177, 190
Interpellation, 37, 40, 96, 108, 121-22, 124, 129-32, 143, 177, 201
Iraq, 55, 118, 251
Irony, 8, 24, 30, 38, 255
Italy, 86-88, 90-94
Iyer, Pico, 153
Jacoby, Russell, 30
James, C. L. R., 9, 17, 29-30, 38-43, 51-52, 57, 70-71, 144, 201, 203, 227-50, 258
Jameson, Fredric, 4, 73-74, 113, 134, 153, 256-58
Japan, 59, 75, 78, 115-16, 170, 225, 252
Japanese Americans, 175, 189
Jen, Gish, 165, 186
Joaquin, Nick, 58
Johnson, Lyndon B. 32
Johnson-Forest Tendency, 239

Jones, Gareth Steadman, 62
Joyce, James, 42
Justice, 12, 29, 38-39, 51, 54, 152, 165, 170, 217, 258, 269-70
Kanafani, Ghassan, 272
Kang, Younghill, 185
Kant, Immanuel, 39, 135-36, 191, 206
Karnow, Stanley, 64-65, 67, 170
Kelly, Petra, 271
Kennedy, John, 32
Kenyatta, Jomo, 56, 229, 233
Kerkvliet, Benedict, 63, 67
Kim, Elaine, 177, 187
Kim Il Sung, 17, 233, 253
King, Rodney, 118-19, 121
Kingston, Maxine Hong, 164, 178, 180, 187, 190
Kipling, Rudyard, 61
Knowledge, 30, 58, 60, 70, 104-105, 107, 110, 121-22, 146, 155, 180, 188, 234, 262, 264
Kogawa, Joy, 190
Kolko, Gabriel, 62, 116
Korean Americans, 130, 166
Kovel, Joel, 131, 181
Ku Klux Klan, 123-24
Kurdistan, 72, 252, 272
Labor, 1, 13, 36, 76, 79, 81, 115-16, 119-20, 122, 125-28, 130, 144-49, 167, 181, 183-85, 187, 190, 206, 221-23, 232, 234, 247, 252, 261, 267, 272; child, 14; division of, 9, 16, 52, 56, 68, 86, 99, 139-41, 155, 161, 166, 191, 221, 252, 254-55, 263; mobility of, 116; segmentation, 6
Labor/Community Strategy Center, 114
Lacan, Jacques, 25, 27, 57, 84-85, 123-25, 143, 200, 255
Laclau, Ernesto and Chantal Mouffe, 165
Lam, Maivan, 16
Lamming, George, 234
Land reform, 32, 80, 93
Language, 8, 22, 25-27, 34, 58, 83-84, 101, 104-105, 107, 125, 132, 143, 152, 166, 188, 202, 210-13, 257, 265; game, 38-39, 57, 59, 75, 177
Larrain, Jorge, 266
Larsen, Neil, 7, 248
Latin America, 100, 217, 253
Law, 13, 122, 125, 131, 218; antimiscegenation, 158
Lazarus, Neil, 267
Lee, Everett S., 117
Lee, Grace, 239

Lefebvre, Henri, 9, 186, 242
Legitimation, 9, 12, 44, 65-66, 88, 144, 165
Lenin, Vladimir, 3, 17, 57, 81, 87, 100, 151, 195, 203, 208, 228, 242, 245-46, 250
Liberalism, 10-11, 38, 59, 68, 88, 113, 130, 135-36, 139, 143, 150, 169-70, 192, 232
Liberation, 12, 20, 35, 51, 81, 106-108, 110, 128, 136, 179, 190, 208, 246; theology of, 12, 269, 273
Libya, 251
Lim, Genny, 187
Lim, Shirley, 177, 179, 187
Ling, Amy, 177, 187
Liu, John, 156
Locke, John, 56, 146
Los Angeles (California), 4, 34, 113-14, 118, 129, 134, 156-57, 161, 166, 174, 220
Lowe, Lisa, 165, 181
Lowe, Pardee, 184
Lu Hsun, 17, 70, 257
Lukàcs, Georg, 9, 57, 127, 147, 195
Luke, Timothy, 262
Lumumba, Patrice, 23, 233, 253
Luxemburg, Rosa, 17, 230
Lyotard, Jean-Francois, 39, 108, 191, 226, 228, 256, 264
Mabini, Apolinario, 78, 218-19
MacArthur, Douglas, 64
Magellan, Ferdinand, 72, 73
Magsaysay, Ramon, 66
Mahfouz, Naguib, 17
"Mail order brides," 13, 45, 170, 224
Makibaka, 44-46
Malcolm X, 129-30, 133, 265
Mandel, Ernest, 3
Mandela, Nelson, 271
"Manifest Destiny," 54, 65
Marcos, Ferdinand, 17, 43-46, 54, 59, 65-66, 73-75, 79, 154
Marcuse, Herbert, 225
Mariategui, Jose Carlos, 17
Market, 10, 15-16, 23, 55, 59, 68, 118, 120, 131, 139, 146, 151, 157, 162, 198, 206, 211, 214, 223, 241, 252, 258, 266, 272; free, 5, 10, 58; labor, 116-17
Marx, Karl, 17, 27, 39, 81, 99-100, 109-10, 120, 127-28, 135, 139-41, 144, 146-51, 181, 183-84, 188, 203-205, 208, 228, 231-32, 236, 260, 273

Marxism, 6, 41-42, 57, 73, 80, 87, 95, 98, 110, 119, 162, 168, 203, 231, 233-34, 238, 246-48, 250-54, 259
Mass line, 17, 35, 41, 51, 77, 80-81, 95-97, 162, 214-17, 228-30, 242, 244-45, 247, 263
Mass media, 11, 24, 26, 36, 38, 72, 133, 169, 233, 248, 262
Mattelart, Armand, 264
Mau-Mau uprising, 56
May, Glenn Anthony, 69
Mazzini, Giuseppe, 206
McCarran, Walter Act (1952), 115, 175
McKinley, William, 68, 218-19
McLaren, Peter, 104, 151, 152
McLuhan, Marshall, 198
McNutt, Paul V., 64-65
McWilliams, Carey, 61
Mediation, 9-10, 28, 42, 92, 95, 97, 105, 139, 143, 146, 150-51, 166, 184, 190, 202-204, 210, 228, 231-33, 236, 238, 268
Melendy, H. Brett, 176
Melloti, Umberto, 260
Melville, Herman, 42, 133, 230, 243, 248-49
Memmi, Albert, 128
Memories of Underdevelopment (Alea), 8
Memory, 18, 52, 153, 176; popular, 22, 258
Menchu, Rigoberta, 12-13, 29-39, 51-52, 112, 265
Metanarrative, 2, 7-8, 25, 38-39, 52, 71, 95, 99, 111, 134, 192, 227, 260
Mexico, 14, 19, 115, 118, 268; Chiapas, 99, 152, 199
Michelet, Jules, 242
Miles, Robert, 117, 126, 161, 221
Miller, Arthur, 187
Miller, Stuart Creighton, 67
Min, Pyong Gap, 158, 159
Minority, 56, 135, 156-57, 246; middleman, 130; model, 133, 160, 163-64, 170-71, 173-74, 181
Mintz, Sidney, 253
Mishra, Vijay, 24
Mocnik, Rastko, 122-23
Mode of production, 86, 100, 144, 191
Modernity, 7, 15, 22, 30, 38, 51, 72, 134, 178-79, 233, 261-62, 266, 269, 273
Monroe Doctrine, 62
Mori, Toshio, 172, 188
Moro Islamic Liberation Front, 77, 196
Morrison, Toni, 56, 225

Moynihan, Daniel P., 159, 176
Mukherjee, Bharati, 190
Multicultural imaginary, 12, 113-54, 187, 192
Multiculturalism, 11, 13, 134, 137-38, 148, 151, 154, 159, 162-63, 169, 172, 183, 191, 220
Murray, Charles, 173
Myrdal complex, 160
NAFTA, 152, 196, 198-99, 261
Nash, Philip Tajitsu, 181
Nation, 1, 7, 15, 43, 86, 89, 98-99, 112, 133, 159, 161, 166, 170, 198, 200-204, 207, 213-14, 225, 234, 249, 252-54, 259, 268
National democracy, 45-46, 54, 77, 87, 254
National Democratic Front (NDF Philippines), 43, 46, 53, 77
National liberation, 3, 17-18, 43, 54, 63, 80-81, 201-203, 211, 213, 217, 238, 253, 264, 270
National-popular, 15, 18, 22, 47, 51-52, 80-81, 93, 151, 161-62, 212, 214, 217, 219, 230, 234, 237, 242, 253, 256, 267, 269-70
National question, 41, 86, 93, 115, 131, 158, 203, 223, 233-34, 238
Nationalism, 7, 15, 67-68, 71, 78, 86, 133, 161, 199-210, 213, 217-20, 228-29, 241, 255, 267, 269
Native Americans, 30, 108-12, 133, 140
Nativism, 59, 159, 167
Naturalization law, 114, 175
Necessity, 36, 95, 98, 138, 151, 219, 260
Needs, 45, 71, 148, 190, 270, 273. *See also* Desire
Negativity, 78, 84, 108-109, 134, 210, 221, 248, 258. *See also* Contradiction; Dialectics
Negri, Toni, 138
Negritude, 233, 235
"Negro question," 244-48
Nehru, Jawaharlal, 208-209
Nelson, Cary, 152
Neocolonialism, 15, 24, 43, 45, 52, 60, 63, 66, 71-72, 75, 78, 167, 211, 221, 269
Neoconservatism, 1, 10, 57, 128, 160, 166, 168, 170, 181, 186, 189, 191
Neoliberalism, 14, 58, 156, 176, 266. *See also* Liberalism
Neruda, Pablo, 21
New People's Army (NPA Philippines), 43, 46-49, 73, 77

"New World Order," 61, 113, 170, 198, 252, 271
New Zealand, 266
Ngugi, Wa Thiong'o, 11, 17, 70, 256, 265, 267
Nicaragua, 245, 268, 272
Nietzsche, Friedrich, 7, 63, 76, 137
Nkrumah, Kwame, 23, 229, 233
Non-Aligned Movement, 98, 99
North Korea, 179
North/South, 16, 96, 98-99, 108, 163, 170, 222, 252, 269, 271
Northern Ireland, 13, 203
Noumoff, Sam, 272
Nyerere, Julius, 233
O'Casey, Sean 42
Okada, John, 172, 180, 187
Okihiro, Gary, 190
Oligarchy, 23, 76, 79, 263
Omi, Michael and Howard Winant, 119-20, 159, 166, 176
Ontology, 144, 166, 172, 186
Oppression, 23, 25, 44, 129, 156, 255. *See also* Exploitation
Orientalism, 9, 72, 84, 113, 160, 170, 179, 235, 265
Osajima, Keith, 165
Other/Otherness, 15, 17, 23, 27, 29, 33, 39, 41, 50, 59, 64, 75, 83-85, 100-102, 108, 111, 115, 120, 126, 154, 177, 181, 202, 204-205, 208, 212-13, 215, 219, 266
Outside/inside, 42, 84
Overdetermination, 37, 70, 80, 121-22, 126, 133
Overseas Contract Workers (OCW), 13, 55, 76, 122, 168, 220-21, 223-26
Pacific Rim, 4, 132, 160, 164, 169
Padmore, George, 229, 233, 235
Palestinians, 252, 267
Palumbo-Liu, David, 129
Panethnicity, 154, 158-60, 163, 165-66, 170, 229
Parkin, Frank, 150
Parody, 26, 38-39, 154, 210, 226
Parry, Benita, 27, 266
Partisanship, 51, 87, 92, 94, 97, 215, 232, 247-48
Pastiche, 35, 73, 75, 153-54, 181, 189, 244, 259, 261
Patriarchy, 44-46, 78, 81, 83-84, 103, 107, 144, 223, 258
Patronage, 63, 67, 171, 262

Peasantry, 45, 47, 78, 86-98, 100, 112, 116, 146
Pecheux, Michel, 132
Pedagogy, 105-107, 176, 211
Peltier, Leonard, 13, 83
Permanent People's Tribunal, 44
Petersen, William, 171
Petras, James, 261
Philippines, 15, 43-52, 59, 64, 69, 76-77, 151, 153, 170, 175, 222, 245, 252, 263, 270-73
Picasso, Pablo, 230
Plato, 12
Pluralism, 11, 29, 44, 47, 55, 58, 69-70, 114, 118, 122, 131, 133-34, 140, 147, 150, 152, 158-59, 162, 168, 173, 178, 191-92, 258
Politics, 30, 97, 107, 233, 261, 267; Manichean, 268; racial, 120, 131, 156, 164, 166, 168, 177, 181, 191
Pontecorvo, Gillo, 103
Populism, 62, 69, 100, 151, 211, 213, 246-47, 256
Portillo, Maria Josefina, 33
Position, 49, 63, 70, 122, 165, 167, 192. *See also* Subject
Postmodernism, 2-5, 9, 16, 22, 24-25, 29, 31, 38-39, 107, 109, 113, 118, 134, 152-54, 163, 165-7, 171, 180-81, 191, 207, 220, 223, 225-26, 252, 254, 267
Poststructuralism, 6, 29, 57, 75, 84, 110, 119, 137, 152, 154, 177, 201, 228, 234, 255, 259, 265
Power, 2, 8, 16, 23, 58, 70, 75-76, 79, 89, 101, 107, 110-11, 123, 137, 149, 165-66, 230, 260, 265, 273; -knowledge, 89, 119
Practice (praxis), 39, 70, 72, 95, 98, 104, 107, 120, 150-52, 181, 192, 231-32, 240, 245, 248, 256, 263, 266
Pragmatism, 16, 52, 61, 67, 70, 137, 147, 166, 213, 230, 258, 263
Prisoners, political, 111
Productive forces, 57, 100, 141, 148-49, 167, 185, 191, 231-32, 242, 250, 270, 273
Profit, 55, 110, 130, 220, 261. *See also* Value, surplus
Progress, 25, 39, 134, 251, 260, 269-70
Proletariat, 4, 88, 90-92, 95, 97, 99, 229, 240-41, 246-47, 250. *See also* Workers
Property, 23, 36, 69, 77, 81, 88, 90, 111, 121, 130, 136, 144, 146, 148, 151
Proposition 187, 113-14

Psychoanalysis, 27-29, 84, 89, 123, 183, 223, 225-26
Public sphere, 49, 69, 88, 138, 263
Puerto Rico, 13, 72, 156
Quiche Indians, 12, 35-36, 38, 50
Rabelais, Francois, 189, 219
Race, 41, 119, 123, 128-29, 152, 178, 208, 234, 244-45, 258
Racism, 1, 5, 11, 27-29, 63, 69, 81, 111, 114, 118-34, 138, 147, 157-58, 161-63, 174-75, 180, 192, 206, 217, 219, 237, 267-69, 271-72; institutional, 160, 163, 165; meta-, 131
Ramos, Fidel, 43, 60, 77, 79, 196, 225
Rastafarianism, 234
Rationality, 39, 49, 75, 106, 119, 122, 130-31, 134, 136, 146, 219, 234, 241, 260, 269
Ravenstein, Edward, 117
Reagan, Ronald, 32, 77
Realism, 34, 36, 38, 49, 186, 240, 257; marvellous, 235
Reality, 10, 28, 34-35, 58, 105, 144, 222; -effect, 34
Realpolitik, 11
Reciprocity, 67-68, 135-36, 147, 243, 270
Recognition, 28, 51, 135-37, 139, 146-47, 164, 167, 169-70, 172, 178, 192, 250
Refugees, 161, 175, 252
Reification, 5, 9, 12, 24, 27-28, 73, 81, 102, 125, 127-28, 132, 144, 147-48, 152, 169, 183, 190, 228, 234, 257, 265
Reimers, David, 115, 179
Relation of forces, 95, 97, 119-20, 139, 141, 148
Relativism, 6, 18, 24-26, 52, 124, 165, 255
Renan, Ernest, 206
Representation, 8, 22, 25, 30, 38-39, 52, 69, 72, 85, 87, 100-101, 103, 108, 121-22, 126-27, 135, 140, 150, 153, 178, 181, 191, 226, 257
Reproduction, 120-21, 130, 165
Resistance, 8, 17, 21-22, 24, 30, 36-37, 43, 50, 78, 80-81, 86, 99, 108, 110, 153-54, 168-69, 228, 256, 258-59, 265, 267-68, 271-73
Resnick, Stephen, 121
Responsibility, 22, 36, 49, 51-52, 70, 104, 106, 167, 210-13, 263
Ressentiment, 13, 124, 269
Retamar, Roberto Fernandez, 18, 49, 70
Revolution, 42, 46, 50, 54, 57, 60, 81, 86-87, 90, 94, 111, 216, 229-30, 233, 249, 258-59, 263, 268, ; anti-colonial,

29; Bolshevik, 96, 117; cultural, 90, 106; green, 272-73; passive, 97; permanent, 39; socialist, 196; Third World, 117
Rex, John, 138
Rhetoric, 8, 11, 25-26, 28, 42, 74, 102, 109, 129, 131, 152, 179, 212, 214-15
Rights, 1, 72, 124, 132-33, 135, 137, 139, 143, 224, 246, 270; human, 1, 46, 79, 272; procedural, 24
Risorgimento, 92, 93
Rizal, Jose, 53, 78
Robeson, Paul, 229
Rodney, Walter, 17, 227, 256
Rostow, W. W., 262
Rousseau, Jean-Jacques, 29, 103, 135-36, 147, 206
Rushdie, Salman, 2, 25, 50
Russia, 88, 90
Said, Edward, 6, 51, 72, 101, 224, 239, 248, 265
Sakdalista, 18, 78
Sandinista, 37, 254, 268
Sangari, Kumkum, 22
Sartre, Jean-Paul, 28, 50, 61
Sassen, Saskia, 118
Saudi Arabia, 222
Scapegoat, 113, 158-59, 163, 170
Schulze-Engler, Frank, 266
Schwarz, Roberto, 17
Segregation, 4, 147, 156, 162-65
Self-determination, 17, 24, 38, 42, 78, 81, 93, 108, 120, 148-49, 165, 177, 190, 199, 203, 210, 212, 245, 258, 263, 270-71, 273
Sembene, Ousmane, 257
Semiotics, 7, 26, 28, 119, 123, 130-31, 165
Senghor, Leopold, 210
Sensibility, 35, 47, 49, 95, 130, 189, 243
Sexism, 45, 63, 72, 101, 103, 110, 141, 178, 184, 267
Shanin, Theodore, 100
Shaw, George Bernard, 42
Sign, 25-27, 72, 84-85, 133, 200-204, 214, 220, 223, 226. See also Language; Rhetoric
Silko, Leslie Marmon, 12, 56, 103, 108
Simulacrum, 29, 31, 34, 55, 75, 113, 153-54, 181, 257, 261
Singapore, 170
Sklair, Leslie, 10, 30
Slavery, 42, 110, 119, 225-26, 229, 235-36, 244-45, 258-59

Sledge, Linda Ching, 178
Smith, Adam, 56
Socialism, 1, 3, 22, 38, 42, 54, 80, 88, 91, 95-96, 98, 110, 148, 196, 200, 203, 208-209, 214, 217, 229, 239, 241, 246, 248, 255-56, 259-60, 263, 267, 272
Socialist Workers Party, 245
Solberg, Sam, 172
Solidarity, 3, 16, 18, 29, 35, 38, 49, 52, 87-8, 90, 96, 99, 133, 160, 206-207, 235, 245, 261, 268, 270, 273
Sollors, Werner, 159, 177
Somalia, 252
South Africa, 67, 252-53, 256, 271
Sovereignty, 15, 65, 103, 117, 170, 199, 203, 213, 219, 222
Soviet Union, 1, 3, 14, 57, 228, 239, 251
Soyinka, Wole, 259
Space, 12, 25-27, 30, 51, 167, 271
Spain, 43, 65, 78, 88
Spanish-American War, 59, 175, 220
Species-being, 128, 148-49, 231, 238, 253
Spectacle, 72, 152-53, 261
Speech act, 15, 26, 36, 84, 109, 120, 202, 204, 218-20, 226
Spinoza, Baruch, 81, 228
Spivak, Gayatri Chakravorty, 6, 22, 56, 85-86, 108, 152, 235, 265-66
Stalin, Joseph, 258
Stanley, Peter, 67
State, 24, 81, 88-89, 91-92, 95, 97, 110, 116-17, 121, 130, 138-39, 150-51, 155, 161, 168, 210, 213, 220, 232, 243, 255, 261; integral, 87, 181; national security, 60, 262; police, 114; postcolonial, 22-23, 38, 44; socialist, 90; welfare, 189
Stauffer, Robert, 67, 69
Steinberg, David, 67
Stereotype, 114, 123, 157-59, 164, 178-79, 181
Stockton schoolyard massacre, 174
Stratification, 11, 13, 89, 131, 143, 155, 158. See also Class; Class Struggle
"Structure of feeling," 3, 11, 40, 47, 55, 134
Subaltern, 8-9, 16, 30, 50, 52, 63, 65, 71, 85, 88-89, 91, 94-95, 103, 107-10, 151-52, 156, 159, 167-68, 178, 207, 225-26, 228, 265, 267, 269
Subcomandante Marcos (Zapatista guerillas of Mexico), 19

Subject, 22, 27, 37, 39, 50, 84, 104, 106, 108, 118-20, 122-25, 130, 132, 146, 148, 152, 158, 191, 205, 232, 248, 255, 257, 266-67, 271; Cartesian, 36; in process, 16, 121; liberal, 33; logo-centric, 25, 167; racialized, 120, 236
Sun Yat-sen, 208-209, 219
Sundquist, Eric, 180
Symptomatic reading, 42, 84, 132
Taft, William Howard, 69, 73
Tahimik, Kidlat, 73-74, 265
Takaki, Ronald, 176
Tan, Amy, 186
Tanada, Wigberto, 77
Tanzania, 23, 272
Tarr, Peter, 68
Tasaday, 74-75, 153
Taylor, Charles, 135-39, 143-44, 147, 154
Taylor, George, 64
Technology, 15, 81, 109, 221, 260, 262, 269-70, 273
Teleology, 25, 57, 159
Temporality, 1-2, 10, 15, 25, 51, 143, 154, 180, 200, 202, 207, 211, 228, 259
Terkel, Studs, 123
Testimonio, 31, 34, 37-38, 52, 272
Textuality, 12, 22, 26, 131, 166, 172-73, 180, 214, 259, 265; inter-, 7, 16, 34, 134, 192
Thailand, 13-14, 170
Theory, 1-2, 24, 57, 70, 152, 242, 248, 260
Third World, 3-6, 15-17, 22-23, 39, 55-56, 60, 63, 68, 80-81, 87, 98, 104, 156, 168, 197-200, 202, 207, 212, 222, 250, 252, 256-61, 264, 266-68, 270-71
Toer, Pramoedya Ananta, 17
Tolstoy, Leo, 135, 139, 143
Tomlinson, John, 15
Totality, 9-10, 23, 27, 57, 87, 97, 111, 113, 119, 121-22, 127, 129, 139-40, 143-44, 149, 151, 230, 232, 253, 257, 260
Toussaint L'Ouverture, 234-38
Tradition, 12, 16, 18, 30, 41, 52, 58, 65, 81, 109, 148, 159, 168, 172, 178-80, 189-90, 256, 269
Transformation, 1, 29, 42, 51, 77, 91, 95, 103-106, 189, 205, 221, 228-29, 235, 241, 248, 256, 259-60, 263, 269
Transmigrancy, 2, 56, 166-67, 214, 220, 254, 261, 271

Transnational corporations (TNC), 24, 69, 98, 100, 113, 115, 117, 157, 198, 261, 264, 270, 273

Trask, Haunani-Kay, 266

Treaty of Paris (1898), 218-19

Trinh Minh-ha, 56, 152, 265

Trinidad, 40, 234, 239, 250

Trotskyism, 42, 228-30, 245, 248-50

Tsetung Mao, 57, 87, 99-100, 265, 272

Turki, Fawaz, 18, 267

Tutelage, 53, 66-67, 71, 208

Twain, Mark, 56, 61

United front, 51, 87, 90-92, 99, 169

United Nations, 100, 260, 262, 268, 270-71

United States of America, 11, 28, 32, 43, 56, 58-59, 65-66, 69, 78, 115-16, 132, 134, 154, 166, 171, 190, 220, 242-43, 249; bases, 44, 73; exceptionalism, 11, 69, 157, 160, 163; foreign policy, 62, 64, 115; imperialism, 11, 18, 47, 62-63, 73, 157, 196, 240-41; -Philippine relations, 63, 67, 154; self-identification, 58, 65, 116, 181, 191; settler society, 152, 165, 183

Universalism, 29, 38-39, 42, 54-55, 58, 94, 97, 140-41, 143-44, 148-50, 186, 188, 200, 229-37, 240-41, 243-44, 248, 250, 253, 267-69, 273

Utilitarianism, 9-10, 54, 70, 146, 160

Utopia, 30, 49, 70, 99-100, 144, 152, 181, 192, 214-15, 217, 219, 223, 254, 258, 269

Utterance, 15, 26-27, 39, 51, 120, 202-205, 207, 210-13, 217, 219

Value, 18, 25-26, 100, 106, 126, 128, 131, 141, 143-44, 147, 149, 168, 195-86, 214-15, 221-23, 268; exchange (money), 140-41, 143, 146, 166, 183-84, 187-90, 257; surplus, 1, 3-5, 57, 100, 147, 161, 169, 184, 198

Vera Cruz, Philip, 81

Vico, Giambattista, 83

Vietnam, 18, 44, 50, 60, 63, 67, 73, 118, 175, 245, 253

Villa, Jose Garcia, 58

Violence, 11, 31, 118, 164, 175, 184, 210-11, 265, 271

Voloshinov, V. N., 204

Voltaire, Francois, 29

Wallerstein, Immanuel, 98, 134, 161, 253, 268

War, 35, 54, 89, 118, 134, 206, 246; low-intensity, 54, 77, 79; people's, 37, 47, 96, 245, 253

"Warm body export," 45, 55, 262

Warner, Michael, 151, 152

Weber, Max, 86, 206, 232, 242

Weiss, Peter, 253

West Indies, 40-42, 219-30, 233-34, 244, 250

White supremacy, 65, 71, 108, 130, 136, 156, 159, 161-63, 165, 171, 191, 208

Whitman, Walt, 133, 230

Wilden, Anthony, 124-25

Will, 95, 99, 131, 146; general, 27, 147

Williams, Raymond, 3, 16, 40, 47, 128-29, 197-200, 269

Williams, Tennessee, 187

Williams, William Appleman, 62

Wittgenstein, Ludwig, 38

Wolf, Eric, 100, 116, 119

Wolff, Leon, 67

Wolff, Richard, 121

Women, 43-44, 102-103, 112, 168, 223-26

Wong Sau-ling, 183, 187

Wood, Ellen Meiksins, 15

Woolf, Virginia, 190

Workers, 34, 46, 49, 87, 90, 95, 107, 114, 116, 146-47, 161. See also Proletariat

World Bank/International Monetary Fund, 22, 43, 60, 63, 77-78, 98, 100, 169, 196, 199, 222, 252, 262-63, 273

World system, 23-24, 33, 39, 41, 55-56, 61, 64, 68, 72, 167, 176, 192, 201, 243, 252, 256, 259, 268, 271-73

World War II, 3, 5, 75, 158, 163, 175, 187

Worsley, Peter, 252

Wright, Richard, 225

Writing, 49, 51, 58, 100, 143, 185, 190-91; emergency, 265

Wynter, Sylvia, 234

Yamamoto, Hisaye, 172

Yeats, William Butler, 42

Yoshihara, Nancy, 170

Young, Iris M., 150

Yugoslavia, 251, 254

Zulus, 135, 136, 143